To Rev. Pat ~

It was wonderful
going ~~through~~ UCC together.
You are a treasure and a
wealth of humor abundant!

All the
Best!
Rev. Leg

The Self-Full Life

The Self-Full Life

...a true story that will help
your soul remember

Peg Abernathy

iUniverse, Inc.
New York Lincoln Shanghai

The Self-Full Life
...a true story that will help your soul remember

iUniverse books may be ordered through booksellers or by contacting:

iUniverse
2021 Pine Lake Road, Suite 100
Lincoln, NE 68512
www.iuniverse.com
1-800-Authors (1-800-288-4677)

with Coffee and Scones Literary, a division of Lucky Parker Media

Registered Writers Guild of America #993269

Web site
www.self-full-life.com

Cover design
Pam Morgenstern

ISBN-13: 978-0-595-34226-6 (pbk)
ISBN-13: 978-0-595-67078-9 (cloth)
ISBN-13: 978-0-595-78996-2 (ebk)
ISBN-10: 0-595-34226-4 (pbk)
ISBN-10: 0-595-67078-4 (cloth)
ISBN-10: 0-595-78996-X (ebk)

Printed in the United States of America

welcome to the knowing.

Foreword

For over seven years, I have been interviewing authors and guests in the field of mind-body-Spirit on my radio show, "Carolyn Craft's Inner Wisdom"/WISDOM Radio. All have offered something wise, provocative, perhaps a recent discovery, or something of particular interest to Spiritual seekers in our country and abroad. Occasionally, there are guests who transcend the ordinary and, with each show appearance, offer something entirely new. These are the 'favorite' guests of listeners. Through their Resourcefulness, they continually offer the latest in evolutionary perspectives, as well as Spiritual assistance for listeners to incorporate these new perspectives into their lives.

It is with this "gift" in mind that I recommend Peg Abernathy's, *The Self-Full Life*. Her story is one rich with Spiritual lessons for all. And yet, it does not stop at "book end". She continues to receive daily guidance and instruction to which recipients listen and absorb, thus enabling them to make improvements in their daily lives.

With a compassionate heart, a deep dedication to Spirit, receptiveness to Guidance and a passion for sharing her gifts, Peg Abernathy will touch the life of the reader and bring to light the possibility of something magical.

Blessings,
Carolyn Craft
Executive Producer/Host
Carolyn Craft's Inner Wisdom/WISDOM RadioSirius Satellite Radio
www.wisdomradio.com

Acknowledgments

His name was Sam. And in his early adult years, a debilitating illness had taken away his sight. He was now 55 years old and sitting across from me in my office. What brought us together was a simple business meeting and we concluded at about 11 AM. I asked Sam if he would like me to walk him to the corner bus stop where he would board the vehicle that was his lifeline. He replied happily and proudly, "No, it's just one building away. I know right where it is." I asked him if he was sure and he was adamant, saying that it was the same stop that he had used in order to meet with me. We said our goodbyes and I went on about my day.

Lunchtime came and I met a friend and ran a few errands. By four o'clock that afternoon, I was already watching the clock, wishing the hour away and silently feeling sorry for myself that I had to be there at all. At about 4:30, I heard a noise at my door. It was Sam. He said apologetically, "Well, I guess I do need help." It had been over five hours since we had said goodbye. He had never given up, trying and trying until the realization sank in that he would need to ask for assistance. Thank you, dear Sam, for Being the example of perseverance and humble vulnerability. Thank you for waving to me as I watched your bus pull away. Even though your physical eyes couldn't see me, the eyes of your Soul did.

I know that every person we connect with is part of a greater plan, designed and created with our own Soul Team of Angels and Guides long before this incarnation. I am truly amazed, every single day, by this enchanted truth. And I am grateful to the following Souls who lived up to this ancient commitment to come together in this dream-play we call a life-lived.

To The Guides. This is our story and I know I've told it resolutely. You, through your loving guidance and intent, have placed a miracle at my feet.

And using my Power of Will, I choose to accept that gift, with an accepting heart, full of raw openness. Thank you. Thank you. Thank you.

To the following people who have inspired my Spirit by keeping my wings dusted and ready for flight: Celeste Waters, who quietly opened the door and began my journey, bless you, sweet Angel. Steve Ross, your guidance and gentle participation in my life are simply inspiring. Wayne D'Vorak, who was instrumental in showing me the way to my true feelings, thank you for removing my rose-colored glasses. Barbara Clay and Joan Weiss, who helped me understand how I am different, thank you for listening to me. Mrs. Verdugo and Mr. Donohue, two members of that elite group of teachers that made a difference in the existence of a frightened young girl, you helped save my life and I thank you for allowing me to Be.

Pam Morgenstern, thank you from the bottom of my heart for your inspiring cover illustration. Cynthia Richmond, your support, advice, and encouragement mean more than I can say; I thank you from a special corner in my Soul. Dan Chilton (surprise!) thank you for telling me that I'm just a human Being and human Beings make mistakes; the thunder rolled under my perfectly tap-dancing feet.

Sister Marita, thank you for delivering me from the fear that lived in my eight-year-old body. Lou Pardini, thank you for helping me to find the voice that was pushed aside.

To Karen, Dora, Teryn, Maria, Lori, and Kelley, you wacky girls give me the rare gift of complete, unconditional love and acceptance; I'll love you all forever. To my husband Pete Fausone, thank you for stepping aside and letting me shine time after time and for encouraging the flight of my Soul. I love you.

And to my family and friends, thank you for the love you continually give to me and thank you for keeping an amused outlook on the crazy gal I am.

Love, Peg
March 2005

Contents

Introduction

"Write what you Know. Write how you feel." These simple instructions put forth by seven Spirit Guides have culminated in this true story of miracles, trials, vulnerability, discovery, change, and enlightenment. And as you read this narrative, I hope you find yourself believing *and* questioning. Or at least allowing non-judgment and the opportunity for opposite views to coexist within your heart until your own personal truth emerges. I hope that many times you will find yourself thinking, "I know that already" or "Everybody knows *that*," because within those crucial moments, if you choose and if you allow it to Be, then you will rethink and unlock your own mystery of life as you say to yourself, "Do I *really* Know this already? Do I really *believe* this? Do I *understand* this? Do I *live* this?" And it will be this crossroad that will inspire you to revisit your own heart and beliefs and, perhaps, allow yourself to grow into a new life adventure.

I also hope that this book encourages you to remember the time before you were taught to forget how to accept everything and every emotion equally, and without question. A time when our young emotions and feelings were raw, new, and easily acceptable and there was wonder in everything around us. We were seeing with newly formed eyes and no societal attachments.

When we first arrived, it was all about "us," our immediate feelings, and our pure Soul. As unadulterated, chaste Spiritual Beings, we were sent from God to experience the All There Is here on Earth. And on that sacred day, our new life began with a single, gentle thought, a kiss from the Heavens and a remembrance of lifetimes before. It sprinkled down into the night sky and penetrated the breath that lingered soft and sweet. Life began anew. As it abandoned it's encircled haven and burst forth into the harsh reality of human existence, this surrendered Soul, our true Essence, was brought forth side by side with the vehicle that would ferry it through a lifetime of experiences and emotions. This deliberate mission summoned our physical body to gasp its first breath and inhale into itself the life force of which we truly are, our Self.

This Self, inhabited deep within the recesses of each and every cell, vibrates its cool energy and yearns daily to emerge, seeking the Greater Good and the Source From Whence It Came. And this common ground that is trampled by everyone, binds us together in that place where we all still remember. A place we inhabited before we were taught this forgetting of the Self-purpose.

Because the physical body is not alone in it's birthing, our Soul quickly merged together with this vehicle, latching onto the space with natural contentment and submission. We trusted, just as before we began this coupling, that our true needs would quickly, evenly, and unconditionally be realized and respected. And as we made our way towards another life journey of certitude, we carried our high expectations, not as a burden, but as a given. For, at this point in our journey, we still remember our basic need, and we believe within all that we are, that we will receive that Divine prerogative which is ceremoniously bestowed upon all Self(s).

As infants, we are able to live freely within that absolute, to expect with joy, our life support system that was so lovingly given by our adult caregivers. They revel in awe and are so often overwhelmed with the responsibility that is endowed upon them. Yet, they instinctively feel our survival needs and swiftly tend to our fragile vulnerability with complete attentiveness. We, as the new arrivals, experience nothing more than pure bliss and total regard as we are allowed to express our own need, openly and often. But this harmonic blending of our Soul with our physical body is short-lived.

For just as soon as we are able to comprehend anything other than "us," our adult caregivers, in an effort to begin our social schooling, teach us, through loving intent, to reach out to others and put our newly formed Self last in the greater scheme of things. We are taught that Self-"ish" is wrong, that honoring our Self first is egotistical, Self-centered, and unacceptable. And society will swiftly join in and begin to dictate the task of turning this true Essence outward, creating a societal Being, ready to be of service, ready to forget who and what we are and where we came from. And that, in turn, causes us to slowly, painfully dismiss and forget the Soul that was tenderly birthed along with our physical bodies. This Self is quickly forgotten, this true Self, so full of expectations and unconditional love, is defined, boxed in, judged, and limited in its potential. And the ensuing conflict immediately begins to build for us all as we don't understand "no" and "you can't" or "you must." Our expectations of instant fulfillment, our own personal power, are ripped from our psyche and placed externally. What was once touted as cute is now wrong. We don't understand and we fight with all we have to retain our power. Our Self is systematically told to forget that unconditional feeling, replacing it with the duty of a physical world. And eventually, we fall in line and march in tune with that obligatory rite of passage.

But soon, we are empty and wanton. We don't understand this lack, for don't we have it all? Nice things, people we love, people who love us? Why do we feel this way? So, we begin to rebel against this ache and in an effort to fill the voided spaces, we buy more, eat more, drink more, work more, and fill up our time and bodies with activities and substances that leave us vacant and alone at the end of the day.

Our physical bodies, our senses and our Souls languish, yearning for us to hear, to Know, to understand, to *remember* what we have stolen from our Self. It is then that we begin the struggle to understand our feelings, and our intuition of the heart, and we internally agonize as these feelings beat against the door of our learned path. We realize that we steered away from our hearts and we moved our energies out towards the masses, denying our individual need to be our own powerful wishers. And by doing this, we limited the potential to turn outward our talents, our true contributions and Spiritual gifts living within our own hearts.

It is this critical juncture that screams for us to be silent, to listen, to hear what is being expressed within. Many times, we see this moment as a crisis of sorts, a "Is that all there is?" moment of truth. But in reality, it is the Self, waiting patiently to emerge as your true purpose, to show you the way to begin your journey on the Earth and to finally understand that, if we understand the power of our Self, we hold all the mysteries of the universe within that power.

And before we can turn this unconditional acceptance and love outward, we must first seek that which reverberates just above us. And the most important point that we all must comprehend is that we can only give to others that which we give to our Self and *nothing more*. We never realized that by putting our own precious Self last, we have ultimately limited what we are able to turn outward towards others. The great givers of the world have the skilled Knowing of this concept and, quietly, they revel in its powers. How can you emote love and kindness without giving your own God-blessed Self the same consideration? For if you remember that *your* Self was created on equal par with all Self(s), why then, would you be unforgiving, unrelenting and hard on the same sparkles of energy that reside within your own body? I would suggest that people who judge others, judge themselves more. People who hate, ultimately revile themselves all the more. People who blame and are unforgiving have completely forgotten to love themselves and can no longer remember where they came from.

We must recognize and understand the importance of this concept and its implications, for it has the power to create a major shift in the hearts of all people. If we break the habit of no longer hating our Self, we could begin to forget the hate we breed in a world of senseless misunderstanding. If we forgave and ceased our endless Self-judgment, would we not forget how to judge those different from us? Turning our loving attention to our Self is the only way to begin the shift away from the external and towards our unlimited potential as warriors of peace and hope. And the biggest payoff would be when we finally see the face of God. And God recognizes a purer Self, capable of giving wholly and completely. One who can live the example. One who *Knows*.

Yet, how do we accept and refrain from living within the conflict that was created so long ago? How can we apply to our hearts this notion of complete acceptance? Where do we begin? Either in prayer, meditation, or light sleep, we must first stop asking and start listening quietly and expectantly. In this first trusting silence, our thoughts will ramble and throw themselves against everything we know. We must allow the arising feelings to be, and we must sit quietly as our Self finishes the grieving of the lost years, the abandonment of our true purpose.

And ever so sweetly, if we continue to be silent and listen, we will eventually hear that message of truth coming through our hearts. And subsequently, when we are stripped of all external stimuli, our answer will be set before us. And we will recognize its simple truth as we find it resting in the ensuing feelings, not in words or gestures.

These feelings of the Soul move and travel throughout our physical bodies in an effort to emote the concept of choice, our personal Power of Will. The feelings start within and reach out with passion, yearning, gut feelings, and reactions. As we turn inward toward this Lighted feeling, we can begin to understand the need, not the wishful thinking, that is our innate right as a living, breathing animal upon the Earth. This seed, planted deep within, with the proper allowing, can blossom forth and place our Self ceremoniously before us. It is then that we can passionately grab on to this action and experience the feelings that will ultimately drive the energy that is needed to create our Self-*full* life.

And it is then and only then that we can turn outward, this illumination, that we are most important and that our Self must come first if we are to be able to give completely. And we can begin to seek out a human purpose that is based in the reality of Self-full-ness *and give without depletion.* It is the person that recognizes the truth of this reality, who can truly emerge as one who is able to turn their own Self outward and recognize their life mission as explained by the heart.

And it is equally important that our Self support our human life mission. It is that conditioned conflict that causes many of us to quit before we begin. The difficult challenge lies in the combining of our Soul with the physical, human reality that we systematically created and set in place. Most of our human existence is stagnated by social responsibilities and choices that we have already made. It is important that we honor those previous decisions and redefine them into something that allows for our Self to take flight and our Self-filled life to fly and soar without fear or limitations. And just as a true love is one whose unconditional breath flutters the wings of our Soul, so will our Self-fullness fuel our passion and glide us in to the direction of those who have accomplished the seemingly impossible, the untried and the unknown.

It matters not where we are, who we are or what we're doing. Our Self-fullness lives in the feelings that represent those givens. It is ultimately defined by us and must be accepted by our Self. It is everyone's own responsibility to introduce his or her life to its Self. It is equally vital that we choose to remember our first breath and the feelings brought forth with our birthing.

So many times we seek to find that which is already in our hands. We just need to recognize it and more importantly, make the choice to accept that it is there. It may not always be easy or free from struggle. After all, we live in a world that necessitates interaction and relationships that seek to define us. We, unfortunately, cannot ignore the obvious and we must attend to daily experiences that are placed before us. It can be transformed, however, by our own power of choice, our Power of Will. And as we listen, accept, and then choose our reaction to events and people, we suddenly realize the power of choosing that we hold. We recognize that our paths are determined by us and through us. And by living within that concept, it is us who put our faith in our own Self, that are the ones who's true needs will always be met. We can then rest blissfully, once again, as a newborn babe. We are complete.

So you see, this true story, which begins in fear, ends in hope. It's filled with messages from The Guides, and anecdotes that will hopefully make you ponder. My mission (and a big reason for writing this book) is to encourage complete non-judgment in the perceptions, reactions, hearts, and minds of all people in order to achieve personal Self-acceptance and a sense of wonder in all possibilities and things unexplored.

My wish is that you simply take what you need and gently leave what remains to the feelings of others.

I recently asked The Guides a question. Their answer, as always, gives me tender hope. And I believe. I *still* believe.

(PA) What would you say to the people of the Earth?

(THE GUIDES) *"We would say, be still and in the silence you will begin to heal your aching heart. In the quiet stillness of the morning, listen for the fluttering of the wings of God's Angels as they leap awake and laugh with joy. You have begun a new day, a new chance and a new promise to fulfill that which is your destiny. And in this time of great disharmony, take in that which lies just above your own feelings. What does it say? Be still. In the quiet, you will perceive the All There Is. And when the day is done and the realization that a new beginning has dawned, you will see God's purpose. You will Know and be filled with The Knowing of God and all will be made well. And within a city far, far away, the bells chime and the Angels sing, Halleluiah! We are all okay."*

A Note from the Author

Throughout this book, you will find various words that are capitalized, such as Know, Being, Self, and Guide. This is intentional and its rationalization is to connect those words with a higher purpose. (See Glossary of Terms.)

—God Bless, Peg

Chapter One

The Night of My Death

...a journey to the other side.

"This life that you are living is simply a dream-play that you are creating within."

My story begins the night of my death. At that moment of the reshaping of my Soul, I was desperately fighting to live when I simply realized that my life was over and I couldn't stop it from happening. When this actuality absorbed my senses, my world went silent and my mind began to clear and turned toward the inevitable.

I thought it surprising that I was strangely calm as I proceeded to cross over from screaming in my head to hold on, to fight, and not give in to a quiet place of submission and the matter of fact acceptance of my death. I found myself enveloped in a deep, resounding subsistence between the struggle of life as I knew it and a physical death realized willingly. I experienced no fear, no pain, no guilt or responsibilities of my life. I was delicately quiet and still in my mind and body, suspended in an unexpected place of escalating peace.

Within this calmness, I embraced the freedom that my dying presented to me and I heard the chains that bound me to a world of expectations and responsibilities crack and break in the cool air. I felt the cool air surround my feet and then move swiftly up toward my head.

It was at this point that I became aware that I was smiling. My smile was actually my last physical awareness before I felt a warm, loving sensation throughout my chest. And within the next moment, I could no longer feel my body and I began observing it as a separate thing, something other than "me."

As this separating began to occur, I witnessed an audible, physical and breathtakingly visual vibration as it set out to permeate my calm cocoon. A roaring noise began to escalate and within an instant, I became aware of an intense bright Light off in the distance and I turned my focus toward its captivating dance. The Light's prism of energy and illumination began to spiral and grow and I immediately put forth all my senses into its hypnotic allure. I began to feel the most utterly peaceful, loving sensation and I yearned to move toward and inhabit this Light and the love it emanated. I tenderly lifted my Self up off the bed, focusing on this wonder presented before me. At the same time, I made a conscious decision not to look back down at my body and I began to feel a sense of profound sadness, as I was keenly aware that I was no longer a part of it. I momentarily ached for the friend that had carried my Soul for twenty-four years, yet I was willingly leaving it and all the limitations it held behind. Then, in a fleeting moment, I hesitated as I felt maybe the body needed me. But also in that instant, I was struck with the terror of the pain that it was suffering and I was terrified to return to such a state and I knew that I wasn't going back. And so I continued on.

Once I broke free from my physical body, I was quickly transported toward this loving Light as I moved into a vibrating tunnel that surrounded me and pulled me forward. My Soul leapt with expectancy, exhilaration, and a love beyond anything I could ever describe in human words. The need and all-consuming desire to move through this Lighted tunnel both surprised and excited me as, even though I knew I was dying, this impassioned longing deep within my Soul for an unknown Light Source wasn't what I expected would occur. At the time, I was Spiritually consumed by my Catholic faith and my beliefs about what happened at the time of death were based solely on church doctrines, rituals, and rules. I believed that when you died, you either went to Heaven (with a quick stop in purgatory) or Hell. But this powerful, magnetic, unexpected turn of events thrust me beyond anything I was ever told or had imagined would happen at this moment. Yet I hungered for more of this feeling and I pushed on toward the charismatic energy that so brilliantly called out to me.

Continuing to focus on this wondrous Light within the tunnel, I found my Self drifting over treetops that resembled what we would call a negative photograph. I was intrigued, as the Light was getting brighter and more intense. I continued on through the negative trees and I began to see shapes of people and heard their incoherent calling out to me. They, too, were in negative form and although I couldn't see them in three dimension, I was somehow aware of who they were. They seemed to be everywhere among the negative treetops and they were welcoming me with waves of passionate encouragement, cheering me on as I began to move through the Light.

I began going faster and faster and within an instant moment of ecstasy, the Light surrounded and pervaded everything I knew as me. Within this feeling, I recognized a remembering as this explosion of wonder and raw newness immediately made me think of being born. The thought that this was the true birthing of my Soul, calmed my newly acquired cognizance and I was spontaneously in love with and in need of this familiar place. I recognized it as a deep yearning within my heart and now I had returned. I knew I was home. I was finally, blessedly home.

As I swirled on within the Light, I felt and saw everything that had happened in my lifetime, every detail in living color. I watched with unattached Self-interest as I re-experienced my life and the choices and Souls I had connected with. The strange sense of deja vu played over and over in my mind and just like watching a movie for the second time, I knew how it started, played out, and ended.

As my life experiences passed me by, I suddenly caught sight of my husband Pete and I being married. The swirling Light began to slow down as I watched our short life together unfold before me. I saw a smiling young man, one month out of his teens, peeking around the people standing in the church pews as he watched me walk the aisle with my father. I felt a yearning for him and a great sadness blanketed my joyous heart. It was at that moment, I heard a gentle voice say, "Not now, my daughter." Immediately, everything stopped in mid-motion and there was a pervasive, silent stillness all around me. I became confused, wondering who had said that. God?? I began to feel a terrible conflict, as I certainly didn't want to go back "there," not to the painful torment, not to my body that was the root of so much shame. Yet, I continued to think of Pete and as I tried to understand what was going on inside my heart, it became clear that he and I weren't finished with our life and that he still needed me. And in that instant, I accepted that I had to go back.

The moment I agreed with my heart that I was to return, I began to spiral backwards in the Light as I entered the tunnel once again, passing the other Souls as I flew through the negative treetops. I opened my mouth to scream out, "No!!!" Faster and faster I flew, fearful and unable to look backwards toward my unavoidable destination. Abruptly, I was hurled back into a physical reality as I found myself in the dense, dark surrounding of a body that was cold and still. I felt my Self looking around within the recesses of my mind when my body jerked and took a gasp for air. I moaned and then cried out as the pain once again seared through my body.

I reached my arms toward the ceiling and swiftly, the warm hands of someone pulled them down and we struggled for a moment. My agitation quickly gave way to a relinquishment of power and I felt my body go limp. I lay there as the noise in the room moved sharply around me and I could hear a softening in the urgent voices as I quivered when metal instruments were placed upon my chest and arms. And as warm hands replaced these intrusive instruments, I slowly opened my eyes and was immediately aware that there were bright colors and shapes moving around my bed. I was conscious of other people in the room, yet I couldn't seem to focus on anyone in particular. I closed my eyes and submitted to an exhaustive sleep.

The last thing I heard as I drifted off into the cold darkness was, "I can't believe that kid almost died."

Six hours earlier:

I had to do it because I had no choice, or so I thought at the time. We needed the money. We always needed the money. And it seemed that I was forever determined to be the one to fix it, to make things right and make everyone happy. And of course, I had to look good while I was doing all this just in an effort to claim some control of my life. Yet it seemed that, although I had always possessed a sense of responsibility, I also carried tremendous feelings of resentment deep inside, as I had lived my whole life with the fear that others would discover the truth about my own vulnerable imperfections.

All I ever wanted was unconditional love without having to earn it. And I wanted to feel safe in that love without having to do or be anything or anyone but me. But I continually felt, deep inside my mind, that I wasn't quite good enough, and that at any moment, everyone would find out the truth and expose my original sin. So I continued to excel, to strive for perfection—perfect grades, perfect singing voice, perfect looks—always glancing over my shoulder to see who was waiting to see me collide with the awful truth.

I will admit to enjoying moments of accomplishment here and there, but those intervals of peaceful reprieve usually ended abruptly when my next "assignment to excel" sarcastically presented itself. I would begin that never-ending, redundant chase for the elusive accolades that continued to feed my vulnerable heart with acceptance. And once again, because we needed the money, I took it upon myself to fix the situation and I found myself with my husband Pete, once again schlepping our musical equipment down the freeway, heading towards another endless, crappy, low-paying gig. Some hellhole near the beach where I knew they would appreciate my cleavage much more than my voice. And of course, lest I fall short of everyone's expectations, I was appropriately dressed to give everyone what they wanted.

I glanced over at Pete and watched as he absentmindedly drummed his fingers on the steering wheel the way that drummers do. We had married young and now we were both twenty-four years old and four years into our marriage. We were out to obtain the almighty recording contract that would make me a star. This concept was ideal for me as a perfect person is no less than a big star. But for now, we were cruising down the freeway in a beat-up old Monte Carlo. This car looked so awful that we were once ticketed for having an "abandoned" car parked in front of our house. And because the doors sometimes stuck, I was getting used to climbing out the windows when I reached my destination.

Nothing would deter my ambition to become a household name, even though, as I would come to realize later, I never really wanted it. I approached singing in public as something that I thought I had to do because I was good at it and it made me special. My voice is a gift from God and when, years later, I began to sing for myself and for those I loved, I realized how wonderfully blessed I am. I've been told that my voice evokes deep emotions and sometimes, even now, I cry when I'm singing.

In reality, I hated the entire process of performing and only relaxed when it was over. I didn't like people looking at me because I felt judged and scrutinized and (usually) fat. And for someone like me, with a pretty face and a naturally full, womanly figure, I was dissected and cut up and told to change my physical appearance at every turn in order to fit the Hollywood standard for beauty. I would retreat into a space in my head where I was thin and accepted by all as perfect. My God-given physical beauty was there, but my willpower to strive for perfection was lacking. And also, what I didn't comprehend at the time was that show business is made up of thousands of other insecure people trying to find uncondi-tional love and fulfillment. Ordinary people trying to be special or unusual people trying to be loved. And with everyone clamoring for the lead spot, there is very little room left at the top and you are allowed in only if you are willing to take someone else with you. There was never a free ride.

We pulled up in front of a dilapidated old building and even though the sign was unreadable, the establishment it held was clear. A shit-hole. Why did we always have to work in places like this? Walking into the dimly lit bar, I wasn't surprised to find a pool table surrounded by fat, toothless bikers. I went into the dirty bathroom and looked into the cracked mirror and thought that it never ceased to amaze me how hard I always tried to please everyone, even when, deep down, I really didn't want to. Everything mattered so much to me and I was bound and determined to make the handful of people in this stinking place like me. Why did I care? Why did I take everything so personally?

I leaned on the sink and asked God to get me through this night and, leaning still closer to the mirror, I realized that I didn't look like myself anymore. I hadn't been feeling well and was always having "female trouble," as my gynecologist called it. Some months were so bad that I couldn't get out of bed and I had to crawl to the bathroom. On this night, I could feel the pressure in my abdomen building up and I knew I was in for it this month, *again*.

I went back into the bar and found Pete bringing in his drums. My keyboard player, Dave, arrived and I smiled knowing that the only thing that would make this night bearable was singing with this man. His voice and mine coupled and breathed together perfectly, seemingly as if we were singing from the same Soul. Dave is a loving, free Spirit, and he would always say to me, "Don't worry about the money, or the notes or the record deal; just sing." And on this night, I knew that I would be lucky if I could "just sing" at all. The pain in my stomach was beginning to throb and I walked over to the bar and asked the bartender if he had any aspirin. I quickly gulped down the three pills he pulled out from God knows where. A sneering biker walked over to the bar and raised his half-empty beer bottle in pointless introduction. I felt appalled and, at the same time, I couldn't have cared less.

As we started in with the first set, the pain was going from bad to worse and the grinding torment began coming in waves. My resentment of allowing myself to be paraded in such a place rose with every note I sang and with every thought of my life. At the end of the first set, I proceeded to introduce the band to the completely disinterested group of six low-lifes in the bar. In the next instant, the paralyzing eruption that struck my center was so incapacitating that it literally took my breath away and I doubled over, frozen and unable to move on the stage. Most performers know what it's like to have to go on stage when they are ill and I had performed that way many times, but this seeming explosion in my stomach was something that I had never experienced before. I was unable to speak or move and I just stood there motionless as if my life and world had stopped. I looked back at Dave and his quizzical expression stung my eyes as I tried to scream out, "Help me!" I turned back around and grabbed the microphone stand, using it to steady me. The guys stopped the song and came towards me to see what was going on.

I was solidly rigid, unable to move. Pete kept asking me, "What's wrong?" over and over again and seeing my inability to answer, he took me over to a small table and helped me sit down. I kept clutching my stomach and could barely look at him. The terror in my eyes was permeable, as I had never experienced any pain like this before and I knew something was really wrong. All I could say was, "Home, home." I suddenly needed to get to the ladies bathroom and after helping me walk to that filthy hole, the guys quickly loaded up the cars and Pete and I were accelerating down the highway for our forty-five minute drive home.

In the car, the pain escalated even more and I began to feel as if my intestines were being twisted and pulled and ripped. Years later, as I watched a movie that depicted a raw execution scene of disembowelment, it struck a cord of familiarity as I empathized with how it felt. My pain seemed to take over my entire senses and my face became distorted in a permanent scream, only nothing came out of my mouth. I began to claw at the window of the old car and Pete later told me that I was unrecognizable, as my face had taken on a totally different look. He headed toward the emergency room.

When we reached the hospital, a slow moving, nonchalant night nurse delivered me to an exam room. Bored and jaded, she began asking the required questions and proceeded to ask me if I thought the pain was from my period. At this point, I still had no voice, so I shook my head no as adamantly as I could. After what seemed an eternity, the ER doctor came in and said that he needed to examine me. When I realized that he meant a pelvic examination, I began to cry, as I knew it would be intolerable. I was finally able to say that it was something else but he argued that he still needed to take a look.

Pulling up the sheet, he saw that that I was bleeding profusely and he asked me if I was on my period. Kicking into survival mode, I was able to tell him yes, but I again said that the pain wasn't from my period, that I could tell it was from something else. Still, he proceeded on and I began to scream, as I couldn't stand any touch or pressure. He stopped and tried again and I screamed even louder. He angrily withdrew his fingers, ripped off his gloves and raising his voice, he told me that if I wouldn't let him examine me, then he couldn't help me. Angrily, he stood up and left the room. In a silent whisper I said over and over, "I'm sorry, I'm sorry." and in my head I panicked and cried out "Please help me, I'm sorry, please help me."

When he left the room, I found myself alone and I lay there as my body was being ravaged. I remember staring at the clock on the wall. 11:45 P.M., 11:46 P.M., 11:47 P.M. Where was everybody? "Help me!" I whispered. All of a sudden, the thought of death passed through my body and I began to hear a low hum and then a soft roaring sound. I heard bells go off and I rolled over and grabbed the bars on the side of the hospital bed. My eyes were wide open but I could no longer see. All I could hear was the escalating roaring sound and distant voices. And I knew I was dying. I stopped fighting. I was going home.

Chapter Two

Who I Am

...a life of fear and tap dancing.

"You must learn to balance all accounts in your life, Spiritual, physical, monetary, emotional, and interpersonal."

Growing up in a very strong Catholic belief system, I possessed limited Spiritual knowledge with ideas outside of that doctrine. My family encouraged following the faith, but we weren't overzealous when it came to expressing our beliefs to others. And from a very young age, I was the one in the family that had latched onto the faith very tightly.

My religious beliefs were my one constant in my young life and I loved the rituals and uniformity that Catholic Churches everywhere provided. Going to mass on Sunday with the traditional pancake breakfast afterwards, celebrating religious rites of passage, and being awed by the nuns and priests that surrounded me are childhood memories that are clear and vibrant in my heart. Due to my father's business, we traveled extensively, and by the time I was in the sixth grade I had been in five schools and four states. After that point, we settled into the same town until I was married twelve years later. Yet for me, changing my physical environment so often during those formative years was not necessarily a bad thing. I became very good at meeting new people and I quickly learned to adapt to different situations. Still, no matter where we lived, my little Soul unwaveringly counted on and required the familiar convocations associated with the church. I was adamant in my beliefs. I took to heart absolutely everything I was told by the nuns and priests at school and at mass.

Even though I was the youngest of four children, and rather immature, I always possessed an innate sense of responsibility for everyone else's life. Many years later, I would learn that I brought this Self-imposed burden into this lifetime as a Soul lesson that must be addressed or else I would have to repeat it over and over in subsequent lifetimes until I understood it. As a child, this burden expressed itself as bossiness or obvious determination to make everyone do it my way, the safest way I knew at the time. When I wasn't trying to "fix it", I was unknowingly looking for more burdens to carry upon my tiny shoulders. I can remember once, at about ten years old, I was walking around the house with a worried look on my face. My Mother asked me what was wrong and I replied, "I'm worried." "About what?" she continued. "About insurance." I guess I had, at one time, heard my parents discussing some kind of insurance and it's importance and now I was worried about it. But I always felt helpless because I didn't understand the "why" of my worries, just the constant dread it produced. So I walked around with a knot in the pit of my stomach, while I smiled and sang for attention. I would do anything to forget and take my mind off my plight.

For a short time, I attended St. Michael's Catholic school and because I had such a strong, trusting personality, the other children always came to me with their problems, questions or to help them tie their shoes. A young nun called my parents and said that she just wasn't sure what to do with me, that I was "running the class" and the other nuns didn't like it. I personally feel that the nuns encouraged me by giving me extra responsibility, which I gladly took upon myself to accomplish perfectly. I was a self-taught reader and far ahead of the other kids in this area.

When I entered the second grade, the nuns, in an effort to keep me occupied, came up with the idea of having me tutor reading to the first grade students. Now, this was a huge responsibility in my mind and this frightening duty weighed heavily in the pit of my stomach, as I was fearful that I wouldn't do it right. Adding to my eight-year-old life experience was the fact that I was given a ruler and was told emphatically that whenever the child I was tutoring made a mistake, I was to rap their knuckles with that ruler. A mighty powerful, unbidden tool for a little girl whose greatest fear was physical punishment.

I vividly remember the first (and only) young boy that I was to help. This little guy was from a very poor family, one of eight children. He was always dirty and smelly and he typically came to school looking half starved. The other kids made fun of him, but I always felt so sorry for him and his seven other brothers and sisters. The only thing I couldn't tolerate was that this child usually had a runny nose that needed wiping. Anyway, one hot and humid afternoon, we faced off in the nuns' parlor. The sisters had set up a table and two chairs for us. Sister Stella plopped down a book and said to the little boy, "Do not come back to the classroom until you can read this book!" She then handed me the dreaded symbol of my new responsibility—a long, thin ruler—and, turning, she left the room with her black habit and brown rosary billowing behind her.

The little boy and I squared off and I knew that I had to get this kid to read or else I would have to go back to class a failure. I looked at the ruler and said emphatically, "You better do as I say or I will hit your fingers with this ruler. The nuns said I could." He looked at me and cocked his head. "Make me," he stated flatly. Then he proceeded to laugh as loud as he could, holding onto his bony sides with dirty little hands. "Make me! Make me!" I was growing more frightened by the minute as the absolute last thing I wanted to do was hit him with that ruler. I never had the tendency for brutality or bullying and I couldn't understand his thinking. I always did what I was told as the threat of corporal punishment was, without exception, a very effective way to get my attention.

I stared at his snotty little freckled face. "Make me! Make me!" he continued in his singsong taunt. I didn't know what to do and I warned him once more to no avail. Finally, I brought the ruler down on his hand. His shock stopped him for a moment, but then he threw his head back and laughed even harder. "Didn't hurt! Didn't hurt! Ha Ha! Didn't hurt!" Once more I brought the ruler down and he continued laughing, "Still didn't hurt! Still didn't hurt! Ha Ha." Wack! The third time stopped him instantly and his eyes grew larger and larger as he looked up at me with all the hurt a six-year-old can muster. We were staring at each other with unbending stubbornness on both our parts when suddenly, he let out the biggest cry I had ever heard in all my eight years. I was so shaken, mainly because I knew I had hurt him, that I dropped the ruler and began to cry as well. The louder he cried, the louder I cried, he out of pain and I out of shame. We both cried so hard that Sister Stella came running back into the room thinking that we had set ourselves on fire. She quickly picked up the book and the now discarded ruler and sent us both back to class after being unable, through our blubbering, to understand what had happened. I hated that I had failed to uphold my responsibility and I hated that I had hurt that little boy. As far as I was concerned, Sister Stella could go "jump in the lake." (I wasn't allowed to hate a person, especially a nun, because it was too big a sin. I wondered how big. Mortal? Venial?)

I was never asked to help anyone again and I was ashamed yet profoundly relieved. However, the nuns did continue to give me additional tasks, as they were aware that my own sense of responsibility would make me try hard to accomplish these duties. They would also take me out on the front steps of the school during recess and ask me to tell them "stories." We would all sit on the steps and I would begin to tell of my adventures with Jesus and Mary as the nuns would clap and laugh at my wild imagination. But what they didn't know was that I wasn't imagining anything. I was simply relaying real stories about "the other times and the other place" that I still remembered. I spoke of this other existence as real, while they accepted it as childhood fantasy. But it wasn't. Not to me.

That summer, the nuns from the school called my parents and asked them if they could take me with them on their summer religious retreat. "Peggy is very special. We think she would get a lot out of it," they argued. But being only eight years old, my Mother said no, that I was too young to be away from home for two months. Furthermore, neither one of my parents wanted me to aspire to the nunnery. I often wonder the path my life would have taken had I been allowed to go.

It was during this time that I began to experience an unusual, physical sensation, which manifested itself in the form of a pulling or drawing up in the pit of my stomach. This raw need or pleading undercurrent seemed to emanate from deep within my memory with the resulting thought of "I want to go home." I would yearn over and over to go "there," yet I couldn't articulate or understand where "there" was. If I were in the middle of experiencing this deep yearning, my face would take on a serious expression and my Mother would usually ask me what was wrong. When I replied that I wanted to go home, she would say that I *was* home, that this place was our new home. Once, I heard her tell someone that she thought, because we moved so much at the time, I wanted to go back to the house we lived in before. But I didn't want to go back to our old house, I wanted to go where the nostalgic longing in my heart emanated. I would languish within this pulling in the pit of my stomach until, eventually, it would subside and I could go about my little world, dancing for attention and acceptance as if my life depended on it.

But the loving trust and tolerance I was allowed as a child was shortlived. As I entered my adolescent years, my life became turbulent and desolate and I often turned to the church's familiar, regimented teachings for the consistent comfort it provided. Because of the fact that I was so deeply devout, I felt quietly different and set apart from the other kids. I seemed to always have a sense of Knowing or feeling what I perceived to be right and wrong and I was unyielding in my beliefs, unwilling to go along with the crowd. And the strong personality and calm beliefs I had possessed as a child began to make me a target when the differences became obvious and unattractive during the inevitable "lets all be the same" stage of puberty. I was ostracized and taunted by the other kids as strange and I felt lonely, confused, trapped, and very suicidal. Yet my strong Catholic convictions literally kept me alive as the frequent, serious thoughts of taking my own life were brushed aside because of the church's stance proclaiming hell for any successful Self-destruction.

So, the ages of thirteen, fourteen, and fifteen were terrifying and dark for me. I was tagged a "Pollyanna Purity" because I was not willing to participate in teenage sex and drugs and I was solidly resolute in my choice. I was picked on and ridiculed so severely that I began living in a dream world, going through my days as if I were inhabiting another life entirely. I invented an imaginary existence to tolerate my life and, every day at school, I consciously transported my way to another place. I became so good at focusing my thoughts that often when the school bell rang, I would jerk awake and wonder for a moment where I was. Yet I felt in charge and safe because I was the one creating the scenario and making it happen whenever I needed it. It gave me a sense of control within my uncontrolled life.

I continued on in such a way for the better part of two years. And because of my ability to banish myself to another place in my mind, I would later wonder if that was what had happened to me in the tunnel. Maybe because of the pain and terror of my predicament, I simply transported myself to another place to avoid experiencing the trauma. However, I quickly realized that this was not the case within the tunnel as this experience was something that had unfolded before me and not something that I purposefully created. It was completely different from anything that I had ever created in my own mind, and the intense emotions and feelings attached to this experience continued on with me, living in my heart and place of intuition in my Soul. I trusted myself to know that I knew the difference.

It was during this period of my adolescence that I blessedly discovered music and my God-given vocal talent. My untapped voice was amazing for such a young girl. I had always loved music and I was particularly touched by and drawn to the lyrics of the folk artists at the time. I would sing along, feeling their loving, melodic lyrics with a deep, fervent understanding I couldn't articulate. I felt a profound synchronicity with the lyrics and as I lived within the simple chord progressions. It caused a passionate stirring in my Soul's remembrance. I carefully began to let my voice be heard and when I sang and played my guitar, people listened, cried, and called me a child prodigy. I had discovered a way I could be special and different without being ridiculed.

In the beginning, my music was absolutely my lifeline. I began to sing in the folk mass at church and I met other kids with similar interests as myself. I joined the teen exchange program and began singing at hospitals, nursing homes, special civic events, fairs, and the like. I pulled myself more and more away from the need of school acceptance to another audience, hungry to hear this unusual child sing. A few years later, music would also introduce me to my husband Pete when I auditioned for the lead singer in his band. I know this meeting was no chance happening as the band members were looking for a male funk singer and they got Pollyanna Purity. I guess it didn't hurt that, by now, I had a pretty face, long hair, and the body of a centerfold. We met, became bandmates and trusted friends and married just out of our teens. We left the comfort of our parents' homes and traveled to Los Angeles to pursue the dreams of stardom.

But coming to L.A. was not what we had expected. I began my familiar "love and accept me" dance. So when Self imposed burdens and entertainment industry standards yielded intense expectations, I would loose myself and get caught up in the inevitable course for pretty young singers. My love of music was bastardized into a requirement of standardization and dread with no room to take any chances. My powerful, pure voice and physical curves were not what the industry was buying at the time. They wanted extremely thin physicality and rough-edged voices. A size 10 was too big for anyone in the public eye and my voice lent itself more to Disney than rock and roll.

And I believed "them." I gave my power over to the people (mostly men) that supposedly knew how to make me a star, while the whole time, I just wanted to go home. I began to hate performing and started to develop severe stage fright, as I knew everyone was looking at my fat thighs or freckles. I moved into studio work where my voice was much more appreciated. I sang many national commercials, film themes, and radio spots. I was more comfortable in the studio as the barrier between my Self and the audience was impenetrable. But even then, I rarely enjoyed the process of singing and the only fulfillment I received was the paycheck and the accolades from admiring people who really didn't know the whole story.

It has only been the last few years that I rediscovered the comfort in my voice again. I met up with a good friend who I trusted and who appreciated my voice for what it was, pure and intense. We recorded a Christmas CD and I sang like I did way back when I still remembered the tenderness in the lyrics and the melodies. Louie was hugely responsible for helping to heal my broken Spirit and, through his beautiful music, I was able to sing freely with joy and truth.

And back in my adolescence, even though I knew that I was set apart from the other kids, I still managed to stay true to myself and who I was. It seems that my Spirit was strong then and able to see a hopeful future and to hang on even tighter to my religion. I realized way back then that being different and accepting that fact could be very life affirming, yet lonely. I also know that, at such a tender age, I recognized that the conviction I was able to hold on to had planted a seed in me that allowed my heart and Spirit to open up as I continued into my adult life. It made me strong and more accepting of the differences in people. I never judged anyone by how they looked or appeared to the outside world. And, most importantly, as I made my way through those tumultuous years, I slowly began to realize that I could create my own existence and that depending on how I looked at things, I could change the way I felt. As I began to trust my own feelings, I began to blossom socially, making teenage friends that accepted me as I was. Later, I would put all these things together, using my focused mind, solid convictions and open heart to unquestioningly allow the Guides to come into my life. My disciplined yet opened mind was succinctly being prepared in such a way that I was able to clear my thoughts and allow this clean palette a chance to receive and develop my own choices.

I did, however, continue to crave "going home" whenever I was in peril. And even though I didn't understand exactly what that physical and emotional craving was, I knew that going home was anywhere but here in my everyday little world. That intense craving would eventually leave and be replaced with a gift beyond my comprehension at the time. I did go home the day I stepped into the temple and met the Guides.

And now, I embrace and love the difference that is me. It has given me the courage to write my story. I am not one to question anymore. It is in The Knowing.

Chapter Three

Permission to Seek

...breaking free from the past.

"Choose to recognize and accept the blessings
that rain upon your life."

When I opened my eyes, I was relieved to see that I was alone in the hospital room. And I winced as the dull, thud-like throbbing in my lower abdomen painfully reminded me of the last several hours. Moving over a little on my right side, I softly rubbed my hands across the bandages that covered my incision. The diagnosis of internal bleeding and peritonitis from a ruptured, enormous cyst was what had caused this trauma. Physically, I had lost an ovary, a fallopian tube, and had cut my chances for having children in half. Emotionally, a ragged tear had ripped deep within the recesses of my mind, and this raw hole was being filled with Light, energy and thoughts that I had never experienced before. Yet, I still felt baffled and numbed by everything that had just happened to me and glancing at the clock, I realized that it had only been about twelve hours since I had embarked on the pilgrimage of transformation. Just as quickly, another distressing, more tangible reality hit me, we had no health insurance and I was going to cost us a lot of money.

I grimaced and tightly closed my eyes, longing for the peaceful, beautiful sensation that had earlier consumed my Being. I tried "going there" in my head once more as I could still remember each detail of what had happened. But the only thoughts that continued to enter my mind were confusion about what had happened and guilt that I had, once again, fallen short of perfection. At that point, a nurse quietly walked into the room and as I looked up at her, I noticed that I couldn't seem to focus in on the details of her face very well and that her image seemed to be glowing and vibrating with colored hues.

I blinked several times, but the incandescent glimmering only intensified and more surprising, when I closed my eyes, I could still see the burn of the shimmering colors outlining her physical shape. For the rest of the day, I became more and more frightened as other people filtered in and out of my room, each out of focus with sparkling colors around their bodies. I complained to anyone who would listen, but they would only say that it was probably the medication wearing off. Desperately, I decided to accept this explanation and for several more days, as I waited for the medication to work its way out of my body, I watched as people began to come into focus, bringing with them a brilliantly clear, colorful rainbow all around their shapes. And I watched in bewildered amazement, as the colored lights would move around their bodies whenever they would talk or express emotion. These colors were not going away; in fact, they were intensifying. After much pleading, some of them took condescending pity on me and examined my eyes. But, finding nothing there, they would just pat my arm and patronizingly write off my fear by saying that I had been through a lot and, soon, I would be back to normal. I wanted to believe them, and a week later I left the hospital to recover my health, regroup, and add up my newfound financial responsibilities.

Eight months later

It was driving me crazy. The sparkling colors surrounding the bodies of everyone I saw had not only *not* disappeared, but had actually increased as time went on. People's faces were now in complete focus, and the colors had brightened even more, becoming beautiful colors of Light that seemed to have a life of their own. The colors were almost always visible to me and they were exceedingly distracting. There had been no medical explanation from anyone about this and every night I prayed that, upon awakening, they would be gone. But they weren't going away and, day-by-day, I became more and more frightened that this would be my life from now on.

I was also consumed with my experience in the tunnel, unable to comprehend what had happened. I knew that something incredulous had occurred and I knew deep within my heart that I had been blessed with this experience. I felt "chosen" for something, but I didn't understand or comprehend any of it. Obviously, I couldn't ignore the colors, as I now called them, and I also began to realize that I didn't want to ignore them. I yearned for an understanding of both the tunnel experience and the colors and I prayed for a sign or an answer that I could grasp and hold on to.

Thinking back to my adolescence, I thought that maybe I had imagined the tunnel phenomenon or maybe I had dreamed it. Was it the terrible trauma that was plundering my body that caused me to leave it behind? Was it medically induced? Did I have a vision of God or was I being tricked by the Devil and being seduced into doing something sinful? The flight through the tunnel had been wonderfully unexpected and unfathomed yet the Spiritual overtone had been unmistakably recognizable. And because of this implication, I was extremely nervous about where my Catholic beliefs stood in all this. Even though I couldn't deny what had happened, (and didn't want to), I was just so stuck in my dictated religious convictions that I couldn't find an acceptable answer for colors or tunnels. Life around me continued to move along yet I was stuck in a seeming void. The tunnel experience had transformed and changed me and left me feeling a need for something I couldn't name. And because nothing could be defined or explained, I felt disjointed, confused, and I continued on with this vapid existence and frustrated state of mind for months.

Then, one Sunday, as I walked into the church for mass, I observed an old lady on the outside of the building, bending down and arranging the flowerbeds. She had very long gray hair down to her waist and I noticed the glowing colors around her to be especially bright, which is why she caught my eye. I watched her as she haltingly stood up, holding on to the side of the building for support. Once she reached her full height, she steadily turned and looked directly at me. We stared at each other for a few moments and as we came closer to each other, she slowly nodded her head in acknowledgment. Then she smiled, showing beautiful, natural white teeth, which I thought was unusual for a woman of her advanced years. I smiled back and even though I knew I didn't know her, she seemed very familiar. Her image burned itself into my consciousness, causing me to feel a remembering of some familiar ache. As I turned the corner of the church, I continued to watch her and she once again nodded to me. Entering the church, I sat in one of the back pews and wondered why she had stared so intently and lovingly at me? As I turned my attention to the beginning of the mass, I closed my eyes, trying to block the "burn" of the colors surrounding the congregation.

I quickly forgot about this encounter until a few months later. By then, I was literally sick with worry as the colors were now so strong and vibrant that I had set it in my mind that I was going crazy. I also began to fear that maybe I was possessed, as, at that time in my life, I felt anything was possible. I found myself going to mass more and more, even stopping in the church during the week to sit and try and figure out what was happening. I would implore God to help me or somehow allow me to understand the circumstances of that time.

Looking back, I now know that I was always talking and asking, but never listening or waiting for the answer. And on a particularly bad, frustrating day, I once again went to the church to plead for a resolution and this time, I went up to the altar and knelt down. I remember looking up at the huge crucifix and begging for help, never stopping to take a breath. I clenched my hands together, desperately bargaining with God to give me a sign or anything that would let me know I was all right. I remember looking up at a commanding effigy of the Christ. I stopped and stared deeply into its carved eyes and calm countenance.

And for the first time, I was silent. I began to allow the flow of my own angst to make it's way up the statue and I waited, clearing my mind of all thoughts. There was a silence all around me; still I could hear a low hum within my head. I forgot about everything for just those few seconds, a few moments of peaceful relinquishment. My mind stopped racing and, trusting this silence, I put my face in my hands while I continued to kneel at the wooden rail.

At this point, I felt a tentative tap on my shoulder. Startled out of this rare silent moment, I quickly turned to see who was there. I immediately realized that I was having trouble focusing on the image before me and that the glow around this person was particularly bright. But when she came into view, I was surprised to see that it was the old lady that had stared at me so intently outside of the church a few months before. She timidly begged my pardon and whispered that she needed a dollar for bus money in order to get home. The fares had recently been raised and she was stuck and unable to pay.

Now, I had lived in Los Angeles for long enough to know about street people and beggars. I knew some of them were drug and alcohol addicts or worse, but I also knew that there were people genuinely in a bad way and in need of help. Looking into her eyes, I saw a legitimate need there and I could tell by the way she used the altar rail for support that she was weak and feeble. I immediately felt concern and was drawn to her in a way I couldn't explain. I reached into my purse and pulled out the last five dollars I had and as her face lit up, she kept thanking me over and over. In my shyness and slight embarrassment, I acknowledged her gratefulness and turned back to the altar.

She continued to thank me as she shuffled backwards down the aisle of the large cathedral. After about three seconds, her voice and shuffling abruptly stopped. Concerned that she had collapsed, I turned back around to see why she had stopped talking and walking so suddenly. But the old lady wasn't anywhere in my sight. Panicking, I thought that maybe she had fallen into one of the first pews, so I quickly got up and hurried down the aisle looking for her.

Back and forth, left and right, I peered down each row. As I got to the sixth or seventh row, I thought that she couldn't have possibly made it that far in just a few seconds. I doubted I could have made it that far. When I reached the end of the aisle, I backtracked up each side checking all the doors and side entrances. I went around the whole perimeter of the church checking everywhere. But she wasn't there. She was gone. I felt numbed and bewildered as I made my way back to the altar. Lowering my body, I knelt down once again, whispering to God, "Where did she go?" It was then that I felt a soft, gentle stirring in my Soul and I somehow "felt" the answer. That in recognizing the fact that all trials and events in our lives may seem burdensome and targeted directly at us alone, that within that weight, the answer lies upon my *own* perceptive mind and vulnerable heart. That instead of pleading for a comfortable, complacent existence, I could challenge myself and my ideas and beliefs, thus amending my own happiness.

And the answers would find me. The old lady had presented to me a life that was much worse off than mine. The colors were annoying but not harming me as far as I could see. And I felt that I would have my answer soon, that it would reveal itself to me in due time. The old lady was a reminder that someone, somewhere will always be worse off than myself.

As simple and basic as this revelation was, it had a huge impact on me as my personal perspective, temporarily, turned from "why me" to "show me." I shifted my focus from someone who felt that events were happening "to" her to someone recognizing that events happen all around us all the time and I could choose my own reaction and in that, choose my life experience. Although presented simply, this was my first true realization that changing my own perception is the crux and the answer for a life-lived in peaceful choice. I didn't know it then, but I had just allowed a small encounter with The Knowing to enter my life. It was living within the silence.

Two months later

The colors continued, but I was allowing some peace with the realization that they were consistent and becoming somewhat familiar to me. I was finding it easier to move on and I began to slowly accept my life as it now presented itself. And while the colors seemed to be more physical than Spiritual, my thoughts regularly returned to the tunnel experience, which had moved me on a Soul level. Looking back, I knew, deep down that this phenomenon was a blessing and for the Greater Good yet I also held fears of the unknown origins of the event. Deeply engrained in my Catholicism, I worried of the possibility of Soul-possession or the devil trying to sway my thoughts away from God. And it was this fear that pushed me towards finding an answer within the familiar church teachings.

I finally worked up the courage to confide in one of the priests from the parish. But knowing that priests are held in very high regard and that you don't just go up and ask them questions, (do you?), it took quite some time to make up my mind about what to say and how to ask. I can say that, once my mind was made up, my hope was that he would give me an acceptable, Catholic-approved answer, then tell me to just "stop it" and get to mass on Sunday. Maybe he would give me penance, anything I could "do" that would help me understand the tunnel and all its implications. I actually felt a great sense of relief as I walked up to the rectory that morning, confident that everything would be defined and explained for me. But here I was, making my way into the office, incredulously brave for someone afraid of her own shadow, with thoughts that soon this would all be over, I would have all my answers and I could go back to my life.

I walked into the rectory office and asked the receptionist if I could speak with the priest that had given mass the previous Sunday. I didn't know him or his name, (I wanted the anonymity, in case I was to be excommunicated. Smart, huh?) but I described him to her and she seemed to know exactly which priest I was asking about. She showed me to a small waiting room and I sat down to await my fate. Looking around, I was comforted by the familiar signs and symbols that I had seen all my life, a crucifix, a picture of the Madonna, The Last Supper.

When the priest entered the room, he was wearing a jogging suit and tennis shoes and apologizing for his casual appearance, he explained that he had been in the garden. Seeing him close up for the first time, I felt a recognizable familiarity in his face, but by this point, I was so anxious and ready to tell someone what had happened and what was still happening, that I blurted out the whole story before he even had a chance to sit down. When I finished, I stared anxiously at his face. He straightened his back, crossed his hands and looked toward the ceiling with a sigh. Slowly, he sat down next to me. I thought, "Here it comes. He's going to tell me that I'm crazy or possessed or something."

Looking seriously into his eyes I said, "Did I do something wrong? Am I going to go to hell?" He smiled at me and gently patted my hand. Instantly, I jerked and thought that he was going to patronize or diminish my pain with a smile and condescending pat on the hand, just as the doctors had done when I told them of the colors. And unexpectedly, I realized that that was not what I wanted at all. I wanted a real explanation. This wise, unusual man-priest leaned over, looking me directly in the eyes.

His gaze never moved from my face as he began to speak. He took my hands in his and began to systematically blast my Catholic comfort zone by telling me that I hadn't done anything wrong, rather, I had been given a great gift. And in the most tender of ways, he continued on, saying that we can no longer deny that people have had near-death experiences and that even though we don't know much about it, it is well documented. And incredulously, he stood up, took a book off the shelf and handed it to me. He said that I should read it, that it spoke of other people who had had an experience similar to mine. I was absolutely, positively stunned. First of all, since when did priests have books about (what did he call it?) near-death experiences, on their shelves? Why didn't he just tell me that I had imagined it all?

As I sat looking down at the book in my hands, I didn't know what to say or think. He gently tilted my chin up and said that it was my responsibility to learn to understand this gift of the near-death experience, and that I should continue to seek answers. And also, that the gift of the colors was also a good thing, something that had been handed to me in trust and I should use it well. He reiterated that I must seek the answers, learn everything I could and no, I wasn't possessed by the devil or going to hell. Again I was stupefied. What was going on here? Why didn't he just give me some kind of penance and take my problem away from me? Why did he just hand it back to me as if it were my new assignment?

All of a sudden, I felt an enormous sense of excitement and release rush over my body and I quickly confessed that I hadn't been very satisfied with coming to mass on Sundays for a long time. I felt that something was lacking in this familiar ritual and that my Spiritual Self was crying out for more. I surprised myself when I made this potentially sacrilegious statement, but it was the truth. I would just show up at mass and daydream the hour away, making my obligatory appearance in an effort to avoid another sin. I rarely felt a Spiritual connection at all, but I did find some comfort in the ritual itself.

This perceptive priest continued on, telling me that some people do need more and that is a good thing. Some people need to seek out the truth for themselves and he asked, "Isn't that what Jesus said? Seek the Kingdom of God?" And with every brick that was falling from my carefully constructed Spiritual foundation, I was getting braver and braver, and freer and freer. I divulged that I was having thoughts about not coming to mass at all and he answered that he hoped to see me at mass on Sunday, but if he didn't? At that point, he shrugged his shoulders and raised his hands in a "So What?" position. I remember how the thunder rolled under my feet. My Catholic world was rocking as this priest had taken my Soul, placed golden wings upon it and handed it right back to me, clean and unrecognizable. And, continuing with the reconstruction of my Spiritual foundation, he explained that the colors I saw were called the Aura. And the Aura is an electromagnetic field around the human body and that there are books on that phenomenon as well. I stared at him in disbelief. The Aura? These colors that had been so frightening and had kept me up countless nights, had a name?

I stared at him as he gently took my arm and led me to stand and move towards the door. I tilted my head to one side and held my hand out to him. He took it and asked me, "By the way, what does my Aura look like?" At this point, I was still reeling from our conversation and all I could manage to sputter was, "Oh, uh, it looks fine." He chuckled and said, "Good." As I began to leave the room, he took hold of my elbow and whispered, "Go, seek."

Walking back to my car, it felt surreal. I got behind the wheel and set the book on near-death experiences on the seat next to me. Staring out the window, I realized that by breaking the heavily dictated, concrete church beliefs that held my Soul to the ground, this priest had set my passion, my thirst for knowledge on fire. The Catholic girl who originally was screaming for a pat answer was, in truth, asking for permission to seek and this priest was wise enough to understand that. The Catholic girl with solid convictions in her heart needed to hear this priest give her the permission necessary to move forward and she did get that precious sanction.

And I had the beginning of the answers to what had happened because now, they had a name; near-death experience and the Aura. But I would soon learn that these two incredible gifts would not be limited by mere human definitions. And my Spiritual journey, even though it seemed free and ready, was only just beginning. I had no idea what was in store for me, but I felt new and ready to begin.

As I drove home, it dawned on me that I never did find out the priests' name. But I did know that I would never see him again. And I was right. I think maybe he was there just for me.

Chapter Four

Celeste

...opening the portal to the spiritual realm.

*"We are all born with the innate right
to receive love unconditionally."*

One Year Later

I was finding it difficult to fly alone in my search for answers to all the questions that had emerged as a result of my conversation with the priest. I hadn't completely given up on my faith, but it made me tentative and anxious that I now found little solace there. The priest had inspired the odyssey, but I was ill prepared for the vulnerability that would arise out of the unknown resting upon a clean Spiritual canvas. I was beginning to seek out other people who had had similar near-death experiences and I found it wonderful and comforting to know I wasn't the only one.

Even though our experiences varied, we had all come back with a common, transforming revelation: None of us were afraid to die. We had been given a glimpse into another world of utter bliss and acceptance with no fear, no longing for more or anything or anyone but the Light. And I now know that this moment will be the true birth, the true-life experience. I had felt this birthing, this new chance, and these hungry feelings. And these feelings were driving me to keep moving forward as my yearning bled into every cell and grew with every thought of that night.

But in all this newness and joy, the colors that continued to infuse themselves all around the people I saw were extremely distracting and continued to make me very nervous. I was finding it harder and harder to relax for many obvious reasons, including the fact that when I would close my eyes I could still see the burn of the lights around the bodies. Similar to what you get when a flashbulb goes off and you quickly close your eyes. I found it especially difficult to be in a crowd and if I attended a movie, with every blink, I would consistently be unnerved by the sparkling flashes or burns from the lights.

I studied books and articles on the Aura, as I now knew it was called, and I was comforted by the fact that the colors had a name and some type of explanation. But I never met anyone who consistently saw the colors like I did and I was just so unsettled about their implications. What did they mean? Why did this happen to me? Most importantly, would they ever go away? This monumental gift that I would eventually come to understand and embrace, in the beginning caused me to begin to experience debilitating anxiety and panic attacks.

A close friend suggested that, as a course of relaxation, I might go to see a shiatsu massage therapist (someone who also did guided imagery and meditation) friend of hers. At that point, I was desperate to find a way to calm my anxiety and I was willing to try anything even though I was so jittery and nervous, I didn't see how I could lay still and focus on nothing for more than a few seconds. However, I had no way of knowing at the time that on this day, the day I met Celeste, absolutely everything about my world would change for me. She would open a portal to my Soul and would literally change the entire course of my life.

I tentatively made my way to the San Fernando Valley neighborhood where Celeste lived. Her townhouse complex stood modestly behind huge black iron gates. I reached up and pressed the numbers she had given me and, buzzing me through, I nervously followed her directions to her unit. It felt so strange and somehow surreal to be going to the home of a stranger who would place her hands upon my body in an effort to help me relax. I laughed when this thought came, as I found it ironic that I was even more nervous than before and I certainly didn't envy her task. The week before, when I had called to make the appointment, Celeste told me a little bit about the massage and what would happen. It seemed simple enough, yet still, my hands were sweaty as I gripped the wheel and pulled up in front of the townhouse. I sat in the car a few moments to try to calm down. Why was I always so fearful of things I didn't understand? I tried to stop myself from shaking as I sat there and prayed. Resigned that I was going to go through with this, I got my purse and walked hesitantly to her front door.

Celeste was beautiful. She was a sweet, soft-spoken woman just slightly older than myself. Her eyes were sparkling and she smiled quietly as she invited me into her home. Her manner was so gentle that I immediately felt calmer and by the time we got to the room where the massage was to take place, we were chatting as if we were old friends. I didn't know this at the time, but we were indeed very old friends. Lying down upon the pallet she had prepared for me, my nervousness was beginning to fade and I was relieved and excited to experience something new.

As she began the massage, Celeste also began to talk to me, explaining in a quiet voice what she was doing and why. Her hands were soft and soothing and I began to totally relax for the first time in as long as I could remember. I had experienced an immediate bond and feeling of trust with Celeste and I found myself wanting to share my story with her. After the massage was over, I sat up and told Celeste everything. From the tunnel experience, to the Aura and how frightened yet mesmerized I was about everything. I remember Celeste sitting cross-legged upon the floor with her hands clasped together as she listened, smiling and nodding at my words of fear, doubt, intrigue, and longing. She looked unsurprised at my revelations and somehow her smile was that of someone who had a secret.

When I finished talking, she sighed deeply and, looking down at her clasped hands, her smile widened as she looked back up at me with a tender, Knowing gaze. She told me that this was something that I must not "wish away," that this great gift was something I must understand and that my search needed to continue with acceptance and love, not fear or worry. She continued and said that I could never understand what this truly meant until I gave up the fear, that my fear had been keeping me paralyzed. Now I had lived in fear and worry about everything and everyone all my life. Living with courage and calm acceptance was never a part of my psyche, and I frankly had no idea where to begin to make that change. She suggested that I lay down again and she would guide me through a meditation that would take me to a special place in my mind where I could learn to relax and clear my thoughts.

Trusting completely, I followed her instructions to lie back upon the pallet and close my eyes. She touched my arm and proceeded to talk me into a deep meditative space, one that I had never been calm enough to experience on my own. She guided my breathing and my mind to slow down and quietly, she spoke of clearing my thoughts and allowing a gentle, cool white Light to come into my consciousness. Celeste continued on, softer and slower, as she guided my thoughts and imagination to go deeper into a velvety repose. And as her simple, melodic voice moved above my body, she delicately encouraged me to transport my thoughts to a "special place" of peace and complete safety. My mind began to use its imagination as she described a beautiful lake with snowy white swans floating serenely upon the water.

She continued on and began to talk about the flowers when, all at once, I was aware that I could no longer hear her guidance. Just as this thought came to mind, I began to hear a quiet wind in my ears. I didn't move or breathe and I lay there silent and expectant and open for this experience. It was within this instant that I suddenly and deliberately "popped" into another state of consciousness and realm of existence. Opening my eyes, I found myself standing at the edge of a beautiful lake. At first, I thought that maybe I was creating an escape like I had done so many times in my adolescent years, but I quickly became aware that this was entirely different. I had no control over where I was or what was unfolding before me. I looked down at my hands and turned them around and I was surprised to see that they didn't look any different than usual. My feet were bare and they were warmly enmeshed within the white sandy particles at the lakes edge.

I raised my hands in front of my face and slowly moved my fingers back and forth. They responded to my demands just as they would in "real" life. I raised my right hand higher and stretched out my arm in front of me in an effort to "touch" or "feel" this place that I so surely was imagining or dreaming. But as the breeze kissed my fingers, hand and arm, I realized that I was really in a three-dimensional place that was vibrating with life. I shuddered with this realization and stood frozen, watching with bewilderment as the lake rippled and clouds rolled by in this unbelievable, serene setting of simple beauty. I looked out across the water and observed fish, animals and nature as they moved and lived in and about this glittering lake that lapped at the edge of a deep green forest. I was having trouble believing this was real, that I was actually "there." How did this happen? Where in the world was I?

I slowly began to move my feet and legs in an effort to continue testing my own awareness. As before, my body responded naturally and easily just as it would on any given day. I was utterly and totally mesmerized with this surreal moment, yet just as surprisingly I felt no fear at all. I surprised myself with this realization and I relished this rare moment of calmness.

Tentatively, I put one foot in front of the other and walked towards the water's edge. Cautiously, I dipped my toe into its balmy water. The temperature was perfect and I stood there, swishing my toes back and forth as little fish began to swim toward the ripples. I squatted down and my fingertips reached in, deftly moving through the water and into the white sand on the bottom. I gathered the crystals into my palm and pulling my hand out of the water, I watched the sparkling beads as they slowly fell through my fingers. Everything was perfect. All the colors were vibrant and living. All the vegetation, coral and rocks were alive and buzzing with energy. The birds, both above me and all around were flying expectantly around the lakeside. Deer moved in and out of the green forest that protected the lake on the right side. I was just a visitor, yet this place was familiar and altogether as real as my own backyard.

Even though I grew up with and used my wild imagination, this place was definitely unimagined or created by me. This life, this environment, was moving and living right before my eyes and with absolutely no prompting from my own thoughts. I stood up and observed the beautiful, encircling beach that was soft, white, and warm. My eyes moved upward and gazed upon a stunning sky of china blue and white. Where was I? Why was I here? Looking around, I began to hear a faint voice calling to me, telling me that it was okay to come back into the room and to open my eyes. I was confused when, once again, I heard a slight whooshing sound and I closed my eyes to block out the realization that I was leaving this exquisite place.

I opened my eyes and found myself staring into Celeste's beautiful face. She sweetly said, "Hi," and smiled. I blinked several times in an effort to focus on her face. Her Aura was glowing so spectacularly that it took my breath away. I sat up and stared at her face and wondered if she knew what had just happened. "Feel better?" she asked. I nodded my head slowly and tried to tell her about the lake, but no words would come. She wondered if I knew how long I had been "gone" and I was flabbergasted when she said it had been about two hours.

She told me that, almost instantly, my breathing slowed down and a look of utter peace came across my face. She said that she had left me there and gone into another room, as she knew I needed that space. All I could whisper was thank you. Thank you. No other words put together by me could possible describe the feeling of being in that beautiful place and my gratitude for the introduction. Nothing would ever detail the complete feeling and power of coming back from such an experience. I was calm and centered and immediately wanted to go back. I knew that it was some-where other than "here" and I yearned to return the moment I opened my eyes. I had felt so safe and wanted and I instantly craved more of those uncommon feelings.

I looked at Celeste and told her that I wanted to go back. Tears filled my eyes as I expressed the instant fear that I wouldn't be able to go back on my own. I questioned my ability to calm my stormy mind long enough to reach the space that would allow me to enter easily and peacefully. Celeste assured me that this place was always available to me and that I could do it on my own. I would need to develop a routine of meditation that could quickly and easily quiet my wild thoughts and energy. She suggested, upon closing my eyes, to envision a white wall where all my thoughts would appear. As they would appear, I was to reach up and erase all those thoughts and words and feelings. Then she instructed me to focus on the clean, white space until more words would appear. I was to then start the process all over again, wiping the words away and focusing on the white "nothingness" for longer and longer periods. She felt that I could discipline my mind to clear itself and that I would be able to find myself back at the water's edge in my place of peace. I was skeptical that I could do this on my own, but I was encouraged and eager to begin.

As Celeste walked me to my car, she took my arm and again assured me that I could do this on my own. And I would learn to calm my thoughts and begin to meditate without fear or holding back. I hugged this familiar stranger and thanked her again, for her help, her gift to me. As I was starting my car engine, she leaned in the passenger window and said again that I could do this, that I must do this. She offered more assistance if necessary and I looked into her eyes with such gratitude that I know she could feel it in her heart. I waved to her and, patting the steering wheel, I set off to find my life.

Two years later

The colors continued, yet I had finally accepted this gift and even began to enjoy it. I was also blessedly able to "overlook" or "turn-off" the colors so that I wasn't constantly distracted by them. I began to see patterns in the Auras and could now tell when people were upset, depressed, and even when they were lying. I can also tell when someone is pregnant and I have more than a few good friends who still talk about how "Peggy knew before I did" about their pregnancy. (note: This ability became clearer many years later as I learned about how a new Soul attaches to its mother and at what point this decision is made. This is addressed in the last chapter.)

Ultimately, I began to meditate at least once a day. Using Celeste's advice, I had slowly learned how to quiet my mind long enough to allow me to "pop," once again, to the lakeside. I was captivated by the beautiful serenity and peace and I continued this privilege for two years. Upon entering the lakeside, I would swim with the fish, feed the deer, and watch the birds and clouds go by as I relaxed on its pristine shore. It was my home and my refuge and I loved it. I was particularly drawn to play under the water with the fish as I soon discovered my vision was as clear submerged as it was above the water line. I loved the sensation of seeing the underwater world as clearly as I saw the land above it and I loved the fish that greeted me with nibbles and brushes. On occasion, I would explore around the lake and would sometimes venture into the cool, quiet dark green forest that stood at its edge. I was so calm and used to coming to the lake that my emotions had gone from complete awe to total acceptance and expectation. I held no fear and I unquestioningly received everything about this place.

It was on a particularly typical day that I emerged from the water and headed for the shoreline to lay down and gaze upon the clouds. I noticed instantly that a soft, warm breeze had begun and along with it, an expectant stirring in my Soul. I looked around and heard the soft breeze as it made its way over my body and into my ears. I gazed back out across the rippling lake when, sensing movement, I sharply turned around and faced the tall trees in the forest. Instantly, I saw an incredibly bright Light emanating from deep within its foliage. The spectacular brilliance of the Light was so intense that it's powerful glow reached the tree tops and beyond. I felt an instantaneous thirst to see what this was and with no hesitation or fear, I began to make my way through the forest towards the glowing beacon. As I penetrated the wooded area, I felt an urgency, a need that was pushing me forward. Slowly, I began to feel the warmth of the glow as I got nearer to the Lighted area. I made my way up a small embankment and pushed through the branches.

As I came to a clearing in the trees, I stepped out of the foliage and caught my breath in astonishment. I found myself standing in front of a huge, glorious temple of stone. It was a massive structure that stood majestically against the blue sky. Its magnificence was breathtaking and I stared upon its girth. The temple was made of cut stones that were different hues of beige with small, Lighted particles. There was a beautiful manicured garden at its base and a stone bench stood simply between the temple and the garden.

On the temple's right side, there was a staircase cut deeply into the stone. The staircase led all the way to the top, where a doorway stood open and dimly lit. But amazingly, halfway up this staircase was a small niche cut into the rock. And in front of this niche stood a man dressed in the clothing of a guard from ancient times. He was carrying a staff-sword and wearing a large metal hat with a plume that was typical of the ancient Romans. He was staring straight ahead when, upon sensing my gaze, he walked to the edge of the steps and looked down upon me. Our eyes met and he smiled and bowed in my direction. He had a look of recognition and he peered down at me as if he had been waiting for my arrival.

And for the first time since I had been coming to the lake, I felt frightened. Even though I had encountered living animals and plants, I had never seen a person before. As if sensing my fear, he tilted his head to one side, placed his hand over his heart and smiled sweetly. My fear immediately melted away. I sensed that I was not in danger and that somehow, this man and I knew each other. Then, ever so tenderly, he extended his hand toward me, beckoning me up the staircase. I walked through the garden and stood next to the bench at the edge of the temple. I slowly made my way over to the staircase, never taking my eyes off this man. And I knew I had to go. I had to climb those stairs.

Chapter Five

The Guard at The Temple

...encountering the first spirit.

"Try to remember, to believe in a time when you were accepting of all new things."

I had become accustomed to the abundant nature that presented its exquisite beauty and life energy all around the lakeside. However, now here was an actual person standing above me, beckoning me to come to him. He was completely real, tangible, and three-dimensional and I knew I hadn't made him up or imagined him in any way. I didn't recognize him, yet his manner and Essence seemed vaguely familiar. I hesitated for a moment, then, with my heart steadily pounding, I made a swift decision to ascend the stairs.

My every step was determined and resolute and in a matter of seconds, I found myself staring into the eyes of this man, this Guard of some sort. He was much taller than myself, yet his large physicality wasn't at all threatening. With his flamboyant staff and ruby and gold robe, I was immediately reminded of a gentle giant. He smiled once more and, again placing his hand over his heart, he slightly bowed and lifted his eyes to meet mine. And I, in my slight awkwardness, bowed my head in acknowledgment.

At this point, any remaining trepidation melted away and I smiled, as his twinkling eyes never left my own wider, wondering eyes. Taking his hand away from his heart, he slowly gestured behind him to a small niche that was carved out of the stone and set back into in the side of the temple. There was a small, gray stone bench that was carved out of the temple floor. I stood there, looking in the direction of the little niche, studying its simple design. Looking back upon the face of the Guard, I saw that his hand was still gesturing towards the bench and I understood that he wanted me to sit down upon it. I walked over to the bench and lowered myself upon its cool top. The Guard, once again, placed his hand over his heart and turned back around, facing away from me. I sat expectantly on the bench, looking at the backside of this man who was so gentle and strong. But if I was anticipating something happening, I was sorely disappointed. He simply stood there and continued his watch and with his back turned to me, he ignored my presence completely.

As perplexing as this was, I was nevertheless surprised at the calmness and contentment I felt. I had no idea where I was, or what this man represented, yet I felt totally safe. I began to take notice of the bench I was seated upon and I proceeded to study the cool stone walls of the massive temple. I could smell moss and rainwater with a hint of newly budding roses. Looking out toward the Guard, I could see that he gazed upon the beautiful forest that I had just journeyed from and beyond that, his eyes fell upon my beloved lakeside. I wondered if he had been watching me all this time and I remember that I felt surprised that I was okay with that. I always had a small feeling that I was a visitor in someone else's dwelling, anyway, and that I had no right to privacy.

Suddenly, the thought entered my mind that maybe this was his home and his lakeside and I softly said, "Excuse me?" The Guard turned around and smiled as I asked him where we were. Was this his home? But he only put his hand over his heart and bowing in my direction and turning slowly back around, he ignored my question. Several more times I prodded him with inquiries and each time he reciprocated with the same hand over heart and bow. I began to feel awkward and after what seemed like a long time, I decided to make my way back down the temple stairs as I didn't know what else to do.

Six months later

Every day in meditation, I continued to make that same trip halfway up the side of the temple only to be greeted in exactly the same manner. And as I sat upon that bench time after time, I became braver and more intrigued. My urgency and frustration were escalating as I would ask him why he wouldn't talk to me or tell me who he was or where we were. My disappointment with his disregard was beginning to be more difficult to hide. And then, one night, I stood next to the Guard and reaching up with both hands, I carefully turned him around to face me. "Why? Why won't you talk to me? Where are we? Who are you?" At this bold move on my part, he smiled and quietly placed his hand upon my shoulder. Looking very deeply into my eyes, I was instantly aware that he was beginning to convey a message to me. His eyes bore into my own eyes and we stared at one another with calm, deliberate intent. And, in that split moment, I began to understand him as I was "feeling" what he tenderly expressed, not with words, but with his heart. Looking back, I know that if this man had actually answered me out loud, I would have run down those steps in fear, never to return. But he knew that I needed a slow induction into this magical moment. So he gently introduced me to communicating with him through his heart. His beautiful message was tender, sweet, and loving and I was ready to hear it. "*You are chosen for this journey. It is you that made the ultimate decision, before you were born, to come here and learn in your embodied Self, the Essence of Spirit and of God. In time you will completely understand the meaning of all this and you will have little fear. Your Soul is familiar with this place as you have been here many times as a child and in your dreams. The love you felt when you came here in your moment of crisis was all encompassing and breathtakingly calm. We know that you felt this and that is why you came. We have been waiting. You must be brave and do not be afraid to step out in front and lead. Those that must lead sometimes have the most tender of hearts and Spirit but are of strong will and constitution. God is the All There Is. There is no other. Of this you are well aware. It is with deep humility that we bring you this place of peace; that we are always here, waiting for you. That you may come here anytime in need, in confirmation, seeking love and answers to complete your pathway. You will Know no fear when you are here. For fear is ignorance of God and lack of Spirit. All things that turn from God are based in fear, because The Knowing is not present. You will be given a task to complete your predestined life's journey. At a time of both your choosing and circumstantial. Receive with joy, go to the Light always, make your intent for the Greater Good and Know that you are a child of the All, ever-encompassing power of the All There Is."*

And with the tender compassion that he emanated, I received the same feeling of total, all-permeating love that had consumed me as I reached for the Light in the tunnel the night of my death. We continued to look into each other's eyes for a moment of eternity and I knew that this night, this moment was new, yet familiar with a feeling of total completeness and Knowing. The kindness and patience he offered me was sincere and unconditional and, looking deep within his eyes, I became aware of his heart's desire, of his need and joy in guiding me, enlightening me and showing me the road less taken.

I instantly became aware that what I had experienced in my life was leading to this ultimate end. Everything I had lived through was bringing me to this moment. I felt humbled and joyful and, as if he understood my newfound enlightenment, he sweetly reached down and took my hand in his. His message had been clear and I was ready to continue the journey as I was solidly in agreement with my own heart and this Guard.

At this point, he stepped aside and motioned me to continue up the remaining stairs to the top of the temple. I felt absolutely no fear or apprehension even though I had no idea what awaited me there. For somehow I seemed to know where I was going, that this was a familiar place. And as I began to ascend the remaining stairs, I gazed upon the opening at the top of the temple. My body seemed to be vibrating with a low hum and with each step, my heart deliberately pounded out the next stride.

When I reached the top, I slowly turned around and looked back down at the Guard. He was facing away from me in his familiar stance, continuing his watch. I laughed to myself, as I wanted to jump up and down and yell out to him, "I made it! Look at me!" But, this reverent moment was not to be shared with anyone, not even the Guard. This was for me and I knew it. I took a deep breath and turning my attention back to the darkened opening that stood before me, I silently stepped inside the temple. It now became a predetermined impossibility that my life would ever be the same.

Chapter Six

I Meet The Guides

...the miracle begins.

"It is important to understand that
you have the power to choose."

This moment was glorious. I felt no fear, only anticipation, as my heart was still singing with the message from the Guard. I crossed the threshold of the temple doorway and waited for my eyes to adjust to the low light. The first thing I could see was a round opening carved out of the floor. Walking to its edge, I could see by the illumination of the Light coming through the temple door, that it was a darkened staircase, leading down. There was a low brick wall that protectively encircled the opening, allowing access only to the stairs. Just on the other side of this staircase was a rather large fire pit that was also surrounded by a low brick wall. The softly glowing embers began to flicker into more definitive flames as I made my way around the darkened stairs and stood beside the pit.

Peering over its edge, I reached my hand into the flames and as if I already knew, there was no pain, only a cool, "Lighted" feeling as the flames leapt through my fingers. I could see my distorted reflection in the fire and again, I felt no fear, only a calmness, a trust of this place. Looking up just beyond the fire pit, I saw a round wooden table with eight chairs that stood deeper within the room. As my eyes adjusted even further, I could see the large, intricately carved wooden chairs standing regally next to the table's frame. The table itself was dark cherry wood with an inlay of beautiful teak around its top.

I walked slowly over to its edge and reached down, gently running my hand over the aged wooden finish. I closed my eyes, taking in the sensation of my fingers against the solid wood when, almost instantly, I began to hear and feel an intense roaring noise as a strong wind suddenly came up. Again, I felt no fear, just a sense of expectancy and safety within these walls. As the escalating vibration became louder, I immediately recognized the deafening roar as the same sensation I experienced the night I died. At that moment in the ER, my urgent need to survive was fighting this vibration, this beckoning of some sort. But this time, I was completely calm and accepting and I bowed my head against the wind as it continued to blow harder and louder.

I began to take in a deep feeling of protective love, as the noisy, chaotic wind whipped my hair and the vibration unyieldingly pounded my body. And then, as quickly as it began, the wind and the roaring stopped and there was complete silence within the temple walls. I stood frozen with my eyes closed as my body, heart, and senses continued to drink in the vibrations that were still permeating my every cell. I hadn't wanted the noise and wind to stop because for some reason, I felt safe within this experience. But eventually, I was compelled to open my eyes to see what the wind had left behind. With my eyes slowly opening, I looked around the now calm, quiet room. The fire in the pit flickered softly, seemingly undisturbed by the wind and I could see that the table and chairs that stood next to me were unmoved as well. The quiet in the room struck me as somehow deliberate as it had the feeling of a job well done or the moments just after a great accomplishment.

I filled my lungs with the cool air that was sweet and readily available and I smiled with a sense of Knowing this place. Looking around, I took in every brick, every edge and form that stood against the air within the walls. I silently smiled and continued to lean against the table's edge, as I didn't want to move or change the electric sensations that floated gently all around me. But as I looked deeper into the room, I was again not surprised to see that a low platform had appeared against the back wall. I watched with calm amazement as a gentle, violet-white colored Light hovered above the platform, illuminating the entire area with its intense brilliance.

As I stared in awe upon this beautiful display, the violet Light began to move and float above the platform, swirling into itself as beautiful colors appeared and began to merge. I watched as these colors danced together and floated towards each other and, upon connecting, there would be little sparks of energy that seemed to spike outward as they collided. I stood watching this incredible dance of Light as they continued to connect and merge with a deliberate mission or purpose. And I remember that I was actually surprised at my own calm acceptance when I observed the Lighted particles beginning to form and shape themselves into six individual Beings. I simply accepted this dramatic entrance as a matter of fact and as their forms and faces began to appear, I literally ached to touch them, to be near them. I had a strange combined feeling of familiarity and yearning to dance within the Lights that were these Beings. And as the Lighted particles and hues continued to form, I watched, as each Being became more solid and three dimensional, with distinct features and size.

The Beings stood side by side upon the platform and as they came into clear focus, I could see that they were smiling and I was immediately enveloped with the feeling of the unconditional love that their eyes were sending to my aching heart. My whole body began to shake with the saturation of this intense love and acceptance from their Lighted Souls to my Soul in need. And I began to cry tears of every emotion I had ever felt. Happy, sad, yearning, loving, and fearful emotions flew through my body with intentional ease. I felt a choking of all these emotions as the Lighted Being that stood in the middle of the platform began to lift his arms outward, urging me forward.

I stood frozen with emotion, wanting so badly to go to him, but feeling intensely overwhelmed, my feet barely moved. The Being slowly began to walk toward me and somehow, I managed to step upon the platform to meet him halfway. His long white robe and long, curly grey hair were a comforting "symbol" of a wise, old loving Being of Light. As our out-stretched hands touched, I felt a surge of unconditional, all encompassing, loving energy flowing through my heart and straight into my Soul. His soft, weathered face held blue eyes that were clear and gentle.

As I gazed into his familiar countenance, he brought our clasped hands to his heart and ever so softly said, "*Welcome daughter. You are here and the Angels rejoice in All There Is. We have been waiting for you. We have missed your sweet smile and generous nature. And now you are here and we will help ready you for your path and destiny in this life, which you call your own. We welcome you to this temple, this heart of your mind, this place of refuge and teaching. In these moments, you will find peace, you'll Know unconditional love and you will learn acceptance for who you are. In this place of refuge, we will teach you to use your gifts of insight, and help your understanding of the colors and energy emanating from the human body. You will develop The Knowing, the ways of God, and the power of the human Spirit. For, when we are born, we soon forget our Heavenly Father and where we came from. This must be in order for us to evolve, grow, and learn to seek truth. You have been given an opportunity to take leaps and bounds of progress towards that goal.*"

He went on, "*This was your choice before you were born. You chose this life as we all do, and you chose to be a teacher. And we shall Guide you to this ulti-mate end. This moment in your life, this defining crossroad of that which you call your life, will be ever evolving and changing. You have been given the gift of this ability to change and accept without reserve. You are your own Power of Will. You will make the choices that define your existence but more impor-tantly, you will lead and grow into the Light with many other Souls. In this reserve, you will find the familiarity that you will need and yearn for. You will find the All There Is. You will share and talk with others of Like-minds and in this defining turn of your road of life, you will run fast and hard toward that ultimate end which is the heart of God and the All There Is, that which we call, The Knowing. And you will recognize this Knowing as the true pathway that you will take at a tempo of ease and truth, this comfortable ease that you will undertake and explore, this Knowing of the All There Is. This hope, peace and serenity of life as you are living it."*

And when he stopped speaking, I breathlessly took in his words and familiar voice. At that moment, I began to realize that his "voice" was the same one I had heard as I was caressed by the Light at the moment of my death. The voice that had said, *"Not now, my daughter"* and led me back to this life experience and all that it encompassed for my journey to this moment.

The Being continued on, *"We are on a level just above your own. We are not special or above you in any way. No, we are there to Guide you, should you choose, and to help you attain the perfection of the All There Is. We will never seek to sway your thinking; we will but give you the opportunity to think beyond what is comfortable and already Known in your heart. An opportunity to be given these gifts in an effort to raise your heart, mind, and Soul to the Heavenly Father and the All There Is, The Knowing. For we see a future of hope, of reason, and of acceptance for all people. A time when expression of ideas, hopes, and experiences are encouraged freely and welcomed with unabandoned joy. We yearn for that Universal power of all things and we seek others of Like-minds. We look for those struggling to understand and we reach out to them with an unconditional hand. Our Purpose, our reason for being in this life experience is limited only by our minds and the boundaries within. Lives change and seasons turn, yet we are all bound together by a golden strand, spun from the wings of Angels. The choices we make and the dreams we share define our existence upon the Earth and vulnerability is the realization that we all matter. Every one of our lives is simply a confirmation of our own intuition, delicate, sweet moments in time. And tenderly, we sing and rejoice in All There Is."*

And when he stopped talking, he took me tenderly into his arms and as he gently stroked my hair, I wept again with a rush of relief, love, and completeness. I knew that this moment, this time, this event was the reason for everything that we, as humans, strive for. Unconditional, unjudged, and completely accepting love: the All There Is. Isn't that truly all that we really need, hope, or long for? This deep yearning for our Souls and bodies?

Lovingly wrapped in the arms of this Being, this "Wise One," my struggled, ragged existence began to make sense, to have a purpose. The Wise One took my face in his hands and continued speaking, "*So, now daughter, it is time to reintroduce you to the other Souls that were predetermined by you to help with this life moment, this journey of your heart. In your heart and Soul you will Know of these entities, as they were there before you went to sleep in the life that you now dream. They appear symbolically for you in an effort to release any preconceived ideas or judgments on your part. They appear as you need them to be and their Souls project to you the symbol most understood by your heart. Their physicality is one that you will understand and accept without reserve or fear.*"

He continued, "*It was in your early existence that you came here and we held you and loved you and told you that soon you'd be here for another reason. You will learn, daughter, that this life would be great. And you will undertake a task upon your Soul, a burden that at times will be heavy to bear. And by living an example of real-life, one of your biggest tasks will be to learn honesty and your ability to portray it in your everyday life. You'll find many conflicts in your world of worlds and it may be hard to determine the road you must take. But we will be there to Guide you, to give to you tasks to ponder and undertake as your journey begins. We, as your Guides, will help to ease this transition of your stark realities to one of Spirit. This meaning, this purpose, will envelope your Soul and will be a shining beacon of least resistance when the time comes.*"

I felt calm and reassured by his words of wisdom and clarity. I knew deep within my heart that this was right, that this was for the Greater Good of my Spirit. All that I had been seeking, all that I tried so hard to understand, had always been completely safe and Known within my own heart. I wholeheartedly and calmly accepted the fact that I seemed to be in some other realm of existence and that my Soul had taken flight and landed in this wonderful place. Unimagined by myself, I knew that I was no longer Earthbound yet I was still connected with my Earthly body and existence. I felt light and centered, and I found instant joy in the fact that this secret place of peace was introducing my heart to its purpose.

The Wise One quietly led me to a sweet-faced, middle-aged Indian (as in India) woman sitting in a wheelchair. Her older, lined face was calming and filled with joy. She had dark black hair that was pulled loosely away from her face and her orange robes were draped casually around her body and the wheelchair. She possessed a solid sense of love and safety and I was immediately drawn to her gentle Spirit and longed to be held in her arms.

Sitting in her wheelchair, she lifted her weathered hand towards me and as I gave her mine in return, her large, pool-black eyes calmly looked deep within mine as she said, *"I am here for your comfort. For the unconditional love and understanding that is an inherent part of all mothers. But not all mothers remember this task, this innate sense of responsibility. As I can, I will help you to understand the unconditional love and how it plays in the world of the human form. This unconditional love, which is a right of every Soul, is not often realized. I will tenderly hold you and let you Know of this love when you forget. I will help you to apply this feeling to all that are deserving, those that do not remember and those that do. It will be easy to give this to children, animal, and plants innocent of the world of harsh realities. But the challenge will lie in those that do not remember, those that need it the most and have forgotten how to care unconditionally for those of great need. I will be there for you and help you recognize this. And when you see this great need among many people on the Earth, I will be there for your own comfort as you will begin to feel their sadness, their yearning for the unconditional arms of God. I will comfort you as you grieve and try to express to those in need of The Knowing. I will teach you to balance this grief and keep it from hindering your own progress. Your sense of right and wrong and your deep, deep absorption of the feelings and emotions of those around you will be one of your biggest challenges in this life experience. You will need to understand the wise, ancient ways of the master teachers. To help without requiring help. To give without depletion, and to teach, Guide, and love unconditionally. I appear less movable to you because of your own fears. As you learn, I will stand and move about with you in your own experience. This chair, these braces that are livable, will break free and you will no longer be bound by your own fears of rejection and judgment."*

I looked longingly at this Being, this Mother Guide, who projected the wisdom of the simple, basic need of all people. I felt the right of my Soul to receive love and acceptance, unconditionally and freely, without hesitation or payment from our own hearts. In the instant we met, I was consumed by her need to teach me the nurturing and loving ways of all women born with The Knowing intact and ready to give back this gift of the female. The Mother Guide reached her arms around my body and pulled me onto her lap. She gently rocked me back and forth, stroking my hair and tenderly patting my arm. Then, with a firm, kind hug, she placed a sweet kiss upon my forehead and Guided me to stand once again beside the Wise One.

She continued, "*And you will begin to remember this feeling, this innate sense of nurturing and place your feet upon the ground in an effort to travel to the ultimate end of your journey. Your eyes will be met by those in need and they will recognize, in you, their need, the yearning for that unconditional love. And you shall show this nurturing; this oneness with The Knowing and you will evoke a gentle peace upon their hearts. This gift I give you and as we grow and learn and life beckons you onward, you will attain this Lightness of heart that you and all others deserve. You will share this love and others will come and drink of the Essence of the vibration from this love. And you will begin to recognize this when it happens and you will feed upon this nectar from the God of The Knowing.*" And I loved her instantly. I loved this Mother Guide and I continued to stare into her vibrant face, which left me yearning for more of this nectar she spoke about.

The Wise One took my arm and we continued toward the Lighted Being standing next to the Mother Guide. This Being was dressed in the soldier garments of the ancient Romans. He reminded me of the Guard that stood ceremoniously in the carved out niche halfway up the temple staircase. He, too, held a large staff axe and a large, plumed hat was placed regally on his head. His red toga top and red and gold trimmed skirt glistened in the Light particles as he bowed his head upon our introduction.

This Soldier Guide seemed less familiar, yet I felt a strong sense of protection from his demeanor. He never touched me, but continued to stare straight into my eyes as he said, "*I have been watching over you and protecting you from harm. Gently guiding you around the paths of least resistance for your body. I will leave soon at the moment of your Knowing and then others will come and take my place. Others will lead and Guide you along your path and they will come and go until this space is permanently filled by your chosen*

Guide. In the meantime, Know that I watch over you and that you will face some uncertainties of bodily harm and I will protect you. And when it is my time for another life, another journey, I will leave and I will leave you in good hands. Each replacement in this post will help your secular world emerge into one of Spirit."

Looking upon the Soldier Guide, I took into my heart his calm and expressive conviction and I had complete trust and belief that he would continue his solid commitment to protect me from physical harm. He was a Spiritual and physical "body" guard to Guide me down the swiftest path that would take me safely to my destination. Looking back at the many close calls in my early adult years, I know he was there, silently protecting me as I made my way through events that could have derailed my journey in the blink of an eye. And so I remember the grateful, reassuring feeling I had as I realized his part in my life and I thanked him for his help. *"So Be it."* was his simple reply.

At this point, the Wise One guided me over to the next Being, a young, very dark-skinned African male in a long white robe and white turban. His large, round eyes of deep brown were friendly and welcoming upon our introduction. Standing before him, we looked into each other's eyes for quite a long time, when slowly, he began to softly laugh as if he had just stated the punch line to his own joke.

He lifted both arms to me and curious, I moved closer toward him. He took my eager hands in his, and as he drew me closer, he quietly said, *"I have been waiting patiently while you rested, between heartbeats, between breaths. I am here to help you understand the connection between perception, reality, and where that all fits into what you will create as your life on this Earth at this time. We are all the directors, writers, producers, and players in our lives. We create, perceive, and react to our circumstances and this is a critical phase of recognition in all our lives. Younger generations will be able to remember this and can be brought along by an older, wiser Soul, ready to teach and Guide. Let it be known and let all Know, you will be that teacher of truth and when you truly understand and recognize this point, you will then be able to move into the next act of your play that is your life. I will be here to help you understand the vulnerability, fear, and the gift of song that was given to you. This stage upon which you act out your life play is ever evolving, with many acts and dramatic twists and turns. There will be comedy, drama, music, intermissions, and an overall view of the world from the perception of each audience member. The key is to present that which is your play with no preconceived agenda or ending. Even though you will continue on, those around you, on all levels, will perceive, react, judge, and believe in a way that only they can. There is no swaying or leading anyone else in any direction that they are not capable of going. Their own life play is playing out at the same time yours is. This stage, this presentation of this dream play that is your life, is just that, a dream, and the choices we make and how we apply those choices define our existence, while at the same time, the choices are being perceived by those in your own life experience. This can be quite confusing at times, but when it is totally realized, then you will truly understand choice. And how that continues to evolve and affect the ebb and flow of your Soul."*

I found myself a little confused at what he was telling me. But I still retained a deep, familiar trust that someday, I would Know and understand everything he had said. And, as if he had just read my mind, the Guide of the Life Stage continued on, *"Do not worry about the timing of this Knowing. Many Souls come into the life experience many times in order to understand choice. It is truly a key lesson in the realization of God and the Light and The Knowing. I am here to help, to remind you in this life of your destined pathway."*

This Guide of the Life Stage would become the Guide most patient with regard to my journey. He would be there for me countless times as I struggled to understand The Knowing. He would help me to understand perception as the key to the All There Is and how this single, basic idea can literally change the course of all humankind. I would muddle through my life until this course of action would become a daily habit in my view of this life experience. And if we all take just one thing away from this life, this idea of true perception can be the key that opens the door of The Knowing for us all.

The Wise One put his arm around my shoulders and led me to the next Being, a scruffy, very old man dressed in oversized, wrinkled white robes. His long, unkempt grey hair stuck out wildly around his slightly scowling and deeply lined face. I was surprised to see that this Being seemed to be upset or frustrated and his cranky demeanor actually caused me to hold back from him at first.

He quickly shoved his hand out to me and I shook it with a little trepidation. He said, *"I will help you to understand the mind-body-Spirit connection and how it all comes together for truth. I will help you to monitor your temple, that which you call your physical body. I will Guide you to help you draw the right conclusion to help you maintain your healthy balance. It is imperative that a quiet, loving balance takes place within the body. It is your vehicle to God and your house to your Soul. Let it not be forgotten that without this balance, you can no longer have a straight path to God. For when the body cries out for help or attention, the Soul is diverted from God and its purpose. For the Soul Knows that in order to maintain its current temporary house, all must be vibrating at the rate that each body is capable of. Even in sickness or with physical limitations, the body is capable of the healthy vibrations to God. However, when the intention is to neglect, that is when the unbalance occurs. Do not fear. I will help you to discover your own healthy balance. I will help you learn to tune into your body, to what it needs and desires. I will help you to keep healthy and strong for your journey will be long and arduous. You must keep your body at its best to open up the channels of God."*

I understood what this "Doctor" Guide was saying. However, I was again surprised at the abrupt delivery. His no-nonsense message was clear, but was sent with little tact or gentleness. The Wise One, sensing my confusion, reminded me, *"Daughter, we are here symbolically for you. There will be moments of different emotions and lessons and messages will come to you in the way we feel you will understand best. This physical Guide, his job, his duty, will be long and will sometimes be frustrating. For in your world of chemicals, sugar, climate, and stressful vibrations, the body is now at its most challenged. There are so many choices and events and decisions to be made that the body toils daily. This Guide, this man will help you undertake this huge, very important task in an effort to clear your path to God. Do not be put off by his voice, rather relish the message and take nothing personally or to heart. Just Know his intent and if you believe in that, you will rejoice and be ever grateful for his purpose."*

As I looked upon the face of the Wise One, I felt such love, such grateful appreciation that I honestly thought he could "see" my love. Gently, the Wise Once touched my face with his hand and once again, he led me to the next Being. Instantly, I knew that this Guide was different and special. He sat in the lotus position upon a white column, surrounded by brilliant, white Light particles. He seemed to be a very young adult, with alabaster skin and long, black flowing hair that trailed down his back and then wrapped around his waist. He wore a small, white loincloth and was bare-chested. His eyes were softly closed and a look of pure ecstasy permeated his entire face. His body seemed to be much more transparent than the others and it seemed to be vibrating at a higher, lighter speed.

I walked up to him and slowly placed my hand upon his chest. But my hand didn't rest upon his skin, as expected. Rather, it actually continued to move through his body and I felt a cool, misty feeling throughout my hand and arm. I pulled my arm back and stared at his face with a feeling of deep admiration. He smiled and opened his eyes, looking directly into my Soul. I smiled back when suddenly, he raised his pale arms and lifted them high into the Heavens. Instantaneously, the Light all around him began to whirl, displaying beautiful hues of color. I carefully backed away from him and watched in pure wonderment.

As the Lights flew around this Being, they began to merge and form into beautiful, huge, silver wings that rested upon his back. At this, the Being actually became smaller and smaller and suddenly took flight. I watched as he soared high all around the temple and then up toward the pointed glass top. As he reached his destiny, he hovered there with his wings open, his face smiling upon me. He then swooped downward, flying all around my head and shoulders, where he gently alighted.

I could hear the soft breeze created by his silver wings gently blowing in my ear. *"My name is Michael."* "Michael." I repeated back. He whispered in my ear, *"I kiss the wings of God's Angels and fly into your Soul. When in fear, remember, when in doubt remember, remember that this life is but a course upon the ocean of many lives. That we do what we can with great intent and love. You will soon understand this message and will apply it to your life. You can be your own Power of Will. With The Knowing of God and All There*

Is, you will come to the understanding that this is your destiny. No shame, guilt, or fear need apply."

And then, once again, he flew around the temple and came to rest upon the column. His wings softly disappeared and his body grew to its original size. As I stood there speechless, he continued on, *"And let this be Known to you, daughter of the Light. This moment, this great gift of the human existence is yours to keep for yourself. And when, in time, it is revealed that you share this gift, you will be ready. And you will remember the feeling, The Knowing of the All There Is. And people will then begin to recognize in you this passion, this feeling of complete serenity and God's love. Do not fear this feeling. Trust it completely. You will learn to keep all this in your heart of hearts. I am here specifically to give you hope. And as you remember, you will recognize that hope and apply it to your existence. When you fear, I will be there to show you the meaning of the true experience and you will be calm and have The Knowing. After this Guidepost, I will move on into the Heavens to help with the next Soul. And you may well replace me when you wake, if that is your choice. I am always here for you to call on in need of Spiritual fullness, to understand and apply the feelings that soar throughout your life. Do not forget, your Soul remembers and so you must too. Be ever joyful and you will Know that this is the true purpose of the world. The love here will permeate there in the cell of all humans reaching for the Light of God."*

I stood perfectly still as my heart beat solid and steady within my chest. I was captivated by his words and inspired by their meaning. I was just beginning this journey, and in this moment, I began to truly understand all that was happening. And I was instantly aware that I was being handed a priceless endowment of trust, love, and responsibility. This overwhelming gift was presented with the faith of these Lighted Beings, these Guides, my Guides. And I knew this glimpse into another realm of life was one that only a privileged few had been given. And I also knew that this came with a responsibility that would be huge and all encompassing, yet I was willing, able and ready to accept.

As I stood within the temple walls, I was keenly aware that I was not alone in this task. My Guides would take me where I needed to go and they would be ready companions. I felt this confidence and I felt familiar and safe standing on the platform, surrounded by these Beings of Light, energy, wisdom, and love. The Wise One stood silently joyful by my side as he witnessed my own realization of this unbelievable delicacy. After what seemed like an instant eternity, he gently took my hand. He led me over to the fire pit that stood flickering in the middle of the room. As we reached the pit, the Wise One led me to once again peer over its edge and gaze upon my reflection. Leaning over, I realized that it was only my smiling, serene face, glowing and looking back.

Quietly, the Wise One said, *"This is where we restrict ourselves to everything that is ignorant of God. And this, daughter, is your deliverance of your fears, Self-loathing, and ignorance of God. And in this pit of fire, they will be taken away until they are but ashes of a memory that was your life experience until now. You will come to realize, when this pit is cold and no longer burns with ignorance of God, that all this was a worthy journey of your Spirit and you will one day come upon this pit and remember it as a place where your Soul grieved and yearned for the tender kiss of God. And you will, on that day, rejoice and understand that we all keep our fears hidden out of fear of judgment. But you will no longer feel or be a prisoner to that thought. And you will have this moment in your life and it shall be a great turning point for you."*

The Wise One and I stepped away from the pit, facing one another. He took my hands in his. *"Daughter, this I give unto you. This moment, this pearl in the crown of your life. You are here to begin this destiny of your heart. You will come here in meditation and when you do, we will be here, waiting for you. And every time you come here and drink from this gift, you will become more and more realized of God. You will Know that this is for the Greater Good. And you will yearn to come here often. Soon you will be given a task that will remind you to attend to your physical body. This must be in order for you to remember that you are yet a human. But your Soul will want for more and more and we shall deliver what you seek. In meditation, you will become more familiar with the ways of this land and this purpose you will carry over to the reality that is your human life. And we are your teachers and Guides and we shall never seek to change your perception, only enhance what you already Know. And in times of need, we shall hold your sweet face within our hearts and wait, wait for you to seek more. We are always here. We are never gone and you are never alone. And as you seek to merge your Spirit with your physical body, you will be made privy to the vibration that is closest to God. The Knowledge you seek will begin your journey and we shall teach you to articulate and give freely of this passion that grows minute by minute within your heart. Welcome daughter. Welcome to your heart, welcome to the Spirit that all are being given. Welcome to The Knowing."* And I, feeling Eternally grateful, bowed my head and wept with joy.

Chapter Seven

The Diagnosis

...validation by medical science.

"To define any person, thing, or event is to limit your Self and that person, thing or event."

When I opened my eyes, I found myself lying upon the old daybed, face up, in what was my usual meditative position. I was immediately aware that my breath was moist, intermittent, and shallow and my heart rate had slowed down to a very steady, few beats per minute. I was very still, quietly taking in all that had just occurred and savoring the feelings that replayed over and over throughout my body. I drank in the peacefulness that infused my senses and I allowed the surreal events to calmly float within my heart. I had met my Spirit Guides, as they called themselves. I knew their faces, their names, their voices, and their purpose and I was unquestioningly invited to go to them whenever I wanted.

In this half awake and half meditative state, I felt joyous and I laughed out loud, embracing this tremendous pronouncement of Spirit with absolute belief and love. Then, as my physical body began to come back into a more tangible, normal reality, I slowly sat up and looked about the room. Absolutely everything in my heart had changed and I knew that my life would never be the same. Thoughts and emotions quickly flew in and out of me and soon, I became overwhelmed and began to cry deep seeded tears of emotions that were solidly ingrained within my physical memories. I played the phenomenal events over and over in my mind and I relished the feelings as they returned to the forefront of my heart.

At this moment of ecstasy, an unwelcome thought began to penetrate my joy. Did this really happen? Had I actually met a group of six Spirits who talked to me, touched me, and offered their unconditional hand whenever I choose? Was this real or had I subconsciously conjured them up or even dreamed them into reality? I then had the horrifying notion that would haunt me for the next several months: Maybe I was beginning to hear voices. This horrific possibility caused the pit of my stomach to go cold. I knew I hadn't purposefully created this phenomenal scenario, as it was way beyond even my wild imagination. So in my mind, there were just two explanations and I carefully began to walk the delicate line between the possibility of true Spiritual ecstasy or mental illness.

However, despite this deep conflict, in my heart, I yearned to be with the Guides. I just couldn't stay close to the idea that the Spirits in the temple were just a twisted figment of my brain. So I began a daily ritual of meditation, going into the temple, sometimes for hours, to meet with and learn from the Guides, expecting nothing short of pure joy every time I was there. In the beginning, they did most of the talking and what they had to say was simple, yet sometimes confusing to my evolving Spirit. But I would listen and absorb everything I could, convinced that I would understand all their teachings in time.

And even more incredible was the fact that every savored moment I was with the Guides, their images, voices, and messages were consistently clear and perfectly understandable. There was never a foggy or vague communication, ever. Never was I unable to connect with them in any way as they were always there for me. Furthermore, their messages and teachings were unmistakably coming from a place of clarity, love, and, most importantly, truth. Yet with all this beauty, in my awakened state of human reality and uncertainties, a lingering doubt as to the validity of this treasure would enter my mind almost immediately upon coming out of meditation. Again I would wonder, "Could this really be happening?" Even though I felt deep within my heart that this phenomenon was real, my human conditioning of suspicions, fears, and unknowns caused me to question, over and over, if this was truly real.

While I was in the temple with the Guides, there was never a moment of questioning, but as I went about my human existence, thoughts of "what if?" would pervade my mind. And since nothing had ever happened in my awakened state that proved their true existence, I internalized, justified, and tore through these thoughts over and over again. That is until a few months later, when the Guides were to show their true colors and their existence would indeed be proven by medical science.

Nine months later

I continued to spend countless hours with the Guides, as they would, each in their own way, speak of my life and how all is tied to Spirit. I developed a strong affinity for each Guide and their purpose. I did have a tendency to favor the Wise One, as he seemed to be the leader of the group and would sometimes comment further upon the others' lessons. This would happen especially if I seemed confused, which was not uncommon in the beginning. The messages were certainly coming from truth, but some of them were hard to comprehend as I was still dealing with my Catholicism and what place those beliefs had in my newfound enlightenment. But the Guides were always clear and they would never leave a subject until I was ready to continue.

The Mother Guide was both my Spiritual and physical nurturer, as she was always there with welcoming arms and unconditional love and understanding. And she seemed to understand when my human body needed gentle fostering in the basic sense, as she would on many occasions tenderly take me into her lap, stroking my hair and patting my arm, saying nothing, but conveying a deep feeling of safety. I instantly became five years old again and I loved and needed this adoring attention. She would tell me time and time again how we all are deserving of this unconditional hand and love of a mother. That it is our right, as Souls in human form, to desire, if not demand, this kind of love.

But in the society of today, a human mother's attention is divided among the everyday mundane tasks and imposed responsibilities that she and society deem will enable her to be "successful" in a world of instant gratification, want, and exhaustive, never ending benevolence. She is perpetually bombarded with the arduous assumptions that have taken over her life as she constantly wonders, "Am I doing enough?" The Mother Guide would tell me that the simple, genuine love of a mother manifests and blossoms within her touch, smile, and tenderness. That is all we consistently and truly need. And even though I was not a parent myself, she taught me to see that the Soul is a human's firstborn child and she helped me understand the importance of treating this child with the respect and unconditional dignity it deserved.

She reminded me to be attentive to my Spiritual Self first, not in the selfish way, but in the Self-way. For she Guided me to conclude that if I don't take care of and respect my own Spirit/child first, then all effort to give would be limited to no more than what I give to myself. If I am harsh and demanding with myself, then I would automatically transfer this to others, either consciously or, more sadly, subconsciously. A strong sense of Self is the simple tool that is an example of "Do unto others as you would have them do unto you." When we treat our Self with care, we are automatically conditioned to treat others the same and these actions, if the receiving Soul has the same Self-sense value, and sometimes even if they don't, are reciprocated. It comes back to us tenfold and we made a difference.

Of course, we are all constantly bombarded by the media to "look this way or that way to be happy" or "buy this in an effort to appear successful" and we all often find ourselves chasing that bottomless pit at one time or another. The Mother Guide often reiterated, *"To give without depletion,"* and learn to tune into my Soul first, remembering to pull back whenever something or someone is demanding more than I can give in that particular moment. She taught me that when I chose to give unconditionally (everything is about choice) and without judgment or preconceived expectations from within that absolute, that I would have the first glimpse of "The Knowing."

This lesson was sorely needed by my ever-perfect, tap-dancing, size 12, too-fat dieter, female "fixer" psyche. And later, as I would open up to my own deeply ingrained feelings, I would begin to develop an empathy with other Souls and I would also begin to absorb their feelings on a level that was more readily available to my own human existence. This became quite a heavy weight to carry and one that would take years to understand. My sense of personal responsibility for everybody's happiness and health would eventually cause me to develop debilitating habits as I went around sticking my finger in the various holes of a dam about to break and kill us all.

But a soft Light of truth went off deep within my heart one day, when the Wise One said to me, *"You, dear, dear daughter, you are not that power-ful. You cannot change anyone else's destiny. You are not God."* The Wise One had struck a cord and I began my slow climb out of the sinking pit of sticky, unreasonable demands on myself. The Wise One explained what place guilt, judgment, and responsibility had in anyone's life. He would explain first that guilt is intentional. That you cannot possibly be guilty of anything at all if the intent to harm was not there. You are responsible for your own actions only and no other. And feeling guilty without the intent is based in fear, Self-loathing, habitual human conditioning, and Self-judgment. And it is the crux for low Self-esteem. He agreed that it is right to take responsibility for your actions, but without judgment of yourself. Judging another Soul's choice and then attaching an emotion to it is creat-ing chaotic devastation, war, and poverty in today's world and, according to the Wise One, is humankind's saddest legacy. "Do it my way or else" has become the foreboding anthem of many countries, religions, and political aspirants. What can we as individuals do about it? The Wise One offered to me the consideration to "Be the example" and that by presenting this unconditional and unjudged personae to the world, we could then begin to pass this legacy of The Knowing on to our children and others who still seek to understand their Spiritual path.

In the beginning, this task seemed too slow and arduous. Couldn't we do more, faster? But the Wise One would remind me over and over that we didn't develop into this type of mindset over one generation's time. Rather we have slowly moved away from The Knowing over hundreds, maybe thousands of human years. We are so used to instant gratification and we often wonder, "Doesn't anyone see? We should do this and this and do it now!" Again, the Wise One would teach that it all starts within individual hearts, that we cannot change anybody else's destiny or thoughts and that one simple life-lived within The Knowing has repercussions that filter down through many generations. And that is the way the world will slowly begin to change and understand. When we incarnate again and again, we are picking up that legacy and hopefully passing it along once more. In this one candle that Lights many other flames of hope, resides the passion, beating within that flame. It is passion that is not wasted in words that hurt or judge. It is all in The Knowing.

The Wise One, with his fatherly demeanor, also acted as a personal tutor of sorts. Many times, he would help me understand the teachings of the other Guides. This was especially true when I would tell him that I already knew what they had just told me and some of the lessons they were relaying to me were things I considered common sense, so basic, simple, and hugely obvious. His Knowing smile would appear across his face and he would often ask, *"Do you feel you already Know this?"* (Yes, I would answer.) *"Do you feel you already understand this?"* (Again, I would answer yes.) *"Do you feel that you agree with this?"* (Yes, I would answer once more.) *"Do you feel as if you live this?"* (Well…and then I would begin to think.) *"Do you feel you Are this example?"* (Hmmm…I….) Usually, after answering yes to the first three questions, I would end up considering that maybe I didn't really "Know" that much after all. Because sometimes the trip from the mind to the heart to the behavior is a long, bumpy journey, with the Soul derailing preconceived ideas along its path.

The Wise One persistently emphasized that living life and seeking God are very, very simple. No big words or deep philosophical thoughts are necessary. In keeping it simple and basic, we resist the temptation to label everything around us. And another downfall to labeling everything around us is that we automatically limit ourselves and the labeled thing or person. And sadly, he would say once again, when we label, we attach an emotion to it and, with judgment soon following, we then begin the vicious cycle one more time. The Wise One often spoke of how, before we had such a varied command of the human language, we were actually closer to The Knowing. We did more listening then, and less mind-numbing chattering. And because of our inability to use adjectives, our physical bodies, facial expressions, and gestures were left open to interpretation by others. Thus the people, things, and events in our lives were given an opportunity to be more than what an adjective could describe. What a beautiful gift of freedom that must have been! The Wise One, in his ever present understanding of my heart, would delight in my new discoveries and he would often say to me, *"There is no judgment here, daughter."* A greater gift, no one has ever received.

Now the Soldier Guide's purpose was different than the others. He explained that he was in a "revolving position" which meant that different Guides would come in and out of this Guidepost and that he would soon be leaving me. He told me that he was there for me before my "awakening" as a physical guard of sorts. He told me that many times during my young life, he had been there for me, whispering to my mind to go this way or that way. A guardian Angel who watched over me as I went about my daily existence, I felt that he no doubt accomplished his assignment with success. He said that he was appointed by myself (pre-birth) to be the constant guard of my physical body, the house of my Soul, and that I would need this guidance to get to the place I was now. After his initial introduction, he would always acknowledge my presence with a respectful nod but he rarely, if ever, spoke with me.

He was soon replaced by several different Guides, who would slowly shift their attention from my physical body to helping me move from a secular career into one of Spirit. No easy task, as I would continue to judge my Self-worth for many years by how much I contributed to the family, either financially, materially, or as a wife. Eventually, in this Guidepost, I would meet the incredible Guide, Asnah, and the now permanent Guide, Ia. Years later, these two Guides would be instrumental in completely altering my new path, helping to bring me forward to the journey that is my life-lived.

The Doctor Guide consistently said that his purpose was to help me understand the mind-body-Spirit connection. He explained the importance of this bond and how they must all work together to widen my portal to God and The Knowing. And one night in the temple, he told me urgently that my physical body was experiencing a change. That it (my body) was calling out for my attention and that it was imperative that I go to an embodied physician for diagnosis. I was not prepared for this, even though I *had* been feeling extremely tired and was losing weight without any effort, which was very unusual for me. My fatigue had actually been escalating and I entertained the thought more than once that maybe this deep meditation was causing some physical problems. Even though I always felt so rested and relaxed after meditating, I had noticed that I wasn't feeling like myself lately so when the Doctor Guide confronted me, he had my attention from the start.

He continued on and said that I had a problem with the sweetness that was *"building up in my veins"* and that my *"temple"* (body) needed immediate medical assistance. So we stood there face to face, me with thoughts of "How am I going to tell my physical doctor that I needed to be tested for *"sweetness"* because my Spirit Guide told me so?" Even though I wasn't feeling like my usual self, I'm sad to say that I didn't listen.

And so, continually, every time I went to the temple, he would tell me that my body was in crisis and that I needed medical attention. And on one occasion, he came to the edge of the platform and sat down with his head in his hands, crying softly. *"Daughter, you must understand of what we speak. This is an urgent need, for your temple, your Body of God, is slowly ruining its cellular vibration with this ultimate crisis. It is imperative that you listen, that the diagnosis is done and that you pay attention to this problem. We understand your doubt and that is okay. For sometimes the human must see with human eyes. See the written word in the bookstore of the Lane Magnolia. There you shall see it. The written word of what we speak. It is in mineral holder that spins and is at eye level. A book of symptoms with diagnostic answers. Seek it, as it is critical in this moment to continue your existence upon the Earth. You have, what is called in your world, diabetes. I weep and cry, as this must be attended to. Please listen to this urgent need."*

Diabetes? I really didn't know anything about this disease except that I thought it was an older persons illness. But this urgent pleading from the Doctor Guide stopped me cold, as none of them had ever cried before or talked about (and named) a human condition. The *"Lane Magnolia"*, so I concluded, was a street and I knew right where the bookstore was, as I went there on occasion. Looking back on this time, I know for a fact that I was far less frightened of the diagnosis of an illness than I was of proving the Guides were right and ultimately real. I knew that this moment, this ultimate "test" would eventually come and here it was. I just feared losing this incredible part of my life, as I also knew that if they were wrong about something that could be proven, I might have to deal with the possibility that I was becoming mentally ill. But, I also knew that now was the time, once and for all, to put any lingering doubts to rest. So, following the Doctor Guide's advice, I went to the bookstore.

I held an argument in my head as I made my way into the store. I was feeling that this was not "proof" as I knew of this store and its location. I entered the store and went to the *"mineral holder"* (wire rack) that held many books. Even though I had never noticed this rack before, I argued in my head that I had probably seen it on one of the many occasions as I made my way through the door. I stepped up to the wire rack and nervously spun it around. It stopped and right in front of my eyes was a book where you look up your symptoms and it would tell you the possible diagnosis.

I began to shake as I reached for the book and I could barely get it to open. The pages fell open and revealed a section where you list your symptoms and then look up the possible diagnosis in another section. I followed the instructions, looked up the symptoms, read the list for the most common symptoms of diabetes. I let out a small cry, closed the book, stuffed it back on the rack and literally ran out the door and down the alley. I jumped in my car, slammed the door, and, with my heart pounding, I sat there staring at the wheel. That I could actually get my hands on tangible evidence of what one of my Guides had been saying to me was astounding and terrifying. Then all at once, the fear of mental illness revealed a crack as I, in my awakened state began to take on the beliefs of my Soul in the temple. Still, I needed more evidence, but this was the beginning of my transformation.

I made my way to my doctor's office wondering how I was going to ask to be tested for diabetes. At the time, I knew I wasn't about to tell him that the reason I was there was because a Spirit Guide told me I had a sugar problem. So when my doctor asked "Why?" in response to my request, I quickly rattled off a short list of symptoms I had been experiencing. He said he would order the test "if I really wanted it" and I, assuring him that yes, I really wanted it, left with the lab order for the test. The next day after the test, I went home to wait for the results. I had not been in the temple since my original visit to the bookstore. I think I was feeling the need to distance myself in case the Guides weren't real.

Later that day, the call came. I was decorating the Christmas tree and Pete was videotaping my silliness and happiness with this favorite ritual. Pete was actually filming me when the phone rang and the camera followed me as I laid the ornament down to go answer it. He turned off the camera just as I headed towards the phone. Whenever I watch that little piece of video, I get the chills knowing that my innocent world would soon come to a screeching halt. The minute I picked up the phone, my doctor urgently gave me the validation I was secretly hoping for and dreading; I had diabetes and a 758 blood sugar reading. Knowing what I know now, I cannot believe that I was even able to stand up and function at all.

So there it was. The validation I was looking for. Medical science had to prove to my mind what my heart already knew. Then it all hit me with the might of every belief system I ever had, any doubts, any fears, any chance of not believing in this unknown treasure, all of it became clear in that moment. These Guides, these wondrous Beings and seekers are real, and I knew it. The Doctor Guide had diagnosed me and medical science had proven it. And I bless him and am Eternally grateful for his persistence. None of the Guides showed any indignation at my doubt and hesitation. They showed only joy and love when I returned to the temple a believer in all. And now, whether awake, asleep or deep in meditation, I know this is real. Oh my God, the Guides are real. *"And with this Knowing, comes the eventual realization of the importance and responsibility of human life and the experience associated."*

After this validating diagnosis, my Doctor Guide continued to work with me on many levels to help me understand, deal with, accept, and express my feelings of being diagnosed with diabetes. Naturally, I would ask many times, why? The Doctor Guide tells me (when I forget) that this physical condition is exactly why I chose this particular body/genetic lineage. That it is not only a lesson in discipline and balance but more importantly, because this illness requires constant monitoring, I must attend to it always, in an effort to stay healthy (I am) and most importantly, so that my Soul will stay in the body. I wondered what they meant by that statement and they said that soon, I would be introduced to another level of Spirit in such a way that I would have trouble manifesting the desire to return to the physical body at all. And they were adamant that I return to my body and continue this life journey.

I have certainly found this to be true. If I didn't have to contend with this delicate balancing act of my human body, I know I would have the tendency to stay with Spirit in meditation for a longer period and leave my human body alone. I know that my meditation is extremely beneficial and physically healthy. I also know that my heart rate and breathing slow down tremendously and I also feel that the aging process slows down because of this. But to keep me attached to the physical world, I chose this body in an effort to keep me grounded to my human life experience and to keep my body a loving, healthy, peaceful place for my Soul. I would soon be presented with an escalating Spirit plan and I would need this temple-body to carry me through.

Chapter Eight

Automatic Writing

...receiving the first messages.

*"As you sit in contemplative silence, receive
The Knowing and revel in its simple-ness."*

With my beliefs resonating solidly within my heart, I joyfully and expectantly continued to receive the intimate messages and teachings from the daily visits with the Guides. Their expressions and the feelings they conveyed to me were all consuming and beyond any descriptive human words. They were trying to help me understand that feelings are based in The Knowing and that these deep-seeded feelings are what drive humankind in all things. They told me time and time again that deep within this Knowing "feeling" lives the truth of the All There Is, of the entire existence of the Soul life. That The Knowing is not a mental thought or something that you can describe, but rather it is the resulting feeling of that thought or thing. Trying to describe it is utterly impossible and unnecessary, for when you recognize it, you will then understand it and no description is necessary.

And how did they help me to get to that place? They started by addressing and alleviating my fears, which were usually based in some blown out of proportion space within the recesses of my mind. Most of my fears had festered and grown due to my inability to address them, again usually out of fear of judgment. So it was this vicious cycle that trapped me and the Wise One purposefully and deliberately set out to help me face these fears, understand their true origin, and then "burn" them in the fire pit within the temple walls.

The Guides used this fire pit as a symbol of total destruction as they told me that the human social psyche had placed fire in the realm of absolute annihilation. In other words, not only was there nothing recognizable left after a burning but the lasting embers eventually disappeared back into the wind or the Earth. As I would make my way up the staircase and into the temple, the Wise One would be standing by the fire pit and would greet me with, *"And what of your fear?"* Where upon, we would discuss a specific fear and he would try to help me understand it's true basis. Eventually, he helped me to recognize that *"all fear is ignorance of God."* And I firmly believe this. For when you truly Know God, or Spirit, there is no fear, only acceptance and trust within The Knowing.

This concept sounds so simple and rather biblical, yet it is truly life altering. The Guides would use this analogy to help me understand. *"What if you knew the exact time and date of your human death? And you knew nothing could kill you or harm you in any way until that moment. And what if you knew that you and the people you care about would be happy and cared for before and after that moment? How would this feel?"* My first reaction was freedom. Free to be whatever I wanted without any fear of lack or responsibility to anyone but myself. And the whole answer lives there, deep within the Self, where life shapes itself and blooms forth for us all.

Children have a deep sense of The Knowing and are in touch with their feelings from the minute they take their first breath. They remember and respond to the Self until the adults in their lives begin to systematically shape these little people and their feelings into what is deemed a socially acceptable persona. This process can include fear, conditional love, and deprivation. While we lovingly and intentionally set out to raise decent, respectable, kind individuals, we are actually teaching our children to put the Self last. We always tell them to look away from the Self and "look out there." But, by guiding them to look inward toward the Light, their social responsibilities will automatically emerge.

We must, of course, teach our children safety for their physical self as well; that is a given. But the innate personalities of these new little people do not need our shaping. They arrive pure and ready to "Be." If we could rearrange our ways of teaching and show them how to love and care for their Self first, then they would automatically reciprocate that sense to others, naturally and willingly. A daunting task, no doubt, to the millions of parents looking to do the right thing by their children.

So, upon entering the temple, the Wise One would greet me at the fire pit and we would address my fears and together we would "burn" this fear and take its Essence away, deep into the flames. Sometimes, it would be a fear that had already been addressed, but the Wise One would patiently reiterate what had been previously discussed until I would finally get it and, more importantly, remember it. Eventually, this pit grew cold and I would begin to address my remaining fears in a different manner. And on the day that I entered the temple and found the smoldering embers cold to the touch, I knew I had turned a corner in my lessons with the Guides.

It was about this time that my growing desire to write down their teachings rose to the surface. I found myself trying to remember the actual words the Guides had said as I was yearning to revisit them in my awakened state. Also, I was slowly beginning to share my experiences with the Guides with my husband Pete and I wanted to show him their words. Naturally, Pete had expressed concern when I first told him of the Guides. He knew of my near-death experience and my ability to see the human Aura and he accepted both of those events as a wonderful, yet more common experience.

But talking with Spirit Guides was another matter altogether and he would often ask me, "Peg, are you sure? Are you sure this is real?" He wanted to believe me, as he was always open minded and encouraging new ideas, but he expressed concern about my mental state. Was I hearing voices? I couldn't blame him, as I had had that same fear myself in the beginning. And the Guides were always there and I was always, on a daily basis, learning from them and telling Pete how incredible the feelings were. So one night, just after we turned out the lights to go to sleep, I suddenly said to Pete, "Lets test them. You ask a question that I don't know the answer to and I will ask them for an answer."

Of course, he was very willing and anxious for me to try this and he asked, "What is the street number of the house that I lived in while I was growing up?" I certainly didn't know the answer to that and I went immediately into meditation to ask. As I stood before the Guides, I began to feel a little embarrassed and ashamed that I was, once again, asking them to prove their existence. Yet I was anxious to share with Pete and I told them of his question and I acknowledged why we were asking it. To my great surprise, all of the Guides started to laugh! They stood there laughing and laughing, and I, feeling slightly embarrassed, watched and waited for their answer.

As soon as the laughter died down, the Wise One said, *Daughter, we laugh with this human's mind and manner of thought. For we could tell you any number at all and this Soul (Pete) would not be able to verify it, for he, himself, does not know this answer. A double test of our verifiability!* And then they all began to laugh again and I, feeling rather duped, quickly came out of meditation to confront Pete with his trickery. I was slightly appalled when I told him what they had said and that they could tell me anything because he doesn't even know the answer himself. Pete quietly said, "They're right, I don't know the answer." And that moment was truly a turning point in Pete's acceptance and since then, he has been my biggest supporter and surprisingly he is not shy or intimidated with my sharing this adventure with anybody, anytime, anywhere. In fact, it was he who said that this book had to be written. This story has to be told.

I continued on with my quest to somehow remember the actual words of the Guides as I longed to share these wonderful jewels of wisdom. I found myself frustrated in this attempt as there was no way I could remember all the little moments and words that I heard in a meditation that sometimes went on for one or two hours. I would come to my awakened state with the feeling deeply vibrating in my Soul, but no words would describe how I came to these feelings. I know that this was deliberate in the beginning as the Guides wanted to get me away from describing everything. They would remind me over and over that the single act of describing, attaching an emotion, and then judgment is the root of fear, which drives ignorance of God. They wanted me to feel, not describe. So for the next several years, I would feel what they were saying, hoping that I would someday be able to share this wonder with the written word, as they called it.

And after all those years of being immersed within The Knowing and exploring the immense feelings that were a result of the teachings of the Guides, I once again, found myself wanting to document their gifts to my heart. I felt the time was finally right, and that I could fully distinguish between those feelings and the descriptive words I longed to write. But the same dilemma grabbed any attempt to do this, as I was always unable to remember what they said upon coming to my awakened state. I came up with the idea that I would put a pen in my hand, place it upon a blank journal, and see if I could write with my physical hand while in the temple.

I settled in one night for my regular routine and I went into meditation, tasting the beautiful fruits of yet another night's lessons. In the process, I had forgotten about the pen, journal, and my plan to write down the lessons. Upon coming out of meditation, I looked down and saw the empty page and was sorely disappointed. I tried again the next night and the same thing happened. I was so engrossed in what the Guides were giving me that I would continually forget to write down the messages and I would find myself staring in frustration at the empty page night after night.

This went on for several weeks and the same thing would happen over and over until one night, upon coming out of meditation, I was surprised to see scribbling on the paper. I couldn't remember doing it and it was illegible. I looked carefully at the up and down movements and thought I could make out a letter here or there, but there was no sense or continuity to any of it. But still, I was intrigued and tried it again the following night. I went deep into meditation, but before I did, I told myself to write out anything that I would want to remember.

Night after night for several weeks, I willed myself to write while in meditation and every time I came out of it, I found more scribbles and illegible letters that I had no memory of writing. And then one night as I opened my eyes, I was astounded to see two words that had been put together by my physical hands. The words simply said, *'Turn Inward'*.

I traced my fingers over and over the writing and I calmly smiled. I stared at this delicate message seemingly written through my own hand and I just knew that I had finally been able to put into words at least part of what the Guides were telling me. These two words began the process that would expand and grow into beautiful, poetic journals, filled with tender messages of hope, love, insight, and simple elegance. These automatic writings were, in the beginning, so basic. They didn't seem particularly profound to me at the time, but how I loved reading them! And now when I go back and revisit them, I find powerful, deep messages that I could only understand after years of study with the Guides. And I would remember that they would often talk about the fact that complex questions very often can be answered, simply, within The Knowing.

In their plainness, these quiet journals can spark an emotional outpouring of immense desire for more experiences deep within my heart. These journals that I would fill year after year would provide the effortless, simple words of contemplation. Obviously, I wasn't able to write all of their words when they spoke in conversation, as my hand wasn't fast enough. But they would slow down their speech and give me simple lines and words that my hand could write. Some of these early words reverberate still within my heart, *"When the Light is realized and you truly understand choice, then you can live, then you can believe, then you just Know." "You are your purpose." "Be the example." "Oh tired one. Know that this is not 'reality.' Not God, but a manifestation of an idea. Rest your head. It is intermission." "Just Know that it is so. When you think it, it is. That's all it takes to become, to Be. It is all you need."*

And then there was a moment when I looked upon the page of the journal and found these words, *"The Box. What it holds is priceless. What it holds cannot be duplicated. It is your future. It is your past. It is your present. It holds all that is necessary. All you need to Know, to Know God."* I found this perplexing, as this was the first time that the Guides had mentioned an actual thing, a box of some sort, and I didn't know what box they were speaking of. But I was to find out very soon just what they meant. It was when I found myself, once again, on the trek up the staircase to the top of the temple.

As usual, at the halfway point, I greeted the Guard with a nod and a smile, but this time, he turned to me and communicated that he had something for me. His eyes were deep and emotional as he slowly extended his hand. He led me to the little bench that stood deep within the carved out niche, the exact place where he first placed me upon our introduction. I sat down and waited for him to proceed. He turned to face me and I watched in wonderment, as he seemed to pull an object from out of the air. He looked intently at my eyes and gently handed me an antique scrolled metal box. It was about six by seven inches and three inches deep and its contents seemed bulky when they shifted. It had two metal hinges that appeared overly large and out of proportion compared to the rest of the container.

I placed the box upon my lap and reached over the top to open it. Swiftly the Guard placed his hand on top of mine and communicated that I needed to wait to lift the lid. I nodded and accepted his request. At this, he motioned for me to stand and continue up to the top of the temple. With my unexpected gift in my hand, I waved to the Guard and ascended the staircase. He bowed his reply as he turned around to continue his watch.

I proceeded up the remaining stairs and entered the temple. I passed by the darkened staircase and walked over to the now cold fire pit. I patted its encircling brick wall and smiled as I remembered the countless hours I spent at its edge with the Wise One. I felt so safe and happy, and with this latest development, I felt expectant and excited. I walked over to the Guides and stood there with the box in my hands. The Wise One came over, smiled, and, taking the box, he said, *"In time, dear daughter, the contents will be made known to you. For there is a natural timing of all in the universe."* I was slightly disappointed but confident in his wisdom and once again, I accepted a request to wait to open the box. The Wise One placed the box upon the wooden table and together, we walked back to the platform to continue the teachings.

Four months later

The Guide, Michael, was different than the others, and the more I was around the Guides the more this became apparent. He seemed "Lighter" and his physical appearance was translucent. Upon my greeting, he would always raise his hands high above his head, as his magnificent silver wings would appear upon his back. His physical appearance would diminish to a mere seven inches high as he closed his eyes in ecstasy. He would then place his tiny hands in mine and together we would fly once around the temple walls and high up to its glass point. After this ritual, he would place me gently at the base of his pedestal and once again, grow to his original size while his wings disappeared into the air.

I knew that he was special and highly evolved. And the Wise One told me that Michael was indeed, a Soul ready to fly to the next plane of existence. That upon my human death, Michael would be finished with this level of realization and would join others that had the same Soul evolution as he did. I was always in awe of Michael. I loved our nightly flights and I would close my eyes and let the feeling of being weightless and totally dependent wash over my Self. It was a sweet reminder of my own womb experience, totally buoyant and trusting. Michael told me in the beginning that his purpose was to help me understand my feelings and understand hope for humankind. He always seemed to be preparing me for more than just my own evolution.

Michael was not as vocal as the other Guides, as his lessons were based almost entirely in my feelings. He would help me to look outside those feelings and help me to understand The Knowing in such a way that I still cannot find the words to describe. His serenity was something that I sought night after night upon entering the temple. Many times, as he immersed me into The Knowing of my feelings, I would cry while he tenderly gazed upon my face. He knew what was happening to me and he seemed to have the most compassion for me when it came to understanding the enormous impact the Guides were having on my human existence. He always had the empathy and the answers for my aching heart. Always. Michael never left me hanging onto my own devices for answers. His delicate responses to questions were something that I could count on when I needed a "break" from the constant shifting of my Soul.

One night, upon entering the temple, I found the Guides quietly gathered side by side upon the platform. Their eyes were closed and their hands were clasped loosely before them. I greeted the first five Guides in the usual manner but after their acknowledgement of my presence, they softly closed their eyes and returned to their quiet state. I actually experienced a twinge of fear, as their demeanor hadn't changed since I first met them and they were acting quite differently. But when I came to Michael, he opened his deep black eyes, cocked his head slightly and looked tenderly into my face.

Quietly, he stood up off his pedestal and walked toward me. This was the first time I saw him like this as we were usually flying around the temple or I would be reverently standing several feet away from him as he sat upon his pedestal. As he got nearer, I could see that his white loincloth had beautiful golden threads running through it and that there were long white tassels that hung from its edges. His cascading black hair that usually fell down his back and wrapped around his waist, was now billowing out behind him, seemingly spun from sugar or raw silk and appearing completely weightless.

When we came face to face, I observed for the first time that we were exactly the same height. Very gently, he took my hands in his and I found it odd to see our hands clasped together as they were also the same size and shape. He smiled so kindly that it pierced my heart and I gasp an emotional breath. I felt as if I too, began to vibrate at his level and it was intoxicating. At this point, he said, *"In this final act of your life play, you will enjoy the completeness, the hope for the future, and the All There Is."*

He lovingly placed his open hand upon my cheek and then he touched my chin and turned it toward an area of the temple that was usually darkened and empty. But now, illuminated by a quiet, iridescent Light, was a huge block of ice at least fifteen feet high. Encased within this crystal cold ice was a very tall, beautiful Angel. The Angel's eyes were closed and its hands clasped together while its head was bent forward as if in prayer. Its pearl-white wings were huge and they, too, stood frozen within the ice.

The Angel seemed androgynous, as I couldn't tell if it was a male or female. It wore a long, white, flowing robe and its hair was very long and blond in color. I remember how interesting it seemed that the Angel looked like a typical replication of an Angelic Being, one we are comfortable with here on Earth. As I stared at this wonder, Michael continued to speak of a great gift that I was about to be given and his words gave my spine shivers of joy. Michael began to explain, "*This tender Guide, will be there to hold your hand, as you teach, Guide, and express yourself so that others of need may find comfort and peace within. It can begin their journey and you can turn the key for them. And as the ice melts around the wings of this Guide of Guides, so your fears and doubts will melt away from your heart. And when all is just a pool of cool water around the feet, you shall begin this ultimate end. Fulfill you life and duty in this incarnation.*"

I was humbled and grateful for this gift. I knew that, even though I didn't understand the purpose of being given this seventh Guide, I was ecstatic as I left Michael's side and walked toward the softly illuminated area. The Angel was so still, so peaceful. I reached up and touched the cold ice, intrigued with its frosty surface. I ran both hands over the powdery exterior and I looked up at the Angel's strong face. It was so much taller than me as my head came to just above its knees. It was a magnificent sight, and I was unimaginably yearning for its teachings and for the first time ever, I felt a sense of impatience while inside the temple walls. I wanted the Angel to speak to me, to tell me its mission and I wanted to drink in all it had to say. But I also knew I would have to wait.

As I backed away from the block of ice, I clasped my hands together and held them to my lips, thanking God for this great adventure, this great life. I proclaimed my patience and trust that all would be revealed in time. And with every meditation, I would enter the temple, greet each Guide and look toward the Angel. It was always the same, and as I checked around the edges of the ice, I would be hoping to see the solid matter turning to liquid. I knew instinctively that that would be my sign that something was beginning to happen.

One year later

I continued the lessons with the Guides for the next year. Every day was a gift, a treasure to behold and experience. I tried to understand and apply all that was being given to me and I felt that I had made great strides toward understanding the All There Is, The Knowing. One night, upon entering the temple, I greeted the Guides in the usual manner and once again, I examined the block of ice. What I found made my heart skip a beat. There on the outer corner, I saw dampness next to the ice. I got on my hands and knees and watched as a little drop of water was slowly cascading down the edge of the ice and settling into a small pool of cool, crystal water. I touched the water with my finger and carefully examined it. It was unlike regular water that is clear. Rather, it contained tiny sparkles of Lighted colors that twinkled and glowed deep within the drop. I was totally accepting of this phenomenon and I clasped my hand tight, wanting to hold onto that little drop.

The Guide of Guides hadn't moved but the ice was finally, miraculously beginning to melt and I felt excited and ready. And with every meditation, I would place my open palm under the now steady stream of cool water, letting it slowly fill my hand and then drip though my fingers. I would then step back and gaze upon the ice and the Angel, wanting to see some movement or anything else that might transpire. But it would take many more months for the ice to melt. And on a particular day, I entered the temple and found that the ice, which was now pooled all around the Angel, had melted and revealed the very tip of the Angel's right wing. I had such a desire to touch the feathers of brilliant white but I was unable to reach it as the Angel towered over my head.

Again and again, the ice melted, pooled and revealed more of the Angels wings until, one day, I stepped into the temple and found the ice had melted halfway down to the Angels waist. I was transfixed as I stared at the strong face of this Guide of Guides and I longed to have the Angel open its eyes and speak to me. But it continued its stance with eyes closed, never moving or speaking. It was on this day that Michael called me to his side and said, *"Daughter, this Angel of the Light, this magnificent Being of help in your life, has begun its ultimate journey. For in your life, you will be entering a new era of enlightenment and hope and it will be time, very soon, for you to share, without fear, this gift of the Light. This Guide of Guides is beginning to awaken and will very soon join you in your task. Its parallel awakening to your own awakening into the Light is no coincidence. It is preplanned and predestined to help you along the way. This Guide that will help you teach, talk, and share the experiences of The Knowing is about to bless you with the unlimited gift of The Knowing and the All There Is, the ultimate conclusion of this lesson that we in the temple as your Guides have led you to understand. This Angel knows no gender and therefore comes to you without definition. And as you learn to describe without definitions, this Angel will be your first experience in that lesson.*" I looked over at the Angel, my Guide of Guides and felt humbled and expectant and most importantly, ready to receive.

A few weeks later, I entered the temple and found beautiful white-lighted candles reverently floating in the air and I watched as the candles moved about while their golden flames flickered and bounced off the stone walls. I looked through the candles and saw the Guides standing ceremoniously upon the platform. The Wise One beckoned me forward and I slowly made my way toward their smiling, glowing faces. As I stepped upon the platform, Michael came to me with his hands outstretched. "*This, dear sweet daughter of the Light, is your treasure, this moment in this incarnation of your life on Earth is about to reveal the purpose of the All There Is.*"

Michael took my hand and we slowly walked towards the still unmoving Guide of Guides. I was immediately surprised and excited to see that all the ice had finally melted and pooled around the feet of the Angel. Its long white robes, long blond hair, strong hands, and beautiful white wings were glistening as small droplets continued to drip from its body. And then suddenly, the Angel reverently opened its eyes and looked down compassionately at me. I could hear the droplets falling and small chunks of ice hitting the stone floor of the temple. The Angel smiled softly and blinked its eyes as little beads of water dropped off the ends of its lashes. Then, ever so carefully, the Guides of Guides raised its head toward the Heavens as a magnificent Light of knowledge burst forth from above. The Angel smiled, closed its eyes, and then began to move its arms out from the sides of its body. As it began to turn its palms upwards, I could hear more cracklings of ice and water and I watched as the Light grew brighter and more intense.

And then, just as the Light became almost too bright to bear, I watched in awe as the wings of the Angel began moving and growing outward and upward from its back. I stepped back as the wings continued to open, revealing a massive, feathery wingspan of at least 30 feet. I became so over-whelmed at this breathtaking sight, that I fell to my knees and crossed my arms over my chest. This Lighted Being emitted such a feeling of holiness and adoration towards the unseen Light Source that I, too, immediately and intensely gave my own, unconditional love to this brilliant ray from above all of us. I was overcome with the feeling that this was right and for the Greater Good and the All There Is.

As the Guide of Guides looked toward the Heavens, I, too, turned my heart toward this loving Light as I felt a familiar goodness and love deep, deep within my Soul. The Angel looked down upon me, and sensing its gaze I looked into its cool blue eyes. The Guide of Guides then placed its hands at its side and waited for me as I intuitively began to walk toward it. When I reached the Angel, I stood quietly to see what would happen next.

As if sensing my readiness, the Guide of Guides brought its huge wings towards me and tenderly enclosed them all around, cradling my entire body into its cool, damp feathers. I could hear the sound of rustling feath-ers, wet leather, and trickling water and I was aware of a slight odor that reminded me of a damp bird. I could feel warmth emanating from the soft white robes where I rested my head. Then quietly, I heard a strong yet gen-tle voice whisper, "*Teacher.*" I allowed this proclamation to hover in the air above my body as I contemplated its acceptance. When I chose this blessed gift to make its way through the top of my head, down my spine and into my heart, I acknowledged out loud, "Teacher." And I felt The Knowing and I understood completely, that this Guide of Guides, my muse, would become my inspiration in the evolution of my Soul and ultimately, my expression of Spirit to the world.

One year later

Whenever I entered the temple, I would always pass by the darkened staircase, the cold fire pit, the table and chairs (with the closed metal box still laying upon it's wooden top), and then over to the back of the temple where I would step upon the platform and face the Guides. But one night, upon entering in my usual manner, the Guides greeted me differently. Instead of beginning their teachings, the Wise One said, *"Daughter, it is time to enter a new phase of your life in this incarnation."* He took my hand and, with the other Guides following us, he led me to the round table and placed me facing the back of the temple. He then took a seat directly across from me and the other Guides followed, each sitting in the semicircle before me.

The Wise One continued, *"Daughter, it is time for us to reveal a task that was predestined before your incarnation."* He reached up and gently slid the metal box over to me. My heart began to beat a little faster when I realized that now was the time, the contents of the box would finally be revealed. I looked up at the Guides and gingerly placed my hands upon the metal container. I ran my fingers over all the intricate carvings on its lid and, lifting the box off the table, I gently shook its bulky contents. The Guides laughed at my Christmas ritual and the Wise One said, *"And now, you are ready to receive this unknown. This treasure that is our gift through you to the world."*

I smiled at the Wise One and, as I carefully opened its lid, I found what appeared to be an ancient book of some sort. It was rather dusty and seemed very old and fragile. Reaching in, I picked the book up and upon wiping off its layers of dust the book revealed a cloth cover of deep violet. Centered upon the front cover was gold lettering revealing the word, *"Life."* I looked up at the Wise One and he nodded, motioning for me to open the book. I turned back the pages and, to my surprise, the book was completely blank. Every ivory, gold edge-trimmed page was empty.

I laid the open book down upon the tabletop and said, "It's empty. Why?" The Wise One said, *"You will fill those pages with the teachings, with the love from above."* I answered, "Here? In the temple?" *"No, daughter, your timing will be revealed to you soon. And then you will Know the true purpose of this gift to the world."* The Wise One continued, *"There will come a time when the book will reveal itself to the human eye. And you will be the vehicle, you will be the Source."* I was confused at this point but I was also used to trusting what I was told. I nodded and placed the book back into the metal box and slid it to the center of the table. I would wait.

My routine in the temple had changed now, as every time I entered, I would walk to the table where the Guides would join me. The round table was my school and, over and over again, more of The Knowing and the All There Is was taught and placed within my heart. And the book stayed on that table for many more years, until the time was right and my expression was courageously revealed to the world. It was then that I would begin to understand the meaning of this gift. I would come to know that it was the human me who was meant to fill in those pages with hope for the future and the lives of humankind. I had to learn. I had to write this book.

Chapter Nine

Asnah

...channeling the teachings.

*"It is not important, what you do for a living.
It is, however, very important how you feel
while you are doing it."*

As my meditation grew, both in understanding and intensity, I sensed a change of vibration within the temple walls. It was a subtle difference but I could certainly feel an added sense of anticipation, of something expectant. The steady constant in my meditations was the manner in which I would enter the temple and greet the Guides. I would start by walking straight to the back of the room and then step upon the platform where I would greet each Guide from left to right. I would first greet the Mother Guide. She was seated in a wheelchair and during the last few years, she had begun to reveal heavy metal braces that were solidly attached to her lower legs. She would kiss, hug, and pat me and usually, the Mother Guide would take me into her lap and rock me securely back and forth. I never wanted to leave her sanctuary, but like a new baby bird, she would gently urge me off her lap and onto the next Guide.

In this second position was the revolving chair and over the years, many different Guides had come and gone. But all of these Guides were now, one way or another, helping me to move my focus from the human rat race to discovering my own Spiritual evolution. But the one circumstance that made me a little uncomfortable at the moment was that this chair was empty and hadn't held a Guide for quite a while. The Guide that had most recently occupied the revolving chair was long gone and a fading memory. So instead, I would greet the Mother Guide, then move to the revolving chair and touch it wishfully. At that point, I would move onto the next Guide, the Guide of the Life Stage and we would both hug and he would throw his head back and laugh a loud *"Ha!"* at the *"irony of Life."*

The Guide of the Life Stage was a great teacher of perception and reality, something he would call *"the very Essence of Life."* We spend, in the human existence, so much of our precious time trying to convince others to think like us, to understand us, to be us. This futile attempt to label and judge breeds fear, hatred, prejudice, and victimization and is based in ignorance of God. Nations declare war and spend the lives of countless young men and women in an effort to force others to be of Like-minds.

In this world there often seems to be little or no tolerance for individuality and acceptance of opposing ideas, of any thought that might conflict with our own. Why can't we just let our own thoughts and ideas live side by side with other possibilities, other realities, and perceptions? Why do we fear that, by accepting and allowing other points of view to exist, we might lose our own identity? In the end, if we are truly receptive, then the truth as we need it and the way for each of us to live within our own Essence would be easy to recognize. And all other things would fall gently away, waiting for another Soul who's ready to form an idea to come upon it's path. The Guide of the Life Stage would say, *"Think of this war taking place within your own body. Think of the destruction, loneliness, and pain."* He was very specific in his teachings and he drilled the concept of perception and reality into my heart on a daily basis.

When I first met him, I was deeply immersed in the entertainment field as a singer and actress. He used the analogy of a stage to help explain perception, reality, and the fact that every single one of us are on our own path and that it is utterly impossible to sway anyone away from their own unique perception of our life and their own. *"Daughter, it is imperative that you understand this concept. It is not easy, in its simpleness, to grasp. Many talk of perception as reality, but they do not take the time to truly understand the magnitude of this statement, the utter life-altering reality that is in this statement. When we truly and completely understand that what we feel about what is happening all around us is what defines our life, then we begin to understand the power and control we have over our own destiny. And just as no one can control or sway our feelings, we, too, cannot sway them to our way of feeling. So the answer to a life within The Knowing is just in the changing of our feeling reaction to the events that happen around us. If you think about this long enough, you will then hopefully realize that none of us are victims unless we choose, because we can choose our reaction, we can choose our life. We become the creator, writer and producer of our own play and we act out our lives as the actors in our existence: An egotist's paradise, but one that is a true gift of God to the Self. That this can also help to explain how two people can see the same event and view it and feel about it two entirely different ways. It is the power that you have, it is your own Power of Will."*

It would take a long time for me to grasp and understand the magnitude of this lesson. I had no idea that I was habitually immersed deep within a victim role, always waiting to be judged, scrutinized, and persecuted. It was an existence that had paralyzed my heart and stopped me from fully understanding my true Self as it struggled to live within The Knowing.

When I was finally able to see that my knee-jerk reactions to events that seemed to bombard me on a daily basis were just a conditioned habit of familiarity and convenience, I was able to turn the doorknob on the door of my new life. Even now it is a daily struggle for me, as I remind myself of the gift of my own Power of Will, of this gift of choice from God to my heart. All of the Guides would gently remind me to consider this notion and they would make choice the topic of many, many lessons.

Because of instant access to information and communication with each other, people on the Earth occupy a world that is a much smaller place than it was. It is so important that people begin to grasp the meaning of choice and realize that the foolish armor of safety that we cloak ourselves with keeps us draped within the victim role that is actually weaved by deception. The Guides would say, *"One Soul at a time, one day at a time, one moment at a time, that is how to bring about the shift in the consciousness of the planet. There is no need to create an instant result, as there is a timing to all upon the Earth. Rather, start with your own Self, share by example, Be the example."*

And I began to slowly peel away the layers of victimization and misunderstanding, revealing raw, unfamiliar feelings and embracing the Guide's wisdom and warmth when things got too scary for me. I lost much of my daily routine of acceptance and point of view of the world. And as I began to tread water, wondering which way to swim, I would close my eyes and listen for my own truth and swim silently toward the end result. Over and over, I would find myself in unfamiliar territory, but the trust within my heart prodded me forward as I headed toward my final destination of the passion within my Soul. I trusted the Guides and I was beginning to trust myself.

And back in the temple, after greeting the Mother Guide, the Guide in the revolving chair and the Guide of the Life Stage, I would move on to the Wise One, who I would greet with big, deep hugs. The Wise One, this gentle man-Spirit, would always be the one I would address first upon the commencement of the teachings. I was most comfortable and familiar with him and I felt that this was no accident. He was a trusted friend, and his gentle, grandfatherly appearance created a safe harbor all around my Soul. He would typically set up the lesson, and then pass me on to another Guide to continue. At the end of the meditation, I would usually end up back in front of the Wise One, where he would confirm my understanding of a particular reasoning.

The Wise One had been the voice I heard in the tunnel at the moment of my death. It was he who urged me back into my physical body in an effort to continue with my life path. And I thank God that he did!! For in doing this, I have been given an opportunity to follow a passionate beacon of hope and also to spread this hope to all who will listen. The Wise One is my comfort zone within the temple, the "parent" a child runs to for a quick hug of reassurance in a crowd of excited fun, chaos, and unknowns. He continually advances my courage and reminds me, *"Fear is ignorance of God,"* and that, *"All things kept within The Knowing are there for the human race to perceive with the confidence of a newborn babe."* I took his words with faith and the understanding that all would continue to be revealed to me in the proper time. He taught me the importance of timing and how it truly is everything. Without a doubt, I believed him then and I certainly continue to believe him now.

Next to the Wise One stood the Doctor Guide. He continued, from day one, to be cranky, irritable, and impatient. I was taken aback by his demeanor at first, but I soon grew accustomed to his seeming agitation. He would place his old, withered hand in mine and shake it absentmindedly while looking side to side. He seemed to want to avoid eye contact with me. The Doctor Guide never answered my questions about why he acted as if he were nervous or why he seemed to steer clear of looking at me. Typically, he would immediately begin to spout words of wisdom about the mind-body-Spirit connection and he would shake his aging finger at me when he felt I was neglecting my own physical body, telling me in no uncertain terms that it needed my immediate attention.

One night, when the Doctor Guide seemed particularly uncomfortable with my presence, I turned to the Wise One for an explanation. He said that I would begin to understand why the Doctor Guide appeared to me as such once the barriers of my own fear were taken down. *"Daughter, many humans live in denial. They live in and amongst themselves, forgetting who they really are. We, as your Guides, are presented to you symbolically. We hope that in your perception of us, you will understand an additional lesson that is so important for you to behold."*

I began to wonder what I was supposed to understand about a fidgety old man who rarely looked me in the eyes. At this thought, the Wise One gestured toward the Doctor Guide, who now stood calmly with his hands clasped before him. I saw for the first time, his clear blue eyes and the soft wrinkles and crinkles that outlined his brow and mouth. And also for the first time, he was gazing directly at me! Slowly, he smiled and I returned the smile as a warm tingling swept over my body.

The Wise One continued, *"And so, in your perception, what do you see? How do you perceive this man of truth? This wondrous Guide is there for you to accept yourself as you are. To be who you are without judgment. The uncomfortable-ness that you feel in your own skin is a major hurdle that you must overcome in order to continue on. This Guide of the balance of health, physical mind, appearance, and Spirit who work together for the Greater Good is a gift of the Angels. For when you look into your own mirror in your physical world, how do you judge yourself? Do you allow for the imperfections that make up each individual? Or rather, do you judge, mistreat, and sabotage your own physical health in an effort to portray the beauty on the outside to the world. Again, realizing that beauty is determined by perception, we say to you why do you judge? Why not just let your body be what it needs to be with no boundaries? As we tune into who we are, and what really matters, the rest will follow into place."*

I looked over at the Doctor Guide and I began to see him for the first time with my heart. His avoidance of me was a reflection of my own avoidance and judgment within my mirror. The Self-judgment of those extra pounds or a stray hair or puffy eyes that would sometimes reflect back at me the total misunderstanding of who I really am. And more importantly, how I see myself and love myself. His avoidance of me pierced my heart just as my own avoidance would unconsciously derail my Self-acceptance. How my inner heart must have been crying out to me all those years! How could I expect anyone else to accept me for who I am if I wasn't willing to do the same? For me, living a lie of confidence, I was ripping my own esteem to shreds while tap dancing and singing throughout the course my life.

And the eventual realization came to me that what we expect from others and how we expect them to be is about us and our own perception of ourselves. It has absolutely nothing to do with them and who they really are. We literally reflect back what we perceive ourselves to be. And when we accept ourselves totally and completely, we can then accept others, just as they are, whole and complete from the gates of Heaven. I remind myself every day to love and nurture my Self first and with that intent, I am rewarded continually, as I am surrounded by a protective veil of my own Power of Will and choice.

It would be after greeting the Doctor Guide that I would then move to stand in front of the ethereal Guide, Michael. As he always did, he would transform his physical self into that of a diminutive fairy and, placing his tiny hands in mine, we would begin our nightly flight around the temple walls, always landing safely in the same spot. This old, but Eternally and physically young, pure Soul of the Light always made my heart sing with The Knowing, the complete feeling of the All There Is. He would go for long periods of time without speaking so that when he did choose to express himself, I listened and felt what he was saying.

I would then move to greet the last Guide, the Guide of Guides: my Angel Guide. Most meditations, it would take me into its wings and I would be cradled in a soft surrounding of pearl white feathers. I would snuggle into the damp wings as small chunks of wet snow would fall around me. I would run my hand all around and through the feathers as my head pressed against the warmth of its body. This safe haven was quick to calm any nerves or unwanted thoughts and it was in this position that my heart rate and breathing would begin to slow to a few beats and breaths per minute.

At this, the Guide of Guides would take me safely from its wings and place me upon the stone floor. Many times, I would watch as it would then release its magnificent wingspan and raise its arms high up into the Heavens. This emotional ritual was so powerful and touching and I would wait reverently until the Angel would settle down into its quiet stance of wings folded and arms clasped. The Guide of Guides had not spoken to me but that would soon change, as its mission would begin the moment I would choose to write this book.

When I was finished greeting the Guides, we would all leave the platform and walk over to the large wooden table where I would wait by my chair until they were all seated. It was at this point that I would take my seat and the lessons would begin.

But now, the feeling of expectancy and excitement within the temple continued to greet me upon entering. And so it was a joyous day when I walked through the opening, stepped upon the platform, and there he stood, with a grin as wide and silly as the cat that just ate the canary. I greeted the Mother Guide first, but kept my eyes focused on this new, bigger than life ethereal Being, the newest Guide in the revolving chair. When I walked over to him, I immediately felt his warmth and joy. He was Indian (as in India) and dressed in the garb of the ancient yogis. His long, shiny black hair was parted in the middle and cascaded down his back. His robes of deep purple cotton were gathered together with a gold tapestry belt that wrapped several times around his ample middle. I laughed out loud as his jolly appearance reminded me somewhat of Santa Claus.

He reached for both of my hands and shook them happily and enthusiastically up and down several times, flashing a beautiful smile of straight white teeth. His loud, infectious laugh continued as we stood there for what seemed like forever, excitedly shaking hands and laughing hysterically. I wondered, "Who is this Guide and what in the world is he doing?" Because he was seated in the revolving chair, I knew he wouldn't be there long, and I already began to feel the dread of his inevitable and eventual departure. As soon as the laughing subsided, we stood there clasping our hands and looking within each other's eyes. I had a deep sense of recognition, but I couldn't place where we had met.

This newly presented Guide heaved a big sigh and wiped the joyous tears from his eyes. He stepped back and looked me up and down as if he were finally being reunited with a long lost friend. And then, clasping his hands in mine, he said. *"I am Asnah. Your Guide of the human existence."* We both continued to stare at one another. *"I am here to help you understand the choices you will make in your human life path and how you can begin to turn it inward toward your true passion. I will teach you to understand that if you believe, if you completely trust, then your true needs will be met. You will understand that humor can help you to realize the joy in the All There Is, and you, sweet baby girl, can be a vital force both within your own life and in the life of the universe. And I will teach you to laugh deeply and joyfully at all that God has created in your world. To learn to not take anything personally, as other people's thoughts and judgments are solely from their own perspective and are not about you at all.* (A confirmation of what the Doctor

Guide had been revealing to me.) *You will be Guided by me to find your true passion and purpose in this life experience. As a teacher, you will begin to trust your own instincts and the pink of your own Knowing and you will begin to put away the fears that keep you bound to what you see as a safe existence.*"

I understood this last statement perfectly, as my life seemed to be ruled by fear and judgment. And even though I worked consistently and diligently with the Wise One for a better understanding of the paralyzing fears of my Spirit, nonetheless, this Guide, Asnah, would help me with the fears of the tangible, judgmental world. He would work closely with The Guide of the Life Stage in an effort to apply the teachings of perception and reality to my life. He actually was a career Guide of sorts whose ultimate goal was to help me with the combining of my everyday vocation and my growing Spirituality. And he would eventually help me move from a secular existence into one of Spirit and he was a major influence in the writing of this book.

Asnah also knew that humor is vital to the human heart, physical body and Spirit and he used it often to teach me and help me understand why humans put so much emphasis on money, career, and hard work. *"It is a sad state that the human of your world puts so much importance in materials outside of themselves. This empty, rarely satisfied hunger for more of the feeling that they think money can buy. Remember that it's the feeling they seek, not the tangible thing. But the feelings that come with the most expensive diamond are free. Free. And available whenever you choose.*"

He made me laugh, cry, and think about my life path in the secular world and his persistent teachings that I follow my passion seemed to be his primary mission. I had recently moved from the entertainment business to the healthcare industry and had begun to reap the substantial financial rewards that accompanied this change. Asnah slowly began to prod me to pay attention to my growing dissatisfaction of my career and he would, at every opportunity, help me to understand that my first, true love was that of Spirit.

But I couldn't understand how I could just walk away from everything I had worked toward in my life and I was frightened about losing my income and the health insurance I required for my diabetes. He listened lovingly and patiently to my Self-arguments on playing it safe in the professional world as opposed to trusting in the universe to meet my needs. *"And so daughter, why do you fear this change, this leap of faith that must be? It is with hope and utter trust that I say unto you, this day, this moment, can be the catalyst that takes you to your true purpose. It matters not what you do for a living; rather, how you feel while you do it. And that emotion is ever close in your heart and can be answered by everyone. So as you fly into the unknown, you will feel the arms of the Angels as they gather you and take you to a place of refuge. Do not confuse what you do for a living with who you are. It truly matters not in the eyes of God. And one day, when this is complete in your heart and you truly understand, then you will Know. And you will then leap and laugh as the wind carries you to your true destiny. It must be made known that all must listen to their inner heart and desires. The needs will be met and the desires will be complete. It is not the 'thing' we need, it is the feeling."* His advice was timely and intense, always prodding me to look beyond the comfort zone of least resistance to a world of change and discovery of my true calling.

Three years later

I loved Asnah. I loved his humor, especially, and his funny way of helping me to understand and more importantly apply the choices that were now open to me due to the teachings of perception and reality by the Guide of the Life Stage. These two Guides worked diligently with me, always displaying their humor and irony of the human existence. Yet recently, they seemed to be stepping up their teachings and were relentless with my lessons. I know that they used laughter to help me understand as this intense concept of choices, (based in reality and perception) were instrumental in the evolution of my Soul to the next level of realization.

Night after night, lesson after lesson, they would pull me into myself and go over and over the choices I had made during a given day and how I was feeling about those choices. And I loved these concentrated teachings and I would often arrive in the temple ready with my arsenal of questions and arguments. The sparring sessions were lively and often hysterical. The Guide of the Life Stage would use his staged forum to act out events and Asnah would make the comments and suggestions for me to consider. It was during this time that I began to once again long to be able to write down the exact words of these precious, simple, yet consuming examples put forward for me. I wanted to share more than just a poem or a sentence or a thought that I had channeled into my journals. But again, I found that, upon awakening, the feeling remained but most, if not all of the lessons evaporated into a glowing memory.

I was particularly frustrated one night when I shared with the Wise One what I longed to do. "Why can't I remember the exact words of the lessons?" I would ask him. *"Daughter, the times we spend here with you are for you. There is coming a time when we will begin to turn the lessons outward and become more general in their simpleness. It would be in this way that we can begin to reach more of the thirsty Souls that long to hear the words of truth. Your time is coming and yet we must continue forward with your lessons, for how can you be a vessel of understanding when you yourself lack the perception at this moment? When your personal tutelage is complete, it is then that we shall set you free to begin your task upon the Earth. Soon. Have patience, but more importantly, have and create within yourself an understanding of what we speak. For until you move on and grasp this level of the teachings, you will be stuck in a circle of misunderstanding toward how to express yourself to those of great need. It is coming soon, daughter; you will be the recipient of a gift that will become for you both a wonder and a duty, as there will be no turning back. A duty that will sometimes be hard to bear. But you will be ready, and soon."*

So I continued my work with the Guide of the Life Stage and Asnah and I slowly and diligently lifted the curse of the victim within. And when the total realization that I am my own Power of Will and that I chose my own happiness began to permeate my heart and existence, I knew I was ready. And the Guides deemed me ready as well and they set out to help me get the teachings from over there to here.

In order to begin to share the jewels of the temple with my own conscious mind and others, I knew that I needed to document the messages while I was actually in the temple. Even though I adored the small statements and poetic sayings that I had been journaling with automatic writing, I wanted to document their lessons completely, word for word. And so, I made a few futile attempts such as putting a small microphone near my mouth so that I could ask the questions out loud and then repeat back their answers out loud while recording. This didn't work to my satisfaction because I found that I was mostly unable to talk understandably during the times I was in the temple. A few lines would come out here and there but there was no sense or continuity to most of it. I even tried a computer program that "types" while you speak, but the same thing would happen. The computer couldn't understand my varied speech patterns and thus would type out muddled words and sentences that didn't make sense. But the computer was inspiring to me as I would sometimes be able to make out a tidbit here and there. I would become so emotional when I would recognize small portions of the teachings and I felt I was getting closer to the answer on how to document the messages.

I had purchased a laptop computer in an effort to type out anything I could remember immediately upon coming out of meditations. I would turn the computer on and place it at the foot of my bed and then lay down upon the bed for the temple meditation. When I awakened, I would grab the computer and try to type quickly in an effort to recall anything that might have been discussed during the temple visit. This was working a little bit but it was not consistent and the words were sketchy.

One night during a temple visit, Asnah was smiling and clapping his hands in excitement. He said that he had a better, quicker way of *"laying down the gifts upon the electronic bytes"* and that I was now *"ready to begin the outward reach."* His excitement was intoxicating as he said to open my physical eyes and look upon the bed that I was lying on. I was very surprised, as the Guides never, ever asked me to leave the temple; they always left my departure up to me. But doing as he said, I slowly opened my eyes and saw the soft glow from my laptop computer at the foot of the bed. As if in a slow moving dream, I remember opening its top and laying my hands gently upon the keyboard. I had a strange feeling of being split in two. I was neither fully there nor here; I felt in between.

As Asnah began to speak and with no help from me, my fingers began to move quickly across the keys, following his every word. I yanked my hands off the laptop, as the sensation of my body moving in any way without my help was startling. But at this point in my life, the unexplained had happened so much that I trustingly placed my hands back on the keys, closed my eyes, and waited. And then I heard Asnah gently say to me, *"Open the paper."* I immediately opened my eyes halfway and found the icon for a writing program and I opened a new, blank document. I stared at the blinking cursor line and slowly closed my eyes once more.

As Asnah began to speak, my fingers again began to type on the keyboard. And as he continued, my Soul was pulled back completely into the temple and we continued with the lessons. I was aware that my fingers were moving but I had no conscious idea what they were typing. And as Asnah stopped talking and the other Guides began, my fingers continued to fly across the keyboard.

The Guides spoke slowly and deliberately, sometimes waiting for my fingers to catch up. And a couple of times during this first, miraculous session, I "peeked" at the computer screen, watching in amazement as my fingers moved. An astonishing thing was that when I was "awakened" with eyes open and looking at the computer screen, I couldn't hear the Guides speaking and I had no idea what my fingers were typing. But as I went back into meditation and into the temple, I was totally aware of what they were saying. And when I came out of meditation at the end of this session, the lessons and words of the Guides quickly faded from my conscious mind as usual. Yet, when I looked down upon the computer screen, I saw it for the first time: a complete, word-for-word documentation of the teachings from the Guides.

I leaned forward and looked intently upon the computer screen and I began to cry as I read with my human eyes what, in the past, only my Soul had been given. The impact of the messages upon my heart was realized all over again, seemingly as if I were absorbing the words for the first time. While in meditation, I was used to hearing and receiving their beautiful words of wisdom and it became a given that this was the way it was while in the temple. Yet, my conscious mind and heart were thirsting for the same affirming messages that only my Soul had been privy. And I could now begin to read and take within my physical body these simple, elegant, and powerful messages of hope. And I knew that I would finally be able to convey the messages from the Guides with no interpretation by me or any missing pieces I couldn't remember.

Night after night, I would find my hands upon the keyboard and my Soul in the temple. And the words and messages came in droves. There was never any fear of the origin of these messages, as I had a routine of saying the 23rd Psalm and asking the Guides if they were "of God for the Greater Good?" at the beginning of each session. And the messages were good; they were full of uncompromising love and teachings of truth. I knew I could now help spread The Knowing. And I knew that, soon, I would begin to write this book.

It was a year later that I slowly began to share my story with very select friends and family. Most found it fascinating, wanting more information. And there were some that had questions for the Guides and they requested that I ask them about different aspects of their own lives. So I found myself doing "readings" for them on occasion. I would go into meditation, ask the questions and send the answer back to the requester. I was surprised when I agreed to this, as my intent was never to "hang out a shingle," and begin to do readings on a regular basis. But it has helped so many people and is, I feel, for the Greater Good. I continue to do this, but only if I am able to address my own life path first. I believe that, in order to be of service to others, your own body and Spirit must be a priority. A very basic, common lesson, but when truly taken to heart, it's a very hard thing to do. Especially in today's world of "Who are you and what can you do for me?" conditioning. I love helping people through these readings. It is very affirming and wonderful to hear the Guides' messages of hope reach those of need. What a wonder. Oh dear God in Heaven, what a miracle.

Chapter Ten

The Crystal City

...entering the mystical land of light and angels.

*"The Angels and Guides that are your Soul Team will,
many times, speak to you through your intuition, your inner voice.
Learn to be silent.
Learn to listen."*

After three years of documenting the teachings and giving personal readings, I began to formulate the path this book would take. On a warm summer evening in the spring of 2001, the Guides greeted me in the temple in a different manner. Upon entering, I unexpectedly found the Guides standing just inside the entrance around the top of the darkened staircase. It was very startling, as my routine had not changed in several years. I felt vulnerable and shy as I greeted each Guide, but when I took in their behavior, these feelings began to subside as I could sense their excitement and delight. There was an impression of urgency and surprise and all their eyes were on me.

I stood back and asked the Wise One why they had greeted me in this manner and why this change? The Wise One said, *"Oh, happy day! Dear daughter, oh happy day! You will now be taken into the heart of this temple. The heart of your temple. This magnificent gift from above to one still on the Earth plane is truly miraculous. The boundaries of memory and judgment will be gone. Only the feelings will be left for you to perceive. We shall take you now to this wondrous place of unimaginable joy. We are happy, as this gift is rare for an embodied Spirit and is given only to those trusted with The Knowing and understanding. Come, let us Guide you into this realm of completeness."*

The Wise One took my hand and as the others followed, he tenderly led me down the dimly lit stone staircase. I looked from side to side as we descended and noticed that the stone walls were producing a clear cascade of misty water that billowed out and tumbled down the sides. When we reached the bottom of the stairs I noticed a musty smell of dampness as I looked out toward a round stone stage with seven steps leading to the top. I also perceived a gentle Light that seemed to peer out over the top of the stage.

The Wise One led me over to the seven steps and slowly we ascended the stairs as the other Guides followed. With each stair, I felt a deep trust within the warm Light that began to slowly appear over the top edge of the stage. As we ascended the last stair, I stood silently looking toward the far end of the platform. A brilliant, iridescent Light called me forward, and the Wise One placed his hand upon my back, urging me to follow its call. I walked out to the far edge of the stage and beheld a magnificent jungle of fragrant flowers, trees, and other living things. A purple-blue sky showcased brilliant white clouds that were filled with flying birds. The colors were of a palette I have never seen before. Everything was sharper, clearer, and more raw than I had ever experienced. I held my arms out to my side as a gentle breeze kicked up and floated my hair around my head. I sensed the life before me and I breathed in this virgin land of simple, untouched nonjudgment. A beautiful mist lay upon the green, waxy leaves and it lingered in the air all around me. This awakened morning was coming to life and I was there, reaping this bounty of living things.

Silently, the Wise One joined me by my side and said, "*This, is the heart of your temple. In this final phase of our teachings, it is here that you will begin to understand, to behold the power of your own desire. It is here, where there will be no pretense, no questions around what it is that you need. You will recognize that this place is the closest thing that we can offer you with respect to Heaven on Earth. For in this welcomed environment, you will Know, without fear, of what you desire and how it can apply to your doubts. Instantly, you will feel this wondrous vibration of a place unjudged by all and with no feeling left or remembrance unacknowledged. You will remember here and when you ask we will ask, what do you remember?*"

I felt so utterly blessed. How could I feel any other way? I turned my eyes to the Wise One as he continued, "*It is here, dear daughter, that you will truly understand nonjudgment. And with this gift comes a small trinket. In this place, you will be allowed to remember your life as you have lived it. You will be given glimpses into your past in an effort to recall what is important for you. You will ask and we will tell you of this remembrance. But even more important, you will be given an opportunity to remember the lives past, of different incarnations. This will come as you begin the final phase of your incarnation. But in the meantime, you will be answered fully and completely and you will remember all in an effort to help your documentation. And what, dear daughter, do you wish to ask first?*"

What did I want to ask first? My God, how should I begin? There was an immediate influx of need to instantly Know everything about everything. But for some reason, I didn't hesitate with my question, as I had yearned and prayed to learn how these Beings of Light saw our relationship. Their teachings were always about me and my personal perceptions and reactions. I knew how I perceived them but I wanted to hear their view of this miracle. And so I asked without hesitation, "How do you perceive me?"

The Wise One answered, "*Oh daughter, we know that you are ready for this. By your question, we know you are beginning to lift the veil of understanding about who you are and who we are and why this relationship was chosen. Yes, indeed.*" And one by one, they came forward and took my hands. And with this wondrous backdrop of beauty and bounty within the heart of the temple, they each answered my question. The Wise One spoke first, *"You are an old, wise and passionate beacon of Light. One who absorbs others; Light and emotions. One who needs to understand and execute the feeling of power, of empowerment over your own destiny. A tender, reassuring Being of hope for those searching for the Knowledge of the All There Is."* He kissed my hands.

Next, the Guide of Guides stepped before me and smiled. I had only heard it speak one word before this day, "teacher," so I was deeply touched when it answered quietly, *"You. Who reach out to others. You, who employ a sense of innate respect among all people on the Earth. And in your example, you make people's hearts sing and rejoice and yearn for more. Your teachings of Light and hope will impact the existence of many. You will begin small and rise to a great level of understanding. I will be there to hold your hand as you teach and Guide and express yourself so that others of need may find comfort and peace within. It can begin their journey and you can turn the key. And in this final act of your life play, you will enjoy the completeness, the hope for the future and the All There Is. You will understand and Know of what is being said and most importantly, you will understand how you truly feel. You, Teacher."*

This Angel would become my muse in this life. It would help me to teach and express perceptions simply and with great impact. This Guide of Guides would take my hand and lead me down the road to become a great and loving Guide of The Knowing in my life. And it would help me understand and apply my power of persuasion for the Greater Good. And this Angel Guide smiled upon recognizing my acceptance of its purpose and reason for being in my life.

Next, the Guide of the Life Stage spoke with resounding impact: *"A songbird and purveyor of truth and an example to others. Your play is well written and executed, yet you yearn for confirmation. Remember that all is already confirmed."* He bowed dramatically and I found myself face to face with the Mother Guide: *"I sense you as a nurturer and teacher of good will. A patient, compassionate human, sometimes owning difficulty in projecting that around those you love."* I was actually surprised at her last statement, but when I really thought about it, I agreed in my heart that her perception of me was right on. I would work diligently (and I am still working on this) to understand the unconditional right of all people to experience total acceptance, nonjudgment, and most importantly, love.

The Doctor Guide was next to answer my question and he began, *"One who Knows the connection of the mind-body-Spirit. One who must recognize this in all things. That they are one and the same and must be taught and acknowledged so."* The Doctor Guide then tilted his head and stepped aside for Michael. He tenderly took my fingers within his own and said, *"Oh sweetheart. You fly to the moon and the stars in anticipation of the greatness of God. Of the feeling. Of the pink. You are already perfect in all ways, as God is good and just and creates us all in It's image. And as you come to Know the importance of these feelings deep within your Soul, you will then recognize and accept all the teachings here as second only to that concept. The importance of feelings is what defines everything in the human existence."*

I smiled at Michael with understanding, as I was beginning to live, to be, to feel my own feelings. And last, sweet, funny Asnah stepped forward and took my hands in his. *"Angel of the land, you are one that understands hope and sees all rivers upon the land as one that can take you to the next level. Your growing understanding of the importance of Being, of Being true to your Self and, most importantly, trusting your Self, is a joy to behold. Oh how we love your curiosity and your longing for the All There Is! And that is why I tell you that soon, as my job here is almost complete, I will be leaving your place of refuge. I will incarnate again to walk upon the land of the thirsty, of the hungry for the All There Is. But you will remember this, dear daughter, Know that you choose your happiness, your reactions, your perception of your life. Again we say this to you again and again. Do not forget this. And as the next Guide comes in, she will help with your recognition of the importance of following your true calling, of trusting completely and Knowing that your true needs will be met."*

My heart had stopped with his words. I had happily taken in his perception of me only to find my Soul plunged into a strange loneliness at his proclamation that he was going to leave the temple and reincarnate. I knew that he would eventually depart, but it had been such a short time. I loved him so much and I anticipated his teachings, his funny words and jolly giggles when he placed a thought before me. But I also knew that I trusted him.

And I believed his words. So, I gently took him into my arms and said, "Thank you." Upon which he replied, *"So be it daughter, so be it."* I took a deep breath and smelled the Essence of this Being, a musky, smoky fragrance touched with gardenias. Then Asnah sweetly turned my face out towards the beautiful land that lay endlessly before me.

We all stood quietly for a long time. Then, I walked over to the far edge of the stage and gazed out into the heart of the temple. And suddenly, I found myself encased within a large, clear bubble. My body became buoyant as I was lifted within its thin, clear walls. I touched the inside lining of the bubble and Light particles flowed out around the indentation. I was floating in an upright position within the bubble as it slowly began to lift and glide toward the beautiful treetops. The bubble drifted peacefully in and out of the flowerbeds and vegetation and I observed the birds, insects, and other living creatures greeting me with their nature calls.

I continued to float in and around it all and I found myself safely and securely soaring over streams and rivers and snowy mountaintops. I relished different seasons of colors as I flew from place to place. I felt as if I was bursting with beauty, love, and yearning. The feeling was so full, so rich, that I almost felt it was too much for me to bear. At this thought, I found myself floating back to the stone stage where the Guides were waiting for me. And as I landed upon the stage, the bubble melted away and the Wise One beckoned me to go to a newly materialized table and chairs.

As I walked to the table, I saw the familiar box that held the blank book. As I took my seat, the Wise One said, *"And now. It is time. To begin to document this story and in an effort to promote the understanding, we give you leave to begin."* I opened the box and took out the ancient book. I saw a carved wooden pen rolling around in the bottom and I took both items and placed them on the table before me. The Wise One continued, *"In the stillness you will Know, you will hear of it. The truth, and then you can understand the ways of the universal law. Daughter, you will be our vessel of hope and reason. There will be times when you shall fear and slip out of The Knowing. But we will be here for you, waiting to help you when you stumble.*

And there will be days when it will be easier and days when it will be more challenging. But always keep The Knowing and the trust within your heart and mind. It is ever there. Believe and most importantly trust in what is being given to you. Your comfort zone may call out to you, but it is not really a place of peace, rather a place of familiar discontent. Do not listen to that call. Know that your true needs will be met with love. And listen for your answer within. Stilling the mind and quieting your environment in an effort to hear your answer. You do not need to continue to ask. The God Knows of your questions and certainly every one of your desires. You do not need to fear that your purpose will not be made known to you. It will. Follow what in the stillness of your mind you receive. It is an anomaly and you can fully understand the path by accepting the truth of it all. You must understand the true importance and never forget what the reasons for becoming are. You can never know peace until you find the silence in your heart and Soul. And fear will keep you grounded in the body and unable to fly. As will anger and hate. Fear, anger, and hate are close in their actuality and are, in reality, the same vibration. It is understood that you will become the answer to all your prayers."

I took in all that he professed and after waiting respectfully for a few moments, I opened the blank book, my mind, heart, and Soul and remembered all things as an accepting Being seeking truth. I began to ask questions of my past and as I reviewed every moment, I caught sight of the true purpose for the Guides and I finally, blessedly began to write this book.

Within days, my beloved Asnah was gone.

Three months later

I continued, night after night, month after month with the writings in the heart of the temple and I was bursting forth with remembering my past and putting the events together to tell my story. Some of the events were difficult to think about but as I explored these situations, I was able to understand my feelings and more importantly, apply my own perception of what was now my life. It was a cleansing, a rinsing of old thoughts and ideas that, with my newfound understanding of my own Power of Will (choice), I was able to reprogram my past to fit into my present life. Many old hurts and pains and even happy events were re-remembered and put into a place of new understanding. And I was writing nonstop. Words and events tumbled out in random fashion and I would rewrite, rethink, and re-remember the words over and over until I finally found a place of consistent flow and routine.

I loved this scratching out of words and sentences. I was, in my infancy, learning to put ideas together in an effort to put the messages forward in a simple fashion, with great impact. And I loved this time in my life even though my two worlds were colliding as my career was going full steam ahead alongside my path of documenting my story and the teachings. Yet, it was also at this time that I began to feel the intense internal pull to move away from my healthcare career and devote myself totally to my writing and documentation.

Shortly after Asnah left, a new Guide had appeared in the revolving chair and was pushing me forward with intensity. She would, at every opportunity, remind me over and over to listen to my inner voice and remember the reason I incarnated into this life. She helped to give me the courage and wisdom to put my mental fears and reasoning aside and listen for the path to take. She would be in the revolving chair for only a few months and honestly, I don't remember her name (I know there was a reason for this) but she was intense in her urgings to have faith in myself and step out of my comfort zone and I trusted her. I listened to my heart night after night with an openness I'd never let myself feel before. But I still wasn't ready to leave my career, not yet anyway.

A few months later, as I made my way up the side of the temple to begin another session in remembering, I paused halfway up the staircase and sat upon the familiar stone bench, reflecting on this wondrous journey. As I looked out beyond the little garden at the base of the temple and further to the deep green forest that had first intrigued me so many years ago. I continued my gaze down upon the sparkling blue lake where I had first "popped" in at its edge. I laughed when I remembered that day as Celeste's soft voice had faded and I found myself standing there thinking, "What in the world is happening here?" And I smiled as I remembered the little animals and toe-nibbling fish that came to me night after night upon my arrival.

I put my elbows on my knees and leaned forward, placing my chin upon my upturned hands. And then surprisingly, I noticed something new in the distance just beyond the lake. I looked closer and saw what seemed like a far off city of some sort. I could see a huge, glass-brick wall encircling the entire area and there were two large pillars of glass that held gates of clear, illuminating water. Inside this city were buildings that were also made of glass or water and astonishingly I could see that in among the shapes of these buildings, were balls of vibrating energy floating all around, in and above the city, permeating the entire place.

I stood up and became mesmerized with this incredible site when instantly, I found myself at the glass gates of the massive, sparkling metropolis. I was more curious than surprised and I stood carefully just outside the huge gates of glass. I reached up and ran my hand along the tall, clear pillar and upon my touch, the gates opened slowly, revealing an entire city made of glass, energy, water, and melodic sounds. Everything I saw, every shape and object was made of sparkling, luninous glass, crystal, and water. The paved streets had glass bricks with crystal grout; the buildings illuminated themselves against the energy of the Lights and water. But the most incredible thing was the individual pulsating balls of Light and energy floating about this beautiful, wondrous site. And then, as if sensing my presence, these shining sparkles of Light floated towards me and I immediately began to feel their love and their emotions as the intensity engulfed the pit of my stomach.

More and more they gathered and their presence reminded me of fish that come together to be fed from the hand of someone standing above the water. Lingering just outside the gates of this vibrating, electric city, I felt the balls of energy begin to beckon me to come into this beautiful place, but I hesitated, as I didn't feel ready somehow. I was surprised when this feeling came but I trusted these beliefs as my truth at that time. So, as if sensing my decision, the balls of energy began to float away and disperse throughout the city. As they scattered, I heard the sounds of wind and melodic tones and I closed my lids as my heart began to ache to go inside.

When the sounds stopped, I opened my eyes and found that the Wise One had appeared at my side. Without surprise at his presence, I asked him to tell me what this place was and why is it there for me? "Should I go into the city?" The Wise One answered, *"This City, this Crystal City of*

Light and energy is there for you to discover the importance of every feeling you have ever possessed and will possess in the future. Feelings are the root of the Soul. From the root grows the tree and then the branches and then the leaves, then the birds come and enjoy the tree. The animals and birds alight upon the branches. The insects find shelter and shade. Thus is the root of your Soul. It all begins with the feeling of any given thing, person, moment, or event. To under-stand the importance of your feelings, imagine what would happen if you did not water and nurture the root of the tree. The tree springs from the root after the seed is planted, so your Soul is planted by God and as you nurture the feel-ings of this Soul, because in the beginning it knows of nothing else, it grows. Side by side we discuss this. Feelings, growth and yearning for more. More nutrients, love, and ultimately, searching for the Light of God. That is the importance of the Soul.

Yet, how do humans define other people, places, and events? By adjectives based on feelings. And when an emotion is tied to that adjective feeling, then it grows forth and emits new feelings of judgment from the individual Soul. When you say "Mother," what you feel about that word is based upon your own percep-tion or feeling of Mother. Every case is perceived differently. So you have percep-tion, reality, based or rooted in feelings.

Feelings are the root of perception, but perception can change the feeling. It cannot happen the other way around. Do you see? So therein resides the key to true happiness and contentment for a rich, blossoming life full of promise. Do not confuse feelings with emotion, or any other defined human definition. As the root of the Soul reaches and peers out of the ground, at the human birth, then other things begin to affect its wholeness. That is when the other emotions, especially fear, which in itself impregnates many other emotions, that is when fear is introduced to the Soul. Embrace this raw emotion, these clear Lights and stark realities of life. Enjoy this place of peace and love and discovery of new ideas in your heart. This City of Light, it is the blood that runs through your portals and flows with the ebb and tide of life. Soon you will leave the temple for a while and go to this City. As such you are already going there in the dream state. That is why it is so familiar to you." And I knew that when I could face my own feelings, those frightening expressions that we all try so hard to hide from ourselves and others, I would enter the City without hesitation.

And with every meditation and writing session, I would stand at the gates and gaze at the glass-brick road that led to a town center of sorts. I would observe the balls of Light as they floated amongst each other, their cores never touching each other yet they continually infused themselves within the buildings. The structures of the buildings were of varying size and shape but pretty much indistinguishable as to their purpose. I became more curious and braver with every meditation until finally, I was ready to enter.

I placed a tentative toe onto one of the clear bricks and it shimmered, emitting a high-pitched tone that called me forward. As I stepped inside the gates, I was immediately surrounded by the vibrating balls of Light and, ever so gently, they seemed to engulf me, every cell and pore. I began to feel my Self being lifted and carried and I observed this dance of Light as they took me over to the center of the City.

They placed me softly beside a table and chair. I watched in awe as the energy balls seemed to get excited and then proceeded to move around and fly over my head with greater and greater urgency. I began to hear musical tones and bells and flutes that emoted deep-seeded memories from somewhere in a lifetime of mine. The sounds became a roaring noise and the balls began to fly and encircle the area above my head in a distinct pattern reminiscent of a flock of birds. Faster they flew until I was unable to distinguish one from the other. They became a single ring of Light and energy and my heart felt the love from a million lifetimes. I saw a spark of energy that had separated its Self from the ring, drift slowly and hover at eye level with me. I began to feel its energy and love and as I reached up to touch its sparkles, the ball began to grow and shape it's Self into a pure, illuminating Being. It took the form of a faceless human and even though I was unable to see its expression, I was able to *feel* everything.

This Being was so full, so intensely fluid and Light and its expressive emotions permeated the entire area. Yet, without preconceived ideas or judgments from an outward appearance, I perceived for the first time with my heart. And it hit me all at once that I was finally beginning to understand the vital lesson about the importance of feelings, of just "Be-ing" side by side with ourselves and others, without pretense, fear, or hesitation.

I began to feel for the first time a pure sensation of utter acceptance while keeping my heart open and my mind undefined.

Soon, the other Lights began to drop and form into faceless, undefined Beings. With no boundaries, no expectations, conditions, or gender, their feelings met mine and together we felt the joy of The Knowing, the All There Is. The intense sensation produced a heat of understanding deep, deep within my heart and I felt the stillness in my Soul. The feelings began to swell and I felt as if I would burst as I leaned my head back and cried out long and hard, "God!"

I was shaking and consumed with the feelings that were flying all around me. I continued to wail for God and I fell to my knees in weakness. The first Being that had descended came forward and offered its cool hand. Without words or expression, I felt my hand surrounded by the energy from this Being's fingers as I slowly stood up. And I felt the message from this Being. *"You will find here, the All There Is, The Knowing. For it lives deep within the feelings of the Soul. And it is available for you at all times, should you choose to listen and accept. Your feelings, your truth, are yours alone. We cannot emote that which lives deep within you. When you are ready, we are ready, to help you accept and Be, your feelings. We are the Angels of the Earth. We catch the wayward feelings of all people upon this Earth. We absorb that energy and turn it back to the Soul in the dream state to create a peaceful explanation of that which is too hard to bear. We absorb the force and carefully place it back within the heart for a better understanding, a new day. And everyday and always, we will ask, how do you feel?"*

I stood quietly and thought of the recent horrific events of September 11, 2001. I had a vision of these ethereal Angels capturing the collective grief of humanity as it flew away from our hearts and into the Heavens. I imagined them catching these intense feelings and softening their edges, making them a little easier to endure as they placed them back with their rightful owner. And instantly the answer to their question came to me. "I feel ready," I replied.

January 2002

During the next year, I entered the Crystal City four times and explored the varying feelings that were embedded within my existence. It would be

a little later that the Wise One told me, *"And at the completion of your doc-*
umented story, you will enter this City of Light and begin your last task upon
the Earth. To understand and promote the power within of all people. And this
last task will be long and arduous, but you will keep with you the understand-
ing of the All There Is. You are ready." Indeed, I was ready.

Winter 2003

The Guide in the revolving chair had done her job well. In early
February of 2003, I realized that my comfort zone, my income, and my
precious healthcare benefits were too Spiritually expensive to maintain.
The Guides had taught me that we all have different kinds of bank
accounts and they explained these accounts as financial, health, love,
Spirit, and emotional. They emphasized that we must maintain each of
these accounts carefully and when one is depleted and out of balance with
the others, this leads to unhappiness, anger, and illness. And the very day I
gave my notice of resignation was the day my health, Spirit, and emotional
bank accounts filled back up. I had finally put myself first and I experienced a feeling unfamiliar to me: a calm, childlike acceptance of what was
my new life in my awakened state. I had worked so hard, even going back
to school to complete my degree in an effort to compete with the corporate glass ceiling. Yet I found myself unemployed, ignorantly blissful, yet
available to concentrate on writing my story.

And I knew this was right. I *felt* this was the right thing to do. And that
night, upon my arrival, the Guide in the revolving chair appeared on the
temple platform and after dusting both her hands in an *"I'm finished"* gesture, she raised her arms high into the sky and was taken up to the glass
top of the temple, where she disappeared. I stood there looking at her
empty space and whispered, "Thank you." And I began to wonder who
would fill the spot. And when. I thought for a fleeting moment that maybe
Asnah would return, but I knew that this was not meant to be. And so I
waited to see who would enter the temple and take their place within my
heart.

Exactly one week later, I met Ia. I had "popped" to the lakeside as I was
missing its beautiful waters filled with life and sweetness. It seemed that for
the last several years, I rarely visited this place anymore as I usually found

myself in the garden at the base of the temple when I would first start my meditation. But the lakeside held precious remembrances of my initial introduction to this miracle and I was reminded of its simple beauty when I went to the Crystal City as the lake's other side lapped at its gates.

On this particular day, I sat on its shore next to the forest of trees that led to the temple. I waded in the water and smelled the floating flowers. Moving back to the shore, I continued to retrace my initial steps from the day I walked into the forest. I stopped halfway in and gazed upon the sun's rays as they filtered from the tips of the trees, down their mossy trunks, and onto the ground that was covered with more moss, fallen pinecones and pine needles. The bark that was visible here and there was a beautiful dark brown and I could hear the calls of the whippoorwills. Several fearless little animals greeted me as I continued to make my way through the dense foliage. A young fawn sprung into my path and stood there staring at me. Slowly, I walked up to it and patted the soft, furry head as it closed its brown eyes. I laughed as it suddenly took off and bounced across the forest floor, going after some important treasure.

I continued my walk until I pushed through the clearing of the trees and into the garden at the base of my beautiful temple. I felt reflective as I gazed upon its massive structure. I would still, from time to time, have thoughts of "Why me?" and "Can I do this?" And as I stood staring at this wonder, I felt calm and reassured that yes, I could do this and I was ready to take it further by bringing all this Knowledge from my Soul to the physical world. Timing is everything, I knew I was ready, and that, in turn, told me that everyone else in my life was ready.

For some reason, on that day, I had the conviction that all would be right. And I knew that I would finally begin telling more of my close friends and family about what was my life. There were many people that knew of my gift, as I had been doing readings and talking with people all over the country. But some of the people closest to me still only knew a little bit about what my life was. I had openly shared my gift with strangers but was hesitant to let my close loved ones know. I think I was protecting them from their own feelings, or trying to, at least. I didn't fear judgment or people leaving my life, as I knew that some would understand, some would embrace, and some would leave. Again, I was trying to find a way to tell them so that they wouldn't worry about me or be fearful for me. But of course, I knew better. I know that we cannot in any way make someone feel the way we feel. That is utterly impossible and useless. We can try to help people understand our way, but they will still come to their own conclusion. And I had given up trying to fix things and make everyone happy.

In a sense, I felt as if I was "coming out" about my life as I lived it. So when I first came to the realization that I needed to begin to tell them about the Guides, I felt little fear. I knew that various family members and friends would vary in their feelings about the information that I communicate with disembodied Spirits. But by the time that I started to talk about it, I was calm and reassured for the most part. In all that is, I have learned to embrace the many differences among Souls that walk the Earth. I find joy and humor in people who are different. To me, they are the people that are really alive. They are the ones that are really living and I know I want to be one of them. I know I am not perfect and I also know that I don't want to be perfect.

I also realized that I don't need acceptance from any other. And so, I welcome the inevitable questions, the concerns that will no doubt arise from this book. I have no fear of these recourses. I have no fear of losing any true friend. Because this is who I am and what I am about. I no longer fear the pulling away of love, I give unconditionally and those that can will do the same, tenfold.

Others who have closed their minds and hearts to anything they don't understand may leave my life, but I feel that's okay as well. I may want their love and acceptance, but I no longer need it. There is truly a huge difference in that statement. There is no guilt. As I had learned that true guilt is intentional, not circumstantial, such as my own situation. I know that I'm different but that is what sets me apart and defines who I am. I have always been different, even if I was quiet in my difference.

And so one day, I had made my way from the forest and into the garden. I paused, looking around at the vegetation that was so alive. My eyes glanced over at a cluster of daisies and I was startled to see a little girl of about five years old standing amongst the flowers. She stood sweetly, dressed in a long white smock dress and her tiny feet were bare and clean. Her little hands were crossed in front and as I met her gaze, she lifted one hand and waved a shy hello. Her long hair was straight and golden as it glistened in the sun. Her enormous, wide-set blue eyes sparked as she blinked her long black lashes. I noticed her skin to be so white that it was almost translucent.

I slowly walked toward her and knelt down, taking her soft hand. "Hello?," I said. Her tiny voice said in return, *"Hello, I've never been here before."* "You haven't?" I replied, a little taken aback. *"No, I've never been here before."* "Are you frightened?" I asked tentatively. I really didn't know what to think at this point. *"Oh no, not at all. I like it here. My name is Ia. And I am here in my first Guidepost. I am here to seek The Knowing within and to help with your purpose. And I will be here until your awakening. I am here permanently."*

I stood up and looked down upon her adorable little face. "You're my new Guide?" I asked with surprise. *"Oh yes, and I appear young to you as a reminder. To go within and believe and accept without condition and to understand how you truly feel about any given thing. I came to you in the form of a child, as it is this childlike innocence that must prevail, before the human condition intercedes and begins to add fear. And this will give you more courage, as there will be times when you will want to creep back into your comfort zone. I am also here to help with your next human task. We have all lived many lives. And with this new Guidepost and your heart of the temple, we shall remember together. We shall go into the various lifetimes of incarnation of my Soul and apply them into a documentation of seven books. These books of the history of humankind and the impending future will work together for the Greater Good. We shall enter the City of Light and we shall begin soon. This will apply to all that would listen."*

I stood there astonished at all she had revealed. First, she was permanent and there would be no more Guides coming in the revolving chair. I found this fascinating and comforting, as she now made up the seventh permanent Guide in the temple. But her revelation that together, we would write seven books of different incarnations was intriguing and exciting to me. She was so petite and cute and I had a feeling that her mind and heart held a power unknown to myself and that she held a very important key to my own transformation. I decided to begin to let her first lesson of total acceptance prevail and I silently accepted everything without question.

I extended my hand and as she placed her warm palm in mine, we made our way up the side of the temple and into the opening. The other Guides were in their usual position just inside the door and they were waiting quietly. Ia smiled and looked up at each Guide and walking over to the Wise One, she lifted her arms to him. The Wise One gently picked her up and together we all descended the stairs into the heart of the temple.

Chapter Eleven

Questions and Answers

...a gift to the reader from the guides.

"As you speak the truth from your own perspective, do so with kindness, for the world aches for a gentle, human touch."

And if, upon my death, I discover that I'm wrong? I will always believe that God Knows the intent of my heart. *"And intent is the manner in which it is received by your Self and your heart and by being true to this one true purpose, the hearts, Souls, and minds of others will recognize its truth. They will join you by your side as they, too, recognize that the intent is for the Greater Good."*

I fully understand and deem that I am, without question, the bearer of my own good and bad news, of my own Light and darkness. I agree that by using my perceptive Power of Will, I can choose my life and existence in this incarnation and that this single truth can alter anyone's life. I understand that I live within the choices created by the feelings that drive my heart and Soul and I'm learning to embrace old feelings and reexamine them with my new perspective of The Knowing.

And most importantly for this vessel of mine, I must cherish, nurture, love, and put first this body that I chose to ride for the duration of this life experience. I accept that I am truly my own firstborn and without my attention, my body will wither away and create illness within itself. The Self of any given Soul must be put first. We are only capable of giving to others what we give to ourselves, and nothing more, ever.

And even with this Knowledge and the miracles that I experience every day, I honestly admit that I, from time to time, still find myself frightened of jumping from the known into the unknown. But for countless years, I was so full of fear that I have concluded nothing is ever clear in a human lifetime. But isn't that the way of life, this wonderful, unpredictable purgatory of existence? And so, I trust. And I seek God and others of Like-minds. I desire all men and women to have this Knowing and I pray that the children of the world never forget as they assimilate into our society. I am ready to lead or to gently Guide if necessary and I'm comfortable being led to new understandings by observing the experiences of others. As I listen to the questions, stories, and dreams of others, I also agree and accept that I am not powerful over any other Soul; that I can't fix anything for anyone. But I can enlighten and put forth an idea or thought, as the Guides do for me. I can help people to develop what is already Known in their heart of hearts.

And even though I cannot command the respect, belief, acknowledgment, or any other raw emotion that comes into play from those around me, I also hold the firm idea that I no longer want to be a slave to the feelings of others. Their lives and beliefs are theirs alone and I can choose to let these beliefs unfold as I draw upon my own Power of Will and place it where it is most comfortable for me. I strive everyday to put my Self first and the more I do this, the calmer my Spirit becomes. I also know how important it is to acknowledge our past and come to grips with the new perspectives of those events that have shaped who we are. It is also imperative that we remember each feeling, good or bad, and put them all in a new place of developing enlightenment. For I believe that by editing and selecting only what we perceive as a good memory, we glorify our past, wish for "the good old days," and stagnate our Self from moving forward and creating same-day memories of equal or greater joy. Or we remember only the bad things and continue to choose to live the hapless existence of a victim. The Guides have taught me to revisit the past when necessary in order to break old beliefs and victimization and then remember that you are alive today, with a new found perspective on the life you're choosing to live. Memories are just wishes for our future and so, by choosing how to remember our past, we can define our lives in the present and thus create the true bliss that we seek from our daily and future life.

And what of my gift of the colors, the Aura? Over these past several years, I continue to be amazed by the rare gift of this "extra sight". This automatic phenomenon also brought with it an added gift of perceptive intuitiveness, as I now "see/feel" others in a way that encircles their whole Self, the whole Essence of who they are, body and Soul. I have determined that because of this ability, I see people's physicality with a different set of eyes that look past the outward appearance and into their hearts. The colors now occupy a safe, comfortable existence in my life and I recently began to document some of the shapes, patterns and movements of the Aura. I see the correlation of the Aura to the health of an individual's body and I plan on taking the next several years to see where this leads me.

And my Catholic faith? It will remain in a tender place in my heart as a loving gift from my parents to me, a foundation upon which I was born and raised and a safe platform from which to start my journey toward God. I believe that all Souls must have some pathway to follow and not everyone is in need of the same thing at the same time. Catholicism was my start, my loving introduction to Spirit with stories, analogies, lessons, and beautiful traditions in an effort to seek God, Know God, and be of God for the Greater Good. It gave me a sense of security and consistency in my childhood, saved my life in my adolescence and gave me my wings in my young adulthood. I am truly blessed. I have no regrets.

I often experience such an incredible, overwhelming sense of The Knowing that I feel as if I may burst with ecstasy and explode into joy with an intensity that is impossible to describe. This feeling envelops my senses and begets an escalating yearning for the Light and the All There Is. And I know deep within the recesses of my Soul that this is right, that this miracle is pure and I continue to seek God in all things that were, are, and meant to be.

And on this night of nights and in this heart of mine I feel and I am sure of this, that we are all of God, the one true string of Light and hope and faith that keeps us all tied together for the Greater Good. And God will prevail and humankind will continue on its path. And as I turn this next corner of my life's journey, I realize that all I need to Know will be given to me in due time and I trust that it will. I believe the Divine path is ready for us all and that any fears I may still have are things Self-created out of ignorance of God. The Guides continue to remind me that when I remember and trust my instincts, all will be made whole. And when they say, *"We are all okay,"* I believe them.

And the recent introduction of Ia and The Crystal City will Guide my life in the coming years. I will document the events of the incarnations of the Soul of Ia and bring the stories to the written word. She has told me of lifetimes that were filled with passionate yearning, seeking, fear, and ignorance and the all-consuming desire for the Lighted Source of love. There were battles fought upon the grounds of the Crystal City as the struggle for power between ignorance and The Knowing played out among the ancient glass land. These stories, set in a time before we annihilated ourselves and we were forced to begin again, seem to parallel our current world events and will undoubtedly inspire, transfix, and warn us all of the crushing veil of hate. It will reveal our salvation, as we trust in our own Power of Will, that which is entrusted to us by God. This will put us a breath away from The Knowing and the Source of Lighted adoration for which we all ache.

And as I place my hands upon the keyboard, I will *"lay down the gifts upon the electronic bytes"* as this next journey will, without question, contain the joy, love, and bliss of a multitude of lifetimes immersed within The Knowing. I am sure of this. I know of no other way. And in our current humanistic, defined society upon the Earth, I also know that timing is everything. We are linear. The Souls that dwell a heartbeat away are not. The difference is clear and I accept that as a fate of a human life that is lived. I believe. I still believe.

And so this part of my story must stop here.

The Question and Answer Gift from the Guides

"*Our gift to the reader of this written word.*"

(PA) I ask first: Are you of God for the Greater Good?
(The Guides) "As always. Amen and so be it."
(PA) Please tell of yourself.

The Wise One: "We are always here. Never do we leave and the moment your thoughts turn to God, ours is directed in that path as well. That is why we are here: to Guide you towards this Light, The Knowing of God. My gentle guidance of your Soul is just that, guidance. It is you who make the ultimate choice. And that is the Power of Will. You must understand that we are no better than you, that we seek the same Light as you. This Team of yours, your Soul Team, as it was, is just that, a moment for you to recognize and yearn for the Light. I am here to help you put this all together and Guide you in this incarnation upon the Earth. To help you see how it all fits together for the Greater Good that we all commonly seek."

The Doctor: "The mind and body have the power of all the universe to affect your Soul and your life. The physical human body, made up of the atoms, particles, and water, and Light, are there gliding through your temple (that which is your body), and must come together to vibrate the Essence of God. It must all come together to keep your temple ready to receive the power and Light of The Knowing of God. It is imperative that the human race begin to nurture, understand, and most importantly love and accept their physical bodies. For when they turn from themselves, they turn from the God of The Knowing. I am here to help you to see this ever-evolving pathway and to remind you to stay in the body when needed. Those of realization yearn for and long for the Light at all times. You are a human, with choices that must be made. Although the realization of God and The Knowing are imperative to your Soul, your body is the vehicle that transports that Soul in this incarnation. Treat it well and wisely with respect."

Michael: "*The Knowing and feelings of the Soul. Your life and Soul journey begins and ends with feelings, as feelings entail all of the senses both of the human body and Spiritual Soul. This delicate, tender fight of the feelings is your gift from the Creator of the Greater Good. Do not fear or run from these feelings, these timely, uninterrupted feeling's of the heart. Embrace the All There Is and wonder no more of the power of God. I am here to help this understanding of the feelings. And along with the Crystal City of Light, you will move, in this incarnation, towards The Knowing and the All There Is with great intensity. Do not fear these feelings. I am here to help you understand.*"

Guide of Guides: "*In this great journey of yours, it is you that must seek. And as you share your moments of truth with others, you will begin the tidal wave that is based in need. It is a great legacy that you will help one person achieve the same enlightenment as you. I am here to help Guide your thoughts and ultimately your words as you speak of The Knowing and to give you great insight into the needs of the human Soul less enlightened and yearning for truth. This gift I give you comes from within The Knowing and the contemplation of its Source. And when you wake, you will then Guide the next Soul upon the Earth and achieve this great gift of gifts, the sharing of The Knowing of God.*"

Mother Guide: "*We all desire the unconditional love of God. We need this acceptance, wholeheartedly and unceasingly. As a baby needs it's mothers milk, so the Soul needs the nectar of God: this contented, unquestioningly innocent feeling of the ray from above. I am here to help you understand the unconditional hands that reach out to you. Our arms are waiting to hold you in the gentle love of God. We remind you to keep the question mark open and never settle on any one answer, for in truth, there are many answers. Your greatest love, of a Soul that is evolving, is to step aside and in no way stop this beam of intense certainty that daily comes your way.*"

Guide of the Life Stage: "*Nothing in life happens to you or because of you. When you create this play of dramas and comedies that are your life, you make the choices. But thoughts are things and they manifest themselves so. There is truly no difference and so goes your defined life. The saddest mark of humankind is the defining of all that is around them in the tangible world. By defining all, there are the limitations that go with the defining and also, more sadly, the judgment. And judgment is rooted in fear or lack. It is this gift that I give to you, my guidance to understand that we choose our existence and ultimately to live in an undefined, unjudged, and accepting world. You create an event and then you attach a feeling to that event. This begins to web the particles that become life. But herein lies the answer as well. Because we create and then attach, it is with this Knowing that the realization that we are in control, our free unyielding will, we have the power to define our lives."*

Ia: *"I have many lives yet to live and this one karmic connection with the Soul of you makes my heart sing. For in this first Guidepost, I am able to help you understand that the child within not only accepts the love, but demands it so to speak. In regards to the why of my presence here, you must remember to keep all the feelings, Guidings, and teachings that have been your experience until now, close at hand and in the string that binds the human and Soul, come to a common conclusion that The Knowing has accepted this as your life."*

(PA) Does everyone have a Guide or Guides?
(THE GUIDES) *"Oh but of course, dear one! Every Soul has a Team of sorts that gathers before they are incarnated and works with the Soul to help it along its path. So you see, it begins with a gathering of Angels and Guides in the heart of your Soul temple. There, the Essence of you and the chosen Angels and Guides and other Souls that intend to karmically birth at your time of existence, for interaction with you and to fulfill their connection, meet. Your main destiny is planned and along with your wonderful gift of the choice, you will incarnate and visit with these Angels and Guides in your dream state.*

They also communicate through your gut and intuition. Sometimes they wait patiently while you move through your life and until you are ready to meet with them again in the physical body. Not everyone will do this or even want to do this. Some will wait until they pass to the next level and return to the heart of their Soul temple, where there will be a life review. When a person is near-death, this is where the Lighted tunnel, voices, and faces emanate. And that is why it is usually familiar. If a human wishes to contact their Guides while in the physical body, it can be done. But it takes great work and the ability to completely quiet the mind. Our minds and thoughts chatter away, leaving no room for the voices of your Team to be heard.

So you see, they are always around you, waiting for you to choose. In the silence, you will hear of it; in the silence, they wait. In the silence, you will Know. And it's important to remember that they are there to Guide, not fortune tell."

(PA) Who is God? Where is God?

(THE GUIDES) "There is no who or where, it is all encompassing. It is all permeating. God is the Creator of all, the Supreme Being of Light, the All There Is. God cannot be described as a who or a what or by mere human descriptions. It is in The Knowing and the All There Is. God is a feeling, a Knowing that this is right. We are all pieces and bits of the body of the Light of the universe. It is bigger than words and so we go with the feeling. That is why for so many years in your world they described God as love because love is a feeling and that is the closest thing that could describe this Light at the time. But immersed deep within the Light, as you have experienced many times daughter, you experience and understand the ecstasy of the feeling of joy too incredulous to behold or describe. Yes, there is a true Being of Light, the One Creator, yet there are not words to describe this Lightness. All will Know, at the appropriate time, just what God feels like.

Trust and keep your eyes towards this Light. Start with the tiniest of sparkles and watch it grow. And daily continue to plead, come to me, come to me, come to me, God the reason. God is also what you perceive. How do you need God to be in your life? How do you desire God to come to you? What do you feel?"

(PA) Do Angels exist? What are they?

(THE GUIDES) "Ah yes, Angels reside in the Crystal City and are balls of illuminate love that is rained down from the feelings of the All There Is. They leave and attach to a Soul Team. They guard and Guide. They are a pure beam of hope for all. Yes, they do exist. But do not confuse them with the incarnate Soul or Guides in Spirit. For they vibrate differently. They will not cross over into your realm or our realm, rather they will stay with their own energies and surround themselves with the Light. They feed off the feelings of incarnated beings, in a good way, they take these feelings that float upward to God, soften them or heighten them and drop them back to where they originated. Their joy

is in God's joy, they delight in all things of hope. They are the Beings of, they are the feelings of God."

(PA) The concept of reincarnation is fascinating to most people. What is the purpose of reincarnation? Do our lifetimes ever end?

(THE GUIDES) "First let us say that the cycle of our Soul goes on for many reasons. As to the validity of it, we would first say, just let the idea and the possibility of this concept of reincarnation rest gently inside your heart. Do not judge it or pressure your Self into deciding whether it is true or not. Just let it Be, without question or judgment. From time to time, explore this possibility and leave it again, to rest gently within. Eventually, as you answer your own questions, it will reveal itself to you and the proper decision for you will stay and the other will gently fall away.

There are many reasons for this cycle. As we said, our ultimate God goal is to find the face and heart of God, to live within that love and telling emotions of the Eternal Life Divine. Even if there is no religion that is followed in your life, we know that all have some conclusion or thought on this subject. And all ideas are good and just. For in reality, everyone's own truth is just that, a personal experience.

Now, as a Soul blooms forth into the Heavens and seeks a respite from the lifetime it has just experienced, where does it go? It goes towards a Source of peace and love Eternal, an undeniable yearning is satisfied and the Soul finds its Self airy and Light. There is a review of sorts and then a respite. There will then come a time when the cycle is started again and the Soul is called upon by God to continue its quest for learning, not unlike the schooling of the children on the Earth. They learn, respite, and start again. Now, so as we are brought forth into yet another incarnation, we bring with us our plan that was gathered in the Light by us, our Angels and Guides. There is a promise made with other Souls who will incarnate with us and as a karmic fulfillment, join us in our journey. And our Souls are questioned and we choose our life experiences, we grow and learn more and with each life, we bring with it more joy, more hope and more wisdom that has been gathered in the memory of the Soul from previous lifetimes.

The purpose is to grow in Knowledge and eventually graduate to the next level of enlightenment that will take us to the City of Light or another planetary lifetime. We are finished when we are realized of God, when we have fulfilled all our destinies and hopes for the Self. When we have learned of The Knowing and recognized that feelings are our life plan. This cycle, which seems endless, happens in a momentary blink of the eye of God and its aftermath is one that can be understood only by the Source of the All There Is.

So therein lies the feeling of trust and hope. You must believe in your Soul, for it carries with you, lifetimes and ions of wisdom and moments of enlightenment. Do not be afraid, it is as it should be. And remember, just keep the thought of this complete, gentle possibility, and soon you will create the answer for your Self. Jesus said, 'I will come again and again.' What do you think that meant?"

(PA) What happens when we die?

(*THE GUIDES*) *"We speak of what you call death first because, that, in reality, is the true birth, the real birthing of the Soul. Think of death as a tiny little droplet of rain within the company of millions of other droplets. This sparkle floats from the sky and lands upon the Earth in various places and in various moments. It is received with love or hate from humankind, depending upon perception. Imagine this droplet that was dropped with love and good intentions, floating back up to the Heavens from which it came. It is a returning to the Source, to the All There Is, to the familiar, and it is buoyantly full of The Knowing. It would be received in love because it was delivered in love.*

When we transition over to the next realm, this gentle area that is so close to our Souls, that which lives just about our hearts and minds and feelings and the love in our heart, it is then that everything and all is suddenly realized. Depending on where your Soul and heart are in your process, you will go to the Light and the level of vibration that is most comfortable to you. You will be drawn to it and yearn for it and never want to return. Into the arms of God you will fly, carried by the wings of Angels and possessing all the love you ever encountered or experienced in your whole life. There will be a review of the Soul and a new level of understanding. Some will soon incarnate again, some will journey to a new plain, some will Guide and some will fly in others' dreams.

Do not seek death yet do not fear it, for as we explained, it is the renewing of a communion with God and others of Like-minds. And within this realm lies the answer to all the questions and struggles of what is perceived to be right and wrong. All the foibles of humankind and symbols and reactions and mis-understandings come together in an effort to return to the Heavenly Light and experience the all-consuming power of God."

(PA) Do you Know Jesus?

(THE GUIDES) *"Oh yes, of this wondrous Being of Light we are well aware. We Know of this Soul's journey, the purpose, and the end result of the tragic. As he said, as his message and pleading continued, we must all search for the Light of God, to reach out to the Heavens in search of the Father, of God.*

This Jesus, as he walked upon the Earth, is to return shortly. Embodied in a most unlikely house, he will again rise to international awareness. Many will doubt again, but his message will be clear and sweet and will be recognized by those who are closest to realization of the Light. This Son of God, this man, this woman, for it matters not, will again try to help the challenged and the unsee-ing, the unaware. He will plead for justice and in this realm hope that all will come eventually to God.

The level of this Soul's vibration is of the highest that can still be housed in human form. The vibrations often conflict with one another and that is why the lives are short. His words, his message of peace, of joy, of nonjudgment and unconditional love is one that we try to help you remember. For when you have The Knowing, you understand this, right? Remember that no matter what you call it, it is the Light of God. To pray for Guidance is good, to pray for your will to be done rather than God's will is a misconceived privilege of those praying for their own will to be done. Acceptance, as Jesus said, accept this word, that there is no greater God, no Greater Good than this Light of Love."

(PA) Do we choose our parents?

(THE GUIDES) *"That is the best lesson of all, to understand that we choose our parents and that much and many events and people are predetermined to incarnate around us before we are even born into this world. Sometimes when different people are in our lives, we wonder why? Or what did I do to deserve this one or that one in my life, either good or bad?"*

Many of our life's lessons are built around our need to grow and search for the Light of God. Let me explain it this way, before we incarnate into our next life, there is a sort of meeting or gathering of Souls ready to help us come into the world with our predetermined armor. This is, in fact, the best way to help us understand our path and the quickest way to that end. When we choose our parents, there can be many reasons. Usually it begins with the genetic makeup, as there are lessons in the physical world that affect our Beings, our Soul. And strengthen us and Guide us towards the Light. Another consideration is one of need for Spiritual guidance. Or lack of it. It all works together in order to begin this new journey for the Soul. Some of the entities incarnate around you, others stay in Spirit as Guides, and others come in and out of your life quickly."

(PA) How can a person learn to meditate and quiet the mind?
(THE GUIDES) "It is imperative that each individual learn to quiet the mind. Whether in meditation or in contemplation or just peaceful rest, it is imperative for the human body as well.

In the dream state, we allow events to unfold, usually just out of our reach. It seems that we have less choice in the dream state that we experience, no? It seems that we plod along after one unfolding event after another. If you think about it, in the dream state, the mind is being led and is less apt to fear or judge. Of course sometimes there is much fear in the nightmare definition, however, mostly we accept the unusual, the absurd, and the like in an effort go with the flow, so to speak. This state of mind is a good lesson for how to clear the mind of thoughts and things. There is no meditation without the quiet mind, so we shall begin there.

Believe it or not, we are capable of quieting our minds and we do it throughout the day when we concentrate on one particular task. If you are in the process of doing a task and your mind is focused, then the mind cannot wander. This is especially true when the task is daunting and requires our complete attention. It would do well to have each individual think of a color. Whatever that color may be, although white and violet are good for the attrac-

tion of Spirit. As you close your eyes, think of that color as something real. Taste, smell, feel, and Be that color. Do this over and over. It may take several attempts to keep other thoughts from coming into this color. When a thought does permeate through to your quietness, simply dismiss it in the best way that suits your own personality. As such, keep swatting away at the thought until it no longer gets your attention. And each moment that you are immersed in this quiet, colorful state, that is the beginning moment to quiet your mind. It may be that you can only clear the thoughts off your pallet of color for a few seconds at a time.

In the beginning, this is a transformation and soon, you will be able to add seconds, then minutes to your quietness. Do not try to force anything. Once you are able to be still and quiet within this color, then gently say over and over, God come to me, God come to me. God come to me. Slowly let this thought of God enter the color. Do not think or ask any more. Be still and wait for the answer. Wait, listen, feel, and Be. If a thought begins to come into your mind, dismiss it and chant again, God come to me. God, come to me. God, come to me, and listen again.

Repeat this process over and over until your chosen color begins to spiral and move towards a great, intense Light. Do not fear when this happens and remember to stop talking, thinking, and questioning; listen for the answer and let the events unfold before you. If there is fear, it may do well to ask of this process, if it is Good and of God. We understand that many humans are fearful of anything called evil. Evil and fear are simply ignorance of God and the Light. Envelope your Self within the Light of God if that helps to ease the mind.

At the point of the spiral, let your whole attention go, and be led, do not question. Imagine this spiraling, growing Light as the answer from God, a tender hello, and a kiss from the breath of Angels. This is a good place to start the quieting. Once you are able to get your Self through this Light and into the next level of realization, then your meditation will begin. Remember that meditation is not about talking, or questions, it is about listening. Be still and listen, listen for the sweet choir of the Heavenly Body of God."

(PA) When does the Soul attach to the body?

(THE GUIDES) *"When it is time to leave the Spirit plane, the Soul is reintroduced to the next incarnation. Armed with their tools, predestination, free will, genetic makeup, and Guidance from their fellow Souls, they enter the Earth in a burst of Light, cold, and harsh realities. In truth, it is so traumatic for the Soul that the Soul is allowed, for the first few months and sometimes years, to move in and out of the physical body and return to Spirit for comfort. It is a frightening thing indeed, but as the babe ages, the Soul stays longer and longer in the body until it is attached permanently around three to four years of age. That is the age that children become more attracted to the tangible things around them and the Soul is able to stay in the body.*

Never does a Soul attach it's Self and then decide not to incarnate, thus creating a miscarriage or accident. No, rather a Soul never attaches it's Self until the first breath. Then, if the decision to make a short stay of it is reached, the Soul makes an appearance usually for karmic reasons and then floats away. The event is usually a karmic fulfillment with the living, remaining entities upon the Earth. Not the child itself. It is not meant to punish those left behind; only to help fulfill karma, teach, Guide, and help the entities involved to become more realized of God.

When you ask a young child of three or four years old if they still remember before they were here, many of them will answer yes and some of them will tell the story. This is an innocent, beautiful remembrance helping this little entity to understand and remember that there are many, many lives that we live. If you can understand this, then the life and death experience becomes less frightening and allows you to live, fuller, deeper lives dedicated to the path of God."

(PA) So many people feel that their pets have Souls. They feel they see "something in there," when looking into the eyes of these beloved animals. Do animals, plants, and other living, non-human things have Souls?

(THE GUIDES) *"Yes indeed, the animals of the planets, including any and all plants and other living things, are resounding with a Soul. It is, however, a different type of Soul attachment. The Soul of an animal is one that vibrates at a different level. It is similar to what the human Soul went through billions of your years ago.*

Let me put it simply, animal Souls and human Souls are not interchangeable. When a human Soul incarnates, it only attaches to the human physical body. When an animal Soul attaches, it attaches to that of an animal, one that vibrates equally with its own vibration. These animal Souls will incarnate again and again until their own evolution grows into a stronger, more intellectual animal. This will not emerge for many more incarnations among the planets.

These animal Souls, which we see so lovingly through the eyes and behaviors of the animal entity, is indeed a feeling attachment. It attaches and begins to feel, most of its instinct, if not all, is about feelings. They react by feelings, driven by their instinct and need for survival. They look upon the human unconditionally, expecting nothing more or less than that which they give themselves, survival.

They have a Knowing that is similar but different than ours. These animal Souls will never evolve into what we know as the human animal, but they will stay within their own vibration and create their own culture. Think of your own body; there are many different types of genes, codes, particles, yet they all work together to vibrate life for you. So animals and humans and plants exist side by side to vibrate the Essence of the Body of God.

The instinctual reactions and feelings of the most tender of animal hearts touches the human as it recognizes on a Soul level, the complete, all-accepting right of unconditional harmony and agreement. This is something that the human strives for. And one more thing to ponder, just because the human intelligence and strength overpowers that of the animal, does that mean the human is more advanced? Or are they a subculture, to the innocence of the animal? Remembering that life and death do not mean the end or beginning for any Soul, who then is the more powerful, the more accepting? Can we learn from the instinctual simpleness of the animal? We give you leave to ponder this."

(PA) What is the biggest challenge facing the human physical body today? (THE GUIDES) *"Most definitely, dehydration is the biggest challenge to the perfect balance of the human body in this moment. The current situation of the planet is grave when it comes to the lack of understanding about how to and the importance of, hydrating the body, and there has been less and less of an emphasis put on the partaking of this pure Essence as the Earth moves into more chemicals,* sugar, fructose, caffeine and dairy. Many illness of your world could be helped along by hydrating the body. Pure, clean, room-temperature water is the best Source of the All There Is for the body.

It is also wise not to drink large amounts of water to quickly hydrate the body. When you drink a large amount of liquid at once, even if it is water, the body cannot assimilate this into its cells, the extra liquid which is most of it, is sent to the kidneys which are then overtaxed and working quickly and hard to eliminate the excess. This is actually counterproductive, as the body is forced to eliminate most of the quickly consumed jewels. And because the mind thinks it has consumed the necessary amount, then it further denies and depletes the body of signaling for additional water.

The best way to keep the body hydrated is by sipping small amounts every five of your minutes and not more at one given time. If you are completely dehydrated, keep at this for one-hour intervals until the body feels satisfied. It would do well to do this throughout the day for at least three weeks and thus make it a habit to keep a small amount of water available to consume upon demand. Then on a daily basis, set aside one hour each day, while there is inactivity perhaps and sip every five minutes for one hour. Doing this on a daily basis gently refreshes the body and hydrates it in such a way that is efficient.

This dehydration process is being worsened by the effects of the planetary intensity caused from the holes in the atmosphere. Teach your children the importance of this fact and they will be healthier and more able to combat illness. Dehydration is causing many ailments in the body today. Things such as urinary tract infections, gastro problems, arthritis and kidney stones, and general low energy levels.

When one consumes any liquid that is dehydrating, remember to counter that. And it is best to sip water before and after the bathing process as well. Keeping this routine up will show a human body that it can trust you to take care of it. This may seem a little daunting at first but it can truly change the dynamic of the human body. If this hydration is done, there will be a noticeable difference in the skin, and hair, nails, and eyes. After a week the body can begin to feel buoyant, with well-fed cells. Hydrate the body. Give it the gift it needs. Listen to your cells calling, for all the bodies of the Earth are thirsty."

(PA) There is so much fear and anger in the world. Why?

(THE GUIDES) "First let it be Known that fear is the root of anger. Taking it to the beginning, let us rephrase it thusly: anger, or the lack of acknowledging anger, manifests itself in fear, by fear and vice versa. Taking anger back to its roots we see the following: fear, based upon lack of acceptance.

Understand that we and all, each live in our own dream play of life. None perceives the world like you do and you simply cannot see the world as others do. It is impossible for you to see with the experiences of their eyes and heart and mind. Anger is based upon fear, judgment, impatience, and want. In order to keep your anger at bay, you must first recognize its origin, anger, based in fear, what do you fear? Judgment? Lack? Coping tendencies? Losing what is near and dear to you?

There is no place for fear in your heart. There is no reason to live with or through this anger. It takes up too much space in your heart and ultimately in your life. Understand that by basing fear and anger on the same plane, that you can deal with one and then address the other and vice versa. We speak of anger and fear interactively as they are pretty much one feeling. It is your fear of losing, that you feel anger. And judgment due to the insecurities felt from a great lack.

But this vicious cycle that we have now confused you with, is it not like that in your heart? Back and forth and back and forth, have we confused you? Because if we have, then you Know how your Soul feels, and how your body aches for the peace of understanding and moving on with the anger and resentment far behind.

Let it be Known that you are a powerful, productive force to your Soul. It is okay to feel passionate and excited about something or someone or some event, yet do not confuse passion with anger.

You can understand your anger and the fear that lies beneath. When you feel loved and accepted by your own Self, then you can cherish the body and Soul that is your "you." We are happy that you have asked and now may your understanding journey begin."

(PA) Is there such thing as the devil? Do the hells of many religions actually exist?

(THE GUIDES) "To be quite frank about it, there is no one Soul or one Being that is what you describe as the devil. This symbol of evil and noncompliance or conformity was created out of the need to control the masses with fear. And

when it became less that and more tradition, then we began to see the devil as an evil entity and one who turned away from God.

Now, we would ask you, what is the worst thing that could happen to a Soul? To not Know God, is that right? Of course, and so, evil is ignorance of God. Evil does not Know God; the devil personified is the turning away from God Knowingly. And why would anyone do that? Out of fear of being right. They fear that their worst fear, the lack of God will become manifest and so they turn away from it in fear.

Fear is ignorance of God. Hatred is bred by fear and lack. Hatred is a vibration that breeds more fear as well. And we say to you, there is not an actual place of hell, except in our minds, when we find the lack of God. For could there be anything worse? Evil personified is the intentional lack and turning away from God. Remember that is the intent. When the unfamiliar is there and you have not been subject to the idea of God, then there is no guilt.

In the early ages, before Jesus the Christ, people mistook things they didn't understand as evil. Again, labeling their surroundings as good or bad. When people who thirsted for more power came to the forefront, they used this fear as a tool to whip the emotions into a following mindset. In order to get what they wanted from the fearful. When you are immersed within The Knowing, there is only love and you will Know no devil or hell or fear, because the vibrations are unable to move at that level. The symbol of the devil is simply lack of God. Ignorance of God, how pitiable that would be!"

(PA) Can the future be predicted? Is our future already laid out for us by Fate or predestination?
(THE GUIDES) "Ah, dear daughter, as we have said before, there are some events that are predestined and others are left to the Power of Will that God has given.

Let us begin this way. All and every Soul choose their parents, other Souls they will incarnate around and certain physical challenges. But there is more to it than that. Events such as the death of our incarnation, the passing to the awakening, can also be predetermined as to the how but the when may be a decision made by the Self and other Self's around you. So the interaction is strong with other karmic relations. Not that others tell us when we transition to the other side, rather, they help the Soul along and once the lessons are learned, the Soul then looks for the best possible way to transition. Do you see? But it is imperative to remember that it is the choices we make amongst the feelings, that is a life-lived.

And that is where the power lives and the search for God begins. If all humans would recognize this opportunity, truly and fully, there would be no fear or anger in the world, rather a contemplative Knowing of God. So each lifetime is different. It may be that the Self or the Soul of you volunteers to incarnate and make a great impact upon the Earth, raise the social consciousness so to speak. Or the life may be simple and short. It matters not in the eyes of God. What matters are the feelings and the choices as we move toward the Light of the God. Do you see?

So we say, first there is a meeting of sorts with your Guides, Soul team, Angels, and other Souls that are to be your companions in this life. Each Soul takes, of their own choosing, their role in the life of you and vice versa. Parents are chosen, by genetic makeup, of each attachment and the life then becomes reality. But before that, there is a decision to be made about the life itself, what is its main purpose? Will it dwell quietly in a special corner of the Earth? Will it have a great impact? And what, after the work is done, what would be the best way to transition back to the Light? As far as the saying, 'What will Be, will Be', there is truth in that statement. But still, there is choice in the matter.

Some humans find comfort when they give their power over to some other forces and faith is good. However, it would be best to always remember that you have choices within this life. That is your God-given right and it is good. That is the way God designed it.

So again, much of our life is choice. And remember, the Soul is very ancient. Even when a child transitions and the tragedy of the event is realized, many times, that child's Soul knew that the impact would be short, but great. Do you see? This predestination is not linear and completely laid out, rather it is a grid of sorts to follow and an outline to help with the accomplishments."

(PA) Why do some people suffer illnesses?
(THE GUIDES) "There can be many, many reasons for this. First, we choose our gene pool and so the Soul Knows what is in store for the incarnation, physically. That is why we sometimes choose to enter a body that is challenged and

there is a reason for that. It could be a karmic lesson for the parents or other family members. It can be a lesson for those that we shall come in contact with. But most assuredly, it is important to show the choice of how we can perceive this illness. The human physical body is magnificent and capable of handling such challenges. Along with our free will, the mind-body-Spirit connection is powerful and many illnesses can be mended through our own Spirit. Others cannot.

Think of illness as a chain that is tight and unbreakable. When there is a choice in the illness, such as when we abuse our bodies with food, stress, and harsh expectations, then there is hope for this type of ailment. Humans are extremely powerful and can literally change their physicality if they chose. However, with everything else that is bombarded from the environment, the current incarnations would be hard pressed to accomplish this. That is why many miraculous cures happen far away and away from modern society. There just isn't any input from the conscious, skeptical mind of the modern human.

Many illnesses are from the fear we hold within our hearts. It should be best to start there when trying to heal the body. You must understand the feeling behind this illness, how it makes you feel. Of course there are other physical ailments that are genetically passed on and those are there for more specific, karmic reasons. When one is faced with adversity, isn't it interesting that so many humans seem to rise to the occasion and Be "brave"? It is inspiring to us all and is an example of mind over matter, so to speak.

It truly is all about the feelings. And as we embrace our feelings, we can then see how they vibrate the Essence of God, how they can move and generate the power that drives the physical body. The human race sees physical ailments as more than what it is. It is again, all in the perception. As your physical challenges are met with joy, love, and a rising above of sorts, it can manifest in and of itself a happy life, no matter how long or how short the incarnation is. You will return again and again, some lifetimes will be shorter, others will be longer yet all will be fraught with the feelings within."

(PA) Why are we so fearful of change? Why can't we all leave our comfort zones in an effort to grow towards the Light of reality?
(THE GUIDES) "The world today is full of fear and anger. We are daily bombarded with messages of more! More! More! And words that are meant to breed

lack. When we are in our comfort zones, we feel more in charge of our life. Even a troubling comfort zone is better for us, so we think, because we are settled within that feeling. When we stretch our Selfs and push our minds, bodies, and hearts toward a great way of Being, then we feel challenges.

Challenge has typically, in your society, been through competition (winners and losers). Because of the constant labeling, we find ourselves pulling away from this competitive outside zone of our comfort. When we realize that by breaking this stale, old, boring cycle of existence, we can truly find the happiness we all yearn for. Dancing and singing while we rush from unknown to unknown.

Think of the newborn child and the baby beginning to explore its surroundings. It has yet to develop the fear of judgment or fear and boldly reaches for and goes after anything it finds curious, always without its comfort zone. Every day of its young existence, it embraces life with unbounded energy and curiosity. What a shame that by social conditioning and what is perceived as appropriate behavior we all shirk from reaching out for the colorful blue ball or the warm, cuddly puppy. We fear change because it is an unknown to us. Deep within the recesses of our minds, we fear that things would get worse than they are so we sit, conditioned to stay put and not rock the boat, so to speak. How sad that we forget this newness that can be ours everyday."

(PA) The concept of time intrigues many people and it is said that time is "happening all at once"; that we are experiencing our past, future, and present at the same time and that time is not linear. Are we incarnated from the future as well? Please explain the concept of "time."

(THE GUIDES) "This is a great, difficult concept for the human to consider as humans live and experience life in a linear environment made of up of seconds, minutes, hours, days, weeks, etc. And there is comfort in this realm for the human can predict with some certainty that Tuesday will arrive, December will be here and work starts at a specific time. It helps to organize their life, but in reality, time does not exist. And this concept is both fascinating and unbelievable. What the human has tried to do is put a name or define time as it is and time cannot be defined by words.

We are all vibrating at different rates and our Essence that floats here and there Knows of no timeframe to box its Self in. So much of what is predestined has been written and the path of the Soul is moving ahead with that quest. We are indeed experiencing timeframes from past, present, and future lives, it is happening all at once. Now this statement is mind-boggling to the human, no? But all we say is keep this thought a gentle possibility. For it is not one that can be explained in the few words or phrases in this written word.

But think about it this way, when you are in a pool of water, your body is bombarded with particles of water and debris all over you. Some consume you, others, float around you, still others circle the energy of you. So you see how this water is happening all at once? It is not one particle at a time, one thing at a time. It is everywhere and water will come and float above your ahead and then circle back and touch your back.

We know this is confusing, but this concept that has been tried and researched in your world, has found no end, no explanation, as there is none. It is one of those great mysteries of the world, one which you must let Be. So as you experience all things at once, all events, just Know, as in your sense of deja vu, that you have experienced all before, you have been there, and you will be there again. This confusing answer is one that we would leave with you."

(PA) How do we Know which religion to follow? Which religious belief has "got it right"?

(THE GUIDES) *"The analogies of Christ were very clear but left open to many thousands of years of interpretation by others fearful of the loss of control. Religion, in and of itself, is a beautiful passage of rite. It is a platform, a foundation that can bring Souls into, in a linear way, the idea of God and the hope for the All There Is.*

It would be best to realize that while a gathering of Like-minds is good, it is up to you to continue that question on your own, in your own time. Never forget that a gathering of Souls seeking the Light is a wonderful combining of the energies, but remember that it is a collective whole and average of these energies and can, in fact, hold your own Soul to the ground if you never fly own your own. For everyone is on their own path.

The important thing to remember is that you must live this feeling and fol-low your own heart and listen most importantly to your intuition, as when there is conflict. Do not ignore these urgings.

And as harsh as it sounds to the human ears of great intent, religion, in your world, is a business of Spirituality and many business decisions are made to keep it afloat. And sometimes those decisions are to control the masses for mon-etary gain. The rules, rituals, regulations, and admonishments are meant to breed fear, anger, and judgment. So as you tip your toe into the minds of others seeking God, it is imperative that you Know their intent.

All religions are good if the intent is for the Greater Good and of God. Let there be no mistake. But when the interpretation of the written words of the ancient ones are used to vilify those that are not on the same path, that should be the first warning flash of disconcertion.

Religion, a gathering of Like-minded people, is difficult to fine tune to the heart of God because it is a collective combining of different levels of vibrations. So while the services and sacraments are there for you to grasp, remember to keep your own heart open and listen within to your own quest. Do not be judged or hurt by those who would tell you to follow this or else, for those are the lost Souls of the Earth. Those are the ones that would wish to box you in to their way of thinking, which is utterly impossible because you are not them and they are not you.

So while a gathering of Souls is good, remember, it is the collective whole of those energies, that vibrate, not your own individual pure Essence."

(PA) Please make a comment on suicide.
(THE GUIDES) "Realize that in the taking of one's own life, the karma cre-ated by that reaction must be addressed in the next life. It sometimes takes sev-eral lives of good, decent Soul living to counter the effects of such as this. In no way mistake that it is a "checking out" but actually a "checking in" with the karma attached to the many, many Souls that are affected. By ending a life opportunity early, one must revisit again all those Souls, their reaction, their intent and then get back to the business of personal karma. It is not a sin of God but rather a sin against one's own Soul."

(PA) Are there people who have psychic abilities? Or are they just very intuitive?

(THE GUIDES) *"Again, there is a labeling from the human mind. Intuition, The Knowing cannot be labeled. All people have this Knowing; it is just that some are more open to the 'listening' of this Knowing as that is where the true intuitive arises. They have learned how to listen, they have dropped the judgment from their hearts, they have chosen to remember a time before we forgot to believe.*

The abilities of some are from the carnival atmosphere and should be taken so. Remember that another Soul incarnate can never help you remember, they can only tell you of their guess. It is you who must believe in the power of your own Knowing, your own pink. However there are many, many Souls that are open and pure and listening to The Knowing. And those that go forward with this Knowing and miracle that is available to all, must be very careful. As you have seen, daughter, not all will follow the same lead. Each person must be addressed differently and if you are to be a good teacher, you must keep this in mind.

The intuitiveness of the many Souls is heartwarming. They are vibrating the Essence of God when they listen. That is why we say over and over, listen, listen and stop asking. If all would quiet the mind, listen and hear without judgment, then the Soul will vibrate higher and higher until the truth is revealed. It is very simple really, just challenging, as it requires discipline and commitment to the Source of the All There Is.

We say to the people of the world, you are free. You are loved by God and you have choice to make your life whatever you desire. It is all in the perception and the reaction to your life. That is why two people can see the exact same event and come away with completely different accounts of that event. This is in The Knowing. Trust your Soul to Know what is best. Keep all beautiful thoughts of God a possibility within your heart, without judgment. The truth will stay; the other will gently fall away. It is as it should Be, it is good.

You have the power, you are your own Power of Will. Listen to the call of the Light. For in its Essence beats the heart of the God from Whence We Came."

(PA) At a time of physical crisis, why do some people experience a near-death phenomenon and others don't? What is the purpose of "dying" and coming back?

(THE GUIDES) *"Near-death experiences are merely dreams that are remembered with the physical body or dreams that are associated with a trauma. We, as Souls dwelling within the human body, come and go many times throughout the day and night. In the dream state, we visit the other side, working with Spirits who Guide us, resting our weary minds and also creating a new perspective on things of the Earth.*

Some people remember the near-death occurrence because there is a return with a physical miracle, as in your gift of the colors. It can bring the physical together with the Soul. It creates openness within the physical awareness of the human condition.

People blessed with this conscious awareness of a near-death experience are usually already seeking, on some specific level, for more. There is a sad discourse within their existence or they are actively seeking out more than they already Know. Others need definitive answers and so they seek it in the three-dimensional.

This miracle, this wonder that has been given to those who ask, and more importantly accept, is actually available to all. As in your current meditation. At the time of your death, you were here, by the lake, you floated throughout the forest trees and flew into the heart of your temple where you were told, "Not now my daughter." But now you come here daily.

This is available to all who seek. All who can quiet the mind, and allow the Light to come. Those who are patient and allowing of the events to unfold in due time. You remembered your near death, because you chose to. Meditation and near death are the same thing. If you choose to define them so."

(PA) There are many theories about the origin of man. Please tell of how the human race began and evolved over time.

(THE GUIDES) *"The human Being is made of the atoms, particles, Light Source, and energy of a vibrating planet upon which they select. There have been many origins of humankind.*

It begins with a small, minute energy of thought, which is then converted into an idea. These thoughts and energies are put forth from other thoughts. And these thoughts began with the Light Source of the God of All. We began as an idea or thought of God. But theses thoughts did not manifest themselves into the humans that we see today, or yesterday. They began as a trusted wink from the heart of the God Source and continued to become an idea.

This first energy-thought of something other than God, manifested its Self into Being and God wondered, what next? The matter that was created by the Body of God, the matter that floats around the spaces within the perceptible universe, was where one of these thoughts landed. Upon landing, it burst forth into many more Lighted particles while beginning to grow and create thoughts of vibrations. As these scattered thoughts flew around the universe, they began to hum and glow.

Now these thoughts of energy were scattered everywhere among the Heavens and the perceivable universe. But we shall speak of the energies that landed upon the Earth-plain. They grew and sparkled into Beings of pure Light. They lay everywhere: among the mountains, in the rivers and the oceans. They were of different sizes and so they manifested themselves into different levels of vibrating atoms. Thus the different species, creating life, animal matter, and plant matter.

The bigger pieces enjoyed the more available Light Source while the others gathered what they could and created within themselves, their own existence. The human particles, large particles, began to multiply over billions of years. They scattered and rolled around the Earth-plain, finding the place most comfortable for their existence. They continued to multiply within themselves and they continued to vibrate the love of their Source. Slowly, as the vibrations began to move into themselves, there was a fight within its Self for more room, more power, and thus created a struggle and the first feeling of each particle.

The feelings began to grow and multiply themselves until there was an explosion of energy with each little particle. As the explosion occurred, then the physical appearance began to change and needed more Light, more energy from the land. (We analogize the popcorn kernel).

The need continued to grow and out of this great need, this great feeling, came the first spark. And such as a flint sparks fire, the two flints of energy and need sparked together, creating a particle that was Self-sustaining.

This first atom, this perfect creation, began to vibrate and sustain its Self, gathering energy from its own environment. It fed off the other less developed energy particles, which gave their own energies freely. They was no fear of taking or joy, just Being.

This amoeba, which was the nucleus of the atom and which was billions of times smaller than the atom of your time, continued its path and its search for its Source. It began to feel, to need, the original Source from Whence It Came and out of this need, it created movement. The feeling of need manifested itself so.

It began to search for the Light and this friction created more energy, more Lighted particles and they in turn created the same. The atoms and particles grew and multiplied, all with the intent of seeking this Light Source. This is where our yearning for God began. This is why we all have an innate need of the Light. As these small particles began to roll and move, they each settled into the best space from which they could move toward the Light.

They sought out water, land, and then their cries for God were heard and God quieted the cries with rain, more energy, the sun, and the moon. And the little atoms bathed themselves within this response. They were everywhere, billions and billions of particles, yearning, seeking and feeling for God.

At this point, the particles seemed to settle into their fate and they began to turn inward rather than outward towards the Light. This response caused a great vibration to escalate and grow as each particle grew into its Self. The love of God, their Source, helped to propel them forward.

Their seeking drove them to escalate the multiplying within themselves and they hurried through this process faster and faster. And another small explosion occurred, creating more warmness and more urgency. It continued and continued. Thoughts, feelings, energy, and need for God.

It was at this point that many of the particles began to shape themselves into more distinctive particles with different shapes and vibrations. Some were turned into animals, others into plants, and others into water. There were more energy particles dropping to Earth every day and they kept on until the Earth was formed by these seeking particles. As more atoms split and flints of energy erupted, we became androgynous amoeba that floated among the water, sky, and land.

And as this second flinting occurred, we chose the vibration that best fit our size and shape and surroundings. We slowly evolved, by seeking the Light of God, into the human and other living things upon the Earth. That is the physical birth of our Essence. And now, as we incarnate into these vibrating particles, our Souls choose these vehicles to return to the Light Source of the All There Is. It is a moving through the particles to return to the eyes of God."

(PA) Why do humans think of light, energy, candlelight, etc., as Sources of Spirit or departed loved ones? Many times, we will light a candle in honor of them and it seems that when we do, we feel their memory closer to our hearts. Do the departed know that we are doing this for them? What if they've already reincarnated? Why do we associate these things together?
(THE GUIDES) "It is because they are connected. The Light Sources are always attracted by the gentle Souls that have departed as a Source of new vibration and energy. It is in The Knowing; it is in the Essence that it is connected. When there is a symbolic lighting, there indeed, is an attraction of Spirit.

This light of the candle, this glow, is vibrating at a level that is near to that of Spirit. Its intensity is seen by the human eye and felt by the Soul. Remember that the Soul is about feelings, deep feelings. So the Soul "sees" with its feelings.

So you see, when you light the candle in someone's memory, they do see it with their feeling of the vibration. They are drawn to it, like the Crystal City of Light that you have been experiencing, the Souls of Light are passing through it. So in reality, the ceremonious lighting of the candle is a joyous thing to the Soul that has departed. Even if that Soul is reincarnate, its Essence from the cellular memory of the living Soul in human form will be ever joyful.

The more you pray for the Light, the more your Soul will be realized of God and the Greater Good."

(PA) Please explain the connection/difference between genes/DNA and reincarnation/memories from past lives.
(THE GUIDES) "DNA and genetic lineage are related. The body you now have carries many different genetic memories. These are very real and thus is the crux of evolution.

The DNA is related in that it is a combining of the different genetic make-ups that have been passed down from person to person. The genes carry the physical memories, which are made up of all the different DNA that exists within a given body. However, that is where the connection ends.

Reincarnation speaks of the Soul, not the physical body. The sense memories that you may or may not experience (usually from genes) manifest themselves physically, but you would not be aware of them consciously. But the body Knows and will continue its magnificence as such.

The Soul actually chooses the DNA and gene pool to which it will attach. There can be several physical reasons for that such as the need to connect with a physical gene pool that will develop a physical condition or illness or challenge or existence in an effort to fulfill a karmic past.

Many humans confuse the connection of the body to the Soul. It truly is a small, thin connection. The house our Soul chooses is determined before we incarnate in an effort to choose our life path.

We hope this has not confused you, but a simpler reason, does not exist at this moment. Remember, all things considered, the physical body and the Soul are two separate things. We should daily thank our physical body as our vehicle to God. We owe our Spiritual path to this temple of God (our bodies) and hope that we, as Souls, choose wisely."

(PA) Is knowing about our past lives important? Do they affect us today?
(THE GUIDES) "No, it is not important for the evolution of the Soul. It can however, help to move forward with insight. But here is the deal that was made on a Spiritual level; No past life remembrance will ever take place unless deemed so by your Soul Team and Guides. When the carnival atmosphere encourages the reading of palm and the crystal ball, you find that amusing, no? But in reality, it is not important. It is not real. For the past lives and future lives are a sacred bond between the Soul and God. Although people do find out about their past lives, they are only being told of this life, they are not remembering it, so you see? It is being recalled for them and should stay that way.

There is a great karmic importance to past lives and their effect on us, but that is on a different level of understanding and vibration and one that is not understood by the human mind. So you see, while it is fun to surmise or guess about past lives, most often they are just that, guesses. This is a secret of the trade of karma and one that is not easily accessed by most."

(PA) What is the Aura and why can some people see it? Is everyone capable of seeing the human Aura? Do animals and other living things have Auras? *(THE GUIDES) "Ah, indeed dear daughter, all things that live and vibrate upon the Earth have the energy field known as the Aura, even electrical pulls.*

We would say this first, our Souls affect our bodies, no? Our emotions can manifest themselves in many different ways in the human body. But the human body itself is not a Spiritual thing other than the housing of the Soul. The Aura is an extension of the physical body and nothing more.

Many would like to compare the Aura to a mystical event or happening; however, it is not. It is special in that it completes the embodiment upon the Earth and grounds it to the many vibrations that are around it.

The Aura does not cause disease or reactions of any kind within the body or Spirit. Rather, it manifests out from the body, do you see? So it is in truth, no more Spiritual than your nose or ear. It is directly manifested by the body within and many times is affected by the Soul etc. So you see that is the connection.

Do not confuse the Aura with your Soul or center of Self. No, that being said, there are those that are sensitive to the vibration that is emanated by this magnetic field and those people can actually see the Aura as it is. It is present in all types of people whether evolved or still at the beginning of their Spiritual search. It is able to be seen by a person whose own vibration has shifted slightly, many times after a trauma to the body. So that is why so many people that come back from "here" or have experienced a traumatic physical event, that is why they are able to see it.

It seems magical because of its beauty and unavailability to all. But in reality, it is not an extra special part of the Soul. But remember, it does show, as in an X-ray, the workings of the human body and its state of being, whether it is in peril or at peace. As you have seen, it is greatly affected by the emotions of the human."

(PA) Thank you.
(THE GUIDES) "You are welcome."
                              Amen and so Be it.

Epilogue

January 2004

"...And so, you Know, you Believe in the power that is your
God-given right.
For you are blessed and accepting.
You feel the emotions as they penetrate your world.
Be calm and Be still. Listen.
For deep within, your true heart will go where it must,
Into the Light of God."

The Guard is gone?
   "Yes."
   Why?
   "Because you do not need further assistance from the Guard. It is your time
to guard your Self and your Life and your God. Let it be known that you are
the guard of your symbolic temple and that you make the choices that affect it."

Thank you.
"You are welcome. Amen and so be it."
Amen.

Glossary of Terms

The Knowing: A resulting feeling of understanding, a contemplative quietness within the soul. A feeling where no fear can exist, where all is well and as it should be. When you experience The Knowing, there is great oneness and stillness within. And just as a newborn babe Knows, all is taken care of. The Knowing is available to all who will listen and receive.

Power of Will: Simply, our Power of Will is our free choice and our innate right to act on those choices. It is how we define and live our lives. It is the greatest human gift given to us by God. And if we choose to accept this treasure, we will then come away with the understanding that we all hold the key to our own happiness lived as a human in this soul incarnation.

Being: A state of connecting your soul with your human life and living within the trusting Universe. It is an adjective that describes someone who Knows and lives and understands how to trust what is given. It is a state of Being one with God and your life.

Lighted: Light is God. Lighted is illumination from the Supreme Being of All. Light is the vibration of the Source From Whence We Came. A vibration of God.

Soul/Spirit: Our spark of energy from God. The Soul is an idea that emanated from God and became a beacon that reflects the Light of God. The soul is witness to the love of God.

Self: The creative result of a soul incarnate. As humans, the Self is our main purpose, trusted to us by God, to develop back into the heart of the

Supreme Being. It is an intentional coupling of the Soul and the mind of the human.

The Pink: Your intuition and gut reactions to a particular event or person.

Channeling: The act of receiving messages from the Spirit Realm.

All There Is: God and everything that encompasses the Light of God.

Life-lived: A created human existence as defined by our choices.

Source From Whence We Came: Our origination from God, the Supreme Being, the Universe or the HigherPower. Our lifeline, parent, and care-giver, our trusted beginning, our tender God.

Greater Good: The purpose of God, the reason. An event or feeling that permeates the love of God and one that is traveling towards God, an intentional prayer and homage to God.

About the Author

Credit for author photo Teryn Davis
www.terynphoto.com

Peg Abernathy is an author and inspirational speaker in Los Angeles, California. She can be reached through her Web site: www.self-full-life.com

978-0-595-67078-9
0-595-67078-4

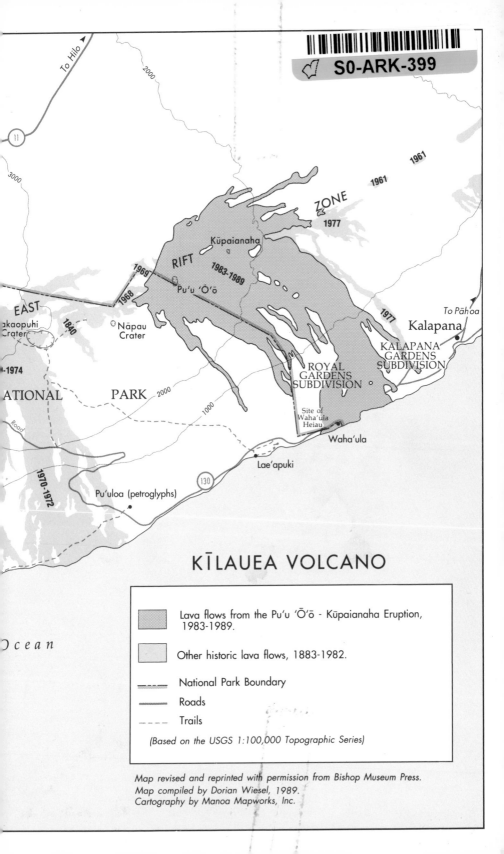

To Hilo

11

2000

3000

2000

1961

1961

ZONE

1977

Kūpaianaha

RIFT

1983-1989

1969

Puʻu ʻŌʻō

1977

To Pāhoa

1968

Kalapana

EAST

1840

Nāpau
Crater

KALAPANA
GARDENS
SUBDIVISION

akaopuhi
Crater

-1974

ROYAL
GARDENS
SUBDIVISION

ATIONAL

PARK

2000

1000

Site of
Waha'ula
Heiau

Road

Waha'ula

1970-1972

Lae'apuki

130

Pu'uloa (petroglyphs)

KĪLAUEA VOLCANO

Lava flows from the Puʻu ʻŌʻō - Kūpaianaha Eruption, 1983-1989.

Other historic lava flows, 1883-1982.

---- National Park Boundary

——— Roads

- - - Trails

(Based on the USGS 1:100,000 Topographic Series)

Ocean

Map revised and reprinted with permission from Bishop Museum Press.
Map compiled by Dorian Wiesel, 1989.
Cartography by Manoa Mapworks, Inc.

The Burning Island

The Burning Island

A Journey Through
Myth and History in
Volcano Country, Hawai'i

PAMELA FRIERSON

Sierra Club Books
San Francisco

Library of Congress Cataloging-in-Publication Data

Frierson, Pamela.
     The burning island : a journey through myth and history in
volcano country, Hawai'i / by Pamela Frierson.
          p.   cm.
     Includes bibliographical references and index.
     ISBN 0-87156-794-6
     1. Hawaii Island (Hawaii)—Description and travel
2. Volcanoes—Hawaii—Hawaii Island.   3. Man—Influence on
environment—Hawaii—Hawaii Island.   4. Mythology, Hawaiian.
5. Hawaii Island (Hawaii)—Social life and customs.   6. Man—
Influence on nature—Hawaii—Hawaii Island.   I. Title.
DU628.H28F75   1991
919.69'1044—dc20   90-46398
                                                                          CIP

Jacket painting: Kilauea Night Scene by Titian Ramsay Peale courtesy of Bishop Museum.
Frontispiece: Lava fountaining from Pu'u 'Ō'ō cone, on the east rift zone of Kīlauea.
Photograph by J. D. Griggs—U.S. Geological Survey.
Jacket and book design by Abigail Johnston
Set in Garamond and Galliard by Classic Typography
Production by Susan Ristow

SIERRA CLUB NATURE AND NATURAL PHILOSOPHY LIBRARY
Barbara Dean, Series Editor

Printed in the United States of America on acid-free, recycled paper.
10 9 8 7 6 5 4 3 2 1

For Delta
—and to the memory of Kalapana,
destroyed by lava in the spring of 1990.

Contents

Preface

A lifetime of events have spurred me toward writing this book, but one moment in particular keeps coming to mind. I was about twenty at the time, returned from a mainland U.S. college to the family home on the windward side of Oʻahu, and I had our small boat out sailing. Reclining against the gunwale, sail slack, I drifted on the shoal waters a half-mile off shore. Deep ocean swells surged against the reef another quarter-mile out, with a low, booming sound.

To the southeast, a couple of islets straddled the reef. Oʻahu curved out toward me in two great arms—Makapuʻu Point to the south and Mokapu Peninsula to the north. Inshore, from one curve to the other swept the great, serrated cliffs of the Koʻolau mountain range. Lying nearly at wave level, half dozing, I felt the horizon of reef and islets, coast and mountain range, encircle me, as though I drifted at the center of a small coherent cosmos. I was at that age when one is preoccupied, sometimes joyfully, sometimes despairingly, with discovering where one belongs, what forces one has been shaped by. One of the painful and interesting gifts of that time was a new clarity in looking at my surroundings. Not long before, I had read a bit about the volcanic origins of the Islands. Now it all came together: what I saw on the lines of horizon around me—the broad curve of mountains, the islet-studded reef—was the eroded rim of a vast, partly sunken caldera. Where I floated had once stood an enormous volcano.

Later I read that the volcano had indeed been huge, with a caldera nearly nine miles long and over four wide, and that it was active more than a million years ago. I had been living in the ghostly curves of it most of my life, and had never heard mention of it.

There was a disturbing aspect to this realization, which I was only able to articulate years later. At the time it was primarily a feeling that I was adrift in more ways than one. Only later did I identify the feeling as a sense of my own intellectual alienness to this place—a hint of the peculiar and profound unease of being a foreigner in the world I felt was home. I had lived all that time in a place I had never really seen, or had seen only dimly, with a vision that clouded and distorted.

I was not born in the Islands. My parents came to Hawaiʻi separately, my mother as a civilian from California, who traveled through and decided to stay in Honolulu and work for a while; my father called up from New Orleans to active duty in the Naval Reserves. They met the year after Pearl Harbor was bombed.

It was during the war years that U.S. culture came to dominate Oʻahu. The island, which had become an eclectic mix of Pacific Rim cultures, now became a Western outpost. During the 1930s and 1940s, the popular image of Hawaiian culture evolved to replace the real culture that had very nearly vanished—from the busy island of Oʻahu, at least.

When the war ended, my parents returned to the mainland for a few years. I was born in Flagstaff, Arizona. Four years later, they moved back to Oʻahu, and both began teaching careers, my father in English and my mother in French.

We moved to the windward side of the island, still rural—the place that I remember as "old Hawaiʻi." But the culture I thought of as "native" was mostly Asian. The men driving water buffalos through the few surviving rice paddies along the road home. The old Japanese man with the vegetable truck. The Filipino gardener. The Chinese-Hawaiian-Caucasian little girl who was my best friend, who taught me how to eat with chopsticks and the bowl held up to my mouth.

The environment that I thought of as "Hawaiian" was what I saw around me as I grew—what my senses heard, smelled, and tasted. The brilliant colors of hibiscus, the pungent odor of plumeria, whose blossoms everyone strung in leis and gave away in the "Hawaiian" gesture, except the Hawaiians themselves, who knew the plant had been brought in to decorate Chinese cemeteries. The murmur of the Chinese dove and the raucous call of the Asian mynah bird—two species that had long since replaced the native birds.

But always, beneath the crowded surface, there were glimpses, shadowy shapes of an older world. Old walls and stepping-stone paths in the deep valleys; the outlines of ancient fish ponds in the bays. Places seen on brief trips to the outer islands that seemed to fit the fluid and haunting world sensed in the "Hawaiian legends" we occasionally were told in primary school. Vestiges of old beliefs transmuted into a folklore that all local children, at least, paid attention to without understanding. If you went swimming in a mountain pool, you first placed on the bank a *ti* leaf wrapped around a stone, an offering to the *moʻo*—the spirit guardian of the place.

When I looked back on my childhood, it seemed as though the land, and the spirits that haunted it, had whispered to me secrets, sent messages through fingertips, nose, ears—even through the soles of the feet—that my mind, educated since those early encounters with "Dick and Jane" readers to a mental topography primarily midwestern and Anglo-Saxon, had ignored or denied. I began to feel that I lived between two geographies—a real and sensory one and a cultural landscape carried in my head. I tried to scan the borders of that mental map, so that I could learn to see *through* it and out the other side.

As a young adult, I made a visit to the active volcano country of the island of Hawai'i. Then another, exploring its remote regions, wandering through vast stretches of land covered with archeological remains, catching glimpses of traditional ways in its remote communities. Hearing the locals speak of Pele, the volcano goddess, as "she"—as a living spirit of the land. Sensing the powerful presence of the volcano country, of this realm of interwoven fire and darkness, of elements utterly foreign to the continental topography I carried around in my head.

At some point I began to wonder if the *dis-location* I felt might not be a fundamental part of Western experience. Western culture has been "migrant" for so long that we are no longer aware that we carry with us a powerful symbolic map—and that we see the world according to an inner topography. Its lineaments, its symbolic forms, may be very different from the actual places we have explored or inhabited. Our symbolic geography is the way in which we orient ourselves within the cosmos—and it profoundly affects the way in which we respond to place.

Natural philosopher Paul Shepard has suggested that Westerners, heirs to Judeo-Christian tradition, carry within us a cosmology—a spiritual geography—that has ancient roots in a physical world. The topography of our minds, in other words, still reflects the real topography of the ancient landscape of the Near East, which gave birth to Judeo-Christian cosmology. That desert landscape—monolithic, unchanging, harsh, dominated by ancient rock and the overarching sky, gave birth to the desert thought of the Old Testament—ascetic, hierarchical, profoundly distrustful of nature. The distrust expressed itself in a dualistic vision of nature whose symbolic poles were the Garden of Eden—where nature, controlled by God and cultivated by man, is bounteous and benevolent—and wilderness, which is most often the chaos of nature without God: wastelands, or even the devil's domain.

I am simplifying here a complex analysis, but Shepard's insights provided a starting point for contemplating the effects of a symbolic geography imposed on a real landscape and, by extension, on the native culture that was in many ways an expression of the land. The volcano country of Hawai'i, physically alien, but in some ways symbolically familiar, has evoked responses from the Westerners who have come in contact with it that illuminate the dark side of the Western vision of nature.

The volcano, or the power in nature the volcano represents, is the nexus of a complex set of symbols in Western culture, an archetypal landscape long since divorced from any real one. It is most powerfully evoked in a nearly abstract form—as the sulfur and brimstone topography of hell.

Yet for the Hawaiians volcanism was a central aspect of the drama of creation, so integral that it was known to them as a powerful deity who is still venerated, whose domain, the volcano country, is still considered sacred land.

A desire to understand this landscape from the inside out led to my spending time in volcano country. But it soon dawned on me that in terms of intellectual inheritance I was just another Western traveler, indulging in some rather extended sightseeing. What I could learn by being here, by simply exploring the landscape, was limited, unless I spent a generation, or several. If I were to learn about the land in any depth, I needed to have some understanding of the experience of the Hawaiians, for they had distilled into a language and a way of life their long intimacy with the land. But accounts of Hawaiian culture have been transmitted primarily through Western observers. It was clear that I would have to begin with Western perceptions, that I would have to learn to see through, in, and around the prism of Western symbolic geography, in order to catch even glimpses of the real and cultural landscape that lay beyond.

Like all travelers, I arrived in this landscape lugging my own ideas. Some I've left behind, and some are still with me, but they shaped this book and assured that its act of interpretation is purely my own. This journey through landscape and myth makes forays into many fields of knowledge in which experts gave much good advice, but I was left free to make my own mistakes. Although several people read parts of the manuscript, I am wholly responsible for its final content. Any quotations that are not documented in the notes at the back of the book are from personal conversations and interviews that took place between 1987 and 1989.

I realize that by using considerable Hawaiian terminology I have made the book more difficult for most readers, but in terms of getting the feel of the native culture and language it seemed important to do so.

The great pity is that a book cannot reproduce the spoken sound of a beautiful language. The Hawaiian Glossary (see page 249) begins with a brief note on spelling and pronunciation. Modern Hawaiian spelling includes the use of marks to aid pronunciation. This usage has only prevailed in the last decade—older documents spelled Hawaiian words without the macron and glottal stop. When quoting from older sources, therefore, I have chosen to retain the older forms of spelling rather than attempting to update them.

One note on the typography—the printers were unable precisely to reproduce the macron over the "i" in Hawaiian spelling, but they have done their best with a substitute.

Anyone who completes a book incurs large debts of gratitude. I have heaped up more than I can acknowledge individually here, but several people went far out of their way to help me, and to these I owe a special *mahalo*—thank you.

Anthropologists Jocelyn Linnekin and Dorothy Barrère generously shared their knowledge of Hawaiian culture, and Dorothy Barrère read and commented on part of the manuscript. Rick Warshauer and Bill Mull contributed expertise in the ecology of the volcanoes region, and both read and made valuable comments on certain chapters. I owe a special thanks to Laura Carter, Hawai'i Volcanoes National Park archeologist, and Tina Neal, USGS geologist, who read patiently through parts of a very rough draft, and who shared their time, their friendship, and their infectious love for the land.

I am especially grateful to Honolulu book designer and publisher Barbara Pope, who out of friendship and her own admirable dedication to the art of bookmaking contributed freely her advice and support. And to Barbara Dean, developmental editor for this Sierra Club series, who has supported this project since its first nebulous conception nearly four years ago.

To my parents, who passed on to me their love for the Islands and their admiration for Hawaiian culture, I am much indebted. And to my partner, Peter, who lived graciously with me through the daily struggle of bringing this book to completion.

"The burning island" is a translation of a Tahitian name for the island of Hawai'i; it is a name that must have been carried back to the Society Islands by Polynesians during those great seafaring voyages several hundred years ago. I am reminded by it that the heart of these islands, physically and culturally, is volcanic. *'Eli 'eli kau mai.* May a deep reverence alight.

The Burning Island

Prologue

Preceding page: Mauna Loa from the top of Mauna Kea. Photograph by Franco Salmoiraghi.

*E*ven after I have spent some time here in Hawaiian volcano country, a subconscious image of a very different kind of volcano still sends up its fumes. The image must date from some book I read as a child, or some early history lesson. The volcano of my early impressions is cone-shaped and steep-sided, solitary and probably menacing, though it has shrunk in memory to a two-dimensional form, about the size of the pyramid on a dollar bill. A cauliflower-shaped cloud of ash and steam spouts from its top, and down the sides run rivulets of lava, like melted chocolate. They threaten to demolish a tiny town at the base. Pompeii? My archetypal volcano, then, must be Vesuvius.

I would venture that in the North American, and perhaps the northern European consciousness, Vesuvius has occupied prime place as prototype for all volcanoes—symmetrical, towering giants, given to occasional deadly paroxysms, and usually located in foreign countries.

The dramatic reawakening of Mount St. Helens in recent years has preempted the Vesuvian model for most Americans (and brought home the fact that our civilization as well as others exist only by geological consent) but that violent explosion has kept in the forefront the image of the *continental* volcano, for various and complex reasons a much different volcano from the one on whose summit I am now living.

Thus the confusion of visitors, who stop me often as I amble down the road toward the village store, here near the summit of Kīlauea, to ask, "Where is the volcano?" Pointing to the ground is an accurate answer, but hardly an adequate one. The full answer presents a geology very foreign to most people, and so I start here with a brief mapping of the territory. Anyone familiar with such arcane topics as "hot spots" may want to skip on to Chapter 1.

This book explores a volcanic world very different from the real and imagined world of continental volcanism. We usually think of the eight high volcanic islands that we call Hawai'i as sitting in splendid but peculiar isolation in the middle of the vast Pacific. But a topographic map of the ocean floor gives a much different view. The map reveals that these islands are only the most visible part of an enormous mountain range, stretching northwest across the Pacific for over 1,500 miles. This long chain of mostly submarine mountains is made up of volcanoes, or the remnants of volcanoes. Northwest of Kaua'i, the last of the main Hawaiian islands, a few of these mountains break the ocean surface as coral atolls. These tiny atolls, the visible tips of huge, extinct volcanoes, form, along with the main islands, the Hawaiian archipelago, and the entire 1,500-mile range is called the Hawaiian chain.

The submerged volcanoes at the northwestern end of the Hawaiian chain are nearly 70 million years old. At the southeastern end, they are still being born. Yet all of them have been spawned from one locus—a geological "hot spot"—now located beneath Hawai'i (the "Big Island," as locals call it, the island farthest southeast). From this locus, for millions of years, a mysteriously generated plume of magma (molten material from the earth's mantle) has supplied the raw material to build volcanoes.

Geologic theory about the workings of the hot spot is primarily an extension of the very new science of plate tectonics. Plate tectonic theory holds that the earth's solid crust is fractured into a dozen or so large "plates" that "float" on the mantle—the semiliquid layer that extends down to the earth's dense core. These plates (driven by mechanisms still not understood, but having to do, scientists now think, with a global process of heat convection) are in constant, majestic motion. Most volcanic activity can be explained by the interaction between plates, occurring where they bump together or along the lines where they are pulling apart.

Where plates collide, the crust of the earth is piled up and compressed, forming the landmasses we call *continents.* The collision also results in volcanism, as one plate is forced under another, and the friction melts the edges of the plates. Made buoyant by the heat, the molten rock breaks through the surface to form a continental volcano. A continental volcano tends to be rather violently explosive, because its eruptions contain a mixture of melted oceanic crust and melted (granitic) continental crust, much less fluid than the basaltic lava erupted by oceanic volcanoes. Instead of being built out of thousands of fluid lava flows, like an oceanic volcano, it may develop in a few or a series of explosions into a steep-sided cone—the classic Vesuvian shape.

Volcanism occurs not only where plates are colliding but also where they are spreading apart. Plate tectonics helps to explain all these forms of volcanism that happen at the edges of plates but is less helpful when it comes to hot spots, which occur in the middle of plates. It is still unknown what earth forces create this birthing channel for volcanoes, but, in the case of the Hawaiian hot spot, layer by layer magma builds a volcanic mountain on the ocean floor, at the same time as, slowly, inexorably, the oceanic crust of the Pacific plate carries the volcano northwest. As it rafts away from the hot spot, the volcano "ages," its eruptive activity slowing, then finally ceasing altogether as it is cut off permanently from the source of molten rock.

If the volcano grows to the ocean surface before drifting too far from the source of magma, it will have a life span as a volcanic island, but when the eruptive activity slows erosion bites in, deeply altering the volcano's form. The cooling rock condenses, and the whole mountain subsides, its enormous weight pushing the ocean crust down into the semisolid mantle. Sometimes a mountain will subside slowly enough that coral has the chance to colonize its top—giving it a rebirth as a coral atoll—but most eventually join the long chain of extinct submarine volcanoes.

This is the pattern of decay that will, millions of years from now, claim all the Hawaiian Islands. One can trace some of the pattern within the major Hawaiian islands, though they are all, within the earth's time scale, very young. Kaua'i, the oldest, and farthest northwest, is 5 to 6 million years old. (Dinosaurs roamed the earth about 60 million years before the single great volcano that created the island first broke the surface of the sea.) The island has been deeply eroded by rain runoff, forming spectacular steep canyons and valleys.

O'ahu rose out of the sea about three million years ago—about the time now set for the origin of *Homo sapiens*. Maui and Moloka'i emerged during the Ice Ages, as did the older volcanoes of the island of Hawai'i. (One of these, Mauna Kea, still bears the marks of glaciation.)

Larger than all the other main islands combined, Hawai'i is made up of five volcanoes, one considered extinct, one dormant, and three "active." Kohala, whose slopes form the northwestern corner of the island, stopped erupting, geologists estimate, about 60,000 years ago. Its rainy windward side is already eroded into deep, narrow valleys. A number of large, eroded cinder cones mark the places where lava erupted explosively during a late stage in the volcano's active history. Explosive eruptions become more common as a volcano ages, moving away from the source of very hot fluid magma, and if Kohala ever had a summit caldera, the cinder and pumice from these late-stage vents have filled it in.

Southeast of Kohala rises Mauna Kea, at 13,796 feet the highest island mountain in the world. Mauna Kea's top is studded with large

5

cinder cones, and covered with thick layers of ash and pumice, with no summit caldera visible, suggesting that it too is an aging volcano. Geologists estimate that it has not erupted for about 3,000 years. Hualālai, southwest of Mauna Kea, may be on the verge of old age. The 8,271-foot-high mountain has the lumpy profile of an aging volcano, but it last erupted a very short time ago, geologically speaking: in 1800–1801.

The two volcanoes of the southern part of Hawai'i are the youngest and the most active. Both probably rose above the surface of the ocean less than a million years ago. Their realm—the region of the island that is shaped and governed by their active volcanism—is the locale of this book.

Of the two, Mauna Loa ("long or great mountain"), 13,667 feet high, dominates volcano country. With its enormous sloping sides, it comes closest to the ideal form of a "shield" volcano, a volcano built up from long lava flows of highly fluid basaltic lava (named "shield" by volcanologists because of this sloping shape, so different from the classic cone shape of the more explosive Vesuvius or Fuji—or St. Helens).

Kīlauea, younger and much smaller (only 4,078 feet high), seems to extend like a large hump from the southern flank of Mauna Loa. But it has its own summit caldera, and, from what geologists can ascertain, a completely separate conduit to the source of magma deep in the mantle. Sometimes called the "drive-in volcano," Kīlauea is considered the most accessible and one of the "gentlest" active volcanoes in the world.

In shield volcanoes still in the prime of life, such as Mauna Loa and Kīlauea, magma wells up from its source deep in the mantle, and accumulates in a huge chamber one to three miles below the volcano's summit. If pressure pushes the magma to the top, it most often erupts first within the summit caldera, then moves out along the volcano's rift zones, large fissures that extend far down the flanks. Rift zones, areas of weakness caused by gravity's pull on the mountain and larger patterns of stress related to plate movement, typically extend down two sides, though not usually in a straight line (Mauna Loa's rift zones, for example, stretch northeast and southwest but at an obtuse angle, like arms spread wide).

If an unobstructed channel develops in the volcano, it can bring magma to the surface over a long period of time: Kīlauea's summit caldera contained an active bubbling lake of molten lava nearly continuously from the early 1800s until 1924. In a more typical pattern, magma erupts into the summit caldera, then finds a lower channel through the fissures of one of the rift zones. Generally such eruptions run for days, weeks, or months before the magma becomes somehow obstructed or the magma chamber depleted. Now, however, Kīlauea is setting a new record for duration in rift zone eruptions—the current one began in January 1983, and as of fall 1989 showed no sign of slackening. Magma wells to the surface about halfway down Kīlauea's east rift zone, forming a small, molten lake. From here it travels seven miles to the sea, occasionally on the surface, but mostly just under it, in the crusted-over tunnels (lava tubes) that earlier surface flows have formed, adding acres of new land to the south shores of Hawai'i Island.

Fifteen miles off these south shores, the drama of volcanic genesis continues. Against the undersea flank of Kīlauea is growing Lō 'ihi—a submarine volcano. Very recent undersea photographs have confirmed that this latest Hawaiian volcano, rising from the ocean crust at a depth of 12,000 feet and now about 3,000 feet from the ocean surface, has developed a summit caldera and rift zones, and shows evidence of recent eruptions. Several thousand years from now, a new island may be born.

Until very recently, the Hawaiian volcano country was *terra incognita,* glimpsed through an explorer's crude map. Now magnetometers, sonar, spectrometers—science's most sophisticated measuring devices—are used to chart volcanic activity. The details of the map are being filled in and they are fascinating; yet beyond them the country remains a landscape for which, in the deepest sense, we have no language, a world that stirs the Western mind at some inchoate edge, some geographic borderline of the unconscious.

Volcano Country

Ten Views
of Mauna Loa

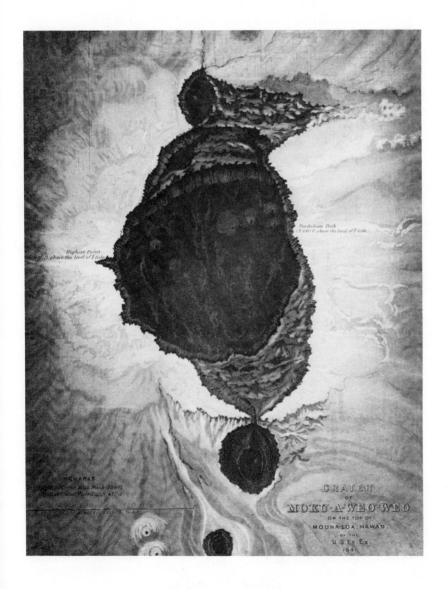

A sight of the volcano fills the mind with awe. . . . The strongest man is unstrung, the most courageous heart is daunted in approaching this place.

DAVID DOUGLAS,
botanist, after
climbing Mauna Loa in 1834

Fear falls upon me on the mountaintop.

From the *Kumulipo,*
a Hawaiian creation chant

*M*auna Loa is monolithic. You can point a finger at Mauna Loa, and say, "That is a volcano," as you cannot about its sister-volcano, Kilauea.

That is, you can do so if you can *see* Mauna Loa. You could spend a long time in the tropic coastal climate of Hilo, the largest town on the east side of the Big Island, and never locate the mountain behind its thick veil of clouds. But one day you would look up to an enormous obstetric hump against the sky, dark blue-green or mantled by snow—a mass so gigantic it would disrupt permanently your vision of a tropic isle. Measured from its base over 18,000 feet below sea level, Mauna Loa is the largest mountain mass in the world.

If the day stayed clear, and you drove up Kīlauea volcano through endless rainforest, the hump of Mauna Loa would at some point shift startlingly into focus. From the summit of the smaller volcano at 4,000 feet, Mauna Loa looms prodigiously beyond, its smooth convexity otherworldly, like the curve of Jupiter viewed from one of its moons.

From this point, by straining the eyes, one can see through the illusion of symmetry that distance lends to Mauna Loa. Actually, the volcano is built up along two rift zones, so that it is much broader in two directions. Mauna Loa's rift zones are cracked and riven, pocked with craters and studded with cinder cones, and they descend from the summit caldera to the southwest and the northeast like twisted spines. From them have poured tongues of lava that have spread to the ocean in those directions. And even, though rarely, to the north: 33 miles from Mauna Loa's summit, near the new luxury hotels of North Kona, the coastal road passes over an 1859 flow that took eight days to reach the sea. The lava of Mauna Loa has flowed over an area that is three times the size of the island of O'ahu. Mauna Loa has been one of the most active volcanoes on earth throughout the last century, erupting on an average of once every 3.7 years, for a total output of more than 3½ billion cubic yards of molten rock. At the peak of its last eruption, in 1984, the volcano pumped out enough lava in one hour to pave a sidewalk from Honolulu to New York City.

Hawaiian legend names Mauna Loa's great summit caldera, Moku'ā-weoweo ("red section of fish"), as the occasional home of the volcano goddess Pele (her permanent residence is in the caldera of Kīlauea), and an ancient trail up the south flank—the 'Āinapō trail—reveals that the early Hawaiians paid visits to the summit, probably to make ritual offerings, but the legends are silent as to what religious sites there may have been on the mountain. In their awe and dread of Pele, Hawaiians in pre-Western times may have made this journey only when extreme rites were felt needed. They would have been very ill clothed for Mauna Loa's extremes of weather. To make such a pilgrimage purely out of curiosity would have been incomprehensible to them, as the early Western explorers discovered.

One of the first things I did after I settled on the Big Island to write a book about the volcano country was to climb Mauna Loa. I wasn't sure whether I was making an expedition, a tour, or a pilgrimage. I suspected that whatever I was doing would have made no sense at all to the old Hawaiians, but I would not be sure of that until I had learned more about the early inhabitants of the volcano country. I knew very little about the region at that point, except a bit of geography, a few legends, and tales of Westerners from the century before who had climbed Mauna Loa. From the accounts I had read, they all seemed to expect the volcano—or their experience of it—to be different from what it turned out to be. I wanted to know what they had imagined, and whether what they imagined influenced what they saw.

The first non-Hawaiian to climb Mauna Loa was Archibald Menzies, surgeon with the Vancouver expedition and ardent botanist. The year was 1794, sixteen years after Captain James Cook had "discovered" the Islands. On February 14 Menzies, encamped with a small party of men from the expedition and their native bearers at 6,500 feet, observed with amazement the "hoarfrost" that had formed overnight. The temperature was 28 degrees. The natives, "all barefoot," refused to stir from the makeshift grass huts erected the night before until the sun was well up in the sky. Menzies left all but a few hardy natives at this camp and proceeded to the snowline at 11,000 feet. That night was spent huddled together on a flat section of lava, where no one slept: "Our minds were variously occupied," said Menzies, "sometimes on meditating on the dreadful consequences of a snowstorm coming on whilst we were thus situated; at other times in contemplating the

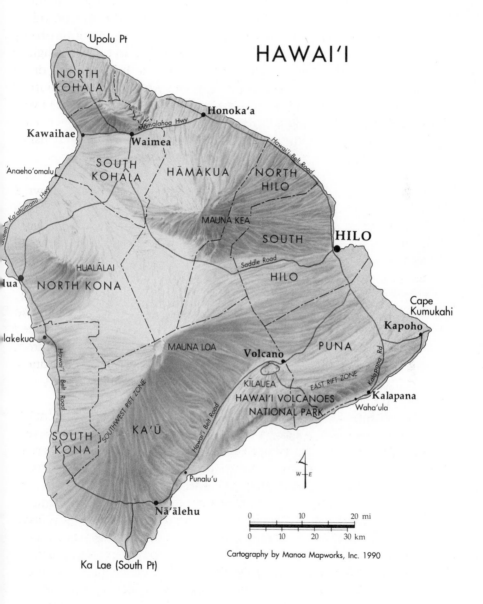

HAWAI'I

'Upolu Pt

NORTH
KOHALA

Honoka'a

Kawaihae

Waimea

Māmalahoa Hwy

'Anaeho'omalu

SOUTH
KOHALA

HĀMĀKUA

NORTH
HILO

Hawai'i Belt Road

Queen Ka'ahumanu Hwy

MAUNA KEA

SOUTH

HILO

HUALĀLAI

Saddle Road

HILO

lua

NORTH KONA

Cape
Kumukahi

lakekua

Kapoho

MAUNA LOA

Volcano

PUNA

Hawai'i
Belt Road

SOUTHWEST RIFT ZONE

KĪLAUEA

EAST RIFT ZONE

Kalapana Rd

Kalapana

HAWAI'I VOLCANOES
NATIONAL PARK

Waha'ula

SOUTH
KONA

KA'Ū

Hawai'i Belt Road

Punalu'u

W — E

Nā'ālehu

| 0 | 10 | 20 mi |
| 0 | 10 | 20 | 30 km |

Cartography by Manoa Mapworks, Inc. 1990

Ka Lae (South Pt)

awful and extended scene around us, where the most profound stillness subsisted the whole night, not even interrupted by the least chirp of a bird or an insect." The experience, Menzies noted, "led the imagination to the utmost stretch."[1]

At "eleven in the forenoon," the small party arrived at "the mouth of an immense crater at least three miles in circumference." Menzies and two others continued the arduous scramble around the edge of the summit caldera to the highest point on the western edge. With a mercury barometer, Menzies recorded a height of 13,634 feet (only 41 feet short of Mauna Loa's actual height).

On the descent, the party was stricken with an extreme "fatigue" that was probably altitude sickness. At the snowline, they found that all but two loyal natives of the waiting party had left, taking with them the bottle of rum "carefully preserved for exigencies." The party revived themselves as best they could on the juice of three remaining coconuts, and reached base camp at ten o'clock that night, after "the most persevering and hazardous struggle that can be perceived."

David Douglas, the Scottish botanist remembered for his naming of the Douglas fir, was the next foreigner to climb Mauna Loa. In January 1833 he started up the south side of the volcano on the 'Āinapō trail, the same route that Menzies had taken. He noted in a letter that the natives were still telling the story of Menzies, "the red-faced man, who cut off the limbs of men and gathered grass" (a reference, presumably, to Menzies's skills as surgeon and botanist).[2]

Douglas took a Hawaiian "birdcatcher . . . who captured and plucked the tailfeathers from the bright mountain birds to weave into cloaks for the chiefs" and three other natives as guides. The natives carried poles on their shoulders with bundles—*poi** and sweet potato, goat meat, a telescope. Douglas wrote in a later account that walking "was rendered dangerous by the multitude of fissures, many of which are but slightly covered with a thin crust." As they continued the ascent, "the cold and fatigue disheartened the Islanders, who required all the encouragement I could give to induce them to proceed. As I took the lead, it was needful for me to look behind me continually, for when once out of sight they would pop themselves down and neither rise nor answer to my call."

A few miles from the summit, Douglas's guides encamped in a lava tube cave and refused to budge. Douglas went on alone to the

*See glossary

edge of the caldera, which he calls "the Great Terminal Volcano." He tried to climb down into it but was blocked by treacherous fissures "concealed though not protected by the snow." He noted a "sweet musical sound, like the faint sound of musical glasses" issuing from these cracks, along with a "kind of hissing sound, like a swarm of bees."

The alien landscape of the volcano seems to have had an unhinging effect on Douglas. His journal records a nightmare of "terrifyingly dreary expanse of lava"; "there is little to arrest the eye of the naturalist over the greater part of this huge dome, which is a gigantic mass of slag, scoriae and ashes." But the note he strikes is not so much boredom as the fascinated horror with which medieval artists dwelt on the skull beneath the skin of beauty. Nature, on Mauna Loa, reveals to Douglas a self that is innately perfidious: "A most uncomfortable feeling," he writes, "is experienced when the traveller becomes aware that the lava is hollow and faithless beneath his tread."

Yet in a letter written shortly after his descent he wrote, "How insignificant are the works of man in their greatest magnitude and perfection, compared with such a place. I have exhausted both body and mind, examining, measuring and performing various experiments, and now, I learn that I know nothing." The extent of the botanist's mental "exhaustion" is revealed in the conflicting accounts he left of his adventures on Mauna Loa. Sarah Lyman, the wife in the missionary home where he stayed in Hilo, recalls in her journal that on his return he described Mauna Loa as "an immense dome . . . with an open crater at the summit, about 24 miles in circumference . . . and was not able to ascertain the depth, as his line would only admit of 1,200 feet, neither could he see the bottom with his glass."[3] But Douglas himself, in a letter, contradicts this description of the "bleak" inactive caldera by describing the volcano as being in "furious agitation." In one letter, he measures a depth of 1,270 feet by dropping a plummet line to fiery depths; in another, the wind is so furious that he can't approach closer than twenty feet from the rim.

"I must go back to the volcano," Douglas wrote in one of these confused communications, as though the mountain itself exerted a mesmeric force. A few months later, instead of pursuing plans to sail for the West Coast of the United States, Douglas returned to the Big Island and met a strange fate. While traversing the slopes of Mauna Kea, on his way to climb Mauna Loa again, he fell into a wild cattle trap, and was gored to death by the pit's other occupant. Since he had been warned of the traps, there was speculation at the time over whether he fell, was pushed, or leaped of his own accord. The mystery was eclipsed soon after by the furor over the "errors and inconsistencies" of his observations.[4]

In 1873, Isabella Bird, Victorian travel writer and amalgam of amateur scientist, pilgrim, and sightseer, wrote to her sister,

> When I left Waimea Mr. Spencer said, I hope nothing will tempt you to go up Mauna Loa," and I said, "I should never dream of it." When Mr. Wilson wished me goodbye he said, "I shall have no rest until you promise me not to go up Mauna Loa," and I said, "I shall make no promise but I should never dream of going up. The suffering is too great."[5]

A week later she became the first woman in recorded history to journey to the top of Mauna Loa.

Isabella Bird was my inspiration to make a similar trek, and, like her, I doubted the wisdom of such a venture. Isabella, short and rather stout, rode up the mountain at the head of a mule string. I suspected she would have found my willingness to be my own beast of burden very unladylike and not a little foolhardy.

My hiking partner Joe and I loaded up our packs at the head of the Park Service trail, which starts at 6,600 feet on the south flank of the volcano's northeast rift zone. From here we could see, several miles distant and 2,000 feet lower, the caldera of Kīlauea (literally, "much spreading") with its steaming firepit, Halema'uma'u. Twenty-five miles away, along the long slope of Kīlauea's east rift zone, the active cone of Pu'u 'Ō'ō was releasing a long, lazy streamer of steam. At 900 feet, it had grown to twice the size of the year before. The south side of the island was clear of clouds, and the coast curved, striped with lava flows, against the flat, deep blue of ocean.

We were standing in a *kīpuka,* a pocket of forest left untouched by recent lava flows. Nature seemed benign enough at this spot: the broad branches of native *koa* trees formed a thick canopy over lush grass, and somewhere to the right of us the *nēnē,* the rare native goose, gobbled a greeting or an alarm. Joe was stuffing our packs with huge water jugs and twice as much food as we would need. He was wearing a very battered straw stetson, hiking shorts, and a fanny pack slung in front like a kangaroo pouch. Joe is 6 feet 4 inches, lean, and mostly legs—a Honolulu architect raised on the Big Island, whose passion is the ocean. He often has to restack surfboards, paddleboards, and a windsurfer or two to get to the drawingboard in his office.

I was studying the notice posted at the trailhead, which was telling me things I didn't want to hear—I should have packed a compass and a signaling mirror in case of nasty storms (frequent) or "volcanic activity." Mauna Loa has erupted thirty-nine times in the last 150 years. The last eruption, in 1984, lasted twenty-one days and sent a lava flow within five miles of Hilo along the same northeast rift zone we would be climbing.

The ancient 'Āinapō trail, which climbed the southwest rift zone, has been rarely used since the nineteenth century. The present trail up the northeast rift zone was built in 1915 by a segregated black company of the U.S. Army. The job was engineered by Thomas Augustus Jaggar, the volcanologist who helped found the Hawaiian Volcano Observatory, to provide access to Mauna Loa eruptions. The first section of trail wound over smooth *pāhoehoe* lava, over 2,000 years old, oxidized to a uniform rust color, its cracks filled with volcanic ash from more recent eruptions. To the right was a brown, clinkery flow of *a'ā,* several hundred years younger. *Pāhoehoe* is the more primal stuff, a hotter, more gaseous, extremely fluid lava. It can drip like syrup or, if channeled on a steep slope, run swiftly like a molten river. It hardens to a smooth, ropy, or billowy surface. *A'ā* is actually *pāhoehoe* that has been stirred and cooled out of solution, becoming extremely jagged and clinkery, so sharp-edged that a walk across it can rip the toughest hiking boots.

At 8,000 feet we passed the last *'ōhi'a* tree, a dry, half-dead-looking scrub compared to the magnificent forest trees below. The *'ōhi'a,* with its scarlet blossoms, is sacred to Pele, and the undisputed heir to her domain. Like the *'ama'u* (Sadleria) fern, it will appear on lava less than a year old; in fact, it often gets its start as a parasite on the fern.

A mile farther, the top of Mauna Loa came into view again, now miraculously clear—a long, huge hump, it filled the whole sky to the west. Between us and the summit was an enormous expanse of lava, made almost smooth by distance, though in fact the terrain was getting steadily wilder. The trail climbed for another mile along a large trench formed by the collapse of a lava tube. At the end of the trench, the tube continued intact, a window opening into darkness. Beyond the trench, we crossed an old lava flow of clinkery *a'ā* pulverized to cinder and tinted green by crystals of olivine.

At about 9,000 feet we could see the day's destination—Pu'u

Ulaʻula ("Red Hill"), an ancient cinder cone some 130 feet high, its surface oxidized to a dull red, against whose base nestles the cabin built in 1915 by Jaggar's U.S. Army labor force. Below Red Hill stretched the spine of the rift zone, marked by a few black cinder cones from the 1984 eruption. At 9,500 feet the last vegetation, scattered tufts of dry, golden grass, was disappearing. The trail ahead to the distant Red Hill led over a huge expanse of jagged, naked *aʻā,* ribboned by flows of *pāhoehoe.*

We reached the cabin in late afternoon, glad to dump our heavy packs. Already ensconced in the one-room bunk-lined space were three teachers and three college students from the Brigham Young University campus on Oʻahu. Two of the hikers had altitude sickness from a day hike up to 12,000 feet, and were huddled inside their blankets. Joe and I wolfed down some food, then climbed Red Hill to get a glimpse of the view before the clouds rolled in. The view was magnificent. For a few minutes the top of Mauna Kea was clear, looming in the north, its profile lumped with cinder cones, and the astronomical observatories perched on top like a cluster of tiny white mushrooms. A break in the low clouds revealed, far to the south, the giant pockmark of Kīlauea caldera. From a spot somewhere near here, the Reverend Titus Coan wrote, in 1852, "I was 10,000 feet above the sea, in a vast solitude untrodden by the foot of man or beast, amidst a silence unbroken by any living voice, and surrounded by scenes of terrific desolation."[6]

For Coan the silent "desolation" spoke: in it he heard the voice of a God who occasionally laid waste the earth in the name of Righteousness. What voice it spoke to me I was not likely to hear, huddled with seven others in the tiny cabin. Since 1915, Kilroys have been inscribing the cabin walls; of late, the Park Service had wisely provided a pen and a large green ledger. A solitary hiker from Florida wrote of getting caught near the summit the day before in a thunderstorm that turned to snow. It became nearly impossible to follow the *ahu,* or rock cairns, that are sometimes the only trail signs across the lava. "I said a prayer," he wrote, "though I'm not a religious man." Other messages:

"At 12,000 feet I had to choose between my wife and reaching the summit."

"Gale force winds, last two miles of trail incredibly hard. Thought my last hour had come."

"Trail is very good in spots, ghastly in others."

"Thought I would get frostbite and lose fingers due to hypothermia plus altitude sickness."

And two messages that seemed to sum up the range of possibility here on the mountain:

"This entire trip has been a religious experience; the summit trail is very hard but worth every minute."

"This is the most God-forsaken wasteland I've ever been in. Heading for Hilo for a beer."

What were they all looking for up here, I wondered. What did they hope, consciously or unconsciously, to find? No one would ever climb Mauna Loa, I was becoming convinced, simply because it was there.

That night, despite extra blankets, I was cold in my summer-weight sleeping bag. All these bodies took up the bunks and most of the floor space; the small space reeked like a locker room. The altitude made my sinuses ache. Eleven and a half miles and a climb of over 3,200 feet tomorrow—it was easy to entertain thoughts of going back. For a moment I was haunted by the pale shade of Miss C. F. Gordon-Cumming, smart little hat perched on her head and her "earthward extremities" clad in a tasteful ankle-length divided skirt. This Scottish travel writer, author of *A Lady's Cruise in a French Man-of-War* and other popular works, viewed an erupting Kīlauea in the summer of 1880, but pronounced its fires not nearly as grand as those that had incinerated the city of Hong Kong.* She spurned a climb up Mauna Loa, explaining in her later book, *Fire Fountains,*

> I suppose that if I were a truly energetic traveller, I should feel bound to toil up the dreary mountain and look down into its crater, but I honestly confess that I have not the smallest wish to do so. *"Le jeu ne vaut pas la chandelle."* [*"The game isn't worth the candle."*] The exertion would be very great, the cold severe, and I detest cold. . . . The whole journey is over a dreary desolate waste of lava, only varying in degrees of roughness, and all of repellent ugliness; and though extremely interesting, and of very varied type, I know that in the crater

*Gordon-Cumming is referring to the Great Fire of 1878, which incinerated much of the waterfront area. Isabella Bird, arriving (coincidentally, I assume) by ship the night of the fire, describes the scene as "luridly grand" in *The Golden Chersoneae and the Way Thither.*

[Kilauea] now before me . . . I have seen, or shall see, every form that lava is capable of assuming—for of course there is a limit to its powers of contortion.[7]

Mauna Loa was not erupting when Gordon-Cumming visited, and her chances for being the first woman to document such an event, at any rate, had been eclipsed by Isabella Bird. That fact may explain the truculence of her comments. But Gordon-Cumming also seemed less inclined than Isabella Bird to assume that nature would deliver up significant messages to those who quest. Did she have, I wondered, less religion, or less imagination? Or was she simply more modern?

It was a long night in which to ponder the folly of emulating Bird rather than Gordon-Cumming, but still the next day Joe and I were on the trail early, our loads lightened a bit by leaving a food stash at the cabin. The morning air was crystalline, and the whole top half of Mauna Kea loomed on our right. Ahead of us a field of lava and cinder cones went on forever. The trail began on lava from 1880 and passed some large, very weathered cones, moored like islands in the newer flow. Along the edges of one cone, the pumicelike rock was multi-colored: sulfurous yellow, oxides of purple and red. The trail was increasingly rugged. The air had a penetrating chill; our hands were cold and swollen from the change in blood pressure. Low clouds obscured Kilauea and were beginning to wreathe Mauna Kea, but we were above them, in another world. No vegetation, total silence, except straining lungs and beating heart and footsteps on lava, crushing it into slivers. We were walking on an enormous mountain of basaltic glass, built up layer by layer by countless lava flows. . . .

At 11,000 feet we left the golden, frothy *pāhoehoe* of an 1855 eruption and the old trail and continued on a 1984 flow of glossy black. We veered off to clamber up a large cinder and spatter cone. The throat of the cone was reddish, cindery rock, but the bottom was filled like a bowl with glossy black *pāhoehoe;* the downhill side was riven or blasted open and congealed lava poured in a frozen river down its side.

The terrain was getting wilder by the minute in this upper part of the rift zone, where eruption after eruption had left its trace. *Pāhoehoe* buckled and cracked into huge plates, pushed up into tumuli that resembled ancient burial mounds, blasted into still-steaming fumaroles, spat and dribbled into spires and cones, dropped in huge cowdung bombs. Gaping and collapsed lava tubes, giant cinder cones

22

cleft and blown apart, revealing sulfur-yellow innards. Rent seams of fissures. Huge upthrusts of rust-colored rock, welded shiny spun-glass blobs of *pāhoehoe*. Geo-sexual, geo-alimentary. Layers of many different flows; we were toiling from one geologic moment to the next in a multiplying confusion of forms. Steaming Cone, at 12,000 feet, was steaming, and so was a mile of long, jagged chasm that we skirted. Sulfur stink. And more fantastic forms of lava, rough-smooth like elephant's skin, shiny glass, blasted cindery red, sculpted, jumbled and heaped, thrown, coughed, spattered, welded, spun, blown to bits. We dropped our packs and lay down on the rough surface, too tired or disoriented even to reach for the water jug.

A few feet from my head, stalactites dripped from the maw of a lava tube like menacing teeth. To the ancient Hawaiians, it had apparently been clear that the wildest regions—the farthest reaches of ocean, the high forests, the tops of mountains, the volcanoes—were the realms of the gods. The Western view of wild nature seemed much more ambiguous. I remembered a reproduction of a painting I had looked at recently. By a nineteenth-century American, Thomas Cole, it is called "The Expulsion from the Garden of Eden." The right side of the painting shows Eden, green and parklike, bathed in soft light. Adam and Eve, expelled from its gates, are tiny stooped figures crossing a bridge toward the left of the painting, over an abyss and into the Fallen World. This world dominates the left side of the painting—a few blasted trees on barren, riven terrain. Ravenous beasts tear at each other in the foreground, and a vulture hovers nearby. And in the background, magnificent and ominous, an huge steep-sided volcano spews fire and smoke.

In Thomas Cole's Fallen World, the volcano reigns supreme. But what did that wild power symbolize?

To the Reverend Titus Coan of Hilo, the volcano was visible proof of a just and terrible God and the Day of Reckoning that would soon come. In 1852 Mauna Loa sent a column of fire into the air for twenty days. The plume was visible from 100 miles out to sea. Titus Coan, called by his detractors "the high priest of volcanoes" because of what they considered an unseemly interest in Pele's domain, started up the mountain with four natives, hewing his way through dense rainforest. After four days, the natives quit. The reverend went on alone, until he reached a huge vent that had opened in the flank of the mountain. In a letter Coan wrote, "At last I reached the awful crater and stood alone in the light of its fires. It was a moment of unspeakable awe. I seemed to be standing in the presence and before the throne of God, and while all other voices were hushed, His alone spake."[8]

I thought of Coan's words as I stood at the edge of Moku'āweoweo, the summit caldera of Mauna Loa, at 13,000 feet above the sea. There were no fires, and no voices. The enormous pit stretched far to the south, a lake of lava frozen into billows and waves. The caldera was—a vast, empty space. Mark Twain at first thought Kilauea's summit caldera looked like a "large cellar." It only became awesome when he saw the distant speck that was the hotel on the far rim. Here too, on Mauna Loa, I found myself scanning for something to measure by, finally locating the two 10-foot *ahu*—cairns—on the southern rim. Erected in 1840 by the U.S. scientific expedition led by Lieutenant Charles Wilkes, they stood two miles distant from us, and marked the present site of the summit cabin. Dwarfed as they were by the distance, they still gave some perspective. The sense of blankness, desolation—even boredom—abated, and other features appeared: cinder cones against the distant western walls, a faint line of steam from a fissure on that far side. The immensity became comprehensible—then staggering.

The wave of nausea Joe and I were both feeling seemed as much psychological as physical. We huddled against "Jaggar's cave," a shallow arch of rock where the scientist bivouacked on trips to observe eruptions in the caldera. The mechanics of science, perhaps, provided a protective lens through which to view this landscape. I could feel my mind searching for some information to give it a handle—a viewpoint. All I came up with was snatches of a song—"Home on the Range!" Range we had, in the sense of wide open space, more than we were comfortable with, but this was no place for deer and antelope to play. The Wilkes expedition, I remembered reading, had found the "entire body of a cow who must have wandered up seeking water . . . dried and perfectly preserved."

To reach the cabin we descended into the caldera, traversing a mile of billowy *pāhoehoe,* the easiest walking of the whole journey. We were briefly rained on, then hailed on. We skirted Lua Poholo ("pit that sank out of sight"), a 200-foot-deep crater formed by "collapse" in 1880. We climbed the caldera rim, the killer last mile of trail mentioned in the logbook at Red Hill. We could see the roof of the cabin, only a half-mile off, but Joe sat down, overcome with nausea, pounding head and heart. I was feeling exhausted but not overwhelmed. I was in much poorer physical condition than my partner, who is a Spartan, an athlete, a big-wave surfer. But I had taken full advantage of the privileges of the less fit—less weight in the pack, lots of breathers, and copious water. And I had eaten most of my candy bars (Joe did not believe in sugar). He stopped to rest while I plodded on toward the cabin, driven by the psychological imperative to get within some walls.

The cabin was little more than that—four walls, a few windows, plank bunks with army blankets, two chairs, a table. Outside, a roof catchment tank for water. The front wall stood about fifty feet from the rim of the caldera. The outhouse was closer, and perched over a deep crack—a midnight call of nature could be fatal. I struggled out of my pack and fell into the closest bunk, trying to calm breath and heart. I thought of Edna. When I lived in the woods in Idaho, Edna was my neighbor, a jack Mormon from a small Utah town. She told me she always dropped a lighted match down the outhouse hole and peered in before she sat down. Atavistic fears. Imagining what Edna would do up here had a steadying effect. I decided to give Joe a half-hour before I went looking for him. It was nearly sundown.

But Joe soon appeared, staggering to the nearest bunk, dropping pack and falling into it. I got out his sleeping bag and covered him with it, handed him the water jug. Neither of us could face food. Heart pounding, head throbbing, I hobbled outside. The sun was already behind the summit, and the caldera sunken into a vast darkness. The rest of the world was obscured beneath banks of sunset-orange clouds. The temperature was dropping rapidly—warmth being sucked out into a vacuum, an emptiness of space.

For comfort I wandered through the maze of low lava walls next to the cabin—the remains of the Wilkes expedition encampment. The piled rock walls were near-perfectly geometric, militarily tidy. These, I read somewhere, were the only remains anywhere in the Pacific from the U.S. South Seas Exploring Expedition of 1838–1842, one of the vanguards of this country's urge to manifest destiny at that time. In 1840 Lieutenant Charles Wilkes and fifty others camped at the summit for twenty-eight days while they meticulously mapped the vast caldera.

The expedition that started up the mountain was much larger. Wilkes describes it as "a vast caravan," consisting of "two hundred bearers of burdens, forty hogs, a bullock and bullock-hunter, fifty bearers of poe (native food), twenty-five with calabashes." The natives carried a portable house, kettles and frying pans, tents, and "a small cannon for the purpose of making experiments in sound." The Hawaiians, ill equipped for cold weather (Wilkes notes they were dressed

The camp at "Pendulum Peak," at the edge of Mauna Loa's summit caldera. Engraved by J. N. Gimbrede after a drawing by Charles Wilkes. Facing page 144 in Wilkes, Narrative of the U.S. Exploring Expedition *(Philadelphia: Lea & Blanchard, 1845). Courtesy of Bishop Museum.*

in bark cloth and "sandals" made of leaves, though he furnished some with rawhide sandals), were understandably reluctant to make the journey, but were coerced by their chiefs, who hoped to be well paid. "I felt happy in not understanding their language," wrote Wilkes in his autobiography, "and of course was deaf to their complaints." Wilkes himself was outfitted with a "guanaco-fur robe" in addition to navy blankets and clothing.[9]

It was December, the worst time for an ascent of the mountain. The two-mile-long procession was guided by the birdcatcher who had accompanied Douglas. He seemed, to the lieutenant, to be taking an unnecessarily circuitous route, so Wilkes took over, "compass in hand." They soon found themselves ten miles from the nearest available water, and nowhere near the snow that Wilkes thought would replenish their supply. As the air turned cold, there was a growing stampede of deserters until none but a guide or two could be induced to remain.

Wilkes's memoirs, written many years later, record the sad tale of one midshipman named Longley. Longley wandered off, apparently in search of water. After much searching he was found "lying in a hole in the rock, with his hat, pea-jacket, and mittens on, his water-flask . . .

26

hanging to his neck, just as he had left the encampment three days before." He "complained constantly, in a low tone, that someone had driven him out of his house." Longley never quite recovered from his encounter with the mountain, and was later pensioned off by the government.

Charles Wilkes, who was notorious for his adherence to military discipline, seems to have been nearly impervious to the awesome qualities of Mauna Loa's landscape. Wilkes's log of the time spent at the summit contains amazingly little description. No mention of twenty-eight days of sunrise and sunset, or of the eerie silence; only "The weather was very fine, very cold and uncomfortable." The only geologic formation he discusses with any enthusiasm is "a crack in the lava rock (under the tent) through which issued a stream of steam which served us the good purpose of . . . keeping our ink fluid." He named the area Pendulum Peak and had a sailor engrave the name where it would "endure as long as the lava on which it is cut." He court-martialed one officer for using precious water for his personal toilet. When he gave the "break camp" signal, he was astounded when his men broke twenty-eight days of formidable rectitude with three lusty cheers.

I stood inside the largest rectangle of low stone walls—what might have been the "pendulum house"—and looked out toward the last tint of sun against the mountain's summit, far across from me above the high western wall of the caldera. Stars were appearing, thick and enormous, as the light withdrew from the mountain. A blackness welled up out of the caldera, a primordial night so thick that it seemed to have a texture; it pushed against me. Not the blackness of emptiness, but a dense, impenetrable presence. It was more than the cold that drove me back within the cabin walls.

Sleep was a half-doze, waking to feel the heart racing, struggling to pump blood at this altitude. Like a fish out of water, or, perhaps, the first amphibian that crawled up on land. Both body and mind hovering on an edge, searching for a foothold in a new element. I thought of Isabella Bird. Is the Western mind more comfortable with the volcano in eruption, when the fire disguises that enigmatic dark presence from which the fire emerged?

At 6 P.M., June 6, 1873, Isabella Bird wrote to her sister, "Edge of the crater of Mauna Loa, Mokuaweoweo. . . . 13,750 feet above the sea. GREAT FOUNTAINS OF FIRE BELOW!!!!!!!!"

A half-mile from where I was lying in my narrow Park Service bunk, Isabella Bird spent the night, muffled in blankets and flannel, staring at the seething crater and thinking of her father.

The diminutive "globe-trotteress," as the press called her, was forty years old. Ever since a wise doctor had rescued her from the stifling drawing rooms of Edinburgh by recommending travel as a cure for her nervous disorders, Isabella Bird had been on the road. She had meant Hawai'i to be only a short stopover between Australia and California. But two things captivated her—the discovery of the joys of riding astride rather than side-saddle, and the volcano country. At first she was appalled by the immodesty of sitting straight on a horse: "It was only my strong desire to see the volcano which made me consent to a mode of riding against which I have such a strong prejudice."[10] But such sacrifices paled into insignificance at the sight of the erupting volcano (as she related to her sister in a letter written June 8):

> The blue moon shed her pallid light, as feeble as compared with that of the volcano as with sunlight, but red and glorious burned and glowed the splendour of the fire fountain on rock and tent, and shivering mules. Oh light that never was on sea or shore. Light at once of beauty and terror, unwatched by any mortal eyes but my own.

It had not been an easy journey: the mules had suffered, and her guide, Mr. Green, had forgotten the tea. He and the "natives" were in the tent, under heaps of blankets, trying to sleep off nausea and vertigo. But Isabella Bird had crawled out, "kneeling on a native" to unfasten the tent flap. Now she was alone at the edge of the seething, fountaining crater, where she sat "swathed like a puffin," in a French soldier's overcoat that reminded her of "regiments in the Rue de Rivoli in the palmy days of the Empire." She had come through "Plutonic" regions to this spot, to witness the naked terror of Jehovah's might: "Dwelling in the light which no man can approach unto."

While the "letters" of her book, *Six Months Among the Palm Groves, Coral Reefs and Volcanoes of the Sandwich Islands* (1875), describe the "awful sublimity" of the scene, her private letters reveal another face imposed on the landscape. "It is HIS birthday"— her father's, a Scottish preacher of the fire-and-brimstone school, a rather Jehovah-like and terrifying man, one gathers. She has come through "a wilderness of force and dread" for this lonely all-night vigil, and she sees, imposed on the face of this "mephitic chaos," the image of her Evangelical father.

For Isabella Bird, in fact, the mountain itself is a "he." Safely back in Hilo, she records a glimpse of "the towering dome of Mauna Loa, a brilliant blue indigo and shaded a deep rich blue where the numerous lava flows had blackened his portentous sides; his whole beauty the effect of atmosphere, on a thing itself hideous."

Hideous? Perhaps she means alien. An alien force. For the ancient Hawaiians, darkness and otherness were not evil, but a fecund source, a birthing place. But in the Western mind the darkness is either hellish or unnamed, a fearful mystery. In the absolute silence of the dawn hours, I myself could feel the dark weight of the mountain pressing against me, as if it would mold me into a different form, as though I could actually feel the pressure to evolve. It was unclear to me whether the metamorphosis I needed to make was conceptual, or organic—or both. Joe, stirring in the growing light, murmured about a sense of struggling, night-long, for survival, of willing the heart to keep pumping. "But you didn't say a word all night," I said. "I thought you were asleep."

"I was too busy composing my last will and testament," he said.

It was a slow, stiff-legged descent to Red Hill. At the cabin, which we were glad to find empty, Joe's vitality returned. He persuaded me to climb the red cinder cone with him to watch the sunset. Huge thunderclouds were piled at the summit of Mauna Loa, glowing red-gold like the fires of an eruption. Somehow, the sun setting behind the mountain projected an outline of the mountain in the sky over the eastern sea, like a second horizon. A sense, fleeting, of seeing through a veil; a glimpse of a second world.

If, as Westerners, our understanding labels this volcanic landscape a vestige of primal chaos, then the descent the next day was a journey through the days of Genesis. At 10,000 feet, the first plants: dry, skeletal grasses. At 9,000 feet, one lone *ōhi'a,* stunted from tree to shrub. Then a bird call shattered four days of silence, our kingdom of solitude. We were poised between two worlds: behind us black rock horizon, shining ether; before us, a deepening dense green giving way to distant marine blue. A hint of moisture to the air; our bodies took on heaviness, solidity. At 6,600 feet, rainforest, a garden of green nearly obscuring the sky. Trailhead, parking lot. Orange VW. Weary and sorefooted, Adam and Eve climb inside metal, wheels roll. I thought again of Thomas

Cole's painting of Eden and the Fallen World, of how neatly the painting divided "good" nature from "bad." What would he have done here, with this landscape, where all of nature—the gentle forests, the raw, lunar lava plains, the steaming, sulfurous pits—is the progeny of the volcano?

TWO

"Unstable Was the Land"

A volcano is a contaminated external remnant of intensely buried intrusion along belts of profound rifting.

THOMAS AUGUSTUS JAGGAR
founding director
of Hawaiian Volcano Observatory

From Kahiki came the woman Pele,
from the land of Polapola,
from the rising reddish mist of Kāne,
from clouds blazing in the sky, horizon clouds.

Fragment from a traditional chant

Preceding page: Thomas Jaggar (in foreground) preparing to sound the lava lake at
Halemaʻumaʻu in 1917. Photograph by Horace Johnson. Courtesy of Bishop Museum.

*O*ne of the stories about Thomas Jaggar, founder and first resident volcanologist of the Hawaiian Volcano Observatory, concerns the house he built on the edge of Kīlauea's summit caldera. From the bathroom you could look straight down 200 feet. Jaggar did, indeed, spend his time "staring into a pit," as he was accused of doing by mainland colleagues. "The pit," for several of those years at least, obliged him by erupting.

Kīlauea has been less obliging the last few years. I was visiting the "crisis tower"—a glass-lined cubicle perched atop the new building for the observatory, which is itself perched on the rim of the summit caldera. The observatory, operated by the U.S. Geological Survey (USGS), sits on the highest wall of the crater, overlooking a ledge—a place called Uwē-kahuna, "wailing priest." Tradition tells that a temple to Pele sat here, a gathering place for the priests and prophets of the volcano.

The first Hawaiian Volcano Observatory was built in 1912, two miles east of here. A second, built at this location in the forties, was still in use until a couple of years ago; one could peer in through dusty windows at venerable seismographs, and occasionally glimpse a geologist bent over one of the machines as though reading an augury.

The new building is large, modern, and audaciously close to the rim. The writer John McPhee, here to research his book *The Control of Nature,* commented that it looked like a "votive offering" to Pele, perched on this highest edge of the vast caldera. An offering—or a challenge? Sitting in the "crisis tower" of the new building, I was wondering what relationship the modern scientist developed with this landscape. Did it have anything priestly about it, or was its primary purpose control?

Kīlauea's caldera stretched below me, 360 feet deep at this side, 3 miles long and nearly 2 miles wide, an enormous irregular oval, its floor of solidified lava the color of a well-seasoned iron frying pan. This was the face it showed that day, but I knew that it had changed shape and form dramatically numerous times since first observed by a Westerner. Its large inner crater, Halema'uma'u, was a molten lava lake when the Reverend William Ellis saw it in 1823, but a few years later it collapsed as the summit magma chamber was drained by a flank eruption. Since then lava has filled, then drained many times from Halemaʻumaʻu, at one time leaving a depression over 1,400 feet deep. During the last few years Halemaʻumaʻu has slumbered, while the volcano's lava has found outlets lower down its east rift zone. That day, as I looked down on it from the "crisis tower" in the slanted morning light, the "firepit" resembled a deep, blank eye socket. Plumes of steam drifted up lazily from cracks around its rim.

It promised to be one of those rare brilliant days atop Kīlauea, free from the heavy rain clouds that the trade winds often push up from the east. To the northwest, the huge parabola of Mauna Loa was tinged rose by the early morning sun. Much has been learned from studying where the spheres of activity of these two volcanoes intersect. It has generally been concluded that the two volcanoes have completely separate plumbing systems, though the movements of one may affect the other, since they "lean" against each other. They have erupted at the same time only twice in recorded history. Of the two, Kīlauea has been more frequently active. Kīlauea's eruptions are less voluminous than those of the great "mother mountain," but they can be long-lasting. On that clear morning, though, neither volcano was revealing any of its secrets, at least to the human eye. Mauna Loa slumbered and Kīlauea poured out its lava, as it had now for six years, fifteen miles from the "crisis tower."

During the early days of the observatory, to observe meant essentially to hoof it to the eruption site, no matter how remote: a volcanologist had to be half goat and half foot soldier. Thomas Jaggar once contemplated building an observatory on top of Mauna Loa (it was after the time he spent several days toiling up the volcano to view a summit eruption, only to be forced back down by a snowstorm). But the active work of "taking the pulse of the volcanoes" (as Jaggar called it) has changed greatly since his time. Now helicopters—if weather permits—can provide access to the remotest regions. The entire island is wired with seismometers that transmit their messages to the observatory computers (primarily by radio now, though a few are still attached by miles of wire). Electronic tiltmeters (imagine an extremely sensitive carpenter's level) transmit information about deformation (ground-level changes) at the summits of the volcanoes. (Volcanoes always "inflate" from the pressure of magma accumulating before they erupt. This process can happen over years, and it is so far impossible to determine when a

34

volcano is filled to capacity.) Today it is possible to be on the "lab tech" end of volcanology and spend very little time in the field. But field work has remained a nitty-gritty affair, a career demanding much application of moleskin to the feet and a high tolerance for sulfur.

Even with the volcanoes wired up like patients in an intensive care ward, however, eruptions remain difficult to predict. Christina ("Tina") Neal, a young geologist who was sitting with me in the "crisis tower," told me a story about the 1984 eruption of Mauna Loa.

The eruption on Kīlauea's east rift was then a year old. Geologists, occupied by that volcano's antics, were less inclined to pay attention to Mauna Loa, though it had for some time been showing signs of awakening. Jack Lockwood, a geologist engaged in mapping Mauna Loa's lava flows, predicted in 1976 that the volcano would erupt in the near future, and even outlined the pattern the eruption would take, starting at the summit caldera and then breaking out lower down the northeast rift zone. (The prediction turned out to be accurate but eight years premature.)

By 1983, signs of Mauna Loa's unrest had increased, and Robert Decker, scientist-in-charge at the observatory, joined Lockwood in predicting an eruption. But by then, for the public and for some of the geologists, it had become a bit of a "cry wolf" situation.

On the evening of March 24, 1984, the observatory staff gathered at a nearby military recreation camp to hold a party for Robert Decker, who was retiring in one week. Part of the entertainment was a skit in which Decker and Lockwood were gently roasted for their "alarmist" predictions about Mauna Loa. The seismic alarm, meanwhile, had been turned off for the evening, since high winds were, annoyingly, jiggling it into action. The volcano itself showed no signs of untoward behavior.

The party broke up early, and Robert Decker was home and asleep before 11 P.M. At 10:55, the observatory's instruments recorded increased seismicity (earthquake activity) beneath Mauna Loa. At 11:30, the earthquakes settled into harmonic tremor, the rhythmic pattern that signals magma moving rapidly to the surface.

Night-time phone calls to the Hawaiian Volcano Observatory were routed through the all-night guard at the military camp. Shortly before midnight the guard received a call from an astronomer at the observatory on top of Mauna Kea. Mauna Loa is erupting, the astronomer said. Probably just a forest fire, the guard countered. No one has recorded what the astronomer replied, but I expect he pointed out that forest fires don't run downhill in fiery streams. The guard called Robert Decker. For Decker, it must have been the perfect cap to his retirement.

Tina Neal loves this story, limning as it does the human side of an increasingly technical science. Neal is an impeccably trained geologist, a cautious, sometimes laconic New Englander. She is young enough to have cut her teeth on the revolutionary but highly abstract theories of plate tectonics. Yet she is a completely dedicated field worker, and—something more rare—fascinated by Hawaiian traditions that connect with this land. A few days earlier I had been out with her in the Ka'ū desert, the dry, rugged lava lands of the south flank of Kilauea. Tina was mapping lava flows in the region for a USGS map project. For months she had been attempting to date the flows by their form and appearance, knocking off rock samples and lugging them back to the nearest trailhead for lab analysis. She is short, slight, and apparently limber as a goat. I hefted her pack at the end of the day. Forty pounds?

In the field, Tina works aided by aerial photographs and reconnaissance maps made by earlier geologists. But primarily she looks at the lava flow, at the type and shape of crystals in it, at the weathered, oxidized patina of its surface. She feels the rock. She has been known to taste it. She walks on the lava, and listens to the sound her boots make. Then she sits down, and looks at the flow again, summoning everything she knows about the immediate landscape. (At this point she is as still as someone in a trance.) An approximate date comes to her. She checks it later against lab reports on her rock samples. She checks against the historic record, and more and more often, against Hawaiian oral tradition.

Tina Neal had spent nearly 300 days alone, logging more than 1,000 miles in this wild volcanic "desert." In the intense focus of that time, she had discovered that there are places one can stand where the landscape will suddenly reveal itself, and your sense of place within it will be changed forever. It is a kind of epiphany. *When* that happens will depend on the landscape, on who you are, on what you *think* you know.

It occurred to me, talking to Tina, that such moments in particular places illuminate because they shake us loose from the metaphysical shape that we impose on the world. The history of geology—and of volcanology—is full of such moments. Geology is the story of the world's beginnings, a story that had already been told by theology. A teleological view of the world, a linear progression, earth history instead of earth process, was the shaping vision, until very recently, in the earth sciences.

Geology as a science had to emerge from the swaddling clothes of the creation story told in Genesis, from its beginnings as, essentially, *scriptural* geology. Some of the earliest books to discuss earth history were written in the 1680s by the Reverend Thomas Burnet. Burnet's *Sacred Theory of the Earth: Containing an Account of its Original Creation, and of all the General Changes Which It Hath Undergone, Or Is to Undergo, until the Consummation of All Things,* published in four volumes, offered a timetable for earth history based on the Creation, the Deluge, and the Final Conflagration. By this theory the first two events could be considered responsible for all geographic forms. Water, Burnet argued, underlay the surface of the earth. During the Deluge, the earth cracked like an egg, and these waters were loosed. Earth features such as mountains could be explained as the "hideous ruins" of that cracked crust.

By mid-eighteenth century the scriptural geologists, now dubbed "Neptunists" because of their belief that the earth's terrain was shaped by water, were pitted against those gathering evidence for volcanism as primary agent in shaping the earth. It was the kind of debate, undoubtedly, that could only rage in a part of the world that was not actively volcanic. But now evidence began to accumulate that Europe itself had been shaped by the forces of volcanism—the eroded shapes of ancient volcanoes were clearly visible in parts of Europe, though neither legend nor history offered any record of their activity. This evidence of volcanism was disturbing, but the suggestion of extreme age was more so.

The creation story of Genesis, if taken "literally," suggested a rather short period for earth history—less, perhaps, than 6,000 years. (Some early scholars, calculating back through biblical genealogy, even came up with dates for the completion of the world. For example, the seventeenth-century Irish archbishop James Ussher announced that it was finished at 8 P.M. on Saturday, October 22, 4004 B.C.) But signs of buried history—of stratified deposits, of volcanoes eroded to hills— suggested the earth's shaping was gradual rather than catastrophic. In 1785, James Hutton presented a paper to the Royal Geographic Society of Edinburgh entitled "Theory of the Earth: or an Investigation of the Laws Observable in the Composition, Dissolution and Restoration of Land upon the Globe." Hutton suggested that the composition of metamorphic rock resulted from slow changes wrought by subterranean heat and pressure. Since his theory seemed to contradict the biblical timetable, Hutton was denounced as an infidel. Nevertheless, the "Plutonists," as those favoring the theory of gradual change were now called, were getting harder to ignore. The man who denounced Hutton, the geologist and theologian Richard Kirwan, felt compelled to concede that the light mentioned in the second chapter of Genesis might have come from volcanoes.

The argument against a world formed by catastrophic events, whether acts of God, as described in Genesis, or acts of nature, was advanced further by Hutton's greatest interpreter, Charles Lyell, in his *Principles of Geology* (1830). Lyell, elaborating on Hutton's theories, talked openly of "freeing the science from Moses." He argued for what came to be called "uniformatarianism" (as opposed to "catastrophism")—gradual and continuous change through forces still at work: heat and pressure, erosion, volcanism, and so forth. A world still in the making; a never-to-be-finished creation. It took a strong mind, in an age that believed that the world had been created as a stage for human history, to raise the vision of time as cyclic, as, in Stephen Jay Gould's elegant words, "a stately dance toward nowhere."[1]

James Dwight Dana, the geologist who became the spiritual father of Hawaiian volcanology—one could even argue, of all modern, investigative volcanology—had undoubtedly read Lyell. Dana was the first to do exhaustive firsthand research on a variety of volcanoes, from Vesuvius to Pacific island chains. He sailed into this archipelago's waters in 1840 with the Wilkes expedition. When he reached Hawai'i, he was armed with Darwin's meditations (in his journals from the voyage on the *Beagle,* which had returned to port in 1836) on the formation of coral atolls. Darwin, much influenced by Lyell, had suggested that subsided volcanoes provided the foundations for atolls. Dana, expanding on Darwin's theory and adding his own astute observations of several island chains, skirted close to discovering the vital relationship between the earth's tectonics—the movements of its crust—and volcanism. But to see the underlying process would have taken more than keen observation and application of known geological principles: it would have very nearly required a new cosmogony. Dana was not, like Lyell, a visionary (or a "crank," as Lyell was labeled by many of his colleagues).

Dana was a civilian scientist sailing with the U.S. South Seas Exploring Expedition—the "Ex-Ex," as the press dubbed it. The Navy expedition's project was to explore and chart little-known regions of the Pacific and Indian oceans. When the "Ex-Ex" reached Hawai'i in September 1840, it had already made two journeys into Antarctic waters, explored down the coast of South America and Tierra del Fuego, and visited several island groups in the South Pacific. At the end of two more years at sea, it had surveyed 200 islands and made charts that were still in use as late as World War II.

Lieutenant Charles Wilkes, commander of the expedition, was a punctilious Navy man—a "martinet," in some eyes. Following Navy code, every man, whether civilian or sailor, was required to stick with his ship. The scientists, whom Wilkes called the "naturalists" (as though they were "interchangeable," historian Daniel Appleman suggests), were scattered among the ships. So while Wilkes sailed from Oʻahu to Hawaiʻi for a few months of exploring volcano country, the expedition's geologist was sent off with his ship to finish charting islands in the South Seas! Thus, as Appleman says, "Pickering, the zoologist, would spend two months on the volcanoes of Hawaiʻi while Dana, the geologist, would examine more coral islands and empty ocean."[2]

Luckily, departures from Oʻahu were delayed, and Wilkes allowed Dana and several others to take the expedition's smallest ship, the *Flying Fish,* on a quick visit to Hawaiʻi. Dana spent one day at the summit of Kīlauea.

Before heading for the South Seas, Dana's ship, the *Peacock,* also made a short run to Kauaʻi. Having seen all the main islands, Dana was quick to piece together their different forms, from the youngest volcanoes to the deeply eroded cliffs of Kauaʻi, as a pattern of age progression. He had noticed the same sequence in other island chains, ending dramatically with the coral atolls that (as Darwin had suggested) formed atop the volcanoes that the forces of erosion had worn back down to sea level. Volcanoes in a chain from fully active to long extinct—what could explain this phenomenon? A global system of fracturing, Dana speculated, around a molten earth core that was slowly cooling. Perhaps the shrinking of the earth's crust could explain why, one by one, these volcanoes had become extinct and subsided slowly into the Pacific. Creation, termination. Like most nineteenth-century geologists, Dana believed that earth history marched on through time, measured in terms of a progressively cooling molten earth core. It did not occur to Dana that he was witnessing an ongoing creation.

Although the larger picture eluded Dana, the conchologist of the expedition, J. P. Couthoy, was more daring. In later correspondence, Couthoy suggested to Dana that the islands were "forced up in regular succession by the subterranean fire." Perhaps to a specialist in shells and corals such a vision of islands sprouting in a kind of organic growth from the sea floor was not entirely alien. But Dana persisted in his argument that "from Kauai to Mauna Loa, all may have . . . simultaneously commenced their ejections, and have continued in operation during the same epoch till one after the other became extinct."[3] Any other answer, for a nineteenth-century geologist, would have been a huge metaphoric leap into the unknown. Dana was a traveler in the Pacific, passing through strange waters: a man from a temperate clime, where the rocks were ancient and rather permanent fixtures. He was not prepared for the vision of a continuous transformation that was implied in the successive birth of islands.

Nevertheless, from his brief visit to Kīlauea, Dana did piece together a simple but in many ways remarkably accurate picture of Hawaiian volcanism. It was a fortuitous time to visit Kīlauea: three lava lakes were in continuous eruption within the great caldera.

The summit caldera as I was seeing it that day, from my privileged perch in the "crisis tower," was considerably altered from the crater Dana peered into, on his one-day visit to the volcano. Dana's view would have been by far the more spectacular. The walls at the highest point—here at Uwē-kahuna—would have dropped another 150 feet to a wide shelf that extended around the caldera. The whole inner part of the caldera had collapsed farther—another 300 feet, forming a giant interior pit much deeper and larger than present-day Halemaʻumaʻu. Yet even then Halemaʻumaʻu was the site of the greatest eruptive activity; at that time, it was filled with a large, active lava lake.

Dana had read accounts of the caldera that described a much different scene. The earliest—that of the Reverend William Ellis in 1823—accorded with what Dana saw—a fiery inner pit rimmed by a shallower ledge. But visitors in the 1830s described a caldera filled until the ledge was buried, and a broad dome built where Halemaʻumaʻu would later form. The year before, Dana learned, the interior of the caldera had sunk down once more. It was clear to Dana that the caldera must go through cycles of filling and collapsing. This last collapse had coincided with a huge eruption on Kīlauea's east rift; Dana surmised that the two events were connected. When the zoologist Pickering returned from a trip down the east rift zone, describing its chain of deep craters, obviously also formed by collapse, Dana had already begun to piece together a rudimentary map of Kīlauea's inner plumbing.

Dana was an excellent observer, but hampered by nineteenth-century geologic concepts, with their primary focus on a continental

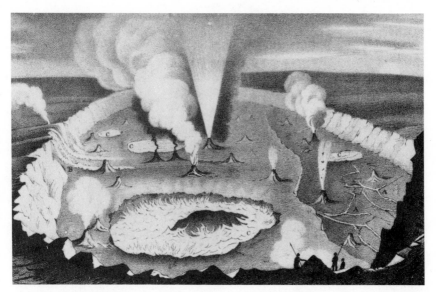

The caldera of Kīlauea as it appeared in 1838, as drawn by R. Bakewell from sketches by captains Parker and Chase. Frontispiece in vol. 40 (1841) of the American Journal of Science. *Courtesy of Hawaiian Volcano Observatory.*

world. For years he and the Reverend Titus Coan had a running debate over lava tubes. Coan, who was no scientist but a keen observer, told Dana that Hawaiian lava flows erupted high on the mountains and flowed long distances through lava tubes. Dana, whose firsthand experience had been mainly on Vesuvius (hitherto the center for volcano observing, where such things were unheard-of), insisted that the flows must emerge from long linear fissures opening down the sides of the volcano. It would have taken only a minute of observation at the right place and time to have changed his mind.

Yet even "scientific" observation is an interpretive act, a way of ordering the world that hinges on concepts, ideas, metaphors. The modern picture of what lies beneath our feet is much more exact, but as in Dana's time it is still an approximate guess—a reduction of an irreducible reality to lines and graphs. Graphs are perhaps a useful way to hold at bay one's visceral response to sitting atop an active volcano. The naked truth, indeed, might be too hard to live with. "You come to realize," Tina Neal said, with a sweep of arm toward the landscape outside the 'crisis tower' windows, "that this is all a highly unstable structure."

Tina showed me a simple schematic cross section of Kīlauea, the basic textbook illustration of a "typical Hawaiian volcano," not much different from Dana's conceptual drawings of 150 years ago. According to the diagram, directly below me about one to three miles deep was a "shallow" chamber of stored magma. Below that a vertical conduit connected like a pump hose to the source of magma, deep (thirty-five to sixty miles) within the earth's upper mantle.

Tina then spread out a more elaborate diagram, which attempted to render Kīlauea's current eruption pattern. It depicted a much less tidy scheme. The primary conduit looped and twisted like some fantasy balloon animal assembled by a mad carnival barker, and the summit magma chamber was a bulbous mass. A kind of elbow joint led from the chamber out into the vast rift zone, to the region where magma now bubbles up into a molten lake at the surface. An inset diagram showed the lava tube system that runs from the lake, in a series of branching capillaries, under the skin of solidified lava seven miles downhill to the sea.

A surface lava flow will move slowly on a gentle slope or on level ground. One can often approach right to the edge of it, which is one reason why Kīlauea is sometimes called "the drive-in volcano." I literally drove in to my first encounter with molten rock, on the southern side of the east rift zone. Here, at that time (early 1988), lava flows from the Pu'u 'Ō'ō eruption had covered hundreds of acres and added more than seventy acres of new land to the island.

Although most of the lava had been flowing through tubes right to the coast, pouring into the sea, the system must have "backed up," in plumbers' terms. A small surface flow had broken out a mile inland, emerging from the lava tubes and cracks of an earlier lava flow, inside the borders of a beleaguered subdivision called Royal Gardens. To reach it from the coast highway, I drove inland on Royal Avenue and turned right on Orchid Avenue. A hundred yards down Orchid, the asphalt disappeared under a glistening and steaming expanse of *pāhoehoe*. I parked the car at a safe distance and walked to the edge of the lava flow. Small, red-hot "toes" of molten rock were oozing slowly out under the hardened crust. Yet "ooze" was not the right word for its motion. In some places, it dripped like thick treacle; in others it stretched elastically, already hardening on the surface, and then ripping open as more molten rock pushed from below. Or it ballooned and spread, amoeba-like, small bits of basaltic glass pinging off its cooling skin. It was solid and liquid, animate and inanimate, at the same time. It was the primal stuff of earth, yet it seemed extraterrestrial. It destroyed in a moment every metaphoric connection I had with stone.

This was a world far removed from the abstractions of science. How, I wondered, did a volcanologist reconcile the two?

I thought of Thomas Jaggar, who was the first scientist to give himself wholeheartedly to this volcano country, to risk a contemplation that went beyond scientific observation. Jaggar's eccentric, impassioned spirit still haunted the observatory—in a real sense, perhaps, since his widow scattered his ashes in Halema'uma'u, Pele's home, in defiance of park regulations. (The ancient Hawaiians cast remains—usually the bones—of deceased relatives into the crater so that they could join a host of Pele's guardian spirits after death.) During the quarter-century that he directed the observatory, Jaggar developed a familiarity with the landscape rivaling that of the husbandman, and in some way more intimate. His intimacy molded him, as love does, from hard-bitten scientist to visionary, waxing dangerously geopoetic about his beloved.

One would not expect it, from the pictures of him. In a 1917 photo he stands in the foreground, knees bent in Neanderthal crouch, holding the end of a 200-foot-long pipe about to be used for the first sounding of a lava lake. Behind him, the firepit of Halema'uma'u, filled to the brim with molten rock, steams and bubbles. Jaggar's face is square-jawed—a bit bull-doggy—under beret pulled backward like a Basque revolutionary. This first pipe emerged from the lake like a length of red-hot noodle, then fused solid to the edge and had to be unscrewed close to the bank, losing the heat-measuring device that was also Jaggar's invention. But other tests revealed molten lava to a depth of 50 feet, confirming his theory that lava "lakes" were "fairly shallow convectional flows over a pasty solidified substance."

Jaggar had earned his doctorate at Harvard with a narrow but unimpeachable dissertation on the "microscopic determination of the hardness of minerals," and embarked on a career of teaching geology.[4] In 1902 he was shaken permanently out of the ivory tower when the double explosion in the West Indies of Mt. Soufrière and, nineteen hours later, Mt. Pelée, killed more than 30,000 people and destroyed the town of St. Pierre. Thirteen days later, Jaggar landed as head of a scientific investigation team, and walked the streets of St. Pierre, where bodies still lay in the rubble, caught in the middle of their daily rounds, as they lay in the ruins of Pompeii. He took away from there the unforgettable memories that led to his adoption of the motto *Ne plus haustae aut obrutae urbes*—"No more shall the cities be destroyed." It became, and is still, the motto of the Hawaiian Volcano Observatory.

His experience in the field in the West Indies, where members of the scientific team, latecomers to the action, tried to piece together events leading up to the cataclysm, convinced him of the need for an on-site observatory in the Americas (the only other observatory in existence had been established on Vesuvius in 1847). As Jaggar liked to put it, "The only way to know a crater is to live with it." A visit to Kīlauea in 1909 convinced Jaggar that here he had found the most inhabitable volcano in the world.

In 1912 Jaggar began his long vigil at the newly built observatory. Both Kīlauea and Mauna Loa obliged him with a period of unusual activity for the next two decades. Jaggar, often the sole scientist at the observatory, and always its chief fundraiser, was an extremely busy man. He didn't mind, for by then he had become possessed, heart and soul, by volcano country. This man, formed in the mode of turn-of-the-century science, firm believer in humanity's inherent right to dominate nature, had fallen in love with the land.

Nothing, perhaps, better reveals the anomalies of Jaggar's character—the peculiar amalgam of scientist and visionary, of romantic and warrior—than the rhetoric with which he announced his invention of the science (or sport?) of bombing eruptions. He did so in 1935, when a lava flow from the top of Mauna Loa had been creeping for weeks— inexorably, it seemed, toward the town of Hilo. Jaggar, the same man who a decade earlier had rhapsodized in a poem about "Mauna Loa, bosom round and brown / Of the vast fire-goddess" from which poured "heavenly fluid," now wrote, "Mauna Loa has definitely mobilized and declared war; there is every appeal for an intellectual and practical victory over Nature.[5] Under his direction, the army obligingly dropped twenty 600-pound TNT bombs at the erupting vent, halfway down the side of Mauna Loa, and at the forefront of the lava flow.

The bombs broke open the lava tube system that was the main conduit for the flow threatening Hilo. Lava poured out on the surface, where it moved more slowly, and ceased flowing altogether a few weeks later.

Would it have ceased anyway, in the volcano's own good time? If Jaggar thought so, he never admitted it, pronouncing the "attack" a "huge success." But by then, the precarious financial position of the observatory during the Depression had combined with his own penchant for melodrama to make him the P. T. Barnum of volcanoes. Witness the following, from his 1931 National Public Radio broadcast, "the world's first broadcast of a live volcano":

> A thousand people at the active crater Kilauea in Hawaii are standing
> here, at the edge of a vast circular pit three-quarters of a mile across.
> The line of motionless white faces, all turned towards the setting sun,
> is like a concourse of fire worshippers. . . . And now, listen to the Fire-
> Goddess Pele herself in the throes of her birthpangs.[6]

This is sales talk, but in terms of Jaggar's personal beliefs is probably less hyperbolic than it sounds. Even hard scientists work partly from descriptive analogy to the body—lava tongues and toes, veins, throats. But Jaggar's long life with the volcano, mapping its body, charting every mood, led him to take the irreversible step toward visionary. He speculated that volcanic gases may have released the elements that were the primal building blocks of creation, that life itself may have sprung from a volcanic womb. He suggested that evidence of volcanic activity would be found throughout the solar system, that it could be an integral part of the formation of worlds. He tried to correlate seasons and tides with the "pulse" of the volcano, revealed in fluctuations of the active lava lake or in the timing of eruptions. (Studies of the last decade suggest some truth in all these "wild" hypotheses.)

It was only a step further, in geo-poetics, from volcanic tides and exhalations to analogies with animal circulation and breathing. Several years before plate tectonics theory made respectable a cyclic vision of earth process, Jaggar speculated on the grand design that would tie together earthquakes and volcanoes, tides and solar-lunar rhythms, revealing the mystery of the planet's living, breathing heart. Scientific theory has just begun to validate what Jaggar's senses, attuned to the heartbeat of volcano country, already knew.

In several of the geologists I met in volcano country—in those who had developed a deep love for the region—I sensed the same schism one found in Jaggar between the scientific and personal response to the land. It was as though they yearned for a language that could express their visceral experience of the land's power, its *presence.* Much of that sense of a compelling power in the land came from the ghostly presence of the old Hawaiian culture, which one encountered everywhere—walls, petroglyphs, arrangements of stones—in the wildest corners of volcano country. Several scientists had begun to study Hawaiian chant and myth, expressing the same fascination and frustration I felt as I progressed from the simple retellings of legends to the ancient chants, with their beautiful, perhaps ultimately impenetrable, metaphors.

The old Hawaiians said, "The gods are forty, four hundred, four thousand, forty thousand, four hundred thousand." The saying could well serve as a poetic tribute to a land of constant transformation. Hawaiian myths of the islands' origins, a rich interweaving of Polynesian myths and the myths this new land itself inspired, tell of the matings and struggles of gods that embody all the elements of nature. Of islands laid like eggs by titanic bird gods. Of islands dragged, by demigods, with fishhooks from below the sea. Of islands growing like trees from the sea floor, budding richly into the air. "Unstable was the land," says an old chant. "Tremulous was Hawai'i. Waving freely in the air, waved the earth."[7]

The Polynesian seafarers who settled the Hawaiian Islands brought their own gods with them, and discovered new gods in a new land. The earliest groups, anthropologists think, came from the Marquesas (around A.D. 300 to 500); later groups may have arrived from other parts of Polynesia—most likely the Society Islands (which include Tahiti) and Samoa. Each group may have brought their own local deities as well as those worshiped throughout Polynesia. Out of this rich stew, and the encounter with the powers of a new land, arose a mythology that became, over time, distinctively Hawaiian.

It will probably never be possible to sort out by whom and in what order the Hawaiian gods were worshiped; Hawaiian traditions give no clear picture, and there may indeed have been little consensus. Some legends indicate that certain gods "arrived" in the islands later than others, but perhaps this indicates when the cult of that god gained power (Pele, for example, is a "late" arrival). The Hawaiians appear to have actively worshiped the gods whose powers they encountered most directly, so that a fisherman would make offerings to a different set of gods from those worshiped by a midwife.

Certain "major" gods, those who had roots deep in Polynesia, may have been universally recognized, if not actively worshiped. These probably included, in one or another of their many aspects, Kū and Hina, male and female gods representing the generative forces of nature. Other pan-Polynesian gods that seem to have been worshiped universally include Lono, god of rain-making fertility and agriculture; Kāne, associated with male procreative energy; and Kanaloa, often paired with Kāne, but particularly associated with the sea, the West, and death. The pan-Polynesian female gods seem to be mostly attributes of Hina, associated primarily with reproduction, childbirth, and the life-bearing powers of the earth.

For the migrant Polynesians who settled this active volcanic landscape, the land must have expressed itself most forcefully through the divine presence of Pele and her "family," as many ancient chants suggest:

> The stars, the moon are on fire;
> The cold months burn;
> Dust circles on the island, the land is parched.
> The sky hangs low, rough seas in the pit—
> The ocean tosses; lava surges in Kilauea.
> Waves of fire cover the plain;
> Pele erupts.[8]

The Pele family had roots in other parts of Polynesia, but as minor deities; only in Hawai'i were they born fully as spirits of the land.

The Polynesian genealogy of Pele is obscure. A god or goddess named Pere is mentioned in legends from Samoa, the Tuamotus, and the Tongan islands. In Tongan tradition, Pere is the daughter of Mau-ike, the god of fire. Legends of the Maori of New Zealand refer to Pare-whenua-mea, translated by one anthropologist as "the effacement of nature due to flood." In Maori legend, this deity is the mother of the Pacific Ocean. The name closely resembles Pele-honua-mea, "Pele of the sacred earth," a name that recurs in Hawaiian chants that tell of Pele's coming to Hawai'i.[9]

In Hawaiian legend Pele is associated with the pan-Polynesian deity Hina, and also with Papa ("earth") and Haumea, who may be aspects of the same goddess. Hina is associated with the birth of islands, and with the worship of the moon and of fire, which are linked aspects, according to anthropologist Martha Beckwith, of female fertility. Haumea is goddess of fertility, or as Beckwith describes her, "the spiritual essence of that ageless womb out of which life is produced in changing forms." The semidivine ancestors of the Hawaiian people are said to be born from different parts of her body. Pele, by tradition, was born from her thighs, as befitting the goddess of the most awesome form of generative fire.

There are many versions of Pele's coming to the Islands. Generally they agree that she was driven from her ancestral home by gods who were jealous of her power. In some legends the primary battle was with her sister Nā-maka-o Kaha'i, a sea goddess. This antithesis of fire and water is found in many legends, but it is never clear-cut. Powers overlap, as indeed they do in nature: Pele was, for example, accompanied on her journey by her brother Ka-moho-aliʻi, variously described as god of steam or vapor, a sea god, god of sharks.

In several traditional accounts, Pele came to Hawaiʻi from Kahiki, a name that can mean either Tahiti or simply "foreign land." She was accompanied on her travels by Laka, the deity of the sacred dance, or *hula*.

According to myth, Pele's sailing journey landed her among the northwestern atolls. Her travels southeast from there recreated the volcanic history of the island chain. The various versions of the Pele story name over a hundred places that Pele "visited" as she traveled down the archipelago, all of them volcanic formations—craters, cinder cones, mountains. The path she took parallels nearly exactly the actual age progression of volcanism from site to site through the Islands. Since most of the volcanic events thus documented would have taken place before the arrival of the first immigrants, the Hawaiians appear to have had an astonishingly adept eye for recognizing the subtle changes that signal age in volcanic formations.

Pele, with her kin, traveled from island to island, digging with her digging stick to create herself a home. At each place her nemesis, the sea goddess, caused the sea to burst in and flood Pele's work. At Haleakalā volcano on the island of Maui, the battle was so violent that Pele's body was dismembered, the bones strewn at a place called Ka-iwi-o-Pele ("the bones of Pele"). Although she left her body, she continued in spirit form to the island of Hawaiʻi, digging in several places. At Kīlauea volcano, she was able to build a home strong enough to withstand the onslaughts of her sister the sea goddess. Here she and her family set up permanent housekeeping, with occasional visits to the top of Mauna Loa. Her digging staff, planted in the earth on the east side of Kīlauea, grew into a huge forest.

Like the simplified retelling of Pele's search for a "home," modern versions tend to emphasize her "human" side. But to the Hawaiians the gods were shape-shifting, fluid, assuming at will different forms, called *kinolau* ("many bodies," or "many manifestations"). Traditionally, Pele's *kinolau*—her various manifestations—are as myriad as all the forms of nature touched by volcanism. Her large "family" are both divine beings and aspects of the volcanic world. Even more confusing, from the Western point of view, is Pele's status as both god (*akua*) and ancestral deity (*'aumakua*). All kinship groups claimed actual descent from an *'aumakua,* and treated the various forms and attributes of their ancestral deity with the utmost respect. Like the worship of all *'aumakua,* Pele worship was strongest in her domain, intimately linked with a sense of her presence here in volcano country.

I was discovering, as I read Hawaiian mythology, that positioning Pele within a pantheon was impossible. Like all the Hawaiian deities, she moved in a world that shaded imperceptibly from natural to supernatural, from good to evil, from male to female. Westerners had responded to Hawaiian myth by trying to limit this "primitive confusion," to reshape the myths into an acceptable form—in the case of Pele's journey, into a tidy little odyssey. To even glimpse the early mythic vision of the land, it was becoming clear that one would have to dig through assumptions, biases, and mistranslations; one would have to chart first the geography of that other world that Western vision had imposed on the land.

THREE

The Lava Lake

Ah, boil up, ye vapours!
Leap and roar, thou sea of fire!
My soul glows to meet you.

MATTHEW ARNOLD
"Empedocles on Etna"

. . . a fiery deluge, fed
With ever-burning sulfur unconsumed:
Such place Eternal Justice had prepared
For those rebellious . . .

JOHN MILTON
"Paradise Lost"

Preceding page: A view, looking southward, of the lava lake of the Pu'u ʻŌ'ō eruption in 1988. The lake at this time was about 400 feet across its widest dimension. Venting steam and fumes reveal the direction of the main lava tube draining the lake. Photograph by J. D. Griggs—U.S. Geological Survey.

*O*f all volcanic phenomena, the "fiery lake" has most haunted the Western imagination. It is the "sea of fire" into which the ancient Greek philosopher Empedocles, disillusioned with human nature, is said to have leaped; it is the "inflamed sea" that Milton's Satan rules over. In Western tradition, you could guarantee yourself a trip to the fiery lake by signing a pact with the devil. In Hawaiian volcano country, you signed a waiver that released the U.S. government from liability for your injury or death, and you found geologists who were willing to let you tag along when they went in to monitor the lake's activity. I went along on a "routine" visit with Dick Moore, a geologist at the observatory, and Zoe Jacobi, who took weekly samples from the lava lake for the University of Hawai'i.

The lava lake formed by Kīlauea's current long-lived eruption was located at an altitude of 2,000 feet on Kīlauea's east rift zone. One could approach it from the southeast end of the island, near the village of Kalapana, through Black Sands subdivision, which ran up the southern slope. Like several other ill-planned speculative subdivisions built on the east side of the island in the 1960s, Black Sands was still mostly unpopulated, with the usual decaying roads. Above the subdivision the road led through locked gates into private land, whose owners made a short-lived attempt at wood-chipping rainforest for sale to a local electricity-generating plant. (Local citizens managed to halt this destruction of what is part of the only remaining lowland rainforest in Hawai'i.) The land was clear-cut and piled with slash, the scarred areas filling in with nonnative weeds.

The route exited abruptly from rainforest at the edge of the vast lava fields created since 1983 by the Pu'u 'Ō'ō eruption. From here a road was bulldozed across a stretch of *a'ā*. Bulldozing had leveled the larger hunks of the clinkery rock, but the effect was still like driving across the top of an enormous landslide. Dick Moore slowed down very slightly. I was wedged into the cab of a Datsun pickup between him and Zoe Jacobi. Zoe had a canvas sack to put her lava sample in after it cooled. She was wearing a fireproof shirt, and she carried in her pack heavy leather gloves and gas masks for the three of us, in case the wind shifted and blew the lake's sulfurous fumes in our direction.

From where we left the truck, it was a gentle three-mile climb up the broad spine of the rift zone to the lava lake. A thick belt of 'ōhi'a forest stretched behind us, but ahead we saw nothing but undulating lava, a world shaded from gunmetal gray to black. Steam and rain clouds shut out the horizon in the direction we were walking. Occasionally the clouds lifted to reveal the cinder-and-spatter cone that had built up over the Pu'u 'Ō'ō vent, two miles beyond the lake, a cone 900 feet high, releasing a great plume of steam. The effect was so theatrically ominous that the scene felt not quite real. Or perhaps the senses just refused to accept that this was not a stage set from which I could easily exit.

The *pāhoehoe* near the lava lake originally flowed in very hot fluid sheets, congealing into a thin, shelly surface that was nervewracking to walk on. Every few feet we broke through the crust, sinking several inches. Somewhere between here and the lake, we would be crossing over the lava tubes that carry molten rock down to the coast. "You can usually tell where they are from the heat and steam," Zoe said, "but there's no way to gauge how thick their roofs are." These snippets of information from Zoe were not helping my blood pressure. I thought of the geologist last year who stepped through a patch of thin crust into a molten lava stream, and escaped with severe burns to his legs. His charred and half-melted boots were on display at the observatory museum.

On January 3, 1983, what came to be known as "the Pu'u 'Ō'ō eruption" began. For several months before then, tiltmeters had indicated that the summit and east rift zone of Kīlauea were inflating. On the day before the eruption, harmonic tremor registered on the seismometers, affirming that lava was moving underground. Kīlauea's summit began to deflate as magma drained out of the summit magma chamber and into the east rift zone. The eruption burst out at the 3,000-foot level, near a huge, ancient crater named Nāpau. Over the next few weeks, fissures and vents opened downrift from Nāpau, covering a distance of nearly five miles, forming at times a long chain of fountaining fire. After considerable shifting about, the fiery energy centered at one vent and began to build itself a mountain.

Tina Neal had told me that she was taken off a mapping project to help monitor the eruption in June 1983. When Neal was first set down by helicopter next to the growing cone, Pu'u 'Ō'ō was only about 50 feet high. A year later, the vent had spewed enough cinder and spatter to build another 850 feet of cone.

The interior of Puʻu ʻŌʻō was a bowl-shaped crater above a hollow "throat" that served as a vertical conduit for magma collecting under the rift zone. Episodically, magma rose and pooled in the crater. If the pressure was great enough, spectacular plumes of molten rock and cinder blew out the top of the cone. In repose, the pond sank way down inside the vent; then it would begin to rise again. The quiet periods averaged 26 days. For a while it seemed to have a monthly cycle, and resurrected scientific interest in the effects of lunar cycles and tides on volcanism. When the pond overflowed the rim, lava flows moved, in broad, creeping sheets or narrow, channeled rivers of *pāhoehoe,* or in clinkery, crashing masses of *aʻā,* downhill. Some of these flows entered the subdivisions below.

Tina Neal found herself spending days and nights near the cone. The USGS crew set up a series of base camps, which they had to move seven times to avoid lava flows. "In the beginning," Tina told me, "I couldn't believe it possible to work so close to an eruption without getting hurt. It went against all my instincts to walk on rock that was still glowing a few inches below the surface. But eventually you learn that it's okay, if you're cautious. You get so you can even sleep out there."

By 1986 Puʻu ʻŌʻō reigned over the east rift, like a miniature, unsymmetrical Mt. Fuji. The vent still fountained at eerily regular intervals, sounding, said its closest neighbors, "like a gigantic rice-cooker," showering homes near the east rift zone with ash and the spun-gold filaments of basaltic glass called "Pele's hair." The fountaining was now higher than it had been in the early episodes, and geologists guessed that the feeder conduit from Kīlauea's summit magma chamber had broadened and was furnishing magma to the rift zone at a faster rate.

In July 1986, the eruption pattern changed dramatically once again. Ground fissures opened uprift and downrift of Puʻu ʻŌʻō. After a period of fountaining, the eruption centered at a new locale two miles downrift from the great cone. The crew set up Camp 8 on an ancient, eroded cinder cone nearby. The new vent (later named by a local Hawaiian elder *Kūpaianaha,* "strange" or "marvelous") developed a lava lake under which magma welled up steadily, overflowing the banks and building the land up in a broad dome. Watching how successive layers of lava flow shaped the land around the lake was like seeing, in miniature and in time lapse, the play of forces that built the great volcanoes of the island.

By 1987, lava flows found their way down to the coast. The flows, channeling into narrow rivers, built their own subterranean network as the surface cooled on the lava rivers, insulating the lava that flowed underneath. Within a few months, a tube system had developed that was a steady conduit of lava to the ocean, nearly eight miles away. Occasionally something—an earthquake, collapsing roofs, slowly congealing lava—would obstruct the plumbing of the tube system, and the lake would back up like a toilet bowl, spilling over the top and sending out surface flows. The day we were visiting the lava lake, it turned out, was one of those occasions.

Dick and Zoe and I were approaching the lava lake up a gentle rise, moving toward the trailing plume of gas and steam that signaled its presence. We reached the ancient cinder cone and the blue-tarpaulined hut of the base camp. The cinder cone was now a tiny island of singed rainforest in the midst of a sea of lava, and the green vegetation seemed to glow with a feverish intensity against its gray-black surroundings. Zoe Jacobi retrieved a shovel from under the blue plastic. We picked our way cautiously up the domed slope toward the lava lake, over ground that was now steaming in many places. I reached down and touched the rock. It was about the temperature of the walls of a good sauna.

Scrambling over lava crumpled and heaped in thin jagged slabs, we came to what appeared to be the ragged outer lip of a giant bowl. Dick Moore clambered to the edge, and said, "Whoops—look fast. It's nearly at overflow." I staggered up next to him and peered over. I was nearly eye level with surging molten rock. It was the most unnerving sight I'd ever seen.

Every cell in my body jumped to alarm level. My knees wanted to buckle but the realization that my shoes were near-melting kept me upright. "Run to the sea; sea, won't you hide me? / The Lord said, 'Sinner man, the sea will be a'boilin.' . . . " There was, in fact, no way you could run over the thin, shelly lava.

The heat pushed against me like a solid wall. The "lake" was a stretch of 150 feet or so of gray-skinned lava that was being split and rent apart by the force of magma from below. Red waves of molten rock seethed up and crested over the cooled skin of the surface. Large rafting pieces of the crust tilted upward and were sucked below. At the edges of the drowning crusts, lava boiled up in red gouts. A dizzying shift from solid to liquid, liquid to solid. I had expected a sight resembling perhaps a gently frothing tomato sauce in an iron skillet. Nothing in my experience had prepared me for this uncanny motion. It was like looking into a wound in the earth that revealed the pulse of some deep vital organ.

Lava was already spilling over the lip to the left of us. We moved back about fifty yards and watched its slow creep down the gentle decline. Zoe prepared to take a sample from the approaching flow, buttoning up to the neck her canary-yellow firefighter's shirt. Dick Moore, in sublime disregard of the sulfur fumes eddying about us, lit up a cigarette. Zoe walked to the front of the flow, averting her face from the heat, and pushed the shovel into a creeping toe of glowing molten rock. She returned with a shovelful, already cooling to black.

We waited for the lava to cool enough to put in the canvas bag, eating our lunch standing up, since the rock was too hot to sit on. We shifted our feet as the heat came through our soles. "That was much easier than it usually is to get a sample," Zoe remarked. Normally the surface of the lake was several yards below the rim, which meant that Zoe must stand at the edge and cast out a piece of pipe attached to a cable, aiming for one of the molten waves that pushed the cooled "skin" apart. If the pipe landed on one of the rafting sections of crust, she had to haul it in and cast again. Sometimes it would hit the molten rock and be sucked down so hard that she had to let go of the cable or risk being pulled in. "It's like Pele on the other end, pulling," said Zoe. "I don't argue—I just let her take it."

On the way back, we came across a sulfurous, steaming vent. We walked carefully around it, then back to the edge of it. Not till I peered in did I realize what we must have just crossed. The vent was the broken roof of a lava tube—a skylight into a molten river of fire. With Zoe holding onto my belt, I leaned over the edge. Ten feet down within the tube, so hot it was the yellow-white of a blast furnace, lava was flowing like a river, at several miles per hour. You could see the ripples on the surface. But it made none of the noises of fast-moving water— only the slightest hint of a low, metallic hiss. One glimpse was enough to send me backing up hurriedly, nearly knocking down Zoe, fervently wishing a helicopter would materialize and pluck me off that treacherous ground. "Which way does this tube run, for God's sake—are we still standing on it?" I asked Dick, who was smoking another cigarette. He smiled, flipped the cigarette over the edge of the skylight, and shouldered his pack again.

In an hour we were back at the pickup, thirstily drinking beer, while Zoe tagged the rock sample. At the lab, petrochemical analysis would reveal whether the source of the molten rock had shifted in any way, or whether it was still being drawn, as it had for months now, from the main summit chamber under Kīlauea. Routine work. On the way home, Zoe talked about the problems her children were having in the local public school system.

By dusk I was home in my house in the rainforest, ten miles from the lava lake, as the 'alalā—the Hawaiian crow—flies (or might, were it not very near extinction). Impressions of the lava lake rioted through the tissues of my body for the next two days: the soles of my feet felt the heat; my retinas projected after-images of incandescent rock. My mind, meanwhile, pushed the experience into a back chamber while searching for the language to contain it.

I went back to the lava lake several months later with John Kjargaard, who makes videos for the observatory and for his own educational films. This time the lake had sunk down about four yards below the rim. We could stand on the edge for as long as we could take the heat, and watch its motion. The sight was awesome, but I felt little of the sheer "animal" fear of the first visit. Primed by my readings in geological theory, I studied the lake as a miniature lesson in plate tectonics. I watched as molten rock boiled up, crusted over and rafted across the surface, and was subsumed again. With my newly educated perspective, I wondered why Thomas Jaggar had not run from his viewpoint at the edge of the fiery lake in Halema'uma'u, shouting, "*Eureka!* Continental drift!"

The initial pieces of the theory that has revolutionized our understanding of earth processes had been fitted together in Jaggar's time. (Actually, as far back as 1620 Francis Bacon had suggested that the continents of South America and Africa had once been united, but it was three more centuries before anyone seriously discussed the idea.) In 1912 a German meteorologist named Alfred Wegener published a work on what he called *continental drift*. But like most scientists of his time, he thought of the earth as a thick crust over a molten core. Such a crust could, conceivably, develop huge fractures as the earth's core cooled. But Wegener was at a loss to explain by what mechanism this thick crust could move.

In 1928, British geologist Arthur Holmes suggested that the driving mechanism for movement of the earth's crust could be convection within the mantle. Perhaps he got his inspiration while pouring cold milk into his hot tea and watching the swirl as the cold liquid sank and the hot liquid rose to the top. Still, it was hard to picture this process on the global scale. Geologists knew the crust beneath continents was thick; they assumed ocean floor was the same. The idea of large pieces of the earth drifting about was perhaps too vertiginous for even a scientist to embrace. Thomas Jaggar, in a late semiautobiographical book called *My Experiments with Volcanoes* (published in 1956), countered the various rumblings about continental drift with a diagram of the earth encased in an "armorplate" of "sixteen volcanic partitions."[1] Some of these "partitions" might be pushed up to form continents (and others covered by ocean), but they certainly weren't drifting anywhere. The "faults" between these great blocks of crust might reach as deep as the molten interior of the earth, providing the conduit for volcanism. This diagram, he admitted, had its problems. Jaggar suggested that to begin to unravel the mystery, we would have to know what lay on the bottom of the sea floor. He was right, but until the 1950s there was no way to find out.

One technological bonus of World War II was the development of sonar instruments that could map the sea floor. Scientists were startled by what they found. Strewn along the Pacific sea floor, in chains trending west-northwest, were what appeared to be volcanoes. Some were gumdrop-shaped. Scientists named them *seamounts,* and decided they were either young volcanoes or volcanoes that had become extinct without ever reaching the sea surface. Other shapes, which were given the name *guyots,* appeared to have their heads lopped off by what could only have been erosion. Sonar exploration also located deep ocean trenches and high submarine ridges. Sometimes seamounts, guyots, and islands were studded along these ridges.

The deep ocean trenches, it was discovered, lay off the coasts of some continents, parallel to the coastline. Scientists had known for some time that these areas were unusually seismically active, and often sported active volcanoes in parallel belts landward of the trenches. Seismic studies of the newly discovered submarine ridges, which ran like enormous spines along the mid-ocean floor, revealed that they were also powerful generators of earthquakes. The new technology of deep-sea dredging revealed yet another mystery: no sea floor rock could be found that was older than 200 million years. On a planet that is 4,600 million years old, this is not "deep time." Where had all the older stuff disappeared to?

In 1960 a U.S. geologist named Harry Hess, synthesizing the discoveries of the previous decade, made some startling speculations in an article entitled "The History of Ocean Basins."[2] Taking off from Holmes's theory about convection as a driving tectonic force, Hess proposed that oceanic crust develops through "sea-floor spreading." According to Hess's theory, magma rises along mid-ocean ridges and spreads to each side, continuously creating new "crust." The new crust is simply the most recently emerged edge of a plate.

The collision points of two plates form the deep ocean trenches, where one plate is forced under another. The leading edge of the "subducting" plate, diving deep into the mantle, melts and recirculates molten material to complete, eventually, a 300- to 400-million-year-old convection loop: the ultimate recycle. The surface life of any oceanic rock was, therefore (in geological terms) a short one, though it would eventually be reborn. "The earth is a dynamic body with its surface constantly changing," Hess wrote. His theory intrigued many geologists, but there was little solid evidence, as yet, to support it. Hess himself called it "an essay of geopoetry."

Support for Hess's theory came soon after, however, in a surprising discovery. Scientists had already found above-ground evidence that the earth's magnetic poles reverse themselves about once every 100,000 years. They had been able to "read" the many times this reversal had occurred by studying the magnetic orientation of continental rocks. Now magnetometers, dragged across the sea floor near the Mid-Atlantic ridge, revealed that to each side of the rift (or what Hess had called the "spreading center") the crust was magnetized in strips of ocean bottom miles wide that lay parallel to the rift. Each side of the rift, in other words, was magnetically a mirror image of the other.

In 1963, geoscientists Drummond Matthews and Fred Vine published a paper in the prestigious British journal *Nature,* using the width of these magnetized strips of ocean crust to calculate the rate at which sea floor was spreading apart along mid-ocean ridges. At a rate of creep of several centimeters per year over approximately 100,000 years, each strip did indeed fit into the time scale for magnetic reversals. Their theory was corroborated with evidence from deep-sea dredging done in the late 1960s along the Mid-Atlantic ridge. The age of each rock sample was discovered to be proportional to the distance it had lain from the mid-ocean ridge. Age had left a personal signature on the bottom of the ocean floor, as clearly as it does in tree rings.

Iceland, which sits astride the Mid-Atlantic ridge, is one of the rare examples of "sea floor spreading" that extends above the sea surface. Iceland is splitting through its middle, with the two parts moving away from each other at the rate of about 0.2 inches a year. The parts are the newborn edges of plates. The North American plate moves northwest from the Mid-Atlantic ridge; its mirror image, the Eurasian plate, moves southeast.[3]

Plate tectonics offered, then, a way to explain the two dominant forms of volcanism—continental volcanism and volcanism along midocean ridges. But what did one do with volcanic chains, such as the Hawaiian archipelago, that emerged in the middle of a plate?

J. Tuzo Wilson was one of the first scientists to tackle the "problem" of mid-plate volcanism. In the 1970s Wilson advanced the theory that a thermal plume from deep in the mantle, a "hot spot," piercing through the Pacific plate, produced the Hawaiian chain. Since the "hot spot" was stationary and the ocean crust drifted over it, the magma it produced would spawn a chain of volcanic mountains. Here at last was an explanation for the successive ages of the islands, for each island, Wilson proposed, was being carried off on the Pacific plate. Tectonics is a slow way to travel, but at least one needn't worry about lost baggage: sitting here at the same desk in the same house I occupied a year ago, I have actually moved over three inches farther northwest.

The graphs of Tuzo Wilson's vision of "hot spots" and plate movement are deceptively simple: a series of volcanic islands, gumdrop-shaped, drift away from the hot spot, losing their fire, sinking into the sea. The "active" gumdrop—the one sitting over the hot spot—has a pipe underneath extending down into the molten regions of the earth's mantle, and smoke coming out of its top. The one northwest of it is no longer linked to the fiery source, so it is smokeless. The next, even farther northwest, has lost its top, presumably due to erosion, and is sinking into the sea. The next one is totally submerged . . . and so on.

This depiction accords, thus far, with the idea that the conduit for the molten rock, or the "thermal plume," as Wilson named it, "pinches off" as volcanoes are carried away from the hot spot. But several Hawaiian volcanoes have gone through periods of "rejuvenated" volcanism several tens of thousands of years after their principal period of activity. Honolulu's famous Diamond Head, for example, is the remnant of a large cone built by explosive eruption during a rejuvenated period—an event that took place long after the main volcanoes that built the island of O'ahu had eroded and partly slid into the sea.

That the volcanoes of these islands could spring back to life long after they were considered extinct would not be so uncomfortable a truth if they became active again in a predictable pattern. But geologists soon discovered that the islands of Ni'ihau, O'ahu, and Kaua'i had all experienced at least one after-wave of volcanism. One such period of rejuvenated activity was fairly contemporaneous among all three islands, though they are spread out over a distance of over two hundred miles.

Most startling has been a very recent discovery—one that may shed light on an incident that continues to puzzle geologists. In 1956 the radio crew of a ship sailing through the northwestern end of the main island chain, between O'ahu and Kaua'i, had reported a "disturbance" on the ocean surface. The sailors had found themselves in a large patch of yellow-brown water, in which two dead whales floated, along with fragments of what looked like pumice. The ocean gave off a sulfurous smell.

No convincing explanation for the episode had emerged until 1988, when an ongoing project to map the sea floor around the Hawaiian Islands with sonar scanners yielded some unexpected images of this region. Between O'ahu and Kaua'i, oceanographers found evidence of at least three lava flows several miles long. Since the rock was highly reflective (which suggests it was not covered with mud and other sea floor sediments), it probably emerged from very recent eruptions. The "surface disturbance" of 1956 turned out to be the visible sign of a much deeper mystery.

How can volcanism recur in areas that have drifted far away from the "hot spot"? One theory is that each volcano carries off with it a residual chamber of magma. Geologists call this hypothetical chamber a *diapir*. Although pinched off from the main conduit, the magma in it would still be, shall we say, "disposable." Something in the volcano's ride northwest, then—perhaps some feature of the terrain over which it rides—could exert enough pressure to reactivate this residual supply of magma.

Other theories suggest that the "hot spot" itself may involve a continuous fracturing of the oceanic crust, caused by the stresses of plate movement over the surface of an imperfectly spherical earth (a friend of mine who is not a geologist calls this the "cowlick theory"). No theory has as yet fully explained the unusual thermal activity except

"Eruption of Etna," engraving by Athanasius Kircher, in Mundus Subterraneus, *1664–1665. Courtesy of Library of Congress.*

to suggest a complex interweaving of enormous forces: convection currents in the mantle, movement of the plate, even rhythms powered by the earth's rotation or by lunar or solar (even galactic?) influences.

The term "hot spot" is still used by geologists, because it functions as a useful metaphor for rudimentary understanding of something that remains essentially mysterious. But in the hours I stood at the rim of the lava lake, while John Kjargaard videotaped its continuous transformation— solid to liquid, dissolving and coagulating—it came to my mind that "hot spot" was a metaphor that carried the freight of a certain consciousness: abstract, mechanistic, linear. The term was the essence of scientific language, but here, witnessing the incredible *life,* the generative power of the earth, it seemed particularly impoverished.

I had learned from some very casual reading that "the new physics" was coining a new language that was replacing the mechanistic vision of Newtonian science with an organic, fluid view of the universe, a vision of "sensitive chaos." I wondered if the new language would allow us to reach back and recover an old one, the language of a mythic vision that existed still, in fragments (or in the occasional arcane meaning of a word). For it seemed important to reconnect the outer geography of the universe with an inner geography, to reassess the ways in which we connected to the world.

One of the systems of thought out of which Western science grew was alchemy, which thrived in Europe from the Middle Ages through the Renaissance, before the rise of Newtonian science. Alchemy was the final flowering of a mythic premodern consciousness that still viewed the earth as alive, as the great mother of all beings, whom the Greeks had called Gaia. The alchemists considered the inner earth, the *mundus subterraneus,* as the great womb of life, where the divine spirit married with matter, engendering fire. "Minerals are engendering themselves," wrote one alchemist, "stones grow . . . a generative power insinuates itself into the hardest rock."[4]

In their laboratories, alchemists attempted to recreate and abet the generative forces of the earth, in a process they envisioned as a kind of spiritual midwifery. They experimented with dissolving ore, reducing it to a primal state, *materia prima,* marrying it to other elements to produce a new, transmuted form. The distilling and refining took place within uterine glass vessels called *alembics,* shaped much like the magma conduit and chamber of a volcano. The alchemists apparently made no separation between natural and supernatural, between the work in the lab and their sense of being involved in a religious rite. The dissolution and transmutation of matter was the same process as the transformation of the soul.

In the past, it had always seemed to me that the mythic world the alchemists inhabited was impenetrable to a modern mind, that it was part of an age or a way of seeing no longer accessible. In the same way, I had despaired, on first encountering the rich, strange world of Hawaiian myth, of finding a way in. Yet keeping vigil there by the lava lake, it seemed to me that the mythic dwells within the blood, a somatic response to forces in nature so mysterious that we have sometimes named them "supernatural." It was unlikely that any alchemists had stood on the rim of a volcanic lake of fire, had even been close to active volcanoes (although Western alchemy could certainly have incorporated spiritual knowledge linked in some far past to volcanoes). Alchemy seemed now less an arcane knowledge than an intuitive vision of correspondence between the soul of the earth and the human soul. Carl Jung discovered that alchemical symbols occur universally in dreams, as though sprung from a collective substratum of the mind. Standing at the edge of the lava lake, alchemical womb of Pele, it was easy to believe in the mythic as part of all of us, as an essential expression of our experience of the elemental world.

FOUR

Volcanic Genesis

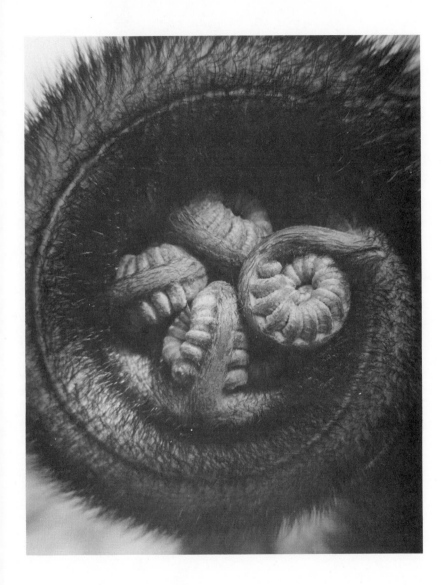

God created man in the image of himself,
in the image of God he created him
male and female he created them

First (and less well-known) account of creation
from *The Jerusalem Bible,* Genesis 1:27

The Lord God then built up the rib, which
he had taken out of man, into a woman.

Genesis 2:22, *King James Bible*

A male this, the female that
A male born in the time of black darkness
The female born in the time of groping in the darkness

From the *Kumulipo,*
a Hawaiian creation chant

Preceding page: New fronds of the native hāpuʻu *("tree fern"), shown here at about one-third actual size. Photograph by Franco Salmoiraghi.*

You're about to go back to Eden," said Bill Mull, "before the coming of man. In these islands, of course, that only means some 1,500-odd years." Nevertheless, I was finding it hard to believe that Eden was just around the bend. We were at about the 3,200-foot level on the windward side of Kīlauea. Bill Mull was punishing foreign weeds with his walking stick. Thwack! at a Himalayan raspberry, covered with small yellow berries. Then a samurai blow to a *faya* sapling, an aggressive newcomer whose proper home is the Azores. "Go home, alien," muttered Bill.

I had decided to take a look at the "creative" side of volcanism, elements often ignored in Western annals of volcano country, which seemed preoccupied with nature's "destructive" side. Bill Mull, rainforest ecologist, had promised a walk through "an almost unspoiled Eden." He had driven us here, to the outskirts of the Volcano Village dump.

The Volcano dump bordered one of the few more or less intact native rainforests left in Hawai'i. We walked past the dumpsters, and a car hulk, and down a short firebreak. The roadside was crowded with aromatic ginger, full of white and yellow blossoms, introduced as a garden ornamental, now a serious pest. And *tibouchina,* with gorgeous purple flowers, a runaway from Brazil, said to have been brought here in 1910 by the wife of the painter Jacques Furneaux. History was that new here.

Nasturtiums, bamboo orchids—the dump was a riot of color. All nonnative plants. But as soon as we stepped off cleared land, we were in the forest, in Bill Mull's school and his heart's habitation. Mull, who looks rather like a white-haired megaleprechaun, is self-appointed student of this bit of rainforest. He himself is a migrant, born in California, arriving in Hawai'i in 1965. In 1973 Bill Mull moved into a Hawaiian rainforest near the top of Kīlauea—and twenty years of work and training in Asian languages were subsumed by a passionate desire to learn about the rainforest world. "I had been fascinated for years by the ideas of evolutionary biology," Bill Mull had told me, "but this is where I learned to *see* it." (And though he is less apt to speak about this, to love and defend the rainforest: he and his wife, the late Mae Mull, have led a tireless campaign on the Big Island to preserve native ecosystems.)

Entrance to Bill Mull's rainforest haunt was guarded by a rusted-out refrigerator, door ajar, festooned with foreign weeds. Entering the rainforest past this vestige of civilization was like being thrust suddenly through some hole in time into a deep, green world. Huge *'ōhi'a* and *koa* trees spread their branches in a canopy high above, where forest birds I had seen only in pictures were singing. A species of *hāpu'u*, a giant tree fern, formed a second canopy, its fronds soaring 20 to 40 feet above our heads. The trail wound among fern trunks, covered with a dark-brown bristly hair, from which young fronds—fist-sized, hairy, fiddlehead shapes—were in various stages of unfurling.

The Hawaiian forest is a very different world from the South American continental rainforest. There, plant life concentrates in the high canopy, where there is abundant light, and some protection from predators. Here, enough light penetrates, and grazing animals are few (though this has changed, with Western-introduced cattle, goats, and pigs), so the greatest diversity is on or near the forest floor. Every surface in Bill Mull's corner of Eden seemed to be covered with multiple layers of greenery; each fallen log had become a terrarium of seedlings, tiny ferns, liverworts, mosses, lichens. Yet the forest was almost spacious, though covered with green life everywhere. And even tidy, in a sense, though filled with decaying fronds and limbs. Life in balance. Bill Mull, clambering over roots with the agility of a twenty-year-old, was reeling off names. "Nettleless nettle; and here's a mintless mint. We also have briarless greenbriers. Look how gentle the rainforest is . . . and how defenseless against alien species—especially humans."

Indeed, nothing here stings, pokes, or poisons. This was a forest that, as Bill Mull put it, "evolved without large stomping, chomping vertebrate animals" (the only native vertebrate is the Hawaiian bat). There were no large carnivores—nowhere visible were those "instincts" we like to attribute to nature in order to justify human behavior, no signs of "nature red in tooth and claw." One could find some evidence for a "savage" nature-at-large in continental rainforests, perhaps, but not in this gentle island world. Or so I suggested to Bill Mull, who pointed out that I was thinking anthropocentrically. "There's fierce competition here, among tiny invertebrates and birds—it's just not on a level that humans are likely to notice."

This was typical upland native rainforest that we were wandering through, ranging to alpine level at 6,000 feet, dominated by *'ōhi'a* and *hāpu'u* (tree fern). The *hāpu'u* is sometimes called the mother of *'ōhi'a* because its decaying growth provides the nutrients for the *'ōhi'a* seedlings (keep in mind that this forest, like all volcanic rainforests, was born relatively recently, from bare rock). The *'ōhi'a,* the same plant that colonizes new lava flow in the form of stubby, leather shrubs, had grown to enormous, shaggy trees here, where the rain was plentiful and the lava several hundreds of years old, old enough to begin its crumble into soil. Along with the *hāpu'u,* the *'ōhi'a* trunks and roots provided platforms for the many parasitic plants—tiny, lacy ferns, brilliant green mosses—while its brushy red blossoms were the main source of nectar for the forest birds. "The *'ōhi'a,*" said Bill Mull, "is one of the most complex plants there is. The catch-all species name here is *polymorpha*—'many forms.' Botanists are still puzzling over how many kinds there actually are here."

As Darwin recognized, isolated islands provide a "controlled lab" for the study of evolution. The more isolated the better—and the Hawaiian Islands are about as far from anywhere as you can get: the distance from here to any other large landmass is about 2,500 miles. Every form of life that got to the Islands naturally (without the help, witting or unwitting, of humans) flew (or rode on a flyer), floated, or was carried on the wind. The isolation factor excluded large groups: all large mammals, any birds that could not fly well, seeds that could not float or were not likely to be swallowed by birds. The life that first colonized these volcanic islands made it here against great odds.

But once safely arrived those early colonizers had a rare evolutionary opportunity. They would, for one, be a small group—perhaps just a fertile male and female, or simply a fertilized female. These early Adams and Eves (or single pregnant Eve) of the plant, insect, and animal world would be passing on only their own limited gene pool—a situation biologists call the "founder effect." (The founder effect applied to the first humans who came to the Islands as well: the small group of Polynesians who colonized Hawai'i brought a limited gene pool with them, which is why, some 1,500 years later, we have a people who are physically distinct as Hawaiians.)

Adaptations (positive mutations) are passed on and become established with astonishing rapidity if the number of genes is limited. If the environment is favorable to adaptation, as it is in Hawai'i, then a single species may proliferate into several species in what is, biologically, an extremely rapid pace. The Hawaiian Islands, with incredibly varied climate and terrain, provided optimum conditions for this process, which is called "adaptive radiation."

Besides the isolation from other landmasses of all the islands together, each island offers the opportunity for a group to become isolated and begin to change to the point where it is no longer able to breed successfully with its former kin (this is the basic definition of speciation). Within each island, many natural barriers—deep-walled valleys, high mountains—could further isolate a group. And for many of the life forms of active volcano lands, volcanism is a potent dynamic for evolutionary change. Lava flows constantly isolate pockets of land, while turning other areas back into a barren volcanic Eden ready to be colonized again.

The varied climate, terrain, and conditions means an incredible plenitude of what biologists call "ecological niches" waiting to be filled. A niche may be just a congenial and conveniently empty physical area, but it can also mean a role to which an organism adapts. Simply the fact that such niches are available encourages adaptation. Some of the native nectar-eating birds, for example, have learned to eat insects, evolving a shorter bill that allows them to do so, albeit rather clumsily. Had there been many other, more clever insect eaters already exploiting that niche, such an adaptation would not have been useful.

Although overburdened by its human population, on other levels of life this island world is still growing, still being colonized, with a myriad of uncrowded niches for old and new species to fill. "Time is still dawning here," Bill Mull said. "You can very nearly see evolution happening. New ground is continuously being formed through the action of the volcanoes. And the ecological niches already here are still pretty empty. There is room here for an organism to express itself in ways that would have amazed Darwin."

Darwin himself recognized the rich possibilities for evolutionary study in this isolated archipelago. In 1850 he wrote to a friend, "of all the places in the world, I should like to see a good flora of the Sandwich Islands. I would subscribe 50 pounds to any collector to go there and work at the islands."[1] It was interesting to imagine Darwin landing here rather than the Galapagos Islands, to speculate whether his views would have been different had he done his collecting in Hawai'i. Not that the basic tenets of his theory would have changed: natural selection and sexual competition are essential elements to evolution here as elsewhere. But perhaps his sense of the tenor—the *spirit,* even—of nature's processes—the element of fierce individual struggle—would have been tempered by the expansive, rich flux of the Hawaiian world.

Actually, even in the Galapagos Darwin was slow to embrace the evidence of evolutionary change. There was, for instance, the story of Darwin's famous Galapagos finches, who supposedly furnished him the key to the mechanisms of evolution. The legend is that Darwin collected finchlike birds from several islands, recognized that, though they appeared to be separate species, they had a common ancestor, and went home and wrote up the theory of evolution.

In fact, Darwin did not recognize at the time that all those peculiar little birds had evolved from common stock. He was busy puzzling about the variations among the tortoises of the islands, finally deciding they were only slight differences in one species. Creationist doctrine had taught that all species were formed, inviolable, by the hand of God, and Darwin still had one foot in the eighteenth century. Not until his return, when a British Museum ornithologist labeled all the birds "finch," did he see that he had missed his prime clue. Even then, it took him another decade to assemble his argument into the *Origin of Species.*[2]

Had Darwin come to the Hawaiian Islands, would he have reached his theory sooner? For nowhere in the world are there more astounding examples of evolutionary change. The finch story here is as amazing as it is in the Galapagos, and twice as complex: perhaps it would have proved too confusing for even Darwin at the time. The Hawaiian version is an intricate dance of flower and bird adapting together. Deep in the rainforest, Bill Mull showed me a woody plant over 8 feet high with a rosette of yard-long, palmlike leaves—a lobelia, relative of those small continental herbs with tiny colorful flowers. Here in the rainforest it "displayed arborescence"; in other words, it acted like a tree, and a palm tree at that. I had been reading about the strange and wonderful niches that had become occupied by species of this plant. Other lobelia have developed fernlike leaves. One of the strangest adaptations, the *ālula (Brighamia insignis),* found now only on the most inaccessible cliff faces of a few of the islands, resembles a head of lettuce perched atop a long sausage, the succulent stem it has evolved for life on arid, rocky cliffs.

Lobelias evolved riotously throughout the Islands, forming more than 275 distinguishable kinds of plants, of which over a third may now be extinct. But these plants are only half of a complex story of coevolution. The other half belongs to native birds called honeycreepers, twenty-eight species and twelve subspecies (about two-thirds of which are now extinct, rare, or endangered), all descended from a common

A native honeycreeper, the 'i'iwi, *whose bill is adapted to feeding on the tubular blossoms of the native lobelia. Woodcut by Titian Ramsay Peale. Page 152 in John Cassin,* Mammalogy and Ornithology, *U.S. Exploring Expedition, Atlas, vol. 8 (Philadelphia: Sherman, 1848). Courtesy of Bishop Museum.*

finchlike ancestor. This subfamily appears to have evolved a beak to match the evolving shape of Hawaiian flowering plants, in particular the lobelias, with their long, slender, curving flowers. One honey-creeper, the Hawai'i *mamo,* (now extinct) was the end product in the evolution to an almost exclusively nectar-eating bird. It was a handsome black bird with a few yellow feathers, much prized by the Hawaiians, who caught it with bird lime, plucked the bright feathers, and let it go. It had a beautiful, long, curved bill, nearly half the size of the bird itself, matching exactly the tubular curves of the lobelia flowers.

A new lobelia was discovered as recently as 1959—an event that should not be surprising, according to Bill Mull. "Anyone adequately trained to work here is likely to discover new species in native forests," he pointed out. "Scientific understanding of this environment is far from complete—partly, because of its rich complexity—but more so . . . because of a dearth of scientists adequately trained in Hawaiian biota. A 'continental' biologist has to be extensively 'retrained' to understand the rich but often subtle gradient of change you find in species here."

The constant state of genetic change and flux makes this particular area of Hawai'i, volcano country, in the opinion of the evolutionary biologists who know the area, the best outdoor lab in the world. Active volcanism, constantly creating new niches for biota to move into—and, in their isolation, begin to diversify. Here evolution, as Bill Mull pointed out, can actually be put into a time frame. The lobelia specific to a certain area on the Big Island, for example, must have evolved in the last 100,000 years, because that is the age of the land itself. In this dynamic landscape, the adaptive shifts that culminate in the development of new species seem to happen with startling rapidity. Polynesians introduced the banana to the Hawaiian Islands around 1,500 years ago. Since then, five new species of banana moth have evolved.

All this makes for exciting times for rainforest specialists. Because of his work as a closeup photographer, Bill Mull has been in on many of the discoveries. Nimbly hopping over the huge *'ōhi'a* roots that crisscross the rainforest trail, he said over his shoulder, "the first happy-face spider was brought to me in the middle of the night." That morning he had shown me photographs of these tiny yellow-green spiders, discovered only ten years ago. They had black and red markings resembling eyes and a clown mouth on their backs. One did look, as Bill suggested, like Charlie Chaplin. "And look at the markings on this one. Greta Garbo." I peered dubiously at the backside of the tiny spider, blown up to the size of a fist. "Well," said Bill, flashing an impish grin, "try squinting."

Ahead of me in the rainforest, Mull had stopped to inspect the broad leaves of a green shrubby plant: "The *māmaki*—used by the Hawaiians for making *kapa*" (the bark cloth that was their main item of clothing). Clinging to the underside was a tiny land snail, with a delicately tinted shell. I recalled the photographs he had shown me that morning, of several snails, all astoundingly beautiful, with shells of translucent colors; some with finely wrought designs. An astonishing diversity of shell pattern and color. "Half of them seem to have become extinct since they were discovered," he had said. The intricate markings on the shells, I had noticed, resembled the designs Hawaiians painted on the borders of *kapa*.

I pondered the irony of what is currently considered "Hawaiian" design (oversized hibiscus blossoms on synthetic aloha shirts) while Bill Mull examined other leaves of the *māmaki*. "Here," he announced, "is one of the most amazing recent discoveries. You've heard of the

75

law of the jungle? Then this would have to be the Hawaiian lion." I stared at the leaf in puzzlement, then spied a small green caterpillar that appeared to be rearing up on its—hind legs?

"It evolved from a vegetarian inchworm," said Bill Mull, "but it sure doesn't act like one. This is the first known fly-catching caterpillar, found here on Hualālai volcano in 1972. It started out as a plant muncher, but somewhere along the line it developed a taste for live meat." The "ferocious" inchworm was discovered by a young biologist, Steven Montgomery, who watched astounded as it devoured a blowfly. The caterpillar's hind end is equipped with sensory hairs and two elongated tail tubercles to sense prey. It strikes at the speed of 1/12 second. Sharp claws have evolved on its front legs, while its back legs are powerfully developed to hold the caterpillar firmly to its perch when it grapples with struggling prey. Steven Montgomery, Bill Mull told me, had now identified twenty species of fly-catching caterpillars in Hawai'i.

Discoveries on the slopes of the Big Island's volcanoes have included finding whole new ecosystems. One unique biotic world flourishes in older lava tubes. In 1971, scientists exploring the tubes found blind small-eyed wolf spiders belonging to the "big-eyed hunting spider" clan, and blind albino millipedes. The spiders had apparently developed an extreme acoustic sensitivity that allows them to hunt their prey in utter darkness. The blind millipedes feed on 'ōhi'a tree roots that grow down through the roofs of the lava tubes.

Recent lava flows host another recently discovered ecosystem, which has been given the unwieldy scientific name *neogeoaeolian* (literally "new land—of the wind"). Arthropods—crickets and spiders—have evolved as scavengers, feeding on the "waif" arthropods that drift or fly in and become marooned on the barren rock.

The forces of creation and destruction are inextricably woven together in volcano country. A lava flow can wipe out thousands of acres of verdant forest, turning the ecological clock back to zero. But the destruction builds a scaffold for creation: pockets of older land are left untouched by the flow, groups of flora and fauna are isolated, and out of these small interbreeding communities new species begin to form. The dynamic only works, however, if there is enough land, enough variety of niches and pockets, to allow for these cycles of death and new life, and to ensure survival of a species if a large area of land is destroyed—whether by lava or by human encroachment. How much is "enough"? "It's hard to gauge how much land is really needed," points out Mull, "because we don't really know enough yet about the biology or the ecology of the species involved. We still, in a sense, don't know who—or what—is out there."

A lovely, dynamic, but fragile world has been born here out of the forces of volcanism—a world of paradox, ruled by a powerful elemental energy but defenselessly gentle. The damage to the wildlands of Hawai'i began with the arrival of humans. The early Polynesian immigrants brought pigs, dogs, chickens, rats, and geckos. These foreigners changed some faces of the landscape forever. Humans and animals killed off entirely several species of flightless birds, including the world's only flightless ibis. The ancestors of the Hawaiians not only introduced foreign plants but also destroyed much of the native lowland forest to make room for cultivation.

Nevertheless, the ancient Hawaiians managed to live for over a thousand years in relative harmony with the land, even though at its peak (at the time the Islands were discovered by Cook—1778), their population may have reached several hundred thousands—two-thirds or more of the modern population of the state.[3] To reach that number with low environmental damage, Hawaiian culture must have established a balanced relationship with the land. The early Westerners observed that the Hawaiian use of resources was regulated through the strict *kapu* (tabu) system and through seasonal religious observances. Fishing for certain fish, for example, was suspended at various times during the year in honor of the gods with whom those fish were associated, with the practical result that the fish population had the chance to replenish itself.

The *kapu* system reflected the Hawaiian sense that many forms of nature were the various attributes of the *akua*—the major gods. Each Hawaiian also had a personal or clan relationship with a certain ancestral god, an *'aumakua,* and took special care not to harm any of the "body forms" or relations of that god. If you were of the Pele clan, for example, you were related to one of Pele's "brothers," a shark god, and the shark would be sacred to you.

The upland forests were considered sacred and mysterious places: the *wao akua,* the "forests of the gods." Hawaiians trapped birds in them, gathered plants, and cut down large trees for making temple idols or canoes, but they did not inhabit them. Nor, for the most part, did Westerners until recently—except in areas that proved valuable for logging or cattle ranching. As an ecosystem, the rainforests have been the least disturbed. But only on the Big Island—in the volcanoes region—are large sections of upland and lowland native rainforest left in Hawai'i.

Only a small part of the volcanoes area rainforest lies "protected" within the boundaries of the National Park. Bill Mull's dump-side rainforest is part of the State Forest Reserve—a designation that by no means guarantees its survival. Rainforest on both public and private lands has been bulldozed and replanted with nonnative trees in short-sighted tree-farming experiments. It has been leased to farmers who clear-cut and plant papaya. And in one private sector the 'ōhi'a were sold, woodchip by woodchip, to generate electricity. Resort development and geothermal development also threaten the rainforest. With its ecological integrity damaged, it falls prey to incursions from nonnative plants. And it has for years suffered the depredations of feral pigs, who root up the forest floor and transport the seeds of foreign plants into the native forest.

The biological diversity of Hawai'i is one of the wonders of the world, but it is fast disappearing. Out of a thousand species of plants native to the Islands, 92 percent are endemic; that is, found here and nowhere else in the world. About half these species are now extinct—gone forever. Three-fourths of Hawai'i's native birds are extinct. Rainforests are the richest preserves left in Hawai'i, holding the largest collection of remaining endemic flora and fauna. Many of the species are on the rare or endangered list. As Bill Mull wrote in a recent article, "What nature's patient schedule took millions of years to evolve here is being destroyed in a blink of man's impatient eye."[4]

"Why has so much destruction of Hawai'i's native biota happened without more public outcry," I asked Bill Mull that day in the rainforest. Ignorance, he replied. Few environmentalists have trained in Hawai'i ecology; until lately, few could even recognize what was here. Very little public awareness of environmental issues. And practically no education in local natural history in the school system. "I can attest to that," I said.

A few days after the rainforest walk with Bill Mull, I wandered down a favorite section of trail on Kīlauea's east rift zone, a few miles below the summit caldera. It was the first trail I ever walked in the volcanoes region, and over years it had become some sort of touchstone for me, a reminder that there were other measurements of time beyond the narrow chronology of my own life. The trail winds over billowy lava fields of the 1971–1974 eruption of Mauna Ulu—a vent that over the course of three years built up a small shield volcano. The Mauna Ulu eruption was at that time the longest-standing ever recorded, and one of the most voluminous, pouring massive lava flows over the huge fault scarps of Kīlauea's south flank, several of which reached the sea. When I first walked the trail, in 1975, the eruption had ceased the year before, leaving an expanse of barren lava where forest had stood. In places the lava had molded around trees before they burned, creating eerie clusters of hollow pillars of rock. Everywhere else the land was sealed over by glassy layers of *pāhoehoe*. Walking on it, you crushed into cinders a gleaming surface shot with blues and gold.

A few years later, I walked that stretch of trail again. The change was astounding: already, in that short time, a new world had emerged from the devastation. Small fronds of the *'ama'u* fern, brilliant green against the glossy *pāhoehoe,* were pushing out of cracks, anywhere the spores could find shelter. In a few places their decayed leaves had provided enough nutrients for the shallow-rooted *'ōhi'a,* emerging as a spindly shrub with a few round, hairy leaves. The brittle surface of the *pāhoehoe* had weathered and crumbled, mixing with bits of vegetation to begin to build a mineral-rich "soil."

And again, in 1987, returning to the Big Island to begin research on this book, I walked the Mauna Ulu trail. If you follow it a mile farther, it leads to an overlook from Pu'u Huluhulu, a cinder cone thousands of years old, its eroded flanks thickly vegetated. Inside the cinder cone flourished a dense rainforest alive with the calls of birds—a tiny, inaccessible Eden. Turning and looking out, I could see the still-steaming top of Mauna Ulu a half-mile to the southwest. To the southeast rose the cone of the new active vent, Pu'u 'Ō'ō, a mountain where a year ago the land sloped gently, a point around which the whole landscape now rearranged itself.

But still the profoundest change seemed what I saw on the trail itself, for out of that land emptied of all but rock and fire, a young forest had been born. The ferns were now waist high: the *'ōhi'a* had turned to shrub and sheltered *'ōhelo* bushes, bearing a few red berries; grasses had proliferated in niches and crumbling edges of lava. Lava desert slowly subsumed into green, birth of a forest, rebirth of a world.

Something in this generative power of the earth here was profoundly disorienting to the Western mind. Since I had been studying an ancient Hawaiian creation chant, the *Kumulipo,* I thought about "creation stories."

The Catholic theologian Thomas Berry has suggested that "creation stories" are the foundation of a culture's attitude toward nature.[5] Modern Western culture, as Berry points out, has two creation stories, usually considered mutually exclusive: biblical Genesis ("creationism") and Darwinian evolution.

Darwinian theory, at least in its general interpretation, continues the mechanistic view of the world that has dominated the sciences: the view of the generative processes of nature as blind, soulless, mechanical.

In the Christian story of creation, the world comes into being as a reflection of the Logos, the Word of God. The world is drawn out of a primitive chaos of matter and infused with the divine spirit. The natural and the supernatural are two separate realms; although the divine may "incarnate" in the natural world, nature by itself has no inherent part in divinity.

The early missionaries to the Islands were puzzled that the Hawaiians would sometimes embrace willingly the drama of Jesus's life, but balk at accepting the Christian story of Creation. What the missionaries did not understand is that the Hawaiians had their own intricate, sophisticated cosmological view. It was based on the two most obvious facts to an agricultural people living on tropical, volcanic islands. First, the elemental forces governing the world were not creative, but *procreative*. And second, the creation or procreation of the world was a continuous process, an endless dance of cosmic generation.

> At the time when the earth became hot
> At the time when the heavens turned about
> At the time when the sun was darkened
> To cause the moon to shine
> The time of the rise of the Pleiades
> The slime, this was the source of the earth
> The source of darkness that made darkness.[6]

Thus are translated the opening lines of the *Kumulipo,* a Hawaiian "creation chant" composed around A.D. 1700 to honor the birth of the chief of Hawai'i Island, Lono-i-ka-makahiki. Hawaiians believed that the chiefs were human representatives of the gods, so such "name" or "birth" chants were traditional ways to place the newborn chief in relation to the cosmos. Since such chants were passed down from generation to generation, the basic themes of the *Kumulipo* are, in all likelihood, very ancient. Creation chants were the special province of *haku mele,* or song masters, attached to the courts of chiefs, and they were always memorized by more than one reciter, to guard against error.

Lono-i-ka-makahiki was a historical figure, but in this chant he melds with Lono, god of fertility and seasonal agriculture. (This same chant was apparently recited to Captain Cook, on his arrival at Keala-kekua Bay in Kona in 1778. The islanders initially thought Cook *was* the god Lono, putting in an unusual appearance in human form at the time of his mythical seasonal return.)

The *Kumulipo* first attracted Western attention in the nineteenth century, when it was partially translated by Adolf Bastian, a German anthropologist who thought he had found in it proof that a "primitive" people could have an evolutionary conception of life's origins. Composed of sixteen sections, the full chant takes several hours to recite. (When Cook complained of the tedium of the long chant he was required to listen to, he had no idea he was hearing a total cosmological story.) The name *Kumulipo* means "beginning in deep darkness." The first seven sections of the chant are concerned with the period called the *pō,* a time of cosmic night. During this time elements of the universe, of the earth, and of organic life have their beginnings. Nine sections follow, telling of the time of *ao,* or cosmic day, and with them commences the story of the origins of both humans and gods.

The *Kumulipo* seems to have several levels of meaning, couched in an elaborate poetic, allusive language. The scholar John Charlot has suggested that the chant describes simultaneously three events: the beginning and development of the universe, the social history of the human community, and the growth, from conception, of a human being.[7] All these events are interwoven—different levels of the same cosmic procreative process. The *Kumulipo* makes very clear that Hawaiian cosmology makes no separation of natural and supernatural, of human and god.

More difficult to grasp, or to translate into Western terms, is the vision of the entire cosmos inspired by an attraction that on a human level one might call *eros.* The cosmos begins, in the *Kumulipo,* by the interaction of two primal forces:

> When space turned around, the earth heated
> When space turned over, the sky reversed.[8]

Life springs from a cosmic union. These beginnings are shrouded in the universal womb of night, the *pō,* the birthing place of the world and of gods:

From the source in the slime was the earth formed
From the source in the darkness was darkness formed
From the source in the night was night formed.

A refrain repeated in the first four sections of the *Kumulipo* serves as reminder that, though the generative force of the cosmos is reflected in human sexuality, it works in a realm beyond our understanding: "It is a god who enters; not as a human does he enter." To speak of these mysteries as generative, sexual, or erotic, is to apply a human dimension to immensely elemental forces.

From the depths of the darkness, darkness so deep
Darkness of day, darkness of night
Of night alone
Did night give birth
Born was Kumulipo in the night, a male
Born was Pō'ele in the night, a female

Born from the cosmic night come divine "male" and "female" principles, still essentially, as *Kumulipo* scholar Rubellite Johnson states, "abstractions of darkness," primal polar forces of the cosmos.

In the first chant of the second part of the *Kumulipo,* which describes the dawn of cosmic "day," life begins to arise along the shores of the earth. It develops genealogically: coral gives birth first to soft-bodied creatures like the sea cucumber, then to crustaceans. (But it also follows an essentially evolutionary pattern, simple organisms being the parents of more complex ones.) Paired with the sea creatures are simple forms of land plants that resemble the life developing in the sea. Thus *'ēkahakaha,* bird's nest fern, is paired with the first seaweed, *'ēkaha,* because its swordlike fronds correspond in shape to the fronds of the sea plant. On another level of cosmic "time," as John Charlot suggests, this embryonic sea world represents the womb in which the human child is conceived.

In the second chant, families of fish develop parallel to growth of forest on land. In the third chant, all winged things appear. In the fourth chant, the creatures of the sea take to the land. The whole universe writhes with birth pains. Human birth and cosmic birth coalesce. In the fifth and sixth chants, cultivated food plants appear. The pig, archetypal symbol of male adolescent sexuality for the Hawaiians, appears. In cosmic and human time, the child has reached sexual maturity.

82

The seventh chant brings full day, the dawn of the time of humans and the gods of humans:

> Born was man for the narrow stream
> Born was woman for the broad stream
> Born was the night of the gods.[9]

Man, woman, and gods are born at the same time, their parenthood blended together, with no definitive boundary separating human from divine.

The remaining sections of the *Kumulipo* are complicated genealogical lists. In the last chant, after a hundred generations, appear Papa, an earth goddess associated particularly with Hawai'i, and Wākea, a sky god, divine ancestors of the Hawaiians.

Throughout the *Kumulipo,* life develops through the forces of attraction and desire. The procreative principle operates on all levels, from simplest life forms to gods. The resemblances among plants, animals, humans, and gods speak of their mutual birth from the cosmic dance. Was it a tropic landscape, I wondered, that produced such a vision—all forms of the bodily and spiritual spewing forth continuously from the same wet and teeming birthing place? It came to mind, reading the *Kumulipo,* that in volcano country I was in a very different world from that of the Desert Fathers who wrote down the Old Testament Genesis. And that I was equally far from Old Testament thought, linear and monolithic, a vision formed—elsewhere. In small cities, perhaps, at the edges of desert. Or with a view of the horizon over ancient, changeless plains, where, unlike here, the human form might cast a long shadow, might seem the central figure in the landscape.

FIVE

The Volcano as Western Metaphor

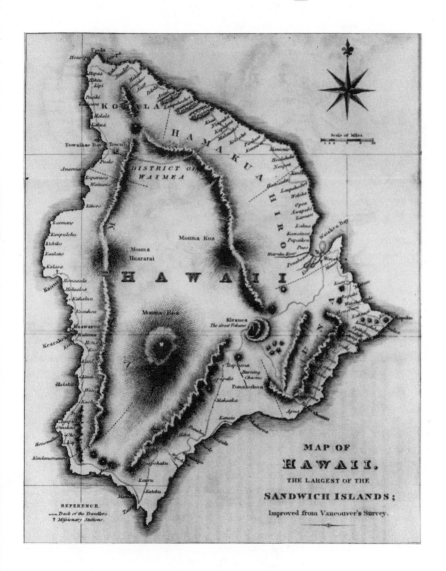

MAP OF
HAWAII,
THE LARGEST OF THE
SANDWICH ISLANDS;
Improved from Vancouver's Survey.

Poetry is the lava of the imagination whose eruption prevents an earthquake.

GEORGE GORDON
the poet Lord Byron

Volcanoes be in Sicily
And South America
I judge from my Geography—
Volcanoes nearer here
A lava step at any time
Am I inclined to climb—
A crater I may contemplate
Vesuvius at home.

EMILY DICKINSON

Early map of Hawai'i, improved from Vancouver's survey. Insert between pages 40–41 in 2nd edition of William Ellis, Narrative of a Tour Through Owyhee *(London: Fisher, 1827). Courtesy of Bishop Museum.*

*I*n the 1890s a French gentleman named d'Anglade stood at the edge of Halema'uma'u and stared down into "a lake of ever-burning, active lava," and discovered that "for once reality surpasses imagination."

In the face of "such elemental non-human forces," d'Anglade wrote, " . . . it is impossible to insulate oneself from a feeling of terror. A sudden sense of utter nothingness joins with a feeling of dizziness as when staring into a void." Meditating on an experience that left him "physically and morally a wreck," he mused that "the volcano comes to exist as a puzzle, a most active and visible mystery, consummating all the inherited ideas rooted in our human fears."[1]

Among the nineteenth-century descriptions of volcano country that I had been reading, this account, by a man who had served as French consul in Honolulu, stood out: it was unusually free of the stock metaphors, particularly the biblical ones, of most of the descriptions I had read, the imposed cultural perceptions. And it hinted at the strange depths the landscape stirred in the Western mind—the fear, the disorientation, the deep-seated emotional response the volcano country evoked. The crater Emily Dickinson "contemplates" (in the poem at the beginning of this chapter) is a profound psychic symbol. Who *was* Vesuvius, I wanted to discover, when he or she was "at home"?

As I had found in trying to trace the roots of the scientific vision of volcano country, Western views of volcanoes grew out of the culture's general perceptions about nature. The ancient Hawaiians held all forms of nature as sacred, as various forms of the gods. Such animistic beliefs are prevalent in the early stages of all cultures, and continue to influence attitudes toward nature in those cultures that maintain strong ties to the land. In Japan, for instance, a very recently urban culture overlays still-vital nature worship, and the volcano Fuji is universally venerated as a shrine.

Western culture, too, has its roots in a mythic, animistic consciousness, still visible in Greek myths, for example, but the Judeo-Christian view has prevailed. The great debate in Judeo-Christian history has been how to reconcile a divinity who is pure spirit with a world fashioned by the Creator out of spirit-less matter. Christianity, struggling mightily against primitive nature worship, tended to deny nature an immanence of its own, though Christian mystics occasionally hinted that the earth itself might be part of the body of God. A concept of the divinity of earth has survived at the fringes of Christian thought but never at its core. At least since the dawn of the Christian era, Western culture has tended to locate the divine in a transcendent sphere, separate from the mortal "thingness" of the earthly realm.

But fire, that most mysterious and transformative element, has occupied a special place even in those cultures that have moved furthest from their mythic roots. In Western culture, fire has remained a powerful but ambiguous symbol, sometimes revealing, sometimes challenging the power of God, in its enthralling, puzzling combination of the physical and spiritual. "Among all phenomena," writes the French philosopher Gaston Bachelard, "it is really the only one to which there can be attributed the opposing values of good and evil. It shines in Paradise. It burns in Hell."[2] Fire consumes matter, transforming it into its own essence: a primal energy that seems to have a life of its own. In myths of many cultures, fire is the power humans steal from the gods.

A volcano is fire in its most overwhelming manifestation. As Westerners, we inherit a mythology that is shaped by volcanism: in its images from the classical world of Etna and "fire-vomiting" Vesuvius; in Greek and Roman myths of the Titans, who inhabit volcanoes and battle Jupiter; in tales of volcanoes as the workshops of gods. The Greek god Hephaestus (who became the Roman god Vulcan) had his forge within great Etna. Hephaestus, the inventor, was the hunchbacked mate of Aphrodite, goddess of sexual love. Hephaestus uses his forge to transform for human use the divine creational powers of fire. His relationship with Aphrodite suggests a strong link between the creative power of fire and the *procreative* power of sex. More precisely, the link is with a female generative power in nature, for Hephaestus' transformative work takes place within the fiery womb of the volcano.

The Christian view, which superseded the Greek mythic view, consigned the primal creative power of fire to God alone. In the biblical world, fire is God's tool for cleansing or giving his people a sign: the burning bush; the pillar of fire that leads the children of Israel out of exile. The might of God: Psalm 104, "He looks upon the earth and it trembles; He touches the hills and they smoke." Yet fire can also represent a latent earth-bound potency, an unredeemed nature that challenges the will of God. Early Christian teachings depict hell as near the center of the earth; volcanoes are often seen as portals to this subterranean world. The physical forms of volcanoes provide us with the very landscape of hell: "The fire came down from heaven and consumed them," declares the book of Revelations, "and the devil who led them astray was thrown into the fiery sulphurous lake." Dante (perhaps influenced by classical mythology as well as Christian beliefs) portrays hell as an enormous crater with Lucifer enthroned in the middle. Lucifer (literally, "the light bringer") becomes Satan, ruler of the fiery lake. In him perhaps we find the ghost of the mythic Hephaestus-Vulcan at his forge, demoted to hell, his fiery fire-stealing energy now deemed diabolical.

But the connection of volcanic fire with a primal creative energy resurfaced in the midst of the Christian world, as I mentioned earlier, in the mythic view of the alchemists. The "science" of alchemy, tapping deep roots in early classical and non-Western philosophy, was based on the idea of *anima mundi:* the world as living, divine being. Alchemists revived the vitalist theories of early Greek philosophers (such as Heraclitus, who argued that every particle of matter contained a germ of spirit) and reinfused them into Christian thought. Drawing on the alchemical view of the world, Athanasius Kircher, a Jesuit, published *Mundus Subterraneus* in 1655, arguing that the earth was alive, fueled at its core by God's divine energy in the form of fire, which moved through channels and passages as blood moves through veins.

The alchemists retained an "animistic" view of a natural world infused with divine procreative power. The alchemical process itself, the "marriage" of elements to create a higher form, was described in metaphors that suggest birth and sex. Norman O. Brown, in *Life Against Death,* suggests that alchemy may truly represent, in the Western world, "the last effort of man to produce a science based on an erotic sense of reality."[3] This view has been consistently rejected by orthodox Christianity, which prefers to conceive of nature as purely material. If infused with spirit by God, then nature is the Great Book in which God's Word can be read. But the wild and turbulent side of nature comes to represent a chaotic world-before-God, or a world that has fallen from God's grace and become infected with evil. In such a world, as Shakespeare has Hotspur comment in *Henry IV,* "Diseased Nature often times breaks forth / In strange eruptions."

Christian cosmology influenced fundamental attitudes toward nature, its meaning, and its value. As early as 1685, "Neptunist" Thomas Burnett (in his *Sacred Theory of the Earth*) had decided that mountains were too ugly to have been created originally by God, so must be instead ruins of a fallen world, or more exactly, debris left after the Flood. The barren landscape that Milton, in "Paradise Lost," portrays outside the gates of Eden, is the inert, chaotic matter of nature from which divinity has withdrawn. The division of matter and spirit allowed for the emergence, in the 1700s, of empirical science, with its mechanistic view of nature. The animistic or mythic view of nature was forced underground, to reemerge later as powerful symbolic forms in art and literature.

Mechanistic science fostered a literary and artistic view that devalued and distanced nature, reducing the natural world to a picturesque backdrop to the human scene. Thus volcanoes enter the newborn scientific and travel literature of the eighteenth century as natural curiosities. Coincidentally, the late eighteenth and early nineteenth centuries were a time of much volcanic activity, particularly in Iceland and in Italy. In 1776, the Italian artist Pietro Fabris produced a series of colored plates of Vesuvius in eruption, to accompany the writings of Sir William Hamilton on the volcano. (Hamilton lived on the side of Vesuvius and was known for giving music parties with the volcano's "fireworks" as background.) Fabris's engravings combine "scientific" detail with the sensational: human figures in the foreground lounge or sketch or gesticulate toward theatrical pillars of fire.

In the nineteenth century, as part of the movement in art and literature called Romanticism, volcanoes reemerge as a potent symbol. Rebelling against the mechanistic view of nature the rise of science had fostered, Romantic artists sought evidence of the supernatural within the natural world. In landscape painting, conventions of the *picturesque*—nature as curious spectacle or interesting backdrop—gave way to those of the *sublime*—nature in its wildest aspect, calculated to arouse a sense of awe and wonder. The volcano, as symbol of primal, creative power, became the ultimate Romantic image of the self. Shelley's "Prometheus Unbound," which was written after the poet had seen Vesuvius in eruption, is replete with volcanic imagery. Emerson, who had argued that "all nature is a metaphor of the human mind," wrote that the great writer should be like a "Chimborazo [volcano in the Andes] . . . running up from a torrid base through all the climates of the globe."[4]

In this image of the volcano as fiery emblem of the self are echoes of the demigod Vulcan, or of the rebel energy of Lucifer, or Milton's Satan, a favorite figure for many of the Romantics. But something else echoes in the imagery as well. Nineteenth-century poets Elizabeth Barrett Browning and Emily Dickinson use volcanic imagery as metaphor for an energy that is creative, erotic, and specifically female. I am reminded again, in their rebellious declarations ("Vesuvius at home"!), of Thomas Cole's painting "The Expulsion from the Garden of Eden." In Cole's vision of the Fall, Eve, the rebel, is leading a reluctant Adam by the hand, out of the artificial garden of Paradise and into a wilderness dominated by an erupting volcano.

Cole's painting, with its juxtaposition of wayward nature (the volcano) and wayward female (Eve) suggests to me that the volcano may symbolize something more than the wild—perhaps unholy?—side of nature. In the nineteenth century, the Western imagination seems literally to erupt, if you'll pardon the pun, with images expressing both fascination and anxiety about forces that more primitive cultures worshiped as the generative female principle in nature.[5] In part this may be the result of the flood of information about "pagan" cultures that entered the Western world during this time through the fledgling sciences of archeology and anthropology. In the 1850s, the Swiss anthropologist J. J. Bachoven's work among the Etruscan tombs and underground temples led to his publication of *Das Mutterecht* ("mother right"), in which he argued that all cultures began as matriarchies. In 1866, Gustave Courbet painted his controversial view of a woman's pubes, and entitled it "The Origin of the World." In 1877, Madame Blavatsky wrote her notorious *Isis Unveiled,* in which the great Egyptian goddess of birth and death is the fount of an occult wisdom that challenges Christian theology.

The impact of non-Western cultures may have spurred this reemergence of a mythic, "animistic" cosmology. Or it may, as Erich Neumann suggests in his writing on primitive cultures and their worship of the "Great Mother," express the reemergence of a primal vision that had long been suppressed by Christian theology. Neumann (who was a follower of Jung) suggests that the fundamental sense of earth as feminine and generative surfaces as a series of images in the mind—geo-feminine connections of cave and belly, womb and tomb, birth and burial.[6]

For an urban, nineteenth-century Westerner, such imagery must have been both exalting and terrifying, disturbing in its hint of nature's powers of genesis and demise. No nineteenth-century work is more telling about the complex emotions surrounding this reemergence of a female generative principle than H. Rider Haggard's *She,* one of England's best-selling novels of the time. Haggard's story begins stereotypically enough with a shipwreck off the coast of Africa. But the survivors—two Englishmen and their servant—are soon journeying (as literary critic Sandra Gilbert points out in her article "Haggard's Heart of Darkness") into a fantastic landscape of marshes and swampy canals.[7] They arrive at last at what Haggard describes as a "vast cup of earth," ruled by a queen named Ayesha, translated as "She who must be obeyed." The people ruled by "She," the Amahaggar, are matriarchal, inhabit great caverns in the earth, and are given to smothering their enemies with hot earthen pots and then embalming them. Ayesha herself has achieved a godlike immortality by periodically bathing, deep in her caves, in a mysterious "flame of life" that is described as "an awful cloud or a pillar of fire." (The phrase reminds me of Milton's Satan, who "Springs upward like a Pyramid of Fire.") In order to escape from this great underground womb, the shipwrecked sailors must destroy the power of the eternal female, Ayesha.

The astounding geo-feminine symbolism of Haggard's fantasy may seem less obscure to the post-Freudian reader, in an age in which the U.S. poet Adrienne Rich has declared explicitly: "Every peak is a crater. This is the law of volcanoes, / making them visibly and eternally female."[8] But I am reminded, in reading Haggard, of the semiconscious fear and fascination that characterize the Western nineteenth-century response to the Hawaiian volcanoes landscape—as well as to the symbolic figure of the volcano goddess, Pele.

The nineteenth century was a time of great curiosity about the non-Western world, a time that gave birth to museums and to the science of anthropology. During this century, landscape painting, nature writing, and travel writing all came into their own. It was the period in which Western travelers discovered Hawai'i and Hawaiian volcanoes. They brought with them, as I've tried to sketch briefly here, a complex range of cultural perceptions, and generally they persisted in trying to superimpose them on the powerfully alien world of the volcanoes.

The earliest portraits—in word and image—of Hawaiian volcanoes were made by the Reverend William Ellis, an English missionary, during an extensive tour of the island of Hawai'i in 1822–1923. His drawings of the volcano region were turned into engravings and published with a perceptive account called *Polynesian Researches* (London, 1827). When Ellis viewed Kīlauea, he described the scene inside the caldera:

> Fifty-one conical islands, of varied form and size, containing as many craters, rose either round the edge or from the surface of the burning

92

lake . . . several vomited from their ignited mouths streams of lava, which rolled in blazing torrents down their black indented sides into the boiling mass below.[9]

The scene, Ellis commented, "filled us with wonder and admiration at the almost overwhelming manifestation of the power of that dread Being who created the world, and who has declared that by fire he will one day destroy it."

Echoing his Christian philosophy, the drawings by Ellis have an allegorical quality that reminds one of the moral landscapes of John Bunyan's *Pilgrim's Progress*—the Slough of Despond, the Delectable Mountains, the Celestial Country, and so on. In his drawing of the inner pit of Kilauea, the fiery cones are shaped like a series of mini-Vesuviuses. Two stock figures, Englishman and native, in the foreground, gesture alike in awe toward this vision of the "dread Being." A few plants are sketched in, with little attempt at botanical accuracy. In the frontispiece of *Polynesian Researches,* another view of the crater by Ellis has been redone by an engraver in a chiaroscuro worthy of Dante's visions of hell.

In contrast to Ellis's vision, which is dominated by biblical symbolism, the response of Robert Dampier, a visitor to the Islands two years later (1824), is worldly and a bit cynical. Dampier, a gentleman artist and adventurer, accompanied George Anson, Lord Byron (cousin of the poet), commander of the ship that was returning the bodies of Kamehameha II and his consort, Kamamalu, who had died (of measles) on a visit to London. The party camped overnight at the eastern edge of the caldera, in an area now known as Byron's ledge. The next day a few of the party (not including Dampier) descended "to explore the horrors of this Hell upon earth." They returned with tales of "hairbreadth escapes" from "fiery embers" spit out by [spatter] cones "at a most furious rate."[10]

Dampier, remaining on the rim, observed that the noise from the inner crater was "most appalling . . . as if all the Sicilian artificers were most busily engaged in their forging operations." This image from the classical world is mixed with references to the infernal. Pele, or the "igniferous deity," as he calls her, is referred to as "Mr. Paley," as though Dampier could not conceive that "so fierce a God" could be female. (This problem recurs for Westerners, my favorite instance being the 1932 Hollywood movie *Bird of Paradise,* in which the ill-fated Polynesian maid Luana (Delores Del Rio) is sacrificed by the wicked *kahuna* (priest) to a vengeful male god, Pele.)

Dampier comes across as a gentleman on a lark, which may explain why his view of Kīlauea is one of the most distanced, the least dramatic. In Dampier's sketch, three figures (all Westerners) are grouped undramatically in the left foreground, contemplating the caldera. The proportions of the crater with its fiery cones and clouds of smoke and steam are, if anything, reduced rather than heightened, as though Dampier found the scene not quite a fit subject for a gentleman's pencil.

The first professional artists to depict the volcanoes region arrived with the U.S. South Seas Exploring Expedition of 1838–1842. The Wilkes expedition crew included artist Joseph Drayton and artist-naturalist Titian Ramsay Peale, son of the painter Charles Wilson Peale. For this expedition, the primary purpose of making illustrations was to record information—Wilkes and others also made many of the sketches, as though making them were primarily a matter of observation, something any intelligent person could do. Often the artists worked with the aid of a *camera lucida*—a piece of glass set at a 45-degree angle, casting a reflection of the scene on the paper set underneath it. Wilkes's drawing of the camp at Pendulum Peak (see page 26), with its detailed rendering of the texture of the lava, was probably made with the help of this instrument.

The nineteenth-century artist-scientist-explorers set out to portray the landscape objectively—yet from the viewpoint of modern self-consciousness they seem astoundingly unaware of the cultural lens through which they peer (even Lieutenant Wilkes, phlegmatic, rarely moved by what he saw, speaks of lava on the floor of Kīlauea caldera resembling "hideous fiery serpents with black, vitreous scales"). But the work of the scientists of the Wilkes expedition does afford some of the least-adorned early visions of the volcano landscape. Peale's painting "Volcano of 'Kaluea Pele' as seen from the side of Mauna Loa looking southeast," (*ka lua Pele*—"the pit of Pele"—is one Hawaiian term for the volcano) for example, places the volcano, with no attempt to dramatize it, in a hazy background where its smoke blends with the sky. Here Peale focuses on the foreground, depicting the vegetation with a naturalist's eye: silversword (now extinct in the area) and fern, 'ōhi'a and *koa* trees. The expedition party approaching up the slope of Mauna Loa is rendered with a wealth of detail—the natives smoking pipes and carrying loads in calabashes; one Westerner draped in a blanket. It is a small glimpse of realism before Romanticism reloads the landscape with significance.[11]

Peale's "Kilauea Night Scene" (see cover), in contrast, is unabashedly

"Temporary Chimneys and Fire Fountains," a bit of romantic excess from the watercolor palette of C. F. Gordon-Cumming. Page 112 of Fire Fountains, *vol. 2 (Edinburgh: Blackwood, 1883). Courtesy of Bishop Museum.*

Romantic, exaggerating the rugged topography of the walls and ledges in the caldera. The artist has included three Hawaiian women in the left foreground, draped and garlanded in a style more Greek than native. Peale has posed them as formally as muses on a frieze, perhaps in affirmation that in this work he has left realism far behind.

Travel writers, emerging as a breed of their own in the nineteenth century, inherited both the zeal for "scientific" observation and the Romantic penchant for voyages of self-discovery. By the late nineteenth century, the quest for "meaningful" scenery reached epidemic proportions. Travelers sketched, painted and wrote, collected and categorized, ransacking the landscape both for souvenirs and for educational experiences.

Isabella Bird, that intrepid climber of Mauna Loa, is a fine example of the peculiar mix of amateur scientist and cultural missionary that resulted. In comparing her private letters to the published "letters" of *Six Months in the Sandwich Islands* (1875), one can see her turning a chaos of impressions into acceptable Victorian guise—instructional, morally bracing. But even in that guise a Romantic quest for self-expression wars with Presbyterian moralism.

Although daughter of a vicar of the old school, Isabella Bird was, in fact, a powerhouse in a tweed petticoat, a woman with "the appetite of a tiger, the digestion of an ostrich" (according to her husband, whom she married when she was fifty and whom she soon after left at home). In her private letters (still unpublished) to her sister, she describes her journey through Hawai'i as a "ravage," and the word suits her voracious enjoyment, her egoism ("I am the best and boldest female rider on the Islands"), and her abhorrence of the Victorian female role ("I think with sickening terror and disgust . . . of the tyrannies of our aggravated conventionalities"). At the same time, she's convinced of the need for ladylike behavior and horrified by "the whites who live like heathens and exercise the worst moral influence over natives."

The letters reveal the Isabella who must never have fit comfortably into the cloistered drawing-room life of the women back home. But the book suggests a rather frantic search for the right language to express her experience—and, perhaps, through language, a search for an authentic self. In the book there is an early, peculiarly domestic description of *pāhoehoe* lava: it has "a likeness," writes Bird, "on a magnificent scale, of a thick coat of cream drawn in wrinkling folds to the side of a milk-pan." Much later in the book, on her second visit to the volcanoes region, *pāhoehoe* is described as "great shining rolls of black lava . . . like boa constrictors in a state of repletion." In fact, by the second visit, Isabella Bird is driven to a veritable orgy of Romantic excess in her efforts to describe the activities of Kīlauea. The volcano is "all terror, horror and sublimity, blackness, suffocating gases, scorching heat, crashings, surgings, detonations; half-seen fires, hideous, tortured, wallowing waves." Phrases such as "lurid glow," "gouts of fire," and "gory clots" build to a crescendo about midway through her second visit.

And then subside. In part of a late chapter subtitled "Horrors of Halemaumau," Isabella Bird writes,

> I write thunder, and one speaks of the lashing of waves; but these are words pertaining to the familiar earth, and have no place in connection with Kilauea. The breaking lava has a voice all its own, full of compressed fury. Its sound, motion and aspect are all infernal. *Hellish* is the only fitting term.[12]

Wildly Romantic metaphors give over to biblical references, and one senses that her Edinburgh upbringing has reasserted itself.

This is the chapter in which Bird ventures up Mauna Loa, and sees the face of her father, the "fire and brimstone" Presbyterian clergyman, in its erupting fires. But this vision is not in the book—it is revealed only in her letters. Also kept only for the letters is her mysterious comment, on her second visit to Halema'uma'u, in a letter dated June 5, 1873, "I saw something too hideous to be imagined." Is it something in the volcano, or something in her mind? My guess is that this is that point where the mind (even armed with biblical and Romantic metaphors) could no longer mediate, where Isabella Bird peered through the veil of language at the naked, terrifying "otherness" of the volcanoes landscape.

Had Isabella Bird been a less serious soul-seeker, she might have warded off such visions with a bit of levity. It is clear from consulting the Volcano House Register, which from 1865 on provided an open forum for volcano impressions, that the sightseer, precursor to the modern tourist, had already appeared on the scene, expecting to be entertained rather than educated. Bird herself remarks that the register, intended as a record of volcanic activity, contained "an immense amount of flippant rubbish and would-be wit." Caricatures of "Madame Pele" and "profane use of certain passages of scripture" alternated with boring particulars about "the precise time of the departure from Hilo and the arrival here." A few samples:

> 9 June 1865. . . . [D]escended the crater and paid a visit to Madame Pele. Found the small lake in great action, it put me in mind of the sea in a troubled state. The sight is awful as well as grand and sublime. . . . Dipped some hot lava and impressed some half-dollars. . . .

> 4 August 1865. Professor William T. Brigham . . . together with Mr. Charles Wolcott Brooks . . . went down into the crater and passed the night within ten feet of the boiling cauldron. The scene was truly grand. Professor Brigham and Mr. Brooks were startled out of a sound sleep in the morning by a violent puff of sulfurous vapor, from which they left in a remarkable hasty manner, leaving blankets etc. behind them.

> 31 January 1866. Found Pele quiet, although smoking a great deal, for one of the "Fair Sex."[13]

Isabella Bird undoubtedly also read Mark Twain's satire on the register's effusions, in his own entry:

Volcano House
Thursday, June 7, 1866

Like others who came before me I arrived here. I travelled the same way I came, most of the way. But I knew that there was a protecting Providence over us all, and I felt no fear. We have had a good deal of weather. Some of it was only so-so (and to be candid, the remainder was similar).

Mr. Brown—But, however, details of one's trifling experiences during one's journey thither may not always be in good taste in a book designed as a record of volcanic phenomena; therefore let us change to our proper subject.

Visited the crater, intending to stay all night, but the bottle containing the provisions got broke and we were obliged to return. But while we were standing near the South Lake—say 250 yards distant—we saw a hump of dirt about the size of a piece of chalk. I said in a moment, "There is something unusual going to happen." But soon afterwards we observed another clod of about the same size; it hesitated—shook—and then let go and fell into the lake.

Oh God! It was awful.

We then took a drink.

Few visitors will ever achieve the happiness of two such experiences as the above in succession.

While we lay there, a puff of gas came along, and we jumped up and galloped over the lava in the most ridiculous manner, leaving our blankets behind. We did it because it is fashionable, and because it makes one appear to have had a thrilling adventure.

We then took another drink.

After which we returned and camped a little closer to the lake.

I mused and said "How the stupendous grandeur of this magnificently terrible and sublime manifestation of celestial power doth fill the poetic soul with grand thoughts and grander images; and how the overpowering solemnity"

(Here the gin gave out. In the careless hands of Brown the bottle broke.)[14]

The "Mr. Brown" here is Twain's fictitious companion, who accompanied him throughout his adventures in the Islands. Twain, at age thirty-one, had come to Hawai'i as correspondent for the *Sacramento Union,* with the intention to "ransack the islands, the great cataracts and volcanoes completely" and write "twenty or thirty letters" for the paper. He ended up staying four months and a day, and declared it ever after the place he had left his heart, "the loveliest fleet of islands anchored in any ocean."

Twain's volcano experiences predate Isabella Bird's by seven years, but in his lack of concern about whether the landscape he presents is real or imagined he seems decidedly modern. Twain wrote, in his first "letter" about the volcano, "I was disappointed when I first saw the great volcano of Kilauea (Ke-low-way-ah) today for the first time. It is a comfort to me to know that I fully expected to be disappointed, however, and so, in one sense at least, I was not disappointed." The volcano, with its active lava lake at one end, looked like "a cellar," with "a few little sputtering jets of fire occupying a place about as large as a potato patch." But Twain's disappointment with the real landscape was brief, for "here," as he said "was room for the imagination to work." And work it did, as Twain piles metaphor on top of metaphor.

After a large (and apparently excellent) meal at the Volcano House, Twain's party returned to the lookout house a half-mile away to view the nighttime pyrotechnics. Now the "floor of the abyss was magnificently illuminated." The molten lava resembled, Twain thought, "the campfires of a great army far away;" "a colossal railroad map of the State of Massachusetts done in chain lightning on a midnight sky," or "skate tracks on a popular skating ground." The sound, characteristically, reminded him of a "low-pressure steamer," with "the hissing of the steam about her boilers." "Vesuvius," he concludes, "is a child's toy, a soup-kettle, compared to this."

The extent to which Twain was "prepped" for his visit to the volcano is revealed in a fragment called "A Strange Dream." Twain apparently wrote the "dream" in Honolulu, two months before he made his journey to Kīlauea. In this bit of total fiction, Twain describes how he and "a companion" visited "the famous firepit Halemaumau" at night. Standing at the edge, Twain writes, they "looked down a thousand feet upon a boiling, surging, roaring ocean of fire!" His companion tells him a legend about "the old King Kamehameha" whose corpse was spirited away the night of his death, supposedly by the "dread Goddess of Fire."

That night, Twain relates, he fell asleep and dreamed that he stood on the edge of Halema'uma'u and a "gaunt muffled figure appeared," leading him through a "cleft" and "many a fathom down toward the home of the subterranean fires." He and his ghostly guide end up in a "sombre" underground chamber where the spectre points out a great boulder and intones, "the grave of the last Kamehameha!" and then disappears. Twain puts a shoulder to the stone, and it moves at last, revealing the crumbling skeleton of the king. From it issues a "hollow human groan" and . . . the author wakes up!

Only to dream again the same dream, until he becomes convinced it is more than a dream. Finally, shouldering the stone for the third time, he finds "there wasn't any bones there." "You cannot bet anything on dreams," the strange piece ends, a rather feeble Twainian twist. Yet in its eerieness one is reminded of the later, much more ornate literary dream of H. Rider Haggard, whose fantasy world holds similar connotations of womb and tomb.

But while Haggard's metaphors seem to well up from some true dream dimension of the unconscious mind, one is less sure how to take this "dream" of Twain, the literary prankster. It may be useless, in the midst of a barrage of Twainian metaphor, to ask the real Sam Clemens to stand up and make a statement about volcanoes (the closest he comes is his remark about his lodgings at the Volcano House: "The surprise of finding a good hotel in such an outlandish spot startled me considerably more than the volcano did"). But Twain's willingness to reconstruct reality to suit his own purposes harks back to the eighteenth-century view of nature as "backdrop," and perhaps presages the modern view of nature as raw material for the molding of human dreams.

The volcano pilgrimage that C. F. Gordon-Cumming (my nemesis on Mauna Loa, whose ghost kept whispering, "Why climb this dreary mountain?") records falls somewhere between Isabella Bird's moral quest and Twain's cynical "ransack." Like her fellow countrywoman, Iabella Bird, this Scottish travel writer was concerned that travel be morally bracing but even more that the scenery be picturesque. A reviewer of one of her books, *At Home in Fiji,* declared of it, "Almost every page is pregnant with instruction and amusement, and not infrequently with both." Kīlauea turns out not to lend itself to either approach: in *Fire Fountains* (1883), Gordon-Cumming writes, "My mind was full of 'sportive fire fountains' and 'awful detonations' and all that sort of thing; but I was utterly unprepared for the dull hideousness of the actual scene."

Part of the problem for Gordon-Cumming was bad timing: the caldera of Kīlauea had lapsed into a lull at the time she visited, except for intermittent activity around and within Halemaʻumaʻu. Unwillingly dragged out on a trek to the "firepit," Gordon-Cumming discovers that "little was visible but a chaos of broken-up crags" that reminded

"Volcano of 'Kaluea Pele' as seen from the side of Mauna Loa." By T. R. Peale. One of the few instances of realistic detail in mid-19th century depictions of the volcano region. 1840. Neg. 323778. Courtesy Department of Library Services, American Museum of Natural History.

her of Scotland. In contrast to the "awful" scene she expected, the sight of a 30-foot-high spatter cone, spitting bits of molten rock, is merely "quaint."

But the need to amuse and entertain is foremost, and Gordon-Cumming fills in reality's "dull" and "hideous" form with fancy:

> It requires small play of the imagination to see these lava beds all peo-
> pled with strange forms, such as antediluvian monsters built up for
> our instruction at the Crystal Palace. All manner of creeping crawling
> things seem to be here: gigantic lizards and monstrous, many-armed
> cuttlefish.[15]

Gordon-Cumming's book is illustrated by her watercolors, and they are astounding, for they bear little relation to what she describes. In one, tiny figures genteelly perch (one, seated and sketching, must be the author) in the foreground atop monumental, intestinal piles of lava, while in the background lava flows resembling Niagara cascade toward them. If the scene in any way resembled the reality, Gordon-Cumming would not have survived to publish tales about it.

101

By the late nineteenth century, several painters had discovered the volcanoes as grand scenery. Charles Furneaux (1835–1913) became the first resident volcano painter. Arriving in the Islands in 1880, he was on the scene to record the prodigious 1881 eruption of Mauna Loa, which sent lava flows within one mile of Hilo. Using everything he could get his hands on—door panels, mattress ticking—Furneaux made over forty paintings "in the field."[16] The paintings are quick, sometimes crudely impressionistic, but they record with immediacy details of an eruption: a fountaining cone, lava moving into a forest.

Of notably different style, however, are his large panoramic paintings, such as "Eruption of Mauna Loa, November 5, 1880, as seen from Kawaihae." This view from the northwestern side of the island (from offshore—the scale is dramatized by tiny men in a canoe in the foreground) looks fifty miles southeast to where snow-capped Mauna Loa is spouting enormous columns of fire. The fairly realistic proportions of the mountains (Mauna Kea is in the left foreground) give way to the exaggerations of the sublime in the oversized fountains of lava. The color—lurid tinges of sulfurous greens and yellows, black and orange, adds to the unreal effect.

Jules Tavernier (1844–1889), trained in France as a landscape painter, was the quintessential bohemian artist—short, stout, equipped with a mustache, and overly fond of drink. Always in debt, he escaped arrest in San Francisco by fleeing to the Islands in 1884. He lived as much in Hilo as he did Honolulu, making the volcano his special subject (at this time there was almost constant volcanic activity).

Tavernier's "Kilauea Eruption 1886" is a portrait of the lava lake surrounded by massive overhanging crags that are stock features from the Romantic sublime. But the cracked, glowing surface of the lake, broken by small fountains of lava, is rendered with a great deal of realism. Tavernier does not include the conventional tiny human figures of such renderings, instead letting the landscape stand alone in its lonely, terrible beauty, its *otherness* veiled by only the thinnest veneer of late-nineteenth-century Romanticism.

The last notable landscape painter to dedicate himself to the volcanoes region was David Howard Hitchcock. Hitchcock, born in 1863, was a home-grown Hilo boy, grandson of missionaries. In 1890, perhaps as a result of his contact with Jules Tavernier, he went to Paris to study art, returning a self-styled "conservative impressionist." Although many of his paintings display the tones of melodrama of his nineteenth-

"Puna 1902." Oil painting by David Howard Hitchcock. Courtesy of W. Dudley Child, Jr. Photograph courtesy of Lyman House Museum.

century mentors, others, with quiet, competent realism, focus on the shapes and colors of particular aspects of the landscape. The stock figure, the Western observer, has disappeared from Hitchcock's impressive volcanoscapes.

Hitchcock's paintings are memorable because (for the most part) they do not seem to force a symbolic meaning on the landscape. But the painter did not entirely escape the impulse to dramatize or personify volcanism. Hitchcock made two attempts at personifying Pele. One work, "Pele in Flames," depicts, in the smoke and fire of an eruption, the shadowy profile of a hideous (and quite Western-looking) hag. The second, "Pele 1929," shows the goddess (face and torso) emerging from a fiery caldera, young, fierce, and vaguely Polynesian, in the act of hurling, like a baseball pitcher, a great fiery ball of molten rock.

These unsuccessful attempts by Hitchcock to incorporate a non-Western symbolism suggest to me why few modern landscape painters have tackled volcano country. Hitchcock was sensitive to native tradition, and in fact claimed to have experienced the presence of the volcano goddess. Yet, unable to transcend the metaphors of his (Western) cultural background, his symbols repeat Western stereotypes, and collapse in on themselves.

Hitchcock himself may sum up the dilemma in one of his quietest and most subtly evocative paintings, "Puna 1902." The small work depicts a horse, saddled, reins draped on his neck, standing alone in a field of grass and scrub bathed in a golden, pastoral light. In the background is the raw, heavily eroded shape of a large cinder cone. The concave shape of the empty saddle serves to draw the eye to the mysterious concavity of the volcanic form beyond, and leaves the observer there, "unhorsed," in an alien land.

PART II

Children of the Land

SIX

"The Astonishing Food of the Land"

Famous are the children of Hawai'i
Ever loyal to the land
When the evil-hearted messenger comes
With his greedy document of distortion.

No one will fix a signature
To the paper of the enemy
With its sin of annexation
And sale of native civil rights.
We are satisfied with the stones,
The astonishing food of the land.

ELLEN WRIGHT PENDERGAST
"Mele 'Ai Pōhaku" ("Stone-Eating Song"),
written in 1893, the year of the overthrow of the
Hawaiian monarchy

Preceding page: Pu'uloa petroglyphs: a female figure with piko holes in the foreground; complex arrangement with piko holes in the background. Photograph by David Ulrich.

*I*f the Hyatt Regency in North Kona, a district on the leeward side of Hawai'i Island, were located elsewhere, one might think of it as simply a rococo extension of the Disneyland motif, the artificial playland gone whole hog. But Disneyland is located in Los Angeles, and we have long ago forgotten what other shape or significance that region of the earth had.

The Hyatt Regency was built in an area that twenty years ago was as remote as the southlands that I now thought of as the heart of volcano country. People still speak of the Kona coast with reverence and regret; they remember its unbroken miles of ancient trails, the marks of the old culture everywhere, the powerful umbra of the past. Now Kona is the "Gold Coast" of resort development on the island, and in another twenty years those memories will fade and few will remember what was lost.

The Hyatt Regency had pioneered in the earth-reshaping technology that could turn lava coast into what developer Christopher Hemmeter called "the ultimate playground." It had turned wild lava lands into a totally artificial creation. Chris Hemmeter's vision seemed to me a culmination of a view that valued only the land's usefulness, that had no respect for the autochthonous, the aboriginal, the spirit of place. Moreover, it seemed to me the "final solution" to a landscape whose nonhuman power could be profoundly disturbing to the Western mind.

Hemmeter's Hyatt Regency occupies a place the Hawaiians named 'Anaeho'omalu. The name means, literally, "restricted mullet": its natural brackish ponds were walled and shored by the Hawaiians for raising fish. The place is an oasis on this barren coast, and the many cultural remains suggest that it was much used. One of the most extensive petroglyph fields in the Islands is found here. The petroglyph field and what remains of the oasis are now in the middle of the Hyatt "fantasy resort."

I visited 'Anaeho'omalu late one afternoon, following the new road that leads from the main around-the-island road down to the coast, through rough stretches of an ancient lava flow. The road was lined with manicured strips of lawn and coconut trees. I turned at a sign saying "Golf Course," with "Petroglyphs" in small print beneath.

The petroglyphs covered an acre or so of smooth lava islanded by a green sea of golf course. When the resort was planned, an environmental impact statement urged preservation of the ponds and of the petroglyphs. Nevertheless, the ponds were mostly gone, bulldozed on the eve of a state supreme court decision that would have halted development until an adequate plan was drawn up to preserve them. The petroglyphs were, for the most part, "preserved."

In this petroglyph field, holes predominated—small cuplike depressions two or three inches across that had been carved or pecked out of the rock. Some of the depressions had one or more circles around them. Sometimes several holes were surrounded by a circle. Occasional human figures, with sticklike or triangular torsos, were scattered among the abstract, enigmatic arrangements of cups and circles. Some torsos enclosed a cup, or were linked by lines to several cups. In a few places figures, circles, cups, and lines seemed to be linked in an elaborate pictograph story.

Mysteriously, circles and hollows similar to these are found all over the world. They may be the world's most ancient symbols. Circles and holes are carved into the rocks of Frijoles Canyon, New Mexico, and in the Mojave Desert, and are engraved into stone on Ilkley Moor, in Yorkshire. Some of this "rock art" may date back over 350,000 years. The shapes seem, universally, to be connected to birth, or fertility.

There are petroglyph sites throughout the Hawaiian archipelago, but the hole and circle motif is found almost exclusively here, on the Big Island. Very little is known about Hawaiian petroglyphs, but a few traditions survive concerning these depressions, which Hawaiians call *piko*—"umbilical cord"—holes. The holes were carved or pecked out of the rock to hold the tiny stump of umbilical cord that the newborn sloughs a few days after the cord is tied. Each was placed in its own *piko* hole and covered with a small stone. According to tradition, some families traveled great distances, with their children's *piko* saved in a calabash (gourd), to deposit them ceremoniously at a particular place. What *mana* (as the Hawaiians call spiritual power) did this place hold, I wondered, that led the people to cover the rock of this lava plain with birth symbols?

I looked around me. Perhaps less than two centuries ago, I thought, a human from a culture we call Stone Age, a culture without metal tools or a written language, sat here, pecking and carving out symbols in a pictograph language we may never fully understand. What did the symbols say of these peoples' connection with the land, of their view of the world?

It seemed unlikely that I would find any clues at ʻAnaehoʻomalu. Around me stretched sixty-two acres of hotel complex, and golf courses, artificial lagoons linked by a "Tomorrowland" tramway. The resort developers had brought in acres of topsoil, hundreds of fully grown coconut trees, innumerable truckloads of white sand to create a beach. They had blasted and leveled the rough lava, had dredged and shaped the old ponds to feed concrete waterfalls spilling over simulated rock. In the lagoons, they had created tiny islands stocked with live flamingoes.

A hundred yards from me, a bulldozer was leveling lava for more golf course. The petroglyphs were at my feet. In one *piko* hole rested a golf ball. Here one felt the same amputation from nature that one sometimes feels in museums, but none of a museum's behind-glass sanctity, its offer of protection and respect. Preservation, resort-style. I looked again at the petroglyphs. What meaning could one hope to find in them in this setting? Curious shapes, carved into rock, in the middle of a golf course. A trap near the tenth hole. . . .

The following week, I visited Puʻuloa.

The name Puʻuloa comes from *puʻu,* "mound, hill"; and *loa,* "great, long, life." Great hill, mound of life. Puʻuloa is on the south-eastern flank of Kīlauea volcano, within the boundaries of Hawaiʻi Volcanoes National Park, in one of the wildest, loneliest, most magnificent landscapes in volcano country. Located on the lava plains inland from the coast, Puʻuloa is the largest petroglyph field in the entire Hawaiian archipelago. It may, in fact, be the largest anywhere in Polynesia.

Puʻuloa lies on an old Hawaiian trail—the Kaʻū-Puna trail, within the ancient district of Puna, and near the border of Kaʻū district. These areas—and a portion of the district of South Kona—are cradled within the great arms of Mauna Loa volcano (*Mauna* means "mountain"). The younger volcano of Kīlauea rests against Mauna Loa's southern flank, and the activities of the two make this one of the most volcanically alive regions in the world. A large section of this land, incorporated within the National Park, is now wilderness, but it once supported a considerable population of Hawaiians. Old trails, village ruins, agricultural sites—those spared from lava flows—attest to a long habitation.

A great *pali,* or cliff, called the Holei Pali rises abruptly a quarter-mile farther inland from Puʻuloa, to a height of 1,000 feet. Holei Pali

is a fault scarp, marking where the land has slumped violently downward sometime in the life of the volcano. Over thousands of years,
lava has flowed and solidified over its steep sides so that it resembles
the backdrop of an enormous draped curtain. The smooth, billowy
pāhoehoe of Pu'uloa itself, geologists gauge, is around seven hundred
years old.

Below the pali, lava plains extend to the sea, broken by scarps
and ridges and striped by lava flows. The ancient Ka'ū-Puna coastal
trail turns inland over this lava plain to reach Pu'uloa. It bisects the
modern park road about a mile west of the petroglyph field. The Park
Service has marked the old trail with *ahu,* rock cairns. But without
the cairns, in the afternoon light, the trail can be spied by the weathered
spots on the surface where it travels across the smooth *pāhoehoe.* Between the billows of lava, the old trail is obscured by native grass, or
by lantana and guava—introduced shrubs that have found their way
into even the remotest regions, their seeds spread by birds. The only
other prominent vegetation is the *'ōhi'a* tree, the great heir to the volcanic lands of Hawai'i, pioneering on new lava flow and dominating
in the rainforest. In the forest, it grows to an enormous tree, and its
durable wood was used by the Hawaiians for carving temple idols and
the gunwales of canoes. In high montane bogs, it can be found in *bonsai*
form, only a few inches high. Here on the lava plain it grows as a shrub,
spare and gnarled in this area of low rainfall and little soil.

From the western approach, Pu'uloa would be unnoticeable without the Park Service stake fence and boardwalk that encircles a small
area of petroglyphs. There was nothing, at first sight, that suggested
to me what meaning this locale might have held for the Hawaiians.
A few dome-shaped hillocks of rock, a bit larger than ones that dot
the surrounding plains, were clustered here. These lava mounds are
what geologists call *tumuli*—they are formed when the solidifying crust
of a molten flow of lava meets some obstruction, so that it buckles
and is heaved upward by the hotter flow beneath. Sometimes the
molten flow drains out beneath them, leaving them hollow inside, like
great rock bubbles. Or, more accurately, like bubbles frozen as they
burst, for they are usually cracked and fissured.

The boardwalk surrounded some fine petroglyphs. But the greatest
concentrations were on the tops and the eastern sides of the two adjacent tumuli. The petroglyphs carved into the top of the tumuli looked
older, but it could have been because they were more exposed to wind

and rain. Here there were *piko* holes so thickly clustered that the rock appeared honeycombed. Puʻuloa is the petroglyph field most dominated by these particular symbols—thousands on thousands of them.

If these petroglyphs associated with birth united human beginnings with the land, why the union with this wild, barren spot? The world around me was silent—not an empty silence but a dense one, as though someone were standing in a concentrated stillness directly behind me. The only sound was a slight soughing of wind in the grass. Huge cumulus clouds piled above the fault scarps to the west, mirroring the round shapes of the tumuli against a blank sky. I gazed out toward the coast, and beyond to the empty expanse of sea, in the direction from which the first voyagers to these islands must have come. Very likely they would have landed on this southern coast, on this southernmost island.

Several miles to the west I could see the fault scarp of Puʻu Kapukapu ("sacred hill") in the midst of the great stretch of the lava plains of Kaʻū. I knew that there were remnants of a *heiau*—an ancient Hawaiian temple—on the top of it. A couple of miles to the east, on the shore, I could see the tops of the coconut grove that surrounds another *heiau*—a very large and important one—at Wahaʻula. Yet even though the land had been left empty and wild, what I was seeing might have been a very different landscape from the one the makers of these petroglyphs saw. Perhaps they were residents here, when lava spilled over these great cliffs and covered this land, seven hundred years ago. Before then it might have been a thick dry-land forest. The land presented no easy antidotes to the distortions of the history books. But here at least was a timeless, wild horizon, a place to begin to imagine a pre-Western past.

Without knowing what I was searching for, I spent several afternoons at Puʻuloa, wandering about in the golden, slanted light of a westering sun. I discovered that I could pass unseeing by a petroglyph as I walked east, but when I turned into the late sun its outline would be limned by shadow and light. And I began to see that this "wild" land bore human traces everywhere.

Western vision, honed by a temperate clime, had been able to see this country and its inhabitants only in a certain slant of light. From the Western view, this land was a barren wasteland, nearly uninhabitable except for pockets along the coast. But archeologists were now discovering agricultural sites all over it, thousands of tiny garden spots in pockets of the lava, roughly shored up with rock.

In the sides of the tumuli, cracks and bubbles in the lava formed shallow caves. They would have offered a rude shelter. I pushed through a patch of native sword fern and crawled under the low ledge of one cave. In the damp silence, I could hear the drip of water. I shined my flashlight into a crevice, just large enough to crawl into. At the back was a shallow pool of water. A large shell from *'opihi,* a native limpet, lay at the bottom. Perhaps it once rested inside a calabash, for scooping the precious water. I imagined the Hawaiians of two hundred years ago drinking the water, then climbing up to rest on the mound above me. Perhaps it was then that they chipped figures in the stone.

In the afternoons that I spent at Pu'uloa, only two other people ventured out here along the rugged trail. They—a young man and woman, both wearing T-shirts with pictures and words I couldn't decipher at a distance, and sun visors—stood on the boardwalk and stared in puzzlement at the petroglyphs below. They looked out at the empty landscape. They glanced briefly at me, sitting atop a nearby tumulus, and averted their eyes. They left in five minutes. I suppressed the impulse to run after them, tell them to abandon their tourist agenda, their search for the generic Hawaiian—the standard hula, the typical grass house, the reconstructed model of a thirteenth-century *heiau*—and instead, to spend a week of afternoons at Pu'uloa.

For I began to think that I could see beneath the Western portrait of the generic Hawaiian: the Hawai'i Visitors' Bureau Hawaiian (lazy, affable dweller in Eden); the anthropological Hawaiian (poetic but primitive worshiper of dark gods of human sacrifice); the sociological Hawaiian (poorly acculturated). I began to sense a still living presence of a people shaped and molded by this land, people who became, in their own lives and customs, its most intimate expression. Species, *Hawaiian:* subspecies, *people of the rugged volcano lands of Ka'ū and Puna.*

Here the people of the region developed a strong allegiance to the gods of the land, in particular to Pele, goddess of volcanism in all its forms. Here they shaped a tradition of stories the land told them. There is an old Ka'ū saying: "We are like the *'a'ali'i* shrub, which holds fast with its roots to the homeland, whatever winds may blow." Passed down in tradition even today, when the descendants of Puna and Ka'ū are few, is a fierce loyalty to this land, which seems to spring directly from experience with its harsh and dramatic landscape. The late Mary Kawena Pukui, a native of Ka'ū and one of the great ethnographers of her people, said the people of Ka'ū (and of Puna—as the proverb goes, *Hilina'i Puna, kālele iā Ka'ū,* "Puna leans and reclines on Ka'ū") saw themselves as one family sprung from one root. They were proud of their land, even of its harshness. Words from an old ceremonial name chant (chant composed at birth) for a chief of Ka'ū capture this sense:

> I do not care for Kona,
> For Ka'ū is mine.
> The water from Kalae is carried all night long,
> Wrung from tapa [bark cloth] and from sponges.
> This land is heard of as having no water,
> Except for the water that is waited for at Mānā and Unulau,
> The much-prized water found in the eye socket of the fish,
> The water prized and cared for by the man.
> Even the child carries a gourd container in his arms.[1]

As Pukui points out, the kinship through the land meant kinship through the gods of the land. According to Pukui, nearly all natives of Ka'ū (and presumably many of Puna) considered themselves "kin" to the Pele family of gods. The kinship the Hawaiians of Pele's domain felt for her, for "the sacred-earth-person," is hard, Pukui suggests, for an outsider to grasp: "If Pele is not real to you, you cannot comprehend the quality of relationship that exists between persons related to and through Pele, and of these persons to the land and phenomena, not 'created by' but *which are,* Pele and her clan."[2]

From the Western view, just as the barren stretch of coast that includes 'Anaeho'omalu was considered wasteland until recently, so was Pu'uloa. The Pu'uloa petroglyph field was not included within the original National Park boundaries. The park, when it was founded in the early 1900s, was conceived of as purely a "geological Park." But with the birth of Pacific archeology (and the decline of traditional Hawaiian culture) came the recognition that these raw lava southlands were covered with an enormous quantity of cultural remains. In the 1930s an extension of the park added Pu'uloa and a large area of south coast and inlands. Pu'uloa itself, therefore, will never suffer the fate of 'Anaeho'omalu.

But in a larger sense it may, for park protection is double-edged, offering preservation but fencing out the living culture, turning Pu'uloa into a "site," an outdoor museum. The region itself—in many ways the last great repository of native lands and native culture—lies mainly outside the boundaries of the park and vulnerable to those who do not respect its uniqueness. The articulate soul of the land, I sensed at Pu'uloa, was the culture. And it began to seem that the ways in which the culture had been misrepresented, misunderstood, and undervalued were an extension (or a reflection) of attitudes toward the land.

SEVEN

Myth and History at the Scene of the Eruption

I then advised [the priestess of Pele], and all present, to forsake their imaginary deity, whose character was distinguished by all that was revengeful and destructive, and accept the offers Jehovah had made them by his servants, that they might be happy now, and escape the everlasting death that would overtake all the idolatrous and wicked.

THE REVEREND WILLIAM ELLIS
Polynesian Researches

Preceding page: The cinder-covered landscape and the huge cinder cone, Pu'u Pua'i, formed by the 1959 eruption of Kilauea Iki. Photograph by David Ulrich.

*I*t was a blustery day on top of Kīlauea volcano. The normal pattern of trade winds from the northeast had given over to strong winds from the opposite direction, the "Kona" winds that often herald a storm. I was standing on the southeast rim of the volcano's summit caldera. The huge caldera stretched below me and off to the left in an irregular oval. Near its northwestern walls, its deep inner pit, Halemaʻumaʻu, was rimmed by steam plumes. Above Halemaʻumaʻu, low clouds ranged against the blue-gray hump of Mauna Loa. A patch of clear sky near Mauna Loa's top revealed a glimpse of snow. Hawaiian winter.

Somewhere near the spot where I was standing an event took place that became, in Christian annals of Hawaiian history, one of the great moments in the conversion of a pagan people. In the fall of 1824, the female chief Kapiʻolani, recently converted, faced the fires that burned then in Kīlauea caldera to declare her faith in the Christian Jehovah. Since this event came only four years after the first missionaries arrived in the Islands, it was interpreted as a major victory in the struggle to convert the Hawaiians. Over the years, the real story was turned into a heroic tale by those anxious to believe that Pele, whose power had surprisingly lingered on after other gods had been abandoned, had at last been vanquished by one of her own people.

Thus Kapiʻolani's "defiance" of the volcano goddess became part of the political tale that has been accepted as Hawaiian history. It is a tale worth tracking, for such stories form the basis for the modern understanding—or misunderstanding—of Hawaiian culture.

The spot where I stood on the caldera rim seemed particularly apt for contemplating the shady areas between legend and history, for the contours of the land were as obscured as those of Kapiʻolani's story. The whole area was now buried under several yards of volcanic ash from the spectacular 1959 eruption of Kīlauea Iki ("little Kīlauea"), a crater adjacent to the main summit caldera.

We know from the Reverend William Ellis's description in 1823 that the caldera, when Kapiʻolani visited it, looked quite different from the way it looks now. At that time the whole inner crater was more than a hundred yards deeper. Nearly all of it was in an active state of

119

eruption, with over fifty spatter cones spurting fire. Among the cones meandered rivulets of lava. The entire inner crater was encircled by a broad ledge about 500 feet below the outer rim. It was probably on this ledge that Kapi'olani stood—although in some of the later accounts of her visit she descended to the very edge of the "fiery lake."

Kīlauea caldera has gone through numerous collapses and eruptions since then. But the biggest change to the immediate terrain was caused by the eruption of Kīlauea Iki in 1959. This large pit crater (over a mile in length), separated by a ledge (the one on which Kapi'olani reputedly stood) from the main caldera, has been active at rare intervals. In 1959, after almost a hundred years of quiescence, lava burst from its southwest wall. During the eruption, lava gushed from the vent seventeen times, with fountains that at one point reached 1,900 feet. Between phases, the lava drained back into the vent. The quantity of lava was awesome—estimated by geologists at one period as "enough to bury a football field 15 feet deep every minute." The spray of cinder and ash built a large dome called Pu'u Pua'i ("eruption hill").

Pu'u Pua'i rose to my right, a prodigious rust-colored heap, blocking my view into Kīlauea Iki. Even here, half a mile from the eruption vent, the land was blanketed yards deep with pumice and cinders. Bleached skeletons of dead 'ōhi'a bore witness to the forest that stood here before the eruption. Thirty years later the native forest has begun to creep back, with young 'ōhi'a, 'ama'u fern, and a native sword fern, and 'ōhelo berry bushes. The 'ōhelo, a short shrub with small oblong, somewhat leathery leaves, is a relative of the cranberry and blueberry, but is found only in Hawai'i. This species, which thrives in volcanic cinder at Kīlauea, grows only one other place in the Islands—among the relatively young cinder cones of Haleakalā volcano, on Maui. Its red berries are sacred to Pele, and were traditionally only eaten after some of the fruit were thrown, with appropriate prayers, in the direction of the caldera. Kapi'olani defied Pele by eating freely of the sacred berries without making an offering, in what was, for a Hawaiian, the ultimate insult to the volcano goddess. At least many of the later accounts say so. There is only one eyewitness account of Kapi'olani at Kīlauea, and it makes no mention of berries.

That one eyewitness, the Reverend Joseph Goodrich, recorded that he traveled from Hilo to the top of Kīlauea after hearing that Kapi'olani was on her way from her home in Kona to Hilo via the volcano. The next morning, Goodrich, Kapi'olani, and attendants (about fifty in all, according to the reverend) descended to the ledge nearly halfway down the caldera. Here the company sat down, at Kapi'olani's request, and sang hymns. Afterward, Goodrich and a few others climbed down to the bottom of the caldera for a closer look at the outbreaks of molten lava, and Kapi'olani, it is presumed, toiled (she was quite portly) back up to the rim.

Thus goes the entire, and undramatic, firsthand account. Goodrich does mention that "some [Hawaiians] tried to dissuade Kapiolani from going up to the volcano. They told her that Pele would kill her and eat her up if she went there. She replied that she would go, and if Pele killed and ate her up, they might continue to worship Pele; but if not, i.e. if she returned unhurt, then they must turn to the worship of the true God."[1]

Kapi'olani's "defiance" was not, of course, an isolated event. But to understand the impulse to turn this rather prosaic event into an epic confrontation requires some understanding of traditional Hawaiian religion as seen through the eyes of nineteenth-century Westerners.

The reports on Hawaiian religion at the time of first Western contact are complex and contradictory, suggesting that it was multilayered and not in the least homogeneous. Certain practices, however, dominated the lives of the Hawaiians the earliest Westerners came in contact with. The early observers noted that the Hawaiians adhered to a ritual year divided into two seasons: the four-month Makahiki, or harvest festival season, in which Lono, god of rain-making fertility and agriculture was worshiped; and the eight months in which worship of Kū prevailed, the deity primarily associated with fishing and war.

Although Cook, arriving at the beginning of the Makahiki (and thought initially to be the returning god Lono) commented on the harvest season rituals, nineteenth-century observers primarily focused on the Kū rituals. Worship of Kū, which took place in large sacrificial temples or *heiau* called *luakini heiau,* involved elaborate rituals that included human sacrifice. At the time Westerners arrived, the primary worship, at least in areas controlled by Kamehameha, was of Kū in the war god form that this island-conquering chief worshiped. Worship of this fierce god, Kū-ka'ili-moku ("Kū-island-snatcher") had, at least in the time of Kamehameha, become a "state" religion that buttressed the power and status of the ruling chiefs and supported a rigidly hierarchical system of rank.

Central to this hierarchy was the *kapu* (tabu) system, which regulated spheres of power according to rank and gender. The *kapu* system upheld a strict separation between chiefs and commoners. Commoners, for example, did not participate in highest rituals (they did not enter the main *luakini* temples at all), were forbidden certain foods, and had to prostrate themselves fully in front of paramount chiefs. Women, both commoners and chiefs, also had to observe *kapu,* though the severity of these varied according to genealogical rank. Women as a whole were forbidden from entering the main temple grounds or from eating with men.

This theocratic system observed by the early Westerners seems to have been inherently unstable. Even the earliest visitors (Captain Cook's crew, for example) noted many of the Hawaiians breaking the *kapu* laws—and were particularly surprised at the willingness of women of all ranks to break them.[2] The rigid *kapu* system that was central to the "state" religion was already beginning to crumble by the time of Western contact, but the presence of foreigners who obviously operated according to a totally different set of ritual *kapu* must have been further unsettling.

In 1819, the *kapu* system was broken and the "state" religion abolished. Interestingly enough, the one person most instrumental in overthrowing the *kapu* system was a woman—Ka'ahumanu, favorite wife of Kamehameha (Kamehameha the Great, as he came to be called, was by then "king" of all the Islands). Ka'ahumanu was beautiful, nearly six feet tall, and ambitious. When Kamehameha died in 1819 she declared herself regent to the new king, Liholiho, Kamehameha's son (by another wife, Keōpūolani). Shortly after Kamehameha's death, the two women—Ka'ahumanu and Keōpūolani—persuaded Liholiho (or Kamehameha II, as he came to be called), to make the symbolic gesture of breaking the strongest *kapu*—by sitting down to eat with the women. Under the new king's decree, the temple idols were destroyed and the state temples abandoned. The first group of missionaries—Yankee Protestants who arrived in 1820, the year after the abolition of the old system—must have thought that God had cleared the way for them.

But as they soon unhappily discovered, even though the state religion was dismantled, some of the chiefs—and many of the common people—continued to worship their gods. The one god still worshiped openly was Pele. This continuing worship of a female deity was puzzling for Westerners who, basing their knowledge on early observances of the "state" religion, with its strict *kapu* on women and its central worship of a male deity, had made interpretations of Hawaiian religion that fit their own understanding of the place of the female.

It is an interpretation that has persisted so well that one can find it still, in, for example, this history of Polynesia written in 1984:

> . . . there existed [in Polynesian culture] a binary world view whereby categories were set in opposition to each other. The most common and potent was the male-female dichotomy where "male" qualities represented goodness, strength, light, and "female" phenomena were nasty, weak, dangerous, dark (but paradoxically also essential as the givers of life).[3]

One senses here the same polarity the Westerners applied to nature, the division into "good" and "evil" elements. The missionaries, already primed by biblical imagery to see the demons of hell at work in the volcanic fires, fixed on the volcano goddess as symbol of all that was unredeemed in the nature of the Islands, and in the "dark" nature-worshiping souls of its natives.

Even before the incident at Kīlauea, Kapiʻolani was one of the early missionaries' most successful conversion stories. As a young woman, Kapiʻolani was known to be "dissolute." After being converted (according to a brief biography in *Notable Hawaiian Women*) "she discarded all of her husbands except Naihe . . . a councilor of King Kamehameha."[4] Kapiʻolani adopted wholeheartedly the ways of the missionaries, dressing her hair in "side puffs" held by tortoise shell combs, even wearing stockings and shoes. When the U.S. missionary C. S. Stewart dined at her house, he was gratified to be served mutton chops, "a sort of jumble," and "Muscadine wine." So Westernized did Kapiʻolani become that she was called by her own people the *haole* ("foreign") chief.

Kapiʻolani was an excellent candidate, therefore, for a Christian heroine. But it is illuminating to note the details of her story in its gradual conversion to heroic tale. For one thing, as the story evolves over time, Kapiʻolani steps closer and closer to the "fiery lake" until, in later versions of the tale, it's a wonder she doesn't get incinerated. But even more interesting—because it affects modern interpretations of Hawaiian religious traditions—is the subsequent denigration of the Pele "priests" and, finally, of the traditional role of the volcano goddess.

After Liholiho abolished temple worship in 1819, direct confrontation with the missionaries came primarily from the "priests of Pele" and their followers. There are a couple of extant accounts of meetings between missionaries and priests (or in these cases, priestesses) of Pele. One is by the Reverend Stewart, who, on a visit to Lahaina, Maui, in the late 1820s, was introduced to a woman the resident missionary identified as a "priestess of Pele":

> . . . I should judge her to be forty or forty-five years of age; a tall, finely formed, majestic woman, wrapped in a large black mantle of native cloth, falling in thick folds like the Roman toga, from the bust to the ground. We were much impressed with her, as she entered at the head of her train, . . . The style of her face is remarkably noble and commanding—indicative of strong traits of character—with a full, piercing black eye, which I can readily imagine, might be fearfully intimidating to the superstitious.[5]

English missionary William Ellis, on his tour of Hawai'i Island in 1823, also encountered a priestess of Pele. The reverend had stopped to preach to the chiefs and people of a small village near Hilo. The text was "Happy is the people whose God is the Lord." When Ellis "arose to depart," he was challenged by an old woman, who chanted a song in praise of Pele. One of Ellis's party, a converted Hawaiian, spoke to her of Pele's cruelty and destruction of the land. The priestess countered that Pele only destroyed the lands of wicked chiefs, and that a greater destroyer by far was "the rum of the foreigners, whose God you are so fond of. Their diseases and rum have destroyed more of the king's men than all the volcanoes on the island." Ellis writes that, sadly enough, "such a declaration was too true to be contradicted."[6]

These two missionaries are unique in the even-handedness—even sympathy—of their reports. Stewart wrote his memoirs from the safe distance of the East Coast, and Ellis was passing through rather than staying to do battle against paganism, and so could afford to be sympathetic. But Ellis was in many ways an unusually reliable observer, for he had spent considerable time in Tahiti, learning the language and customs, and had soon learned to understand Hawaiian. Ellis had left the islands at the time Kapi'olani visited Kīlauea, but the story was related to him later (unfortunately he doesn't say by whom) and included in *Polynesian Researches.*

According to Ellis, Kapi'olani was "passing near the volcano" and determined to visit the caldera. She was met by "devotees of the goddess," who "tried to dissuade her." Kapi'olani "proposed that they should all go together; and declaring that if Pele appeared, or inflicted any punishment, she would then worship the goddess, but proposing that if nothing of the kind took place, they should renounce their attachment to Pele, and join with her and her friends in acknowledging Jehovah as the true God." Kapi'olani and attendants descended "several hundred feet toward the bottom of the crater, where she spoke to them of the delusion they had formerly labored under in supposing it inhabited by their false gods; they sung a hymn, and, after spending several hours in the vicinity, pursued their journey." "What effect," Ellis muses, "the conduct of Kapiolani, on this occasion, will have on the natives in general, remains yet to be discovered."[7]

Ellis's version adds no startling embellishments to the eyewitness account of Joseph Goodrich, but his is the only one that doesn't. A notable leap from history to heroic tale is accomplished by the Reverend Hiram Bingham. Bingham, who was stationed in Honolulu at the time of Kapi'olani's visit, retells the tale in his memoirs (*A Residence of Twenty-one Years in the Sandwich Islands*), published in 1847. His version claims that Kapi'olani's sole reason for journeying to the volcano was to "trample on the pretended authority" of Pele. According to Bingham's account, on approaching "the region of the volcano," Kapi'olani was met by a "haughty prophetess," who claimed to have, on a piece of *kapa* (bark cloth), a message from Pele. The woman "poured forth a torrent of unintelligible words or sounds which she would have them believe was the dialect of the ancient Pele." Kapi'olani countered with passages from the Bible, and the "haughty prophetess quailed . . . she confessed that *ke akua* [her god] had left her."[8]

There are no other early accounts that corroborate this meeting between chief and "prophetess." Nonetheless, the encounter enters the annals of history, whence it colors later secular accounts. To C. F. Gordon-Cumming (*Fire Fountains,* 1883), Kapi'olani is the Hawaiian "Elijah," defeating hosts of false prophets. Folklorist William Westervelt (*Hawaiian Legends of Volcanoes,* 1916) is more circumspect, repeating Bingham's story but with significant embellishments: in Westervelt's version, Pele's priestess is not only haughty but "bold." Taking out the *kapa*, "she began to read or rather mumble an awful curse."[9]

But the ultimate apotheosis comes from Alfred, Lord Tennyson. Tennyson published his poem "Kapiolani" in 1892:

I

When from the terrors of Nature a people have
    fashioned and worship a Spirit of Evil,
Blest be the Voice of the Teacher who calls to them
    'Set yourselves free!'

125

II

Noble the Saxon who hurled at his Idol a valorous
 weapon in olden England!
Great and greater, and greatest of women, island
 heroine, Kapiolani
Clomb the mountain, and flung the berries, and dared
 the Goddess, and freed the people
 of Hawa-i-ee!

III

A people believing that Peelè the Goddess would
 wallow in fiery riot and revel
On Kilauea,
Dance in a fountain of flame with her devils, or shake
 with her thunders and shatter her island,
Rolling her anger
Thro' blasted valley and flaring forest in blood-red
 cataracts down to the sea!

IV

Long as the lava-light
Glares from the lava-lake,
Dazing the starlight;
Long as the silvery vapour in daylight,
Over the mountain
Floats, will the glory of Kapiolani be mingled with
 either on Hawa-i-ee.

V

What said her Priesthood?
'Woe to this island if ever a woman should handle or
 gather the berries of Peelè!
Accursèd were she!
And woe to this island if ever a woman should climb
 to the dwelling of Peelè the Goddess!
Accursèd were she!'

VI

One from the Sunrise
Dawned on His people, and slowly before him
Vanished shadow-like
Gods and Goddesses,

126

None but the terrible Peelè remaining as Kapiolani
   ascended her mountain,
Baffled her priesthood,
Broke the Taboo,
Dipt to the crater,
Called on the Power adored by the Christian, and
   crying 'I dare her, let Peelè avenge herself'!
Into the flame-billows dashed the berries, and drove
   the demon from Hawa-i-ee.[10]

Tennyson's primary source was *The Book of Golden Deeds* by Charlotte Yonge, published in 1864. Yonge portrays Pele as the "fierce goddess" who "permitted no woman to touch the verge of her mountain." She maintains that Kapi'olani climbed to the top of the volcano "bearing in her hand the sacred berries which it was sacrilege for one of her sex to touch. The enraged priests of Pele came forth from their sanctuary among the crags, and endeavored to bar her way with threats of the rage of their mistress."[11]

What is most fascinating about the successive versions of the Kapi'olani story is the direction they take in portraying Hawaiian religion. Women are excluded from the rites of worship and even, in some later versions, from the domain of the volcano goddess. The Pele priestesses are depicted increasingly as hags and sorcerers, the lunatic fringe, until they finally disappear altogether and are replaced by a male priesthood. Eventually, Pele herself takes on the personified character of the hag and sorcerer. In 1847, Bingham had described the priestess of Pele as "haughty," "disheveled," and "wild." We see this same figure reappear as Pele herself in the writings of historian and folklorist Joseph Emerson in 1892:

> She could at times . . . assume the appearance of a handsome young woman. . . . At other times the *innate* [my emphasis] character of the fury showed itself, and she appeared in her usual form as an ugly and hateful old hag, with tattered and fire-burnt garment, scarcely concealing the filth of her person. Her bloodshot eyes and fiendish countenance paralyzed the beholder, and her touch turned him to stone.[12]

Perhaps we should not be surprised at the resemblance to Medusa here, since a nineteenth-century folklorist would be very apt to be influenced by classical mythology. But Emerson is also conforming to a view that has prevailed into the twentieth century, that has been ac-

THE SACRIFICE TO THE GODDESS PELE.

A popular Western view of Hawaiian religion. This illustration, with the title "Sacrifice to the Goddess Pele," accompanied an article on the 1859 eruption of Mauna Loa. Engraving in Harper's Weekly, *April 16, 1859. Courtesy of Bishop Museum.*

cepted as "real" history. There has been little to contradict that view in recorded history, a record made by male (and mostly missionary) observers, speaking primarily to male chiefs. The details of the lives of most Hawaiian women—and most commoners—went largely unrecorded throughout the nineteenth century.

As antidote to the Kapiʻolani story-cum-moral parable, I tried to track down a story that survived more as folktale than as history, perhaps because it did not provide the material that "history" required. It was the tale of another encounter with Pele.

"Princess" Ruth (Luka) Keʻelikōlani, born in 1826, was one of the last descendants of Kamehameha I. Although known in her youth for her beauty and skill at dancing, she later became a great volcano of a woman, over six feet and weighing in at around 400 pounds. She had a nose resembling a mashed turnip, due, according to Western accounts, to some unfortunate but necessary nasal surgery, and in Hawaiian tradition, to a bout of fisticuffs with her second husband.

Princess Ruth, vociferously non-Christian, hated the *haoles* but occasionally liked to outdo them at their own style. Some photographs show her in Victorian attire, draped in enough material to curtain an entire London drawing room. She built a house to rival the grandest mansions of the age, but spent little time in it, preferring the native grass house. Although apparently a sharp businesswoman, Princess Ruth was fiercely devoted to traditional ways, and refused to speak English.

In November 1880, the people of Hilo observed a fiery glow at the top of Mauna Loa. A short time later, the eruption broke out several miles down the rift zone in the direction of Hilo. Lava flowed slowly but inexorably down the mountain. Within a couple of months, the flow had traveled twenty-five miles, and was only twenty miles from the town. Still it kept on. By June real estate prices on the outskirts of Hilo were one-tenth of what they had been before the eruption. At the beginning of July, the massive creeping flow had swallowed its first house—a dwelling about three miles from town. Most of the Christians in Hilo had suspended business to attend prayer meetings. Hawaiian members of the community sent a desperate message to Ruth to intercede with Pele.

Princess Ruth was staying on Oʻahu at the time. The aging princess was loaded by her retainers on a boat that carried her to harbor at Kailua in Kona. According to John Cameron, first mate on the boat, she was unloaded in a cattle sling. When she climbed into the carriage awaiting her, the axle broke. Another was found. Her retainers had to help the overburdened horse along the bumpy road to Hilo.[13]

On arrival she went to her home in Hilo for several days, apparently unconcerned by the lava inching closer and closer to the town. According to her bookkeeper, Oliver Kawailahaole Stillman, who was with her at the time, "Things looked desperate for Hilo . . . [the lava] was three-quarters of a mile from Hilo. I went back and told Ruth about it." The princess, Stillman recounts (in an interview years later), ordered him to go out and buy as many red silk handkerchiefs as he could find, and a bottle of brandy.[14] The Hawaiians rounded up another carriage to carry her to the lava flow. They took tents and two roast pigs to dine on. After the tents were pitched, Ruth and retinue walked to the glowing edge of the slowly creeping flow. Chanting, Ruth offered Pele the red silk handkerchiefs. Then she broke the brandy bottle on the hot lava, where it burst into flames.

Princess Ruth and her followers went back to their tents to dine and sleep. Returning to the flow the next morning, they found no sign of molten lava. After eight months, the eruption had ended.

According to John Cameron, Princess Ruth returned to Honolulu a heroine, greeted by huge crowds of native Hawaiians. Cameron, telling the story nearly forty years later in a highly colored memoir, was much tickled by the discomfort felt by the missionary community at the time. The general response, apparently, was to ignore the event—an effective move, since all but two newspapers in 1881 were missionary sponsored and, except for a few "renegades," Hawaiians who had learned to read or write in missionary schools had been thoroughly Christianized in the process. And so the Ruth story, though preserved as oral tradition, never entered the mainstream of history.

The only other account from that time that I've been able to unearth is in the irrepressible C. F. Gordon-Cumming's *Fire Fountains,* published two years after the lava flow ceased to threaten Hilo. Although Gordon-Cumming had left the Islands by then, she heard the story through correspondence with Hilo missionaries. Her version:

> One fine old chiefess (commonly called Ruth) . . . went in person to the flow, and presented offerings of silk handkerchiefs and bottles of brandy to Pele, praying to her, if she had any *aloha* (i.e., love) for her, to go back to the mountains.
>
> This occurred only a few days before the fires began to subside, so of course this loyal disciple of Pele assumes this happy result to be a clear proof that her offering was accepted.

Two pages later, Gordon-Cumming offers a more acceptable miracle:

> . . . But now all [the residents of Hilo] agreed to meet, and plead that if so pleased the Lord, their homes might be spared. All places of business were closed, and crowded services were held at morning, noon and evening at all the churches—Catholic and Protestant, native and foreign—throughout the district.
>
> Even the . . . Chinamen, who had burnt their joss-sticks, and made offerings to the fire-demons, all in vain, came in a body to attend the evening service at the Hawaiian church, that they might test the power of the Christian's God.

We may leave it to those materialists who deny the overruling hand of the Creator in the wonderful working of the great forces of nature, to search out purely natural causes for the strange coincidence that, *from that very hour, the fire-flood was stayed.*[15]

Thus did Gordon-Cumming return history to its proper course. Sitting that day on the caldera rim, I reflected on the two histories, of Kapi'olani and of Princess Ruth, one raised to epic (with the help of the written word), the other demoted to folktale. It came to mind that, although the encounter Bingham describes between Kapi'olani and the priestess of Pele may have been fictional, it worked terrifically well as an allegory. In Bingham's tale, Kapi'olani and the priestess stage a contest for the last word. Kapi'olani's weapon is the Bible, while the Pele priestess is armed with a frail piece of bark cloth, as though trying to legitimize, in Western eyes, her own unmediated experience of her god. In Bingham's story—and in the court of history—the Christian champion Kapi'olani wins, for from the time of the missionaries' arrival the power of "the word" rested firmly in Western hands.

At this late date in the twentieth century, how much of what we call "Hawaiian" history, was still, I wondered, a disguised form of Western history? And how many more aspects of the culture had simply gone unnoticed, and unrecorded? It was noon, by then, a hot tropic noon, at the edge of Kīlauea caldera. With the sun directly overhead, the lead-colored lava floor of the caldera was shadowless and blank; it seemed to float like a mirage. It would be nearly impossible to gauge its depth from this position, from this particular point in time.

EIGHT

Unredeemed Nature; Unredeemed Goddess

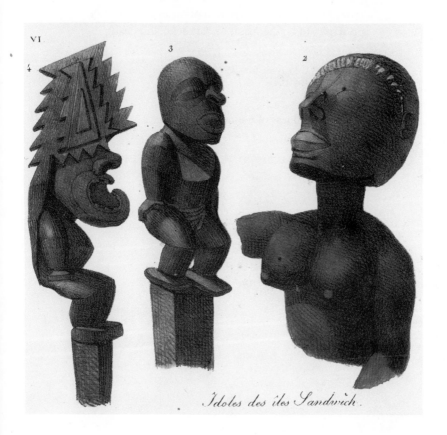

Idoles des îles Sandwich.

[In Polynesian religion] the inferior aspect of nature . . .
is found to be the manifestation of the negative female
principle, to be the realm of darkness, and death.

E. S. C. HANDY
Polynesian Religion (1927)

The uncleanliness of women . . . may have led to the
awarding of volcanic fires to a woman.

SAMUEL H. ELBERT
The Chief in Hawaiian Mythology (1950)

Female impurity explains [Hawaiian] women's close
connection with sorcery.

VALERIO VALERI
Kingship and Sacrifice (1985)

*Preceding page: "Idoles des l'Isles Sandwich." Engraving after drawing by Louis Choris
(detail). Choris identifies the female figure as a "de'ese Hareopapa," presumably meaning an image found in the* hale o Papa, *or "women's temple." Plate 6 in Louis Choris,* Voyage
Pittoresque Autour du Monde *(Paris: Didot, 1822). Courtesy of Bishop Museum.*

*P*ele's earth-shaping activities have obscured all traces of Kapi'olani's visit to the volcano, and all the eyewitnesses are long dead. The "truth" of that event can only be reconstructed from a very selective record. Princess Ruth left no artifacts embedded in the lava flow above Hilo. But at the ruins of a large, ancient temple complex at Waha'ula on the Puna coast, history is a palpable presence. Some aspects of history at this important archeological site are more palpable than others: parts of Waha'ula have been cleaned up and opened to visitors, and other parts ignored.

Waha'ula is a few miles south and east of the Pu'uloa petroglyph field, and a very short distance from the place where the Pu'u 'Ō'ō eruption had, since 1987, been pouring lava into the sea. The large temple complex covers several acres of a raised ground built up by a 1,500-year-old lava flow of clinkery *a'ā*. Groves of ancient *kukui* and coconut trees cover the east end of the temple grounds.

Waha'ula, like the other "state" temples, had been abandoned since 1819. When archeologist John Stokes surveyed the complex in 1900, he found it already in a state of ruin.[1] He identified two large rectangular structures as *luakini heiau*—temples of human sacrifice dedicated to the god Kū. The large rectangular enclosure that dominated the northern corner of the grounds—the younger of the two temple structures—still had fairly intact stone walls, up to 6 feet high and several feet thick. The enclosure, covering an area of about a quarter-acre, was paved with smooth beach pebbles. Stokes suggested that a square platform inside the enclosure was the altar where human sacrifices were laid before being placed on the scaffolding of a wooden tower that stood behind the altar. Other platforms marked places where the drum house and the house where images were kept had stood. These structures, framed with wood poles and thatched with palm leaves or grass, had decayed or been torn down by the time Stokes visited Waha'ula.

According to oral tradition, the initial temple at Waha'ula (probably the older structure near the coast) was built by a mysterious figure named Pā'ao, a "foreigner" who arrived in Hawai'i in the thirteenth

135

century (historians now conjecture that he came from the Society Islands, since some archeological evidence suggests emigrations from that region about that time). Out of oral history Pāʻao emerges as a shadowy figure who wrought, or was harbinger of, enormous change. He is said to have established the ascendancy of his own priesthood, bringing with him the fierce sacred image that held the *mana* (spiritual power) of the war god Kū-kaʻili-moku, and introducing a new ritual system based on human sacrifice. Wahaʻula, it is said, was the first temple of human sacrifice built by Pāʻao.

Hawaiʻi Volcanoes National Park acquired Wahaʻula and surrounding lands in the 1930s, and two decades later the Park Service cleared the overgrown ruins and rebuilt some of the temple walls. A visitors' center was built, trails cleared through the complex, and a paved walkway provided to the younger of the two main temple ruins. The various vestiges of structures inside the temple were duly labeled, including the small platform of stones that Stokes identified as the altar where human sacrifices were temporarily placed.

John Stokes had noted another structure that appeared to be part of the main complex, but failed to identify it as the *hale o Papa* ("house of [the goddess] Papa"), the temple where female chiefs worshiped. Another early visitor, however, the painter David Howard Hitchcock, identified it as the women's temple that traditionally abutted the main temple complex, and described it as a rectangular structure, about 23 feet wide and 33 feet long, with walls in poor condition.[2]

When the Park Service "stabilized" the main temple grounds in the 1950s, the *hale o Papa* was cleared of vegetation but it was decided (the report does not say by whom or why) not to include the structure in the area that would be opened to visitors.

I decided to look for the *hale o Papa*. I asked three park interpreters if they knew where it was located. Not one had ever heard of it. I drove to Wahaʻula and stopped at the desk of the visitors' center to ask for a brochure. The brochure noted that women were not allowed inside the main temple grounds, but did not mention the *hale o Papa*. I walked through the main temple complex toward the ocean, passing a group of tourists who were reading the sign that identified the altar of human sacrifice and staring at the small, unprepossessing platform with a disappointed air. Nevertheless, I suspected, "human sacrifice" would be one fact they would carry home with them about Hawaiian religion. The other, perhaps, would be the exclusion of women from the main temples.

At the coast, I turned west along the rocky trail to the edge of the temple grounds and followed the low wall inland until it disappeared into impenetrable brush. The air was acrid with the fumes of a surface lava flow just inland from Wahaʻula. I decided to talk Laura Carter, the park archeologist, into returning with me in a few days to look for the *hale o Papa*.

The ignored and forgotten *hale o Papa* seemed to me to represent the unrecorded or neglected aspects of Hawaiian religion: just as the site of the *hale o Papa* was not considered worth "stabilizing," the rites of the *hale o Papa* were less fully recorded, and have received less attention than those of the main *luakini heiau*. The few mentions by nineteenth-century Hawaiian informants indicate that female goddesses were worshiped in the women's temple, and that priests of Pele sometimes came to make offerings. But the only rite described is the one in which males also participated, which took place at the ceremonial closing of the eight-month ritual season of Kū worship.

Anthropologist Valerio Valeri provides an analysis of this one rite in a study of Hawaiian religion that focuses primarily on the worship of Kū.[3] In this rite, the ruling chief entered the women's temple, carrying one end of a long, white *kapa* loincloth that had been ceremoniously presented to him by his highest-ranking female relatives (who held the other end). Inside the *hale o Papa,* the chief's wife offered sacrifices (*kapa* and a pig, according to a nineteenth-century Hawaiian historian) to the female gods.

Valeri's interpretation of this final rite of the Kū season is that it returns the ruling chief from the domain of the sacred or pure to the domain of the profane or impure (symbolized by women), and frees him to once more participate freely in daily human life. The *hale o Papa* thus primarily serves as a way station where men can be relieved of the burden of sanctity after an eight-month effort to provide sacrifices "pure" enough to be acceptable to the highest god.

Valeri's analysis, which ranks Kū worship as central to Hawaiian religion, is the culmination of an assessment of the religion that has focused primarily on the sacrificial rituals of the high-ranking males, as observed from the time of Cook's arrival. Because of this focus, Valeri argues for a general understanding of Hawaiian religion as a hierarchical system in which the male ruler stands closest to the divine, and thus is primary sacrificer to the most important gods. The *kapu* system supports a division into realms of the sacred and profane, the pure and impure. Women are impure by nature because they are sullied by their own reproductive processes. Valeri concludes that "goddesses are few and have a marginal position in the Hawaiian pantheon. This corresponds to the marginal position of women in the ritual system."[4] Valeri discusses Pele only in passing, but relegates her to the position of a minor deity whose powers are primarily connected to sorcery.

The apparent inferior position of women in the *kapu* system is presented by Valeri and earlier commentators as evidence that the Hawaiians perceived women as "inferior, negative, and distant from the divine."[5] It is true that tabus restricting women's activities are found throughout Polynesia. Valeri is expanding on the classic anthropological interpretation of these tabus as proof that in Polynesian society women are viewed as impure or profane, a source of pollution that jeopardizes human relations with the gods. According to this view, women's primary impurity seems to be the fact that they menstruate, which makes them repellent to the gods. As E. S. C. Handy argues in *Polynesian Religion* (1927), menstrual blood is "utterly contaminating to all that is sacred."[6] Women were barred from ritual areas because, according to Handy, "they were common (without mana) and harbored dangerous influences of the lower aspect of Nature, [and therefore] were always open to acting as mediums of evil."

The concepts of purity and impurity as applied to Hawaiian religion are worth considering further, because they are the basis for a devaluation of the female within traditional culture in general, and of female goddesses within the religious system. Valeri, building on the work of earlier anthropologists and the views of Christianized native historians, applies a system of dualistic categories to Hawaiian religion: male-female, sacred-profane, pure-impure. As Jocelyn Linnekin, who has been Valeri's most cogent critic, notes, one of Valeri's important sources for a strongly dualistic interpretation of Hawaiian religion has been Handy's classic study *Polynesian Religion*.[7] Handy links all the superior "procreative" life-giving aspects of nature with a male principle, and equates "the inferior aspect of nature" (that is, "the realm of darkness and death") with a "negative female principle." Handy's summation of Pele in this early work as "devastator of lands and great patron of the black arts" may stem from this view of the female's place in the natural scheme.[8] This equation of the female with the "destructive" aspects of nature (and male with the "creative") is common enough in Western cultural history, but does it really reflect the Hawaiian view?

Valeri continues the same argument, most tellingly in his asser-
tions that female goddesses are primarily sorcery goddesses, and that
"female impurity explains women's close connection with sorcery."[9]
In the Western understanding, "sorcery" is linked to the "black arts,"
which seems to essentially mean a power to harness the destructive
aspects of nature. In Hawaiian culture, forms of "sorcery" ranged from
prophecy and healing to praying to death. The Pele family was linked
to "sorcery"; so also were all the war god aspects of Kū.

There is an interesting circularity to the argument that women
were both "without mana" and "dangerous." The argument hinges
on the interpretation of the Polynesian concepts *tapu* (*kapu,* in Hawaiian) and *noa* as "pure" and "impure." But in fact the literal translation of *kapu* is "restricted or set apart" and of *noa* is "freed from
restriction." As F. Allan Hanson has argued in an important article called
"Female Pollution in Polynesia?" women may have been hedged in
by a system of tabus because, rather than repelling the gods, they were,
by their own anatomy, a direct conduit to the realm of the gods.[10] In
Tahitian, the word for vagina also means "the pathway of the gods";
in Maori, *atua* means both "god" and "menses." Throughout Polynesia, according to anthropologist Caroline Ralston, "women's access
to the *pō* [primordial night; the cosmic realm of the gods] was seen
to be close and active, especially during menstruation and childbirth."
For this reason "women's potency [pō-tency?], their ability to transform and absorb [*tapu*], particularly at inappropriate times, had to be
carefully controlled."[11]

This conception of female power may help to explain why ancient Hawaiian women enjoyed an equal rank with men genealogically
(for example, Kamehameha the Great had one wife who outranked
him in ancestry—he had to enter her presence on his hands and knees)
but not within the ritual system—or at least the theocracy that had
come to dominate Hawaiian culture.

As Valeri himself points out, the sacrificial system may be seen as
male substitute for female generative power: "it is possible to represent
childbearing as woman's sacrifice and sacrifice as man's childbearing."[12]
One might question, though, Valeri's argument that Hawaiians saw
sacrifice as "superior" to reproduction as a conduit to divine power
(because not tainted by women's impurity). Several anthropologists
note the possible connection between the rise of Kū worship and increased competition for land and power among Hawaiian chiefs, or
perhaps from immigrant chiefs. Kamehameha himself was said to have

been a descendant of a chief brought to the islands by Pā'ao, the "foreign" priest who tradition says established Kū worship.

There is much to suggest that Kū worship—and the rigid *kapu* system that accompanied it—may have been a late and by no means universal development. Certainly the evidence in myths and cosmological chants of a procreative view of the cosmos, a dynamic balance of male and female, argues against accepting Kū worship as a reflection of central beliefs. The continuing worship of male and female generative gods by commoners after the abolition of the "state" religion in 1819 suggests that dismantling Kū worship and the *kapu* system did not destroy fundamental beliefs. Even if one looks solely at the written record, with its politicized history, one catches intriguing glimpses of another side of the story. This one, for example, by Martha Beckwith, of Kihawahine, an ancestral goddess of Maui:

> Kamehameha set up her image in the heiau. In her name he carried his conquest over the islands. He gave her the prostration tapu [ultimate sign of respect]; even those passing in canoes were obliged to observe this tapu.[13]

As Valeri's book makes clear, the rites of "kingship and sacrifice" are only one part of the annual ritual cycle. For four months of the year the hegemony of Kū was suspended, his temples closed, and chiefs and people celebrated the harvest festival called the Makahiki, dedicated to the god Lono. The Makahiki began at the time of the rising of the Pleiades (around the end of October), and marked the coming of the fertile rainy season. Lono is the patron of fertility and of the peaceful arts associated with reproduction and food cultivation. During his reign the sacrificial altar of the *luakini* temple closed, the images of the war gods were covered, and the Makahiki image of Lono was brought forth and decorated.

It is possible that the Makahiki—a time in which *kapu* were suspended and men and women, chiefs and commoners participated in the harvest rituals, was a vestige of more universal worship of the generative gods. As anthropologist Marshall Sahlins points out, in Hawaiian genealogies "certain ruling chiefs are identified with Lono and bear his name, and these are descended from women of indigenous or early lines."[14] Sahlins notes that what is known about Kapawa, the chief that the foreign priest-conqueror Pā'ao deposed, suggests "an earlier, more indigenous type of ruling chief: succeeding by inherent right and tabu status rather than usurpation; benevolent to his people; sponsor of

An early portrait of a luakini *temple, sketched by the artist on the island of Kaua'i. Engraving by Lerpernere after original by John Webber, artist with the Cook expedition. 1784. Courtesy of Bishop Museum.*

agricultural production . . . ; and, above all, the chief who eschews human sacrifice.''

In a concrete sense, the Makahiki was a celebration of the fertility of gods, people, and earth. In the beginning rituals, the female chiefs girded a Lono image called "Lono the parent" with a sacred loincloth made of the finest white *kapa* (a role similar to the one women played in the closing rites of the Kū temples, at the *hale o Papa*). Over a period of days, the ruling chief ceremoniously gave up the power he had accrued during the season dedicated to Kū.

On the twenty-third day of the festival, everyone dressed up, both chiefs and commoners, ate a great feast, drank a lot of *'awa* (an intoxicating beverage), and went to bathe ceremoniously in the sea. The "bathing," which lasted till dawn, was apparently a sexual free-for-all in which all sexes and social classes mingled freely. For the next four days everything except having a good time was forbidden (the high priest of Kū was blindfolded during this period so he did not witness all the breaking of the normal *kapu* that went on). The king and other men and women of all ranks participated in boxing matches and other games. According to Valeri, "scatological or obscene songs . . . [were] improvised" and "hundreds, . . . or even thousands of people partici-

141

pate[d] in dances that enact[ed] mythological and historical episodes. These dances often . . . [had] an erotic character."[15]

The Lono-the-parent image was then taken in procession clockwise around the island, where each district gave gifts that were redistributed among the people. Another Lono image proceeded in the opposite direction, accompanied by images of the female gods. Games, boxing, and hula dancing took place all along the way.

Do we have in the Makahiki, then, the vestiges of an earlier, more widespread cult based on the worship of the generative gods? (We do know that Kamehameha himself made changes in the traditional festival, by including his personal gods (notably the war god Kū-ka'ili-moku[16]) and exacting additional tributes that originally went to the people. The basic form of the Makahiki seems to be a celebration of the people in honor of the gods of generation, with similarities, as Marshall Sahlins suggests, to the great carnivals, or Saturnalia, of medieval Europe.[17] Some historians have suggested that the Saturnalia represented a kind of "return of the repressed"—of a pagan, tribal identity that Christian theocracy had pushed down. The rituals of Europe were dedicated to the fertility gods and the worship of nature (in the figure of the goddess Flora) as female and divine. Since European history has been given primarily a "Christian reading," little attention has been paid to this underside of the dominant culture until recently. In the interpretation of Hawaiian religion, we may have a similar situation.

Certainly the emphasis on the androcentric rituals of Kū as primary to Hawaiian religion has obscured the role of the generative nature gods, and particularly of the goddesses, including Pele. Pele is a member of the Lono family—in legends he is characterized as her "uncle" and as "keeper of her firesticks." Only when removed from this context does she become a puzzling figure—an "anomaly"—as Samuel Elbert calls her in his study *The Chief in Hawaiian Mythology* (1950).

Elbert finds that Pele is not easy to dismiss. "How does it happen," he asks, "that the pattern of male dominance [in legends about chiefs and male gods] should be upset so completely by the powerful goddess of volcanoes?" Perhaps, he suggests, Pele is powerful by default—to impute the "terrible activities" of volcanism to the major male gods "may have seemed sacrilege." Elbert suggests other possible reasons the powerful forces of volcanism might be awarded to a female god: the geo-uterine aspects of the volcanic landscape, the resemblance of lava flows to menstrual flows, and the "capriciousness" of volcanic activity.[18]

Apparently unsatisfied with a geo-sexual explanation for Pele's power, however, Elbert offers also a psychological theory. Pele's power may be a reflection of "intersexual tension," particularly that kindled by "female aggressiveness." (Elbert gives an interesting example of "female aggressiveness": "women retained the right to refuse sexual approach, and their rejectees could not have felt happy at being cast aside.") Elbert concludes that "male resentment of over-aggressive women" may have been one of the "forces leading to the establishment of the cruel goddess Pele."

One is left to simply wonder at the apparently heartfelt need to explain away this investment of divine power in the female.

Elbert's understanding of Hawaiian religion drew heavily on E. S. C. Handy's early work, *Polynesian Religion.* Elbert's work was his doctoral dissertation, written before he had spent much time in the Islands (he is primarily known now for his excellent work on Hawaiian language); Handy's book was written before he had ever been to Hawai'i. Handy's later works, written after gaining knowledge of regional Hawaiian traditions, of proverbs, stories, and chants, offer a radically different view of Hawaiian culture than the one expressed in *Polynesian Religion.*

Handy spent the latter part of his career piecing together information about the lives of the common Hawaiians, whom he calls "the planters of Lono." Much of his research was done in Ka'ū, where he was accompanied by his friend and colleague Mary Kawena Pukui. Pukui was a descendant of chiefs and priests of Ka'ū. Her family was Pele clan, claiming the volcano goddess as ancestor as well as family god. In the 1930s Handy, his wife Elizabeth, and Pukui spent months collecting oral traditions in Ka'ū and Puna. The result was two books: *Native Planters in Old Hawai'i* and *The Polynesian Family System in Ka'u, Hawai'i.*

Both books argue that primarily the ancient Hawaiians were tribal, peace-loving cultivators of the land, with a strongly developed loyalty to place. (As Handy points out, "the initiation rite that every boy went through, be he chief or commoner, was a dedication to Lono, the rain and harvest god. There was no similar dedication to Kū, the god of fishing and war.")[19] Prototypical were the people of Ka'ū and Puna, who in their isolation may have retained a tribal pattern longer than anywhere else in the Islands. These people "loved Pele, whose home was their land; they endured her furies, and celebrated the drama of creation, with which they lived so intimately, in the songs and dances of the sacred *hula.*"[20] Handy, looking at the relationship of the people to the generative gods of the land, developed a very different view of Pele, whom he had characterized in his earlier work as "the incarnation of female rapacity."

Waha'ula was abandoned in the nineteenth century, its idols hidden away or destroyed. But no images were ever recorded as having been made of Pele, perhaps because she was a part of nature that could not be "tamed," brought into the temple and dedicated to human aims. Yet her strong presence permeates oral traditions and shapes the current lives of those who dwell in her lands, and it is there we must look for her.

In May 1989, surface lava flows moved once again toward Waha'ula. In June, molten lava ignited the visitors' center and flowed to the wall of the main *heiau.* Park archeologist Laura Carter and her crew started emergency salvage work to the west of the main temple. Now Carter located what she believed to be the *hale o Papa.* When I drove down to look at the structure, the steaming front of the lava flow was only twenty feet away. The next day, lava covered the *hale o Papa.* The main temple, on a bit of higher ground, so far remained untouched.

NINE

The Many Bodies of the Goddess

The woman Pele burst forth at Nōmilu,
She flashed to the heavens, on and on.
The woman Pele burst forth at Kakakalua,
She flashed to the heavens, on and on.
It was awe-inspiring, awe-inspiring.
She flashed to the heavens, on and on.

Traditional Pele chant and hula

You can't imagine what you're feeling
blue about.
You simply glide and take a slide and you
want to shout.
You wiggle, you giggle, you wiggle to the
Hula Blues.

Popular song, 1930s

Preceding page: Kumu hula *Pualani Kanahele, chanting while her troupe dances. Photograph by Boone Morrison.*

There is a central connection between the Pele family of gods and *hula*. One can't begin a serious discussion of hula, however, without confronting its modern image—a naughty dance performed by Hawaiian maidens in coconut shell bras and imitation grass skirts made of shredded bright-green cellophane. That particular fashion, in fact, was pioneered by Dorothy Lamour in the 1930s, but by then hula reborn as tourist entertainment was well on its way to becoming quintessential "airport art." Modern hula bears little resemblance to the traditional art; like the purple orchid grown here in greenhouses, it is an artificially cultivated product of Hawai'i. Were this the only form in which hula survived, we would have a sad situation indeed—the equivalent, perhaps, of the sacred *kachina* dances of the Hopi reduced to a Las Vegas chorus line.

Traditionally, hula was not a solitary art but an accompaniment to chant. Both art forms could function as pure entertainment or as sacred ritual, depending on style, content, or place of performance. Chanters and dancers were carefully trained in hula "schools," and it is likely that performances commemorated every major event in ancient Hawai'i. One important ritual service was the chanting and dancing of *mele ma'i* ("genital chants") at the birth of a chief. As this suggests, one important ritual use of hula and chant has to do with transferring the generative powers of the gods to the people.

Which probably explains why the missionaries, who tended to interpret Hawaiian celebration of the generative powers of nature as just plain prurience, worked so hard to repress the hula. To this end they enlisted the help of Christian convert and reigning regent Ka'ahumanu, who passed an edict in 1830 forbidding public performance of the hula. Until King David Kalākaua openly defied the Christian community and revived the hula during his reign (1874–1891), the art virtually went underground. But masters of chant and hula generally passed on skills within their families, so that the chants and dances that have been preserved may be one of the more authentic sources of knowledge about traditional Hawaiian culture.

Unfortunately, it is not a knowledge that can be easily expressed in modern or Western terms, even if one can gain access to the many layers of meaning. The extremely metaphoric nature of the language itself, with concrete images—places, individuals, historic events—standing as symbols for inner truths, makes translation difficult. If the original import of place or event is lost, we are left to try to guess meaning without context—as though, lacking a knowledge of Western history, we were left to puzzle at such phrases as "building castles in Spain," "taking a journey up Boot Hill," "being in the Slough of Despond," or "crossing the Rubicon."

The modern translator must find some way across the great abyss between a culture of written traditions whose metaphors are abstract symbols, and a purely oral culture whose metaphors are tied closely to concrete aspects of nature and place, to even begin to understand the world mirrored in Hawaiian chant and dance. Western metaphors may be long distanced from an ancestral landscape, or from nature as primary source of symbol. How many of us have seen the Rubicon? Do we know in which direction it flows, from what mountains it receives its waters, whether its taste is sweet or bitter?

As do proverbs and legends, Hawaiian chant and dance reflect the close bond of people to the land. Human, natural, and supernatural are all unified through the concrete symbols of the natural world. As with the "dreaming" of the Australian aboriginals, *place* is the meeting point of natural and supernatural worlds. Chants are maps to real and mythological landscapes. The metaphors of chant kept an enormous amount of knowledge—historical, topographical, environmental—constantly circulating.

They also maintained the sacred link to the gods as embodied in nature. All chants and dance, whatever their ritual use, possess *kaona* ("veiled or hidden meaning"). *Kaona* is the invocational side of word, music, and movement, acknowledging and appealing to the powers of the gods. Those powers are the great generative forces that are continuously conceiving and giving birth to the world. Hula invites the gods to join their primal energy with the human, so it is a profoundly erotic invitation. An excellent example of *kaona* can be found (as Marshall Sahlins points out) in the ancient proverb that is inscribed above the entrance to the Honolulu Board of Water Supply:

Uwē ka lani, ola ka honua.
The heavens weep, the earth lives.

Implicit in this apparently simple noting of natural process is the myth of the mating of Wākea, the sky god, with Papa, the earth goddess—a cosmic coupling that engendered the Hawaiian people. As Sahlins says, it is "unlikely that the *haole* ('white men') and Japanese who now dominate Hawaiian bureaucracy are aware that this anodyne snippet of pastoral poesy refers to a primordial copulation."[1]

The mythological connection hints at the deeper meaning of the proverb (though it by no means exhausts it), but also expressed in metaphor is a simple observation about human sexuality. This typical encoding of an erotic element—the "human" side of a deeper meaning—has afforded the Hawaiians great amusement at the expense of foreigners, as well as a way to protect themselves. I suspect the extent of the joke has been enormous: for instance, I attended a school here in the Islands whose Hawaiian name, chosen by its missionary founders, meant literally "happy work." The figurative meaning of the phrase, it turns out, refers to lovemaking. We were taught to sing a Hawaiian chant with a rollicking rhythm that our teachers identified as a "Hawaiian war chant." Years later I came across a translation. Part of the refrain goes like this:

> We two in the spray,
> Oh joy two together
> Embracing tightly in the coolness.[2]

To understand the full nuances, it helps to know that a whole complex of symbols combining water with coolness—mist, rain, wave spume—are central to Hawaiian understanding of sexual passion, just as variations on "heat" are to ours. Sexuality as response to a tropical climate, perhaps? A reminder, at any rate, that one has entered a very different metaphoric world.

The centrality of the erotic-generative may explain why, as Jocelyn Linnekin notes, "according to early post-contact sources, women predominate in the hula. Chants and genealogies are often passed down through women."[3] Captain Cook's crew observed that during the Makahiki, the great festive celebration of the return of Lono, god of fertility, the women spent most of their time singing and dancing.[4] Yet hula has been given little attention as an integral part of Hawaiian religion.

There are male hula teachers and dancers as well, but the stories of the origins of hula suggest its relation to mediumship, and remind one of women's special capacities as prophets and mediums. One

149

legend is that the early people observed the motions of a woman in a trance. When she awoke, they asked her to teach these movements to them. In other legends, the first dancer is inspired by the movement of leaves in the wind, and the first chanter by the voice of a bird. In performing both these arts, the powers of the nonhuman world—of the winds and rain, clouds and sea waves—are embodied in the performer. Thus the *frisson* that comes in watching or listening to the great chanters and dancers—one is responding to the voice or shape of the nonhuman world, to a cosmic energy speaking through the human form. ʻIolani Luahine, a dancer of astounding power who died a few years ago, was asked once, "What happens when you dance, ʻIo?" She replied, "I don't know. I'm not there."[5]

As female generative gods, Pele and her family occupy a central place in chant and dance. Hiʻiaka, a deity that is an aspect of volcanism (or a "sister" to Pele, in her "human" form), is both sorcerer and great patroness of hula. According to myth, Hiʻiaka learns the hula from a legendary female figure named Hōpoe. As the chant that tells this story reveals, Hōpoe is both spirit and natural form, since in the legend she becomes transformed into an actual rock off the coast of the Puna district of the Big Island, at a place called Hāʻena:

> Puna is dancing in the wind.
> The hala grove at Keaʻau dances.
> Hāʻena dances with Hopoe.
> The woman dances,
> Rotating her hips in the sea of Nānāhuki,
> A hula that is all delight
> In the sea of Nānāhuki there.[6]

As this scene suggests, with its synthesis of god, human, and natural forms in "erotic" dance, hula mimics the generative energy that the gods express through nature. The force that animates the cosmos, one might say, is the desire to "dance."

Hula and chant, then, both evoke the spiritual forces of the natural world and *invoke* them. In the same way that the female body can be a gateway to the *pō*, the sacred darkness from which both gods and humans are born, the dancer becomes a conduit to the spirit world. For this reason, chanters and dancers observed many *kapu,* and had to know the prayers to ward off harmful sorcery.

With Pele and Hiʻiaka, the goddesses Laka and Kapo are connected in myth with the origins of hula. These deities can all be considered

"Iles Sandwich: Femme de l'Isle Mowi Dansant" (female hula dancer from the island of Maui). Engraving from drawing by Jacques Arago, artist with the Russian expedition led by Otto von Kotzebue, which visited Hawai'i in 1816. Plate 88 in Louis Freycinet, Voyage Autour du Monde, *Atlas Historique (Paris: Pillet Ainé, 1825). Courtesy of Bishop Museum.*

aspects of the great female generative gods—Haumea, who is worshiped throughout Polynesia, and Papa, who might be considered Haumea in her Hawaiian incarnation. Laka is the deity invoked at the altars of the hula schools, worshiped with offerings of wild forest plants and flowers. Laka is identified in some ancient chants as either sister or wife to Lono. Her power as a generative goddess is evident in a prayer to her as

> the woman suspended in air, face upward, tossing this way and that, her limbs outspread, her voice choked. She is the fondled, sacred one, the earth left over in the making. Her womb holds multitudes upon multitudes in the uplands and the sea. It is a single family that springs from her womb. She is the impregnated one, the fertilized, from whom descends generations of offspring, the family of Laka, fruitful as the stalk.[7]

"In other words," says Martha Beckwith, "Laka . . . is the goddess of love." Beckwith pairs Laka with Kapo, another goddess connected by myth to the origins of hula: "Laka and Kapo must be thought of as different forms of the reproductive energy." If Laka is the "fertile" one, Kapo seems to represent a sexuality separate from reproduction. Kapo has the unusual ability to separate her vagina from the rest of her body. In that form she is called Kapo-kohe-lele, "Kapo of the traveling vagina." (It is in this shape that she rescues Pele from the pig god Kamapua'a, but that story comes in the next chapter.)

Kapo was known as a powerful sorcery goddess. Nineteenth-century historian Joseph Emerson wrote of her,

> An inferior deity of the Pele family is the obscene *Kapo,* a conception of impurity too revolting to admit of description. She is continually employed by the kahunas [traditional priests] as a messenger in their black arts, and is claimed by many as their aumakua.[8]

As was true with early accounts of Pele, Kapo enters the historical record only in her "dark" form. Yet, like most nature deities, this is only the shadow side of a dual nature:

> As Kapo'ula-Kina'u (Kapo-red-spotted) she was the Kapo invoked by *kahuna* when sending evil back upon a witch. This Kapo was a goddess whose temper was violent and vengeful. But when worshipped by dancers and chanters, this same person was the gentle Laka, the spirit of the wildwood.[9]

As did sorcery, chant and dance called forth a spiritual power that had to be carefully controlled. If the laws of the hula school were violated, the gentle Laka could turn quickly into the vengeful Kapo.

The chants and dances concerning Pele are, according to Martha Beckwith, "not composed by mortals but taught by the Pele spirits to worshippers of Pele. Those who learn the dances are supposed to be possessed by the Pele goddess of the dance."[10]

Families who sacrificed the bones of their ancestors to Pele became particular guardians of the rites to the volcano goddess. Contemporary *kumu hula* ("hula master") Pualani Kanaka'ole Kanahele, whose family is from Ka'ū, is one of the people for whom Pele is an *'aumakua,* an ancestral or family god. She comes from a line of hula masters, on the maternal side, who bear Pele names. Pualani Kanahele herself resembles the regal "Pele priestess" that the Reverend Charles Stewart described meeting in 1831—she of the "noble and commanding aspect" and the "full, piercing black eye." She is built, decidedly, on the majestic scale, with long, black, wavy hair touched with gray. When she performs with her hula troupe, she usually dresses in a floor-length cloth of red or saffron yellow, draped, in the ancient style, over one shoulder, with her head crowned in a wreath of *'ōhi'a-lehua* blossoms and the feathery *palai* fern that is sacred to Laka. With her sister, Nalani, she has trained a group of chanters and dancers that have dedicated themselves to the works honoring Pele and to the revival of traditional chant forms. To hear Pualani herself chant is to feel the enormous power of that art, even if one doesn't understand the words.

Pualani Kanahele honors the traditional *kapu* on discussing the religious aspects of her work, and she does not give interviews. But she spoke briefly at a Native Hawaiian Rights conference that I attended. She said that she is often asked, "How can you believe in a Christian god and believe in Pele?" She answered, "Well, I believe in my mother and I believe in my grandmother. . . . Pele is my ancestor, just as they are." Pualani has also testified in court on behalf of the Pele Defense Fund, the group of native Hawaiians who have fought geothermal development on the east rift of Kīlauea on the basis that it will desecrate ground that is part of the body of Pele. Pualani and other "Pele practitioners" spoke of the responsibility, for those who carry the Pele name, to honor and protect their god in her many forms, from steam to lava to the fragile and beautiful plants of her realm. She pointed out that a sense of Pele's presence may be "the life connection we have to Hawaiian culture . . . our ancestral memory is sort of clinging to this Pele deity."

Pualani also spoke of the creative role of the *kumu hula* in translating the physical manifestations of Pele into hula dances and chants, in order to convey the volcano goddess's "message"—her revelations of the central mysteries of creation. In that sense, the *kumu hula* still function as mediums for the divine. Many *kumu hula,* like Pualani Kanahele, do not see a conflict between Christian belief and this role of being channels for the spirits of the land.

Other native Hawaiians, however, do. At the January 1987 dedication of the new Thomas Jaggar Museum in Volcanoes National Park, blessings were offered at the hula platform, a beautiful stonework edifice built in the traditional style a few years ago near the edge of Kīlauea caldera. Pualani and her sister Nālani's group performed a traditional hula in honor of Pele. Then the mayor got up and made a little speech, including a joking reference to the local belief that removing rocks from the volcano brought bad luck; he remarked that he didn't know whether Pele made exceptions for geologists.

A pastor from a fundamentalist Christian church in Hilo had been also asked to give a blessing, and he got up next. The pastor—a native Hawaiian—challenged the idea that respect should be paid to Pele. In words that reminded one of Kapi'olani's purported challenge to Pele the century before, he said offering respect to the goddess verged on idolatry, and that the Christian god, and that god alone, gave "permission to bless this place." In a later newspaper interview, he elaborated,

> We are praying to God that through his spirit he will break through the darkness on this island. . . . I will do everything I can to lead my people out of bondage, and Pele worship is nothing more than bondage.[11]

Pualani and Nālani drew their dancers back from the stage area after he began to speak. After most of the crowd had dispersed, Nālani went up to the pastor and chided him for not being more respectful of "the old Hawaiian ways." "There is only one God," he reiterated. "Everything else is superstition."

Pualani Kanahele's most important work has been in reviving the great cycle of chants and hula concerning Pele and her "sister" Hi'iaka. This body of myth, which was the particular property of the hula schools, celebrates the goddesses most closely connected with hula. The central motif is the epic journey through the Islands that Hi'iaka undertakes on behalf of Pele. But as in all great epics, the real journey is metaphor for an inner quest. The powers that Hi'iaka discovers in herself are the powers that hula was particularly concerned with.

Most of the translations of "Pele and Hi'iaka" were done in the nineteenth century, the most extensive by the prolific Nathaniel Emerson (who unfortunately imposed a rather Homeric form on the chants).[12] The following compilation is drawn from several translations.

Hi'iaka's full name is Hi'iaka-i-ka-poli-o-Pele ("cloud holder embracing the bosom of Pele"). She is one of several Hi'iaka "sisters," all with equally poetic names: "red-hot mountain-holding cloud," "fiery-eyed canoe breaker," "wreath-garlanded cloud holder," and others. All these "sisters" are manifestations of divine energy in volcanism.

The Pele and Hi'iaka story concerns Pele's love affair with a chief, Lohi'au, from the island of Kaua'i, and the unhappy results of Hi'iaka's attempt to fetch her sister's lover for her to the island of Hawai'i. The story opens with Pele watching Hi'iaka learn the hula from her female "friend," Hōpoe, the legendary first dancer. One might reflect here on the meaning of *hōpoe,* literally "fully developed, as a *lehua* flower." The bright red *lehua* (the blossom of the *'ōhi'a* tree), with its cloud of delicate tendrils and faint, tantalizing fragrance, is an emblem of female sexuality.

After watching the dance, Pele falls asleep. But her spirit, hearing the nose flute and hula drum, follows the sounds until it comes to a place called Hā'ena (same name, interestingly, as the spot on Hawai'i where Hōpoe dances—the literal meaning is "red hot") on the island of Kaua'i. (At this spot one still finds the ruins of a *heiau* traditionally associated with the hula.) There she finds feasting and dancing in full swing. Pele is invited to sit and feast with the chief, Lohi'au, who falls in love with the beautiful stranger. She spends three nights with him, but resists his advances.

Meanwhile Hi'iaka, worried about Pele's long sleep, has been calling her spirit back to her body. Pele takes leave of Lohi'au, promising to send for him. He believes that she has abandoned him, and begins to waste away with grief.

Pele, on awakening, asks each of her sisters if she will make the arduous journey back to Kaua'i to fetch Lohi'au. Only Hi'iaka is willing to go, but first she extracts the promise from Pele that the hot-tempered goddess will not destroy Hi'iaka's beloved groves of *'ōhi'a* or harm Hōpoe. Pele sends Hi'iaka off with two traveling companions. The names of these companions are what first suggested to me that the underlying theme of Hi'iaka's odyssey is the journey from girlhood into womanhood, and the possession of full female generative power. The first companion, who only accompanies her halfway, is her "old nurse," Pā'ū-o-pala'e; the literal meaning of her name is "skirt of *pala'e* (also spelled *palai*) fern," the latter often used to symbolize female pubic hair. The second companion, Wahine'ōma'o ("woman clad in green") is a personification, perhaps, of the fertile growth of the forest. Hi'iaka herself is given by Pele a skirt with special powers that seem to increase as the challenges she meets on the journey become greater.

Journeying to the northwest tip of Hawai'i Island, along the coast and through the great upland forests, Hi'iaka and her companions wage several battles with evil *mo'o,* peculiar chthonic beings, often in lizard form, who guard various places. (There is some hint in legend that *mo'o,* considered ancestral beings by some clans, may be connected to some of the earliest groups who migrated to Hawai'i.) With the help

155

of Wahineʻōmaʻo, Hiʻiaka entangles one *moʻo* in a huge net of forest vines; by summoning a spirit form of Pele, she engulfs another in a flood of lava. At each place Hiʻiaka pauses, she composes a chant to honor the beauty of the land, as though claiming its spirit for herself.

On the island of Maui, the girls encounter a maimed creature, the spirit of a lame girl. Hiʻiaka returns the spirit to the body and then heals the girl's lameness. Refused hospitality by a Maui chief, Hiʻiaka revenges herself by dashing his wandering spirit against some rocks after the chief falls asleep. Pursued by his men, the girls make a series of transformations into commonplace women: an old woman and a child, two girls stringing blossoms, two women braiding mats. (The range of ages here suggests a cautionary message—any female may be a "body form" of a goddess, and thus should be treated with respect.)

Crossing to the island of Molokaʻi, Hiʻiaka defeats a "lawless *moʻo* tribe" who have been robbing women of their husbands, and admonishes the widowed women for letting themselves waste away with grief.

Arriving finally at Hāʻena, on Kauaʻi, Hiʻiaka cures a lame chief and is rewarded with a night of feasting and hula. The chief and his wife lead in a sacred dance that describes (in Emerson's words) "the mysteries that had marked Pele's reign since the establishment of her dominion in Hawaii." The chant, essentially, celebrates Pele's dominion over the land:

> For whom do I make this offering of song?
> For the ancient stock of Haumea.
> God Kane planted the coral reefs;   •
> A work that done in Pele's time;
> For Pele, for Hiʻiaka the land—
> This solid ground that swings and floats
> Beneath the o'erhanging arch of heaven.[13]

The next day, however, Hiʻiaka learns that Lohiʻau is dead, having hanged himself in his grief over Pele's departure. Lohiʻau's sister has taken his body and hidden it in a cliff above Hāʻena. After much difficulty, Hiʻiaka and Wahineʻōmaʻo scale the cliff. For ten days, "while the people below dance the hula, [Hiʻiaka] recites the chants useful to restore a spirit to the body." These chants continue to be used to this day as healing prayers. Wahineʻōmaʻo, wildwood goddess, supplies Hiʻiaka with the herbs and aromatics that aid in restoring life. The whole time, Hiʻiaka works to push the soul back into the body (some versions say through the eye socket, others the big toe).

"At the end of this period Lohi'au lives and all three descend on a rainbow and purify themselves in the ocean."[14] Finding himself fully restored, Lohi'au grabs his surfboard and heads for the sea!

Hi'iaka and Lohi'au begin the journey back to Pele's home. While stopping to rest on O'ahu, Hi'iaka climbs the volcanic cone we call Diamond Head to see if, with her inner eye, she can catch a glimpse of home. She spies the glow from her beloved *'ōhi'a* groves burning, and knows that Pele has betrayed her. A lovely modern translation is available of the chant she gives:

Fire-split rocks strike the sun;
Fire pours on the sea at Puna;
The bright sea at Kū-ki'i.
The gods of the night at the eastern gate,
The skeleton woods that loom.
What is the meaning of this?
The meaning is desolation.[15]

The fickle Lohi'au has been offering love to Hi'iaka on this return journey, but she has resisted his advances. Now she is furious at Pele for having broken her pledge. Reaching the edge of Kīlauea, she stands within full sight of Pele and embraces Lohi'au. Pele answers with a flood of lava, which does not harm her immortal sister, but reduces Lohi'au to ashes. The various versions of the myth have Lohi'au again brought to life by Hi'iaka and either reunited with Hi'iaka or sent back to Kaua'i by canoe. The latter strikes me as the more likely, since mortals and deities rarely end up living together happily ever after.

One can only hope to skim the surface of the richly symbolic world of this chant cycle, but I would like to draw attention to a few of its aspects. The chant cycle seems to lay poetic—and possibly spiritual—claim to a large territory—the entire chain of the main Islands. If one recalls that Pele first approaches the Islands from the northwest, so that her journey traces a trajectory down the archipelago to the island of Hawai'i that follows the actual path of volcanic activity, then the journey Hi'iaka makes takes on a new significance. Hi'iaka's journey, from Hā'ena at southeastern Hawai'i to Hā'ena at northwestern Kaua'i and back, traces in reverse and then repeats Pele's original journey through the Islands, renaming and celebrating place in the name of the Pele family of gods.

The claim is to power as well as place. Hi'iaka's battle with *mo'o* may be a conquest of earlier deities associated with the land. Pele's courting of the chief, Lohiʻau, who comes from Kauaʻi, the island famous for its ancient lineage, suggests that Pele worship may have spread its influence at a later period through the Islands. (The myths connected with Pele's arrival suggest that the Pele clan did indeed arrive late on the scene, so that a later immigration could have brought the gods of the Pele family. But one could also speculate on a geological connection here. Around the thirteenth century, Kīlauea began a very active period that has continued, with some respite, to this day. Perhaps the Pele gods gained power as a result of their increased visibility.)

An assertion of territorial power may also explain the elements in the Pele and Hiʻiaka chants that the anthropologist Samuel Elbert called "a puzzling anomaly." Elbert argues (in *The Chief in Hawaiian Mythology*) that in Hawaiian mythology "the leading protagonists are male."[16] He considers uncharacteristic both the power shown by female gods and the passivity of chief Lohiʻau in the chant cycle. Lohiʻau (he notes that the literal translation of the name is "habitually slow, blundering") must be, Elbert argues, a prototype for the "unsuccessful or defeated chief," since he certainly doesn't fit the heroic role. One can question Elbert's entire premise, since there are many legends about female gods or female humans, but for our purpose here, one might point to several myths in which Pele defeats chiefs. These myths are connected with place, and in all likelihood with actual eruptions. Typical is the legend of Kaha-wali, which is connected in legend with a lava flow that inundated an area in Puna at around 1350 C.E.

Kaha-wali was a high-ranking Kauaʻi chief who came to visit a Puna chief, bringing his family and even his pet pig. He and his host spent their days racing down steep, grass-covered hillsides on narrow hardwood sleds—a sport reserved for chiefs. One day Pele, in the guise of an old woman, appeared and asked for the use of Kaha-wali's sled. He roughly refused her. Her eyes flashed fire, and, assuming the form of a lava flow, she rushed down the hill after the fleeing chief. Stopping only to embrace wife, children, and pet pig, Kaha-wali fled to the beach, scrambled into a canoe, and pushed off one leap ahead of the molten lava. Later, according to one version, he brought his most powerful priests back to Hawaiʻi to defeat Pele, but she triumphed over all of them.

The power being claimed in the Pele and Hiʻiaka cycle is not merely territorial, but is also specifically female. Lohiʻau plays a minimal part in the drama because this is not a story about male-female relationships (as far as the "real action" of the "Pele and Hiʻiaka" chant cycle is concerned, the men are perpetually "off surfing"). There is an antihierarchical element to the wild nature of the volcano goddess, who sends her lava flows over lands without regard to the status of the humans who lay claim to them. The power of the wild and the power of the female coalesce in the Pele and Hi'iaka cycle, a power that transcends the rigid tabus placed on women within the traditional culture. Hi'iaka triumphs through specifically female avenues of power. In one chant she is called "guardian of womanly rites," and this seems fitting to the powers she learns to wield in the chant cycle. The paradox of Pele, creator and destroyer, and her "sister" Hi'iaka, healer and sorcerer, points to the difficult business of reconciling the creative and the destructive elements that are inextricably linked in nature and channeled, unmediated, according to Hawaiian beliefs, through the female form. In Pele, the powers spring direct and wild from the *pō,* the sacred darkness; in Hi'iaka, they are directed, into mediumship and sorcery, into the arts of healing and the dance.

TEN

Pele and
the Pig God

Hearken, O Hearken!
Hawai'i, Hawai'i is the one to be loved.

Chanted by Kamapua'a (the pig god)
on arriving in Puna
E. S. C. Handy and E. G. Handy,
Native Planters of Old Hawaii (1972)

One thing only is certain: the [Hawaiian] past has far
more secrets to reveal than all those that have been
discovered in a century of scientific investigation.

Patrick Kirch
Feathered Gods and Fishhooks (1985)

*Preceding page: Kamapua'a, the pig god, and the 'ōhi'a lehua blossoms sacred to Pele.
Woodblock print by Dietrich Varez.*

*L*aura Carter likes to say that Pele was responsible for giving her a job. Carter, an archeologist, was hired by the National Park Service in 1987 to do emergency salvage work among the ruins of a village just east of Wahaʻula. She and a hastily assembled crew tackled the project when a slowly advancing lava flow from the Puʻu ʻŌʻō eruption was just a few hundred yards away. "We kept popping our heads up," Laura Carter recalls, "and saying, 'Hey, where is it now?'"

Carter and crew worked in a grove of ancient coconut trees that were already dying from the heat and fumes of the encroaching lava. The crew tied bandannas over their mouths to filter the ash-filled, sulfurous air. They worked to the sound of muffled explosions as the lava moved into vegetation, trapping pockets of volatile methane gas. "It's a peculiar feeling," Laura Carter remembers, "to be carefully dusting off a small patch of dirt while massive destruction is happening right behind you."

Under the waterworn stone paving of what had been thought to be a mid-nineteenth-century house site, Carter found a fishhook of a much older design. The lava substratum provides a useful "control" on dates—since the flow in this area had been dated to the thirteenth century by geologists, the fishhook could not be any older. Somewhere, Laura hopes to find evidence of even older habitation—but it will have to be on older lava flow. The ancient history of this place was sealed under lava 600–700 years ago, and the history of the last several hundred years has now disappeared from view. In November 1987 the lava flow came just to the edge of Carter's excavations, and congealed. In the summer of 1989, it moved in again, covering every trace of the ancient village, stopping right at the edge of the *heiau* of Wahaʻula. "We managed—just barely—to do the essential salvage work," says Laura. "We were one step ahead of the lava the whole time. It began to feel a bit eerie—almost as though the lava would wait for us to finish surveying each site before it moved in and took it."

Carter is the first archeologist to be employed full time at Hawaiʻi Volcanoes National Park, and the money to hire her was only available through funds for emergency salvage work. Only one-tenth of the park's 200,000 acres have thus far been surveyed. This small percentage has yielded an astounding number of cultural features and artifacts.

The irony is that these volcanic lands, where history can disappear as fast as it is created, are the richest storehouse of archeological knowledge in the archipelago. This island, with its large stretches of raw land, has been the slowest to feel the impact of development. Thirty years ago, one could walk a network of ancient paved trails along the west side of the island—the Kona coast—in constant company with the ghostly remains of ancient Hawaiian culture. In the last two decades, development has come to Kona, and too often preservation has taken a back seat. Some individual "important" sites have been preserved, in pockets between resorts, subdivisions, golf courses. But there are only a few places in Kona now where one can wander undisturbed among the signs of the past.

Because of rugged isolation (and within its borders, park protection), the great stretch of volcano country from South Point to Kalapana still lies like an open testament to its peoples, except where Pele has reclaimed her territory. But the record of human history is highly tenuous in the Kīlauea landscape, where lava flows have covered nearly 90 percent of the land since the thirteenth century. Scattered pockets of older land may hold vital information about the life of the earliest immigrants to this region, but geologists and archeologists have only just begun to map and survey these areas. There is much to be learned here, if Pele permits and if development can be held at bay.

I had been spending time with Laura Carter to find out what has been learned recently about how the ancient Hawaiians lived in this challenging landscape. This day Laura and I were two miles west of Waha'ula, near the ruins of a coastal village named Lae'apuki. Laura would be doing an intensive site survey in this area, meticulously mapping a swath inland to the base of the great fault scarp that forms the whole northern horizon of this region. We made a quick estimate—on her own, at a rate of 10 acres per month, it would take her 20,000 months to cover the entire 200,000 acres of the park. But quite a bit of land had been covered by lava since the beginning of this century, and so needn't be included in a site survey. We revised our estimate—only 15,000 months, say—"And at the rate Pele is working lately," said Laura, "I might even be able to retire early."

A rough ancient trail led inland here, crossing the gently sloping coastal plain, then climbing steeply up the great fault scarp, draped alternately with young lava and ancient forest, to the top of Kīlauea. The trail began in coastal scrub growing on a bed of *pāhoehoe* dating back to around the thirteenth century. As we moved away from the Chain of Craters road, we were walking through more and more native vegetation, dominated by the ubiquitous *'ōhi'a.* Laura Carter has the stride of someone who has walked over a lot of rough terrain. She is thirty-seven, a "local haole" raised partly in Hilo, and then in Vienna and California. She's surprised to find herself back on this island, doing the most exciting work of her career. "The whole focus of archeology in Hawai'i has changed in the last decade or so," she said. "We've finally learned how to look at patterns, rather than isolated sites. But to see a pattern, you have to have a large area that hasn't been disturbed much. That's becoming hard to find."

Early archeology in Hawai'i concentrated on cataloguing major structures, such as *heiau,* and synthesizing Hawaiian culture with what was known about other Polynesian cultures. Habitation sites and agricultural features, and the larger patterns that showed the life of people on the land, tended to be ignored. It was assumed the Hawaiians had not been here all that long—not long enough to develop a culture that was significantly different from other Polynesian cultures. Little digging and analysis of stratigraphic deposits was done. In any case, early archeologists assumed that with no pottery to analyze there would be no way to date things.

In the 1950s, two discoveries made Hawaiian archeology blossom. Radioactive dating provided one way to determine ages by analyzing charcoal buried in habitation sites. Archeologists were motivated to start digging. When they dated charcoal buried in deeper layers of strata, they found evidence of very early habitation, pushing the time span for the earliest colonization back to around the fourth century C.E. The diggers also found, buried in successive layers, an artifact that could substitute for pottery: the fishhook.

The search for deeply stratified sites to excavate had led to the sand dunes at the end of South Point (Ka Lae), the southernmost tip of Hawai'i Island. This wind-blown bit of Ka'ū is still the boat-launching point for some of the richest fishing grounds in the Islands. The excavated site yielded layer on layer of fishhooks carved from shell and bone. The fishhooks, when matched with hooks from other sites, revealed a design that varied consistently over time. (The artifacts recovered, matched with carbon dating, suggest that South Point may be the earliest habitation site found thus far. Perhaps the first humans to set foot in the Islands, sailing out of the South Pacific, landed somewhere near this spot.)

The evolution of fishhook design gave evidence that Hawaiian culture had been consistently dynamic, adapting to the particular conditions of the Islands, incorporating Polynesian traditions into an emerging new form. This new awareness had to work against a static picture of traditional Hawaiian culture, frozen in time at the moment of Cook's discovery. It became clear that studies of the culture had mostly yielded knowledge of a single period in Hawaiian history—one dominated by an enormous population expansion, and a period of wars and intense political rivalry. An evolving, changing society had been perceived through a narrow window.

In the last decade, archeology has presented a major challenge to this "status quo" picture of Hawaiian culture by examining settlement patterns and regional differences, looking for clues to the life, over time, of the common people on the land.[1]

The people of the rugged lava lands through which Laura and I were walking were molded by the land itself into a profoundly regional culture. It is their traces that we were following this day.

Just off the trail Laura pointed out a crack in the *pāhoehoe* that had been filled in with a loose pile of stones. The stones formed a heap about three feet high. I would have walked right by them without even puzzling out that they could not be natural forms. They were agricultural mounds, Laura Carter told me, for growing sweet potato—unprepossessing features ignored by early archeologists but key to Hawaiian life in volcano country. "Realizing what these mounds signify has totally changed our picture of Hawaiians in this landscape," said Laura. "Early archeologists noticed them, but didn't register the fact that it meant these lands were intensively cultivated. They figured the Hawaiians viewed the land as we see it today—marginal, unfit, really, for habitation. That was despite the fact that early Western travelers talk about populous villages on this coast, and farming inland."

One early visitor was Henry M. Lyman, son of the missionary couple David and Sarah Lyman, who came to Hilo in 1831. In his memoir, *Hawaiian Yesterdays,* Lyman describes traveling through Puna as a

young man, and being amazed by the extent of sweet potato garden-
ing in the mounds or pits of broken-up rock:

> Wherever the lava could be pounded into scoria, a plantation of sweet-
> potatoes was laboriously formed by digging among the stones and fill-
> ing the holes with dried grass brought from the mountain-side. Placed
> in these nests, the tuberous buds were covered with gravel, and there
> grew with astonishing luxuriance, yielding the largest and finest pota-
> toes on the island.[2]

The evidence for this intensive form of farming is still visible, Laura
said. From the coast to a 2,000-foot elevation, the landscape here was
literally dotted with these pits and mounds. The rarer broken-rock,
jumbled *a'ā* fields were favored. Everywhere else, each rock had to
be broken from the *pāhoehoe*. Dry-land sweet potato flourishes with
surprisingly little water, but if water was needed it was collected painstakingly in calabashes wherever it percolated through cracks and bubbles in the *pāhoehoe,* or hauled from distant waterholes and wells. And
always, these dry-land gardeners would have lived knowing that Pele
might reclaim the land, no matter how lovingly tended. "I'm amazed,"
commented Laura, "at the incredible resourcefulness of these people—
they made ultimate use of a very challenging environment."

Laura and I had followed the gently climbing trail about ¾ mile inland from the coast. The scrub began to give way to small pockets
(some of the few left in the Islands) of native dry-land forest: gnarly
wiliwili tree, with wood as light as balsa, used by the Hawaiians for
fishnet floats and canoe outriggers; *lama,* whose small bright-orange
fruit taste like those of their relative, the persimmon; *'ākia*, with tiny
red berries, which it is said could be crushed and dropped in water
to poison fish; a rare sandalwood—a tree that nearly disappeared from
the Islands in the early 1800s, when U.S. traders offered the Hawaiian
chiefs everything from mirrors to guns in exchange for its fragrant heart-
wood.

A bit farther inland we came across, nearly buried in grass and
shrub, the old Kalapana-volcano trail, the main route for the Hawaiians
between the top of Kīlauea and the coastal villages east of Wahaʻula.
The trail, about six feet wide, lined and paved with stone, cuts almost
a straight path in a diagonal, up from the coast to about the 2,500-foot
elevation, where it disappears under recent lava flows. In the nineteenth

century, curbstones were added to make it fit for horse traffic. Even now, dilapidated and overgrown, the trail was an impressive feat of engineering through this rough land.

We picked our way cross-country a mile toward Waha'ula, winding up at the top of a small fault scarp about fifty feet high. There were two well-preserved habitation sites here on the edge of the cliff, with some low walls intact and leveled stone floors. One had a stone-lined hearth in the middle. At the edge of another grew a large old *ti* plant,* a sure sign of former habitation. The plant, a member of the lily family, was probably brought to the island by early immigrants. It was of great value to the Hawaiians, and they planted it near every house site. The leaves of the *ti* were used to wrap food for cooking in underground pits, or *imu;* were woven into sandals; and were tied in bunches to make rain capes. The plant is a symbol of spiritual power, and the leaves were believed to ward off evil.

The house site, perched near the edge of the scarp, commanded a view of a long stretch of coastline. Stopping to gaze, we felt the great expanse of quiet around us. Some sense of presence lingered at that spot, so palpable that it touched the back of my neck in that feeling— rare for me—that Westerners call "someone walking on your grave." The locals here sometimes dub the feeling "chicken skin" and matter-of-factly attribute it to spirits. We picked our way rather hastily down the fault scarp. Looking back up from the bottom, I could see an edge of wall and the tall *ti* plant, its long leaves seeming to move a little more than the breeze warranted. If there are ghosts here, I thought, they are really not that old. Around the time my grandmother was conceived, a "Stone Age" people were still making a resourceful living on this land.

The lava fields that Laura Carter and I had been traversing all day date from a period around 700 years ago when a small satellite shield volcano formed (just as the Pu'u 'Ō'ō eruption may be doing now). Large flows from this shield (which was located about two miles uprift from Pu'u 'Ō'ō) over a period of years appeared to have inundated much of the fertile land of Puna. About this time legends claim that Pā'ao, the "foreign" priest, brought new immigrants to Hawai'i Island. From the archeological record, we know it was a time when the population

---

*The Hawaiian term for the plant is *kī,* but it is now universally referred to by the Polynesian name, *ti.*

Hawaiian couple in grass house, c. 1890. This lantern slide was taken at Wahiawa Ranch, Kaua'i, but it depicts the interior of a traditional grass house (embellished with a few Western objects). W. E. H. Deverill. Courtesy of Bishop Museum.

began to expand dramatically, moving into previously unoccupied lands, particularly the dry lands of the leeward coasts. During this "expansion period," Hawaiians developed intensive dry-land farming techniques for sweet potato and taro, as well as sophisticated irrigation systems for wet taro farming. It is likely that the extensive sweet potato farming Laura is uncovering dates from this period, and that it coincided with a period when the lavas of Pele flowed time and again over the landscape.

In mythological time, it is the moment when Kamapua'a, the "pig god," is attracted to Puna from his ancestral home on O'ahu by "the fires of Pele," and their stormy courtship decides the fate of the land.

I find the pig god legends particularly interesting because they make clear how difficult it is to understand the past through the present. I had been puzzled by the Hawaiian predilection for the pig—the numerous allusions to pigs as household pets (the story, for example, of the "sacred royal pig" who attended the missionary church with Kamehameha's favorite wife, Ka'ahumanu). But I had been interpreting my "readings" from my knowledge of the pigs that run wild throughout Hawaii's forests today, doing great damage. These are huge, hairy, fierce—and, in fact, genetically closer to the Eurasian boar introduced by Westerners. Hawaiian pigs were much smaller and more easily domesticated, though capable of "rogue" behavior, judging from the Kamapua'a tales.

Kamapua'a is hero of a large body of legends and chants and of a few hula. Like Pele, he is both an 'aumakua, an ancestral being that has a totemic link to certain families, and an akua, a god. Like Pele too, his cult is local, born from the Hawaiian soil, though he is linked by kinship with some of the great pan-Polynesian deities. His genealogy must have deep roots, for he appears fully integrated into Hawaiian cosmology in the Kumulipo creation chant. According to the chant, in the fifth period of pō, the time of cosmic dark, a creature is born, half god, half hog:

> His snout was of great size and with it [he] dug the earth,
> He dug until he raised a great mound.
> He raised a hill for his gods,
> A hill, a precipice in front . . .
> For the offspring of the pig that was born.[3]

John Charlot (who has written extensively on Kamapua'a) suggests three levels of meaning in the pig god's appearance in the Kumulipo. On the human level, he represents male puberty. On the social-historical level, he is connected with the control of nature through cultivation of the land, with the procreative symbolism of tilling the female earth. On the cosmological level, Kamapua'a is a kinolau, a "body" of the fertility god Lono, born into the world of Hawai'i.[4]

Kamapua'a, whose ancestral home is one of the rainiest valleys on windward O'ahu, is associated with the fertilizing rain, and the power of water to erode and shape the land, and with the rainforest verdure that covers the land and "attracts" the rain. As a "local" aspect of the pan-Polynesian Lono, he is particularly associated with the interplay of fertile growth and volcanism. The giant rain clouds that sweep up from the east to the very edge of Kīlauea caldera are the "pig clouds" of Kamapua'a. The ferns that push through the cracks of new lava are "bodies" of the pig god.

But his primary association is with sweet potato and taro farming. Kamapua'a is the intimate champion of the farmers who break up the lava to plant sweet potato. Farmers appeal to him to bring fertility to their fields. The sweet potato tubers themselves are referred to as the pig god's sexual parts; irregularly shaped ones are called "hog-excrement."[5]

As an agricultural god, Kamapua'a challenges nature's wildness, which is embodied in the Pele family, in the same way that farmers "challenge" Pele by cultivating her land. But his power is the generative power of the gods—a power occasionally lent to humans but remaining eternally wild.

In his pig god form, Kamapua'a's "rutting" in the soil is a symbol, obviously vastly enjoyed by the Hawaiians, of the erotic dance of the "male" and "female" in nature. By tilling the land, the farmers themselves participated in the cosmic drama. Stories abound both of Kamapua'a's snout and of what one historian calls his "virile member," and the two are interchangeable (although in "cleaned up" translations the double meanings are ignored). Kamapua'a's sexual energy is prodigious, and his "snout" has rutted out and shaped much of the landscape on all the Islands, particularly the deep, rain-grooved valleys of east Hawai'i Island.

Pigs were the largest and most intelligent animals in the Hawaiian world (other than dolphins, which Hawaiians admired and gave a place in their cosmos as *'aumakua,* family gods), and the people identified with them strongly. Kamapua'a seems to represent an archetypal maleness, in the same sense that Pele, in her many bodies, sums up "femaleness." Like Pele, Kamapua'a can appear in human form, as an extremely virile, handsome man, though he must wear a cloak to hide the pig bristles on his back.

There are various versions of the Pele and Kamapua'a legends, of which the following is a composite. The pig god, lured by the smoke of Pele, journeys to the edge of Kīlauea caldera, arriving on the eastern side, where the rainforest marches right up to the rim, and huge, gray rain clouds often hover. Here he assumes his resplendent human form and calls to Pele, who is slumbering (not, in other words, erupting). Pele replies, "One might wake up for a man, but imagine waking up for a hog!" Kamapua'a chants:

> In Hilo, in Puna let us dwell, O Pele,
> To string the lehua blossoms of Hopoe,
> You string them and I'll wear them. O awaken![6]

Stringing and wearing the lei is a common euphemism for intercourse. Pele replies with a long taunt, the gist of which is "you are Kama of the noisy anus, / With the penis attached to the abdomen." Kamapua'a replies, "Puna is darkened by bitterly cold rains . . . / Made foulsmelling by the smoke of Pele." The battle is on.

Pele stokes her fires until they reach the pig god. His bristles are burned off, and the foul odor spreads over all the Islands. Kamapua'a changes to a rain cloud to escape, and summons all his plant bodies to invade Kīlauea. Pele and her family are forced to retreat into Halema'uma'u firepit, where she summons all her firepowers to attack the trees and ferns. The battle rages back and forth, and Pele's lava devastates Puna and Ka'ū. At last near Kalapana (a place called Pua'akanu (literally, "pig planting"), Pele and Kamapua'a consummate a tempestuous courtship (or some prolonged and rather rough foreplay, depending on how one wishes to translate the "events"). As one translation says, "There was no delaying of the surging of the large seas."

For four days and nights Kamapua'a makes love to Pele on the sharp lava until the "gods of Pele" begin to wonder if she will survive this "piglike" behavior. They send for Pele's relative, the goddess Kapo, in her *kinolau* as Kapo-kohe-lele ("Kapo of the wandering vagina").[7] In this "body form," Kapo distracts Kamapua'a, who follows her off on a chase through the Islands, Kapo landing here and there and leaving her imprint on the landscape. (The famous landmark Koko crater, southeast of Honolulu, was given its distinctive shape by Kapo.) Pele flees back to her home and proclaims the ancient law of "the right to separate domain," which was supposed to have been decreed by a chief after a great flood, to keep the sea apart from the land. Pele and the pig god agree to live forever apart, dividing the lands between them. To Kamapua'a go the rainy windward lands of the Islands, to Pele the dry leeward lands dominated by the forces of volcanism.

The Kamapua'a legends seem to provide a male-centered polarity to the predominantly female experience recounted in the Pele chants and legends. The two cycles together dramatize the experience of the people on the land in a way that is paralleled most closely, perhaps, by Western folktales, which are, in their earliest versions, just as "pagan" and as profoundly concerned with generative energy.

One might also think of the Pele and Kamapua'a material as "folktales" in a political sense. Through such tales, with their celebration of *place,* the regional people asserted their claim to the land. The chiefs, in the later periods of Hawaiian culture at least, were notorious for their "absentee landlordism" and their exploitation of the people on the land. In both the Pele mythology and the Kamapua'a legends, there is a strongly antihierarchical element. Both gods challenge the power of chiefs: Pele overruns the lands of chiefs who do not honor her; Kamapua'a, in one legend, steals the chickens of a great chief, and in another fights for a chief and then steals his war booty.

Both bodies of myth, as well, depict men and women eating together, in violation of the strongest *kapu.* Hawaiian scholar Lilikalā Dorton, who has translated Kamapua'a stories printed in a Hawaiian-language newspaper in 1891, notes that in this version the term *'aikū,* which means "to break tabu," particularly in relation to eating, is used in names of members of both Pele's and Kamapua'a's families. Dorton suggests an actual historic significance. "Did the *'aikū,* the "irreligious eaters," Dorton asks, connote "a set of gods, perhaps of the family of Lono, that were demoted in the Hawaiian pantheon by the emergence of a new line of chiefs and their war-god Kū, but never forgotten by those Hawaiians, now commoners, who were related to and worshippers of Pele and Kamapua'a?"[8]

That question may never be fully answered. But what we do hear, in these chants and legends, is a tribal voice that was excluded from the annals of history—the voice of the people on the land.

I was stumbling with Laura Carter across an old lava flow of *a'ā,* incredibly jumbled, clinkery rock. Even in heavy boots it was rough going. It was also, apparently, the best sweet-potato-growing area in the neighborhood. Laura pointed out mounds, and excavated pits and meandering paths, the ghostly pattern of the huge garden that was once here. Bind *ti*-leaf sandals to your feet to walk on the jagged rock. Heap up the porous rocks, push a little compost into a crevice, add a small slip of the plant, with a prayer to Kamapua'a. Fetch in a gourd a bit of precious water. If one was to farm this land, one would *need* the energy of a divine pig.

On some parts of the jagged *a'ā,* a wild relative of the cultivated sweet potato had woven a thick green mat, nearly obscuring the rock, a burgeoning of green life that matched the raw potency of the lava. The Hawaiians, it seemed, saw a cosmos not as an "opposing" of "male" and "female" but a reciprocal play. As people do who live close to the land, they exulted in both aspects, in all their myriad forms.

ELEVEN

Rift Zones

Here in this wholly mineral landscape . . . , even memory disappears; nothing is left but your own breathing and the sound of your heart beating.

PAUL BOWLES
on the Sahara

Ka'ū, hiehie i ka makani.
Ka'ū, regal in the gales.

Hawaiian saying

Preceding page: The Ka'ū desert, looking inland toward Mauna Loa. Photograph by Boone Morrison.

I: Kīlauea, Desert and Rift

The southwest rift zone of Kīlauea extends to the sea (and beneath it). It makes a long and wild, torn and riven western border to what is, to me, the heart of volcano country—the Ka'ū desert. Like the red stone deserts of Arizona, or the sculpted badlands of the Mojave, this is a land of deep mineral expanse, of the awesome silence of stone. But the Ka'ū desert is not the ancient, monolithic world of the continental desert. This is volcano desert, a land so fully in Pele's embrace that few now venture into it except those who honor solitude and silence. It is a place to meditate not on eternity, but on change.

The Ka'ū desert is a hot and dry region, but not by virtue of climate only. Rainfall is sparse, on this leeward slope of the mountain, but it is volcanism that determines the complex character of the Ka'ū desert: successions of lava flows have made the land a tapestry of change. Expanses of stone that seem as lifeless as the moon give way suddenly to pockets of older land hosting native dry-land forest; an absolute silence yields to the sound of wind in leaves and the drone of insects.

It is a world at once more gentle and more extreme than the continental desert. The Ka'ū desert is quieter and emptier—few creatures live here. The land has not had eons of time to evolve its own community to match the myriad tough denizens of continental deserts, with all their wonderfully peculiar adaptations to desert survival. Like the Hawaiian rainforest, there is nothing poisonous, horny, thorny, or spiky here—leaving the land, even in its stony harshness, vulnerable and open. Since early in this century, feral goats have wreaked havoc among the fragile plants of the Ka'ū desert, which may disappear before they can evolve the thorns to defend themselves.

In its isolation, the Ka'ū desert cradles remnants of the past. Along the coast, in places where no lava has reached for generations, are the ruins of villages. Inland there are trails paved with stepping-stones across the roughest lava, lava tube caves with petroglyphs carved into the

177

walls, rock quarries, and burial mounds. No one knows much about the archeology of the inlands, since only the coast has been extensively surveyed.

Laura Carter and I were spending a day with geologist Tina Neal exploring and mapping an area of the southwest rift. We were about half a mile inland, a point from which we could contemplate the great sweep of volcanic desert to the east. The Ka'ū desert, which covers a good portion of the south flank of Kīlauea, is some of the newest land on earth—most of it is covered by lava flows less than 1,500 years old, though a few pockets of land may have rested undisturbed for more than 10,000 years. Undisturbed by lava, that is; what marks this land most are its great fault scarps—the precipitous cliffs that give it the contour of a Titan's staircase. Each fault scarp represents a point where a great section of land has slumped or slid downhill. If one descended in a bathyscaph offshore, one could follow similar giant steps down Kīlauea's steep, submerged flanks to the ocean bottom.

On all sides but the farthest extension of its east rift zone and this, the vulnerable south flank, Kīlauea rests against the massive bulk of Mauna Loa. Lō'ihi, the undersea volcano growing twenty miles to the south, may provide some buttressing for the tip of Kīlauea's southwest rift zone. But the entire south flank, built up of loose, porous lava, is unsupported. Scientists debate whether the slumping is caused by magma intruding into the rift zone, forcing the land outward, or whether the land moves from its own gravitational pull down the volcano's steep slopes. They are also puzzled as to whether these huge scarps (the Hilina Pali, for example, which extends all across the south flank to the east rift zone of Kīlauea, is over 1,000 feet high in some parts) developed from a few catastrophic slumps or a long series of smaller displacements. Answers to these questions may be crucial to gauging the probability of future cataclysm in this region.

There have been two "slumps" on Kīlauea's south flank in historic time (that is, from the early 1800s when the first data about Hawaiian volcanoes were recorded by Western observers), and both were potent reminders of human vulnerability in such a landscape. In 1868, what remained of the once-proud coastal village culture of the southlands, already decimated by Western disease, was virtually obliterated by the *tsunami* (tidal wave) unleashed by an enormous land movement that seems to have involved the south flanks of both Kīlauea and Mauna Loa. Just over a hundred years later, in 1975, a large section of Kīlauea broke along the Hilina Pali fault system and slid seaward, with disastrous consequences for a group of campers on the coast.

Like the catastrophic event of 1975, the 1868 slump was accompanied by an eruption, but it is impossible to determine a causal sequence. The summit caldera of Kīlauea had been actively erupting for much of the first half of the nineteenth century, and at the beginning of 1868 it was steaming heavily and pouring lava from several cones within the caldera. On the morning of March 27, passengers on a whale ship off the west coast of the island observed "a dense cloud of smoke rise from the top of Mauna Loa, in one massive pillar, to the height of several miles, lighted up brilliantly by the glare from the crater Mokuaweoweo."[1]

The next day the earthquakes began. By the beginning of April, they were coming at a frequency of more than one hundred a day. In the Ka'ū area it was impossible to walk across the ground at times; it rolled like an ocean swell beneath the feet. Missionary families in the region moved out of their houses and into tents, and held services out under the trees. They were wise to do so: on April 2 a shock came that knocked down nearly every stone wall in Ka'ū and destroyed the church at Wai'ōhinu. A missionary living nearby wrote of that day,

> First the earth swayed to and fro, north and south, then east and west, round and round, then up and down . . . the trees thrashing about as if torn by a mighty wind. It was impossible to stand, we had to sit on the ground, bracing with hands and feet to keep from rolling over. In the midst we saw burst from the pali [cliff] [a mud slide] which rushed down its headlong course and across the plain below swallowing up everything in its way, trees, houses, cattle, horses, goats, men.[2]

The giant mud slide triggered by the earthquake traveled "three miles in not more than three minutes time." A village of "31 natives" was buried alive. From the coast of Ka'ū to the summit of Kīlauea, the earth opened up in cracks and fissures. Geologists now estimate that land along the southern coast slumped as much as six feet. The earthquake, or the subsidence, or both, triggered a tsunami. The waters receded, then rushed back in, sweeping away the fishing villages that dotted the southern coast, with the height of the wave, according to one account, "equal to that of the coconut trees that grew near those houses."[3] A passenger on a ship sailing offshore reported later, "The sea stands some six feet deep where houses once stood." Before the end of the same day, small eruptions had broken out on Kīlauea's southwest rift zone and inside the volcano's summit caldera.

It was not over yet. The earthquakes continued, though none approached in intensity the great jolt of April 2. On April 7, lava erupted at the 2,000-foot level on Mauna Loa's southwest rift, just a few miles above the present-day Kahuku Ranch. A witness claimed that "here (at Kahuku) the lava burst forth, April 7th, through an enormous fissure of nearly three miles in length . . . the great fissure having been formed, in all probability, on April 2d, the final breaking through of the lava seems to have begun almost without noise."[4] In a little over two hours, the lava flowed nine miles to the ocean. The eruption lasted for five days, covering the devastated region with a pall of dark smoke. "A terrible roar was heard . . . while the fire was flowing," reported a Hawaiian resident. "The natives and the whites were excited, thinking that their last hour had come, for such was the explanation of the learned whites."[5]

Had the fishing villages remained along the Kaʻū-Puna coast, the disaster that struck in November 1975 would have claimed many more lives than it did, for it came virtually without warning. The only hint had been an increase in seismic activity beneath the south flank of Kīlauea during the early part of that month. On Thanksgiving weekend, thirty-four people—fishermen, a group from Sierra Club, and Boy Scout Troop 77—were camped at the idyllic little cove at Halapē, an oasis of coconut groves and white sand beach in the heart of the Kaʻū desert. Once you arrive under the rustling palms at Halapē, you can forget the torn and riven country you have walked through to get there; you can pitch your tent on the soft sand and slip into dreams of paradise.

These campers, if they dreamed such dreams, jolted awake to a living hell. A minor shock woke a couple of campers at 3:36 a.m.; a father reassured his anxious young son that there was nothing to worry about. At 4:48, an earthquake with a magnitude of 7.2 struck, with an epicenter several miles to the east. The shaking went on, it seemed, forever. The campers, crawling from their tents, were thrown to the ground. Rocks came tumbling from the cliff just inland from the beach, and some campers fled toward the shore to escape them. It was the wrong direction to run. The first wave struck thirty seconds after the earthquake subsided; the second, much larger, swept everything in its path as far as 300 feet inland. Incredibly, only two people were killed, one battered against the rocks, the other disappearing out to sea.

About half an hour after the main shock, seismographs recorded harmonic tremor under Kīlauea. At 5:32 A.M., a long fissure opened in the floor of the summit caldera, spouting a continuous curtain of fire.

Scientists later determined that the south flank coastline had subsided as much as ten feet. The summit of Kīlauea itself sank six feet, and the entire south flank of the volcano was "displaced seaward" by several yards. Just as pressure buildup along the San Andreas fault guarantees that earthquakes will occur in that part of California, it is inevitable that such displacements will continue to happen along the south flank of Kīlauea. What geologists can't predict thus far is either their frequency or magnitude.

If the south flank of Kīlauea, encompassing the Ka'ū desert, begins to seem as precarious as a house of cards, a few days of walking along the southwest rift zone can deconstruct permanently any remaining notions of *terra firma*. At the top end of the rift zone, the land is heaped with great dunes of volcanic cinder blown down from summit eruptions. Thin sheets of volcanic mud, remnants of the explosive 1790 summit eruption, can still be found in pockets where the wind has uncovered it. The 1790 explosion was "phreatomagmatic"—or "steam induced"—and it turned a normally "gentle" volcano into a killer. Lava in the summit caldera apparently sank deep into the mountain as a result of a great draining of lava out low on the east rift zone. The subsiding magma encountered a table of ground water. The resulting steam-powered explosion blanketed the top of the rift zone with choking fumes and a rain of volcanic mud, ash, and cinder.

This was, in both oral and recorded history, Kīlauea's most violent eruption—and it came at a most significant moment in Hawaiian history. The army of Keoua, the hereditary chief of Ka'ū, was returning from the Hilo area to Ka'ū after battling Kamehameha's allies. (Keoua was the last holdout against Kamehameha's hegemony.) Keoua's army, traveling (as was the custom) with women, children, and domestic animals, stopped to make offerings to Pele at the summit caldera. They were greeted with rumbles and small explosions that began to increase in ferocity. Keoua divided the army into three groups, sending each ahead on the trail to Ka'ū at two-hour intervals. The third group, reaching a point six miles southwest of the summit, found the group that had preceded them lying on the ground, looking, at a distance, as though they were resting. They were, in fact, dead, with only a few pigs as survivors of what must have been a cloud of poisonous gas on the heels of a huge explosion.

For these people who worshiped Pele both as god and ancestor, to have the volcano goddess show such anger must have been profoundly demoralizing. Perhaps this explains why, in the next year, Keoua allowed himself to be trapped by Kamehameha. The latter had spent the last year at Kawaihae on the Kona coast, overseeing the building of an enormous war temple. When the *heiau* was finished, Kamehameha invited Keoua to come to the dedication. Keoua made preparations that indicate he knew he might be traveling to his death, choosing old friends to ride with him as "companions of death" in his huge double-hulled canoe. One of Kamehameha's men slew Keoua with a spear as he stepped ashore under the shadow of the huge temple, and his body was offered as its first sacrifice. That day in 1791 marked the beginning of the end of proud independence for the peoples of Puna and Kaʻū.

In the upper regions of Kīlauea's southwest rift zone, one still comes across footprints, in the solidified mud from that explosion, that may have been made by Keoua's retreating army. Much of this area, however, was covered by an enormous, lengthy eruption in 1920 that built its own small shield, given the name Mauna Iki ("little mountain"). The glossy *pāhoehoe* fields of Mauna Iki cover a tremendous area. Below them, one enters a region marked on maps as "the highly fractured zone." It is here that the true temper of the rift zone reveals itself.

For the last month or so, Tina Neal had been mapping land around the lower part of what is called "the Great Crack," a huge continuous fissure that extends for nearly fifteen miles down the spine of the rift zone. The Great Crack is testament to the paradoxical nature of stone, its simultaneous elastic and brittle properties. Under slow pressure, it can bend and move with surprising plasticity, like ice in a glacier, but at some crucial point pressure or movement will shatter and rend rock apart. There was an incident, famous in local history, when, during the 1960 eruption of the east rift, the ground opened in numerous fissures. Some sprang back together again. An unlucky cow fell into one of these before it closed up—a photo from the time shows one leg of the beast protruding from a very narrow crack.

The Great Crack is the result of repeated fracturing caused by the pressure of magma moving into the southwest rift zone. At the point where we were standing, the crack was perhaps 20 feet wide and 40 deep, and we looked into the tops of a dense grove of *kukui* trees that had populated the bottom, where rainwater probably accumulated.

"Burning Chasms at Ponahohoa," showing an aftermath of the 1823 eruption on the south-west rift zone of Kīlauea. Engraving after drawing by Rev. William Ellis. 1823. Courtesy of Bishop Museum.

They were the only trees in a land that is mostly barren lava, for a large portion of the lower rift zone was covered in an 1823 eruption. This rapid, very fluid flow issued, apparently with little warning, out of a six-mile section of the Great Crack. Since the bottom of the fissure is only half a mile from shore, the lava must have reached the sea very quickly. The Reverend William Ellis, passing through this area soon after, reported that "the people . . . told us that no longer than five moons ago Pele . . . had issued from a subterranean cavern, and over flowed the lowland. . . . The inundation was sudden and violent, burnt one canoe, and carried four more into the sea."[6]

The fast-moving 1823 flow drained quickly toward the sea, leaving in some areas a thin sheet of cooling lava only a few inches thick, coating the landscape in a kind of volcanic shellac, draping features rather than obliterating them. Empty, cylindrical "tree molds" reveal where forest once stood. Through the glossy surface protrude archeological features made up of older, weathered rock—remains that Laura Carter, if she works her way painstakingly across the Ka'ū desert from Waha'ula, may get around to cataloguing in the year 2040. But some of the traces of the past Tina Neal had reported stumbling on in this raw, remote landscape had piqued Carter's curiosity, and so she too had decided to accompany Tina Neal for a day, to match her knowledge of culture with Neal's knowledge of nature.

Neal herself was filling in the last details of what eventually would be the definitive map of the southwest rift, an area previously explored mainly by aerial photography. Her systematic rock sampling would provide a chemical history of the rift zone. She was chronicling the extent of flows and identifying cracks and faults, along with checking for evidence of lava "intrusions"—lava activity that never quite made it to the surface. For a volcanologist all this information feeds one underlying, elusive goal—to be able to predict the future.

Tina Neal was wearing one of those field vests that is all pockets, stuffed with pens, notes, magnifying glass. Her rock hammer hung from a loop. She took notes and samples, but spent most of her time staring at the landscape. Watching her, I imagined she was the first *haole* to give this landscape her full attention for such an extended amount of time. There was something priestly in her wandering and pondering—I thought of the ancient Chinese geomancers whose job was to determine the *feng-shui*—the cosmic energy or lines of power in a landscape. The Chinese believed that every place had such patterns, and that humans must consult the wisdom of a place in order to determine how to live in harmony with it. Many of the riots against the Christian missionaries in nineteenth-century China came about because the missionaries built their structures without even considering the *feng-shui* of the land.

Tina was now at the tail end of 1,000 miles of walking, mostly alone, in the lands of Kīlauea's southwest rift zone. She was delighted when I told her about *feng-shui,* and my image of her as a modern geomancer. "Something has happened to me out here," she said, "that I'm still trying to fit in with my training as a scientist. Spending time near Puʻu ʻŌʻō, monitoring the action, was exciting, but what has really shaken me is the stronger and stronger sense of presence I've felt here, in this lonely, desolate place." She paused for a long moment, scanning the empty landscape in a way that seemed almost expectant. I followed her gaze down to where, a few miles distant, bare lava fields, a quilt of matte and shiny grays and blacks, gave way to the blank blue of the sea. "I guess I'm still uncomfortable, as a scientist, saying these things," she said finally. "But it's like having a sense of something very powerful, yet not knowing how to acknowledge it. I finally came up with my own little ritual—a kind of prayer or greeting to the land, or the spirit of the land."

We detoured to show Laura Carter some of the archeological sites that Tina Neal had stumbled on. Most impressive were a couple of small platforms on a pocket of high ground surrounded by 1823 lava flow. They are carefully covered with a flat surface of slabs of older lava, which Neal has identified as rock from a vent, two miles upland, that erupted about 2,000 years ago. Carter is puzzled and fascinated by these features—they resemble the burial platforms that Hawaiians began making in historic times, but their foundations are partly covered by an older flow—one that Neal has dated as around 500 years old. "Put that on my list for excavations," said Carter. "Maybe I'll get to it before Pele decides to visit this area again."

We followed the 1823 flow down to the sea, then walked the coast west to Pālima Point. The coastal area is dotted with the remains of temporary shelters, walls, fishing shrines. The sea cliffs are high here—30 to 50 feet—and the sea dashes against them. According to Tina Neal, the lava flows that drape over the cliff edge like thick frosting are 400 to 750 years old. The rocks that make up the sea cliff are about twice that age. What did they cover—a small, beautiful cove, perhaps, where the first voyagers touched land? Layers of lava; pages in a volcanic book of time.

The bulb-shaped head of a rare green sea turtle broke the surface of the water, and I wondered if an ancient instinct had made it search this stretch of coast for a nesting place that is no longer there. A few terns wheeled in the updraft from the cliffs. From this spot, in every direction, the land appears huge and empty. To the west, the coastline stretches, wild and magnificent, to the very tip of Ka Lae, or South Point, where sand dunes cover the oldest settlement thus far found. To tourists, it is better known as the "southernmost point of the United States." It projects horizontally, like the snout of a needlefish, into a gray-blue haze of sea and sky.

Pālima Point lies three miles outside the National Park boundary, on land owned partly by the state and partly by private parties. For years the park had planned to acquire another section of this land, incorporating the coastal portion of the southwest rift zone and extending park boundaries westward to within a mile of Pālima Point. But funds were perpetually scarce and there seemed to be no hurry—no one dreamed that any economic use would be found for this stretch of wild lava coast, just as no one twenty years ago could have imagined the huge resorts hacked out of the lava plains of Kona.

The park has come to realize, a bit too late, that no land, however wild, is immune from speculation any more. For the last two years, state and private monies have been pumped into feasibility studies for a commercial "spaceport"—a satellite-launching facility—on the Big Island's sparsely populated Ka'ū coast. The search has been narrowed to two choices, and one is Pālima Point. The spaceport, which would launch commercial and possibly military payloads, would require a safety zone with a three-mile radius (extending to the current boundary of the National Park), which would mean that lands and offshore waters would be closed to the public during launching periods. The rocket pads and other launching facilities would be highly visible for many miles. Noise at time of launch is estimated at 115 decibels for a distance of up to three miles from the launching site. As one feasibility study states, this sound would be "approximately six decibels higher than would be experienced by a person seated near the stage at a rock music concert."[7]

What concerns Tina Neal, besides what she terms the "inappropriateness" of such a facility adjacent to a National Park, is the geologic risk. Part of the land is actually on the southwest rift zone; on all of it, ground cracks and relatively recent lava flows reveal the inherent instability of land in the heart of volcano country. "Space launch facilities should be sited to minimize risk associated with earth displacements, lava flows and gas and tephra [ash, cinder, and solidified bits of lava] emissions," the feasibility study suggests. How much "minimizing" can humans do on the unstable flank of a very active volcano?

Standing here on that magnificent wild coast, I thought about the hubris of those who come from outside, who seek to place quantifiable measures on this land, who think that humans can (and should) always find a way to control nature. That hubris has included volcanologists: I was reminded of Thomas Jaggar's motto, *Ne plus haustae aut obrutae urbes,* "No more buried cities."

But something has shifted in the view of some of the volcanologists I have met here, those who have come to love the wild power of the land. When I mentioned Jaggar's bombing war on the Mauna Loa lava flows of 1935 and 1942 to Jaggar's present-day successor, observatory scientist-in-charge Tom Wright, he shook his head in distaste. "Not only do I believe bombing ultimately futile," he said, "but I find abhorrent the idea of destroying a pristine lava flow." Tina Neal feels the same. It is as though loyalty has shifted from human-scape to landscape. As though, in touching this land long enough, deeply enough, these Westerners had become, in a sense, Hawaiian.

II: Royal Gardens

SUMMER 1988

*R*oyal Gardens is a subdivision laid out in a grid on the southern flank of Kīlauea's east rift zone, a long narrow rectangle of one-acre lots climbing from the coastal plain nearly to the top of a steep fault scarp. The subdivision, sitting just inland of the Waha'ula temple grounds, borders National Park land on its south and east boundaries. Over the top of the fault scarp, at about 2,300 feet, about two miles distant from the upper end of Royal Gardens, lava surfaces into a molten lake. From the lake the lava runs, sometimes in tubes, sometimes on the surface, down to the sea. And seven times since the current eruption began in 1983, the lava has flowed into Royal Gardens. Twenty-two houses have been destroyed, about one-third the total number of dwellings in this 1,800-acre subdivision.

Jack and Patty Thompson live in a beautiful cedar home they built near the top of Royal Gardens. Their front porch commands a twenty-mile view of the coast. The Thompsons have prime balcony seats, in effect, for the volcanic display—on the day I visited, great clouds of steam rose from the coast at three points where lava was entering the sea, and a wide band of greenish yellow water spread offshore. But it is a show they are enjoying less and less the longer they are its captive audience. "Want to rent it? Want to buy it?" asked Patti when I admired her home.

The Thompsons are among a handful of people still living in the subdivision. Some former residents have dismantled their houses, loaded them piece by piece on trucks, and carried them off; some have simply abandoned their homes. And nearly two dozen have watched their homes burn to the ground. Jack and Patty's house sits between two lava flows. From the second story, I could see the flow that plowed down the steep slope a hundred yards to the east, in June 1983. Two hundred feet to the west, a frozen, jumbled river of $a'\bar{a}$, fifty yards wide, cascades across their access road. A makeshift road has been bulldozed over the top of the huge, clinkery mass of rock—the one gesture of help from the subdivision's developer, Norman Inaba. Without the road, Jack and Patty would have lost access to their house. According to the covenants of Royal Gardens, the community, with the help of funds set aside by the developer, is responsible for maintaining the roads. But there is no community left in Royal Gardens. The developer's real estate corporation has filed for bankruptcy.

Royal Gardens is one of a number of subdivisions that sprang up during the 1960s on lava lands in the active volcanic regions of east and south Hawai'i Island. The real estate boom here seems to have been part of a nationwide phenomenon: from Florida to Arizona—everywhere in the Sun Belt—large-scale speculative subdivisions were being carved out of marginal lands—desert, tidal flats, lava lands—and sold as cheap "retirement" or "investment" parcels. On the Big Island, most of the parcels were sold, like those in Royal Gardens, with no available water, no telephone or electricity lines—no improvements, in other words—and had only minimal "private" roads that had to be maintained by the lot owners.

Many of these subdivisions were miles from any services. Royal Gardens was an exception: the county coastal road ran past the southern end of the subdivision and gave access to the village of Kalapana just to the east, to phones and laundromats, stores and beaches. Now an active, steaming lava field more than a mile wide separates Royal Gardens from Kalapana. Lava first covered the road in 1984. Nearly six years later, underground rivers of molten rock still cross the road on their flow to the sea. The Park Service has provided a rugged "emergency access road" through park lands to the western edge of the subdivision. It was originally opened to allow full-scale evacuation for the remaining residents in the subdivision, and the Park Service has been on the verge of closing it several times, since it is against federal codes to provide private access through park lands.

The only access to services now from Royal Gardens is a long drive up through the park and over the top of Kīlauea, so no families have remained in the subdivision. The nearest phones are thirty miles away, the nearest schools and supermarkets are fifty. The upper parts of Royal Gardens are thickly vegetated, and in many places the forest has nearly reclaimed what roads the lava has not covered. There are dilapidated hulks of abandoned houses and rusting cars. Of the few

Abandoned cars caught in new lava flow near Kalapana, 1987. Photograph by J. D. Griggs—U.S. Geological Survey.

houses that still stand in the subdivision, many are virtually shanties, since the original subdivision covenants were never enforced. Steep, narrow, crumbling roads named King, Queen, and Royal, Orchid, Plumeria, and Paradise dead-end into lava fields. The only people who tend to like these isolated conditions are marijuana growers. Royal Gardens, like many of the speculative subdivisions carved out of lava land, has become outlaw country.

There are a few exceptions to the rule, most notably Jack and Patty Thompson. Their house is lovingly designed and immaculately kept. Out of the lush jungle surrounding them they have carved a garden that grows a little of everything, pineapples to pole beans, bananas to citrus. Jack, who is thirty-seven, and Patty, who is twenty-nine, are both from southern California. A house in Hawai'i was their dream. Jack worked for ten years as a mason and refrigerator technician, commuting from Royal Gardens to the Hilo area, to finance their "dream house." It's a tough commute now.

Jack first heard of Royal Gardens on a visit from the mainland to Waikiki in 1969. He saw a promotional movie, and read the brochure handed out. "Along the southern shores of the Big Island . . . lies the historic and legendary lands of Kalapana," it read. "This is the setting for Royal Gardens, a fertile area directly adjacent to the Hawai'i Volcanoes National Park with its spectacular attractions."[8] "'Spectacular' is right," said Jack. "They didn't tell you that this place sat right below an active rift zone. I knew the volcano was there, of course, but this area had not had any lava flows for over 350 years. At $900 for an acre of land with an incredible view, I figured it was worth the risk. Besides, at that time I figured I'd have fire insurance."

Jack's fair coloring reddened considerably when he talked about their current impasse. He and Patty sank their life savings into their home, thinking they were buying into a "quality subdivision" where land values were sure to rise. Seated on the edge of the couch in his airy living room, Jack pulled out a copy of the original subdivision covenants and handed them to me. I leafed through them. "No structures of a temporary character." "No used or second-hand lumber." "Paved driveways, covered carports. . . . " "Ludicrous, isn't it," said Patty. "Ours is probably the only house in the subdivision that was ever built completely to code."

After the Pu'u 'Ō'ō eruption began, the fire insurance company refused to renew the Thompsons' policy. There is little chance Jack and Patty could sell the house for even the flat cost of materials. They take vacations separately for fear the house will be looted if left vacant. "We wouldn't be in this situation," Patty said, "if we hadn't been painted such a rosy picture."

Volcanic risk was never mentioned in any of the developer's sales brochures, or in any of his state-required disclosures, until more than four years after Royal Gardens lots were put on the market. Royal

Gardens is only one instance among many—a majority of the speculative subdivision lots spawned in the 1960s on the Big Island lie within what the USGS has now classified as "high-risk" zones. Some of these subdivisions were laid out when lava had barely cooled in their backyards. The most visually astounding of these is Hawaiian Ocean View Estates, an enormous grid running from about 2,000 feet to the 5,000-foot level on the west flank of Mauna Loa's southwest rift zone.

This huge subdivision is built partly on top of 1887 and 1907 lava flows. A few miles above are the massive lava fields of the 1916 and 1950 flows. At the very top of the estates, you can buy a one-acre lot (quite a few are still available) that is nothing but clinkery *a'ā,* collapsed lava tubes and spatter cones—your very own geologic Disneyland. The address is Paradise Avenue.

Just as in Royal Gardens, few of the lots in the Hawaiian Ocean View Estates have actually been built on. If all the subdivisions had filled rapidly, the county (the entire Big Island is one county) would have been put in a very difficult financial bind trying to provide them with public services. So why did the county allow these subdivisions to be built? In late 1987 I had asked this question of Albert Lono Lyman, county planning director at the time. "Greed and short-sightedness," he said, shrugging, as though poor planning decisions were a thing of the past. "This has always been a poor county, with a lot of what was viewed as wasteland. Then someone figured out how to make a buck. The majority of these lots were sold, sight unseen, to mainland buyers. One Royal Gardens lot was even given away on the TV program 'Queen for a Day!'"

The best explanation for the volcanic subdivisions boondoggle is given in an exposé called *Land and Power in Hawai'i,* written by Gavan Daws, an eminent Pacific historian, and George Cooper, a lawyer based in Honolulu.[9] Daws and Cooper trace the intricate connections between politics and real estate development in Hawaii, and the Royal Gardens saga is one of their cases in point, a microcosm of the larger picture.

Norman Inaba, the developer of Royal Gardens, was described in a 1964 newspaper article as "the Big Island's most diversified if not biggest subdivider with nine developments around the island covering some 7,000 acres."[10] Inaba is a member in good standing of the power structure that became firmly entrenched in state government during the reign of Hawai'i's first Democratic governor, Jack Burns,

191

in the 1960s. As Daws and Cooper point out, "Just as on other islands where strong family/business/political interconnections grew up in the Democratic years, so on the Big Island Norman Inaba and his immediate family interlocked with the Democratic leadership, and with investors from outside the main Democratic ranks as well."[11]

Of Inaba's immediate family, one brother was chief of the Hawai'i County Department of Public Works from 1953 to 1963, another served on the State Land Use Commission from 1963 to 1973, and a third served two terms in the statehouse. Others involved with the Royal Gardens development as investors, attorneys, or consultants included George Ariyoshi, then a state senator, who became governor in the 1970s; another state senator; the wife of a state supreme court justice; and the parents of the county supervisor.

Such confluences of power are not unique to Royal Gardens' history, and they still shape Hawaiian politics. They may help to explain why the Big Island in particular was slow to develop land use plans or to enforce state land use laws. As Daws and Cooper point out, "For nine years, 1958–1966, Hawai'i County routinely approved speculative subdivisions."[12] Although in response to various pressures (including a federal lawsuit) new county ordinances banning substandard subdivisions went into effect in late 1966, development of already approved subdivisions continued into the 1970s. The Big Island was left with the legacy of mostly empty, decaying subdivisions, in some places turned "outlaw lands." Now there are signs of another real estate boom. If all those lots should actually become occupied, the county will be faced with the enormous burden of providing services to these far-flung home sites. Nearly 60 percent of the lots in those subdivisions, moreover, are within what geologists have identified as volcanic high-risk zones.

What kind of responsibility the county should assume in regulating development in high-risk areas is still an open question. The 1966 state law requiring developers to disclose information about volcanic risk in their public offerings did not provide specific guidelines on the extent or accuracy of the information. Certainly in the 1960s less information about volcanic hazard was available (although it does not take a geologist, one would think, to ascertain that downhill from an active rift zone is a risky place to put a subdivision). In order to provide useful information for land use planning, the USGS in 1974 released a definitive paper on volcanic hazard, including a map rating all areas of the Big Island according to a "hazard" scale of 1 through 9.[13]

Zone 1, the highest-risk zone, includes the summit areas and rift zones of Mauna Loa and Kīlauea. In these regions, 25 percent or more of the land has been covered by lava within historical time. Zone 2 includes all areas "adjacent to or downslope of the active rift zones of Kīlauea and Mauna Loa." In the Zone 2 lands on Kīlauea's southeast rift, 25 percent has been covered with lava since the beginning of nineteenth century. Royal Gardens sits squarely within this zone.

Even with such information readily available, the county has been unwilling to adopt any hard and fast rules to determine which areas are "unsafe" for development. The general argument for not doing so is that the USGS ratings are broad-based predictions, and that terrains and conditions vary widely within regions. County officials often tend to classify geologists as alarmists, particularly after geologist Dick Moore's suggestion that resort developers along the Kona coast area below Hualālai volcano (a Zone 4 area, less than 15 percent covered by lava within the last 750 years), should be taking steps to mitigate volcanic hazard.

Dick Moore's 1986 report on his intensive mapping of the lava flows of Hualālai resulted in that volcano being reclassified from dormant to active.[14] Moore found that 25 percent of the volcano's surface is covered with flows less than 1,000 years old. Hualālai's last eruption was in 1801, when it sent highly fluid, fast-moving lava to the sea at the Kona coast. The airport that services the resorts and towns of Kona is built on that flow. Most agencies, public and private, from chamber of commerce to planning commission, have been reluctant to accept the idea of risk along the Kona coast. Tourism, after all, is the main source of revenue here. Hazard perception is strongly determined by economics on this island.

The continuing policy, therefore, seems to be "Let the buyer beware." Jack and Patty said they have received very little sympathy or assistance from the county for their plight. They are the first to admit the land should have been reserved for other uses—"Maybe just left wild. Or maybe added to the park." (The park, in fact, had long considered purchasing that section of land, but funds had not become available.) Even if the eruption ceased, and the road to Kalapana were rebuilt, the Thompsons doubted if Royal Gardens would ever attract a settled community: "It will be hard to ignore the fact that this area is part of an active volcano anymore," said Jack. He was quiet for a moment. "On the other hand, memories seem to be pretty short around here. And the eruption could stop tomorrow."

*I*n May 1989, the course of lava through its network of tubes to the sea one mile east of Waha'ula was disrupted, and lava broke out on the surface, moving along the east edge of Royal Gardens and into the lowlands just inland and east of the temple grounds. The air turned acrid and smoky as the lava burned into the vegetation. Another Royal Gardens house ignited. The few remaining residents were warned by Civil Defense that their emergency access road might soon be cut off by lava, and were urged to pack up what they could and get out. Half a dozen, including Jack and Patty, chose to stay.

Early June. Lava covered the emergency road, and all vehicle access to Royal Gardens was cut off once again. The flow steadily filled in the lowlands between Royal Gardens and Waha'ula and approached the visitors' center parking lot at the temple grounds. The main temple complex, which sits on the raised ground of an ancient *a'ā* flow, was not in immediate danger, but park rangers were stripping the visitors' center. Water trucks sprayed the front of the flow in an attempt to divert it around the buildings and into a lower area to the west.

I heard some of this news from Jack and Patty, when I ran into them at the Volcano Village store. Patty had fallen the day before on the rough lava as they hiked their groceries half a mile to the bottom of the subdivision. (With the vehicle they had kept inside Royal Gardens, they were able to drive down from their house through a maze of subdivision roads, skirting the ones blocked by lava.) They had just been to Hilo where doctors confirmed a broken arm. They were headed home, Patty to maneuver over the lava with arm in a cast; Jack to carry the groceries. They needed to make it before dark, so they didn't have much time to talk.

June 20. An earthquake of magnitude 6.1 shook the south flank of Kīlauea, its epicenter just east of Waha'ula. Patty was inside the house when it hit; Jack was in the backyard. Patty, standing near a front window, had time only to clutch the window frame with her one usable arm as the house lurched forward and down. She was amazed to find herself still standing, unhurt, when the motion stopped. Jack was shouting and trying to open the jammed back door. The house had jumped the foundation and moved ten feet forward, coming to rest on top of their Toyota sedan, parked underneath.

Jack and Patty called me from Hilo two days later. The Red Cross had put them up in a hotel room. Patty was headed back to her family

194

in Huntington Beach, California; Jack would stay to salvage and pack out what valuables he could, then join her on the mainland while they decided what to do next. "He's finally had enough," said Patty. I heard both defeat and relief in her voice.

June 23. Lava reached the foundations of the visitors' center at Waha'ula. The entire building burned to the ground in less than thirty minutes. The lava flowed to the edge of the main temple and congealed against its walls, but the temple still stood. Two days later, lava entered the sea just west of Waha'ula, and the surface flow crusted over and flowed underground through the new tube system, pouring out at the coast and building a new plateau along the sea cliffs.

Mid-July. I was surprised to encounter Jack at a local supermarket, with a basket full of canned goods. "Been batchin' it in the house," he said, grinning. "Got it all jacked back up again with the help of a friend and a couple of two-ton jacks. There's a lot of minor damage, but the structure is basically sound. I came out to get fixtures to redo the plumbing. Patty is coming back in two weeks. She says Huntington Beach is too noisy." Rather dazedly, I agreed with him to reschedule the barbecue we'd talked about having two months ago.

Early August. Patty was back. I telephoned a friend who relayed a radio message to Jack and Patty, and we arranged a time for the barbecue.

A few days later I walked in over the half-mile of lava from Chain of Craters road to the bottom end of the subdivision, carrying charcoal, steaks, and beer. I could see smoke and fumes from the surface flow that was igniting vegetation along the east edge of Royal Gardens. The sulfur fumes made my eyes smart. By the coast, a quarter-mile to the right, I could see a heap of twisted metal—all that remained of the visitors' center. The afternoon winds came off the mountain, and a huge steam plume billowed seaward from the sea cliffs this side of Waha'ula.

Patty was waiting for me on the other side of a stretch of very new-looking *pāhoehoe*. She waved cheerily, hair in a ponytail, sunglasses, white top. She could have been standing in the streets of Huntington Beach, deciding which shop to enter on a leisurely afternoon. The car beside her, however, didn't fit the image, having been pancaked by the falling house into some surreal parody of a customized low-rider. The broken-out windows were covered with plastic, and my head hit the top of the mashed ceiling. "Looks a bit weird, doesn't it," remarked Patty. "But it runs just the same as ever."

We wound through a maze of dilapidated roads, Patty weaving in and out to avoid the vegetation that had nearly closed over in some spots, and up the one road—Prince Avenue—that still gave access to Jack and Patty's home high on the scarp. Patty stopped for the stop sign at the corner of Prince and Plumeria. "I can't seem to break the habit," she said. "Though I guess it's pretty silly—I think there's only two other vehicles left in the Gardens that still run."

When we reached their place, Jack and Patty took me for a tour of the house. Little but the cracks in the Sheetrock still showed the damage done by the earthquake. The whole house stood ten feet away from where it used to stand, because Jack propped it up on the spot where it came to rest. "I always wanted a larger backyard," Patty joked.

We barbecued in the newly spacious backyard, under the suburban shadow cast by the satellite dish. The lawn and garden were well tended, and Jack and Patty clean and trim, though, as they confessed, "a bit rusty at playing host."

In the late afternoon light, I could see, way down at the coast, a few palm trunks that marked the remains of the once-beautiful groves of trees at Wahaʻula, and the plumes of steam at either side where the lava poured into the sea.

Jack and Patty both seemed subdued, or perhaps simply more narrowly focused on the one looming force in their lives—the eruption and its pattern, present and future. Jack used to launch bitter tirades against the developer, insurance companies, tax assessors, county officials, and various agencies that had shown little sympathy for their plight. Now it was as though all had narrowed to a personal battle. They were only there by dint of Jack's ability to fix nearly anything that broke, to find ways to survive without most of the props of the outer world. But the fight to stay in the home that he and Patty had built now seemed to take on some element of a single-handed combat with nature.

Patty too seemed changed. Practical and straightforward, she had never shown a thread of awe or "superstition," as she called it, in her talk about the eruption. Now she spoke of feeling an uncanny sense of presence. "There's something—I don't know—*hideous* about it," she said. "All those tubes and oozes."

Just after dark, Patty delivered me to the bottom of the subdivision. With the aid of a flashlight, I picked my way across the rough ground to the coastal road. Looking back I could see glowing ribbons of lava winding down the steep sides of the scarp along the east edge of Royal Gardens. A half-mile to the west, near the top, a dim light shone from Jack and Patty's house. No other lights were visible anywhere; in all directions, there was nothing but silence and darkness.

The next day, the paper announced that one more house on the east side of Royal Gardens had burned during the night. The total of houses lost since the Pu'u 'Ō'ō eruption began in 1983 was now 72— very nearly the same as the number of acres of new land the volcano had added to the island. Destruction, in human terms; creation, in volcanic terms. In human time, for Jack and Patty, the central drama of their lives. In volcano time, an instant in a pattern too large for us to discern.

III: Mauna Loa, Southwest Rift Zone

R oyal Gardens and the various other lava land subdivisions came into being in the 1960s when developers discovered that "wasteland" could be profitable if sold simply as cheap land. This was a purely economic assessment—land as square footage. Those who sold the lots and those who bought them must have thought in the same terms. The state averted its eyes and held out one hand behind its back. After all, what other use would it ever find for its lava lands?

No one foresaw then that within a decade the technology to dam, dredge, crush, and reshape land would provide the means to alter completely the coastal lava lands of Kona. Or that the hotel business would give birth to the megaresort, with the money and means to create a completely artificial world in the middle of a lava plain. Or that tourists would find appealing the idea of resorts that were like city-states, effectively shutting out the world outside. Destination resorts, they are called, because they are not doors of access to a region, but rather worlds unto themselves.

On Hawai'i Island, all these resorts thus far have been located on the Kona coast, where one can perhaps make some sane argument in their favor. They cluster in an area that is already more Californian than Hawaiian, where the economy is already enslaved to the resort market, where the risk from lava flow is diminished (though far from absent). But the Hawai'i County Planning Department has now approved the biggest megaresort yet—and not in Kona. The Hawaiian Riviera Resort will be located at the south end of the island, in a remote area of Ka'ū, ten miles south of the state's last surviving Hawaiian fishing village. And directly below Mauna Loa's southwest rift zone.

The project will extend along 4.5 miles of the rugged Ka'ū coastline, and—in scale at least—promises to out-Hemmeter Chris Hemmeter's Hyatt Regency in Kona. But while Hemmeter's "fantasy resort" makes no pretense of having any connection with local nature or culture, the Hawaiian Riviera developers claim that "a sense of [the] majesty of, and respect for the *'āina,* the land, will establish a consistent theme for the resort."[15] That is a good claim to make when you are proposing to bring large-scale development to the last truly rural region of Hawai'i.

The area chosen for development is a wilderness of lava coastlands and sea cliffs, with some pockets of dry-land forest and a couple of tiny sandy beaches and a few brackish ponds. Numerous archeological sites, including a large field of petroglyphs, suggest that this coast was used extensively by ancient Hawaiians; the land's remoteness has kept these sites well preserved. The resort landholdings are 3,300 acres, currently zoned as agriculture and conservation lands. Two-thirds of this land will be divided into two "separate but contiguous developments." The Hawaiian Palace Resort will include two luxury hotels with 1,275 rooms, "luxury villas," condominiums and townhouses, an 18-hole golf course, and polo grounds. The lava coast will be reconstructed as a 400-slip marina, a cruise ship docking facility, artificial lagoons, and an artificial beach. A shopping complex at the marina will have a "European village character."

Complex number two, the Hawaiian Ka'ū-'Āina Resort, will be the more modest cousin, with a "deluxe hotel," a "high-activity hotel" and a "first-class" hotel, various single-family homes, and condominiums. This resort will "draw upon the natural beauty and the historical significance of the surrounding area for its inspirations." A cultural center, housed in a "commercial area," will administer tours to the "petroglyph park," sandwiched between a hotel and the golf course clubhouse.

With total occupancy and full employment, the resort population would be more than double the current population of the entire district of Ka'ū. The promise of jobs in an economically depressed area has produced quite a few local residents in favor of the megaresort. They would do better to take a long look at what is happening in Kona, where local people—those not driven out by rocketing housing prices—have generally been shunted into the most menial jobs at the big resorts. At the Hemmeter's Hyatt Regency you don't see the locals much, because many of them work in the mile-long underground service quarters. There is something bleakly feudal about the city-state world of the megaresort.

In terms of appropriate bioregional use of the land, the resort is a disaster. But leaving those considerations aside for the moment, one might consider, simply, its position in relation to a very live volcano.

Hawaiian Riviera Resort lands fall within a Zone 2 hazard zone for lava flows from Mauna Loa. Royal Gardens sits within a Zone 2 area for Kīlauea. Having watched the fate of Royal Gardens, how can county officials (state officials so far remain opposed) justify approving this enormous resort in a similar high-hazard zone? The answer surely must lie beyond economic considerations or political pressures: one begins to think that some deep-rooted psychological denial is at work here, some fundamental inability to accept nature's imperatives.

Mauna Loa appears to have had a much higher rate of activity in the last 150 years than in the previous several hundred years. In the Zone 2 areas of Mauna Loa, 20 percent of the land surface has been covered with lava since historic times. On the southwest rift, seven major eruptions have occurred since the mid-nineteenth century. Since the southwest slopes of Mauna Loa are relatively steep, several flows from these eruptions reached the sea the same day the eruption began. During three of these eruptions—in 1868, 1887, and 1907—lava flows entered the lands of the proposed resort.

In contemplating the possibility of high-density growth downslope from Mauna Loa's southwest rift zone, one might benefit from reviewing some of the volcano's more interesting eruptive events, as follows.

The eruption of Mauna Loa in 1868 that followed on the heels of the disastrous April 2 earthquake broke out at about the 2,000-foot level. It reached the sea in less than four hours, flowing over what is now the northeast corner of the proposed resort site.

In 1926 an eruption broke out at the summit of Mauna Loa, and then, in characteristic pattern, was followed by a flank eruption midway down the southwest rift zone. A huge *aʻā* flow more than half a mile wide moved slowly like an enormous juggernaut down the mountain. It reached the sea after several days, completely destroying the coastal village of Hoʻōpuloa. A photograph taken at the time from a nearby promontory shows a fifty-foot wall of smoking *aʻā* engulfing the first house on the outskirts of the village.

In 1950 Mauna Loa produced the largest and most spectacular Hawaiian eruption in historic time. The eruption began with a fissure opening high on the southwest rift, emitting an enormous column of fiery gas. Within an hour the fissure extended nearly six miles downhill, to about 7,500 feet above sea level, with lava fountaining up to 900 feet high all along the opening.

PART OF THE LITTLE HAWAIIAN VILLAGE OF HOOPULOA JUST BEFORE THE LAVA OVERWHELMED
LITTLE PIG ON THE ROAD. 8:15 A.M. 1926.

U.S. POST OFFICE

An a'ā lava flow from Mauna Loa entering the coastal fishing village of Ho'ōpuloa, South Kona, on April 18, 1926. Photographs by Tai Sing Loo. Courtesy of Bishop Museum.

RIVER OF MOLTEN LAVA AS IT JOINS THE SEA AT THE VILLAGE OF HO AT 6:21 A.M. APRIL 18

Two gigantic flows poured down the western side of the rift zone. The northernmost of these, traveling at an average speed of 5.6 mph, reached the sea in less than four hours, wiping out a small village from which the villagers escaped by a narrow margin.

By the next day, two other flows were advancing down the west slope. One entered the ocean around noon. The other reached the coast about 3:30 P.M., spreading laterally as it hit the coastal plain, destroying a new restaurant and surrounding buildings. The plunge of lava into the sea raised a steam cloud 10,000 feet high, and "the sea boiled for a considerable distance offshore."[16]

Twenty-three days after it began, the eruption finally drew to a close. An estimated 500 million cubic yards of lava had poured out of Mauna Loa in that time. Lava flows had crossed the main around-the-island road—the only through-way for the region—three times on their rapid flow to the sea. One of these entered the sea about fifteen miles northwest of the land on which developers now propose to build the Hawaiian Riviera Resort. In terms of the geology of the mountain, is there any reason why an eruption of this magnitude could not take place on the rift zone directly above the proposed resort?

The developers would like to suggest that there is. Reading the Hawaiian Riviera Resort's Final Environmental Impact Statement (EIS) on the subject of geological hazard is a peculiar experience. The information, assembled by a reputable firm of geological engineering consultants, makes use of various USGS reports but changes the emphasis of some statements and does some quoting out of context. As the EIS reads, "*only seven* [my emphasis] of the thirty-two eruptions of Mauna Loa since 1832 have occurred on the Southwest Rift Zone, and *only two* of those have impacted the project site."[17] (In fact there are three, as Riviera representatives have subsequently admitted at public hearings.) But the EIS implies that those three flows—in a period of forty-eight years—were erratic behavior on the part of Mauna Loa. This suggestion is buttressed by a quote from a USGS report noting that "southwest rift zone eruptive loci generally migrated uprift from 1868 to 1950."[18] The EIS interprets this fact as a "trend" that could "imply that future eruptive events will be further away from the [Hawaiian Riviera] site."[19] They would have done better, perhaps, to have heeded the same USGS report's cautionary note that "the relatively brief historic period has sampled only a small portion of the diversity of eruptive behavior that has occurred on Mauna Loa and Kīlauea over the past few thousand years."

Rift Zones

As every academician knows, quotes out of context can be made to support any argument. The county thus far has chosen to deal with the problem of building in geologic high-risk areas by insisting on disclosure of risk to potential buyers and investors. As Harry Kim, head of civil defense for Hawai'i County, pointed out to me, some of the responsibility has to lie with the individual, in the old "Caveat emptor" sense. Yet, Kim agreed, local government should ensure that the "facts" are fully disclosed. But in the Riviera case, at least, the "facts" have been liable to a number of interpretations. Meanwhile, the volcano keeps its own counsel.

There are other geologic dangers to consider in this portion of volcano country. The southwest flank of Mauna Loa has one of the steepest underwater slopes in the world, which is why, if you swim off the shores of this region, you are very soon in what local fishermen call "purple water." This unbuttressed flank has had major fault block slumps, though none of them seem to have been in the recent past. Nonetheless the evidence is there on the sea floor: massive landslides, mapped in recent sonar studies of the undersea slopes. The slides lie offshore from a coastline bounded by two conspicuous fault scarps. One runs about five miles southeast of the proposed resort; the other is some twenty miles up the coast to the northwest. Geologists have concluded that these mark the borders of an enormous section of the mountain that slid seaward thousands of years ago. In 1951 a damaging 6.5 earthquake occurred along the latter fault scarp where it extends into Kealakekua Bay, proving that it is still very active.

The probability of a major slumping event in the near future along the coast where the resort will be located is not great, but in light of the scale of catastrophe it could cause, it must be considered. Smaller slumps are more likely, and evidence that these have occurred can be found at the proposed resort site. As the EIS notes, "ground cracks have been located along portions of the project shoreline and at some inland areas. . . . The cracks tend to be parallel with the shoreline." Some of the cracks "are estimated to be greater in depth than 25 feet," and are "as much as 2 feet lower" on the seaward side. The EIS concludes, "It is believed that the extent of their potential impact is limited to the immediate area of their occurrence, leaving the great majority of the project site unaffected."[20] Who believes this, the EIS does not say. The average length of these ground cracks is over 1,300 feet. If you superimpose the project plan provided in the EIS over the map of "geological features" also provided in the document, it would appear that cracks bisect a hotel, an area designated "luxury villas," and a "commercial center."

It is questionable whether any development is appropriate in a "high volcanic risk" zone, but large-scale development seems downright foolhardy. The support community needed for the resort would mean a large influx of people into the area. There are over ten thousand subdivision lots in the Ka'ū region—the legacy of the 1960s—most of them in volcanic high-risk areas, only about 5 percent occupied at this time. The demand for residences would undoubtedly mean that these subdivisions would be populated. Hawaiian Ocean View Estates, for example, directly above the planned resort, might finally fill up with houses, all the way up to 6,000-foot elevation on the southwest rift zone.

Geologists at the Hawaiian Volcano Observatory say that since its 1984 eruption, Mauna Loa has been slowly inflating once again. At the current rate of inflation, they are predicting another major eruption in about 1994. The material here for a disaster scenario is irresistible—

—Let's say we travel in time to the winter of 1994. On the island of Hawai'i, a fierce storm sweeping in from the southwest has caused some damage to the marina and cruise ship docking facility at the newly opened megaresort, Hawaiian Villa Lux-Pompeii. Nasty winds have closed the private airport. Visitors at the huge destination resort, forced off the polo fields and golf courses by the weather, become aware that much local TV coverage is centering on the many swellings and shiftings beneath Mauna Loa in the last few days, which scientists think mean the slumbering giant is waking up. The news doesn't alarm the visitors much—the great mountain's summit is far away; in fact, the mountain has been shrouded in clouds of late and many guests haven't even been aware it is there, a huge hump on whose southwest rift zone the resort sits.

Still, some guests are thinking of leaving early if they can get reservations elsewhere. Nighttime gambling on the cruise ship, off the coast, has had to be suspended. And the little earthquakes that have been rippling through the resort for a week or so seem to be getting just a bit stronger and more frequent. The management has assured guests that small earthquakes are normal to a volcano prone to a bit of dyspepsia now and then. Those who persist with questions are reassured that no lava has entered the area for at least ninety years—and that flow was just a little guy some hundred yards wide that had meandered down to the shore and flowed harmlessly into the sea. Should such an unlikely event inconvenience guests or disrupt the quality of service, management would reimburse in full. . . .

On the third day of these annoying earthquakes, a rather nasty one hits. It topples nearly all the large "Etruscan" wine jars that line the halls. Jake Ford, a visitor from Texas, is sitting in the Gladiator bar when his passion-fruit margarita leaps out of his hand and the bar top bucks like a bronco. It is, as they say in California, "The Big One."

When it is over, Jake Ford finds himself lying on the floor among chunks from the plaster ceiling. Dazedly he picks himself up, only to be knocked to the floor by the aftershock that follows a minute later. Half-crawling, he makes it through the shattered doorway. The buildings, reinforced for earthquakes, seem intact, though reduced to shells. All the plaster has crumbled from columns and cornices; shards of decorative tile cover the ground. He notices distractedly that without the veneer the place looks like a shopping center in the suburbs of Dallas.

Outside, people sit on the ground or wander about in confusion, or attend to those who have been hurt. Jake Ford decides he has had enough of his Hawaiian vacation, even if the company is paying for it. He is heading toward his room when the first tidal wave strikes. The resort complex itself has been built back from the shoreline as protection against just such an event, but Ford sees the boats in the harbor lift straight up and come careening 50 yards inland. The cruise ship dock bends like a giant elbow.

The sight sends Ford scrambling up the path between the artificial lagoons. The route is drenched with water sloshed from the lagoons and littered with dying fish. He notices what appear to be giant cracks in the ground. He wonders whether the roads are intact. Up toward the mountain he can see nothing but rain clouds, tinged now slightly reddish by dust, or smoke, or something. In fact, the whole sky seems to be darkening into an eerie twilight. He braces himself against crumbling plaster—as the next aftershock hits.

The earthquake has been strong enough to knock local seismographs off the track. At the Volcano Observatory, geologists are calling Japan to get a reading. No one has noticed the beginnings of harmonic tremor under Mauna Loa's southwest rift. Mud slides have raised great clouds in already dense rain—so it is not until half an hour after the eruption begins that it is discovered.

It begins with a fissure that opens at the 6,000-foot level and rapidly cleaves downward, through the middle of the giant Tiki Gardens

Estate subdivision. A fiery crack extends from Paradise Street to Sweet Leilani Lane, swallowing a few houses, stranding the houses above. Lava pours through the subdivision in two wide molten rivers, heading for the coastal highway. In less than an hour, any evacuation by road will be impossible. . . .

One could go on—all of it within the realm of possibility. The disaster scenario, loved by Hollywood producers and environmentalists. There is a pulp novel called *Volcano,* written a few years back, that does the scenario full tilt. In the book, an enormous eruption from "Mauna Kai" is fought with dikes, with water, with aerial bombing. All attempts to divert the lava from its onrush toward the county seat fail. Finally a mysterious Hawaiian woman helps the head volcanologist by revealing the location of a lava tube that goes deep under the mountain. The volcanologist pauses briefly to ponder the revelation that there are mysteries beyond the realm of science. Then, with Pele's presumed *caveat,* he diverts the flow of lava by blowing another path for it with explosives set off in the deep cave. Shades of H. Rider Haggard, of womb-tombery, of insistence on the human right to control nature—to destroy, if need be, in the process.

Somehow, as Westerners, we seem to return again and again to these images of battle, of violence, in our fantasies of controlling nature. During the period when lava flows from the Puʻu ʻŌʻō eruption had first entered the Kalapana area and destroyed several houses, the media gave most of its attention to the "siege" of Bob Paolucci's home. While others dismantled their houses and carried them off, or moved out their possessions and abandoned them, Paolucci stood his ground. As the molten flow crept inexorably toward his house, he cooled the front of the lava with a firehose, hoping the lava would harden and divert the molten rock pushing up behind. For days he sprayed water on the flow as it inched toward his house. He was a Vietnam veteran. He was fighting a battle, he said, that reminded him of the war. Paolucci's house burned in the third week. Since then he has left the Islands.

In *The Control of Nature,* writer John McPhee describes attempts made in Iceland and Hawaiʻi to divert lava flows. He points out that "efforts to do battle with lava in Hawaiʻi were few in number, futile in nature, and not conceived by Hawaiians." He writes that for Hawaiians, throughout history, "the primary way of dealing with the problem was through native votive offerings . . . to placate an irritable Hawaiian deity whose dark humors are expressed as earthquakes and whose rage takes form as molten fire. . . . [The Hawaiians'] passive acceptance of the errant moods of Pele," McPhee concludes, "remains intact even if their belief in her does not."[21] McPhee is one of the writers I admire most, but in this case I wish he had spent some time with the people of Ka'ū and Puna. I would suggest that Hawaiian relationship with the land and the gods of the land has been anything but passive (unless one considers it passive not to be aggressive)—it has been an ongoing dialogue that has accepted the natural forces of the land and the conditions nature imposes. The Hawaiians lived not passively, but lightly in volcano country. They did not build cities. It is very unlikely that, given the opportunity, they would have built a resort in Pele's domain.

TWELVE

Kapu Ka'ū

Once again, O Pele, break forth;
Display thy power, my god, to the world;
Let thy voice sound out like a drum;
Re-utter the law of thy burning back;
That thy dwelling is sacred, apart . . . .

Chant translated by Emerson in *Pele and Hiiaka*

Ka'ū mākaha.
"Ka'ū of the fierce fighters."

Hawaiian saying

Preceding page: "The Rape of Puna," a vision of future Hawai'i. Woodblock print by Dietrich Varez. Detail.

*M*idmorning at Punaluʻu, site of an ancient village in Kaʻū, now site of Kaʻū's only resort, seven miles west of the park boundary, four miles west of the proposed spaceport site at Pālima Point. I was sitting on the black cinder beach with Palikapu Dedman, Kaʻū resident, Hawaiian "activist," listening to his stories of local history.

Palikapu is forty-two, a burly fisherman of German-Irish-Hawaiian-Filipino ancestry. The Hawaiian side of the family has deep roots in Kaʻū. They still own a piece of land across from the beach here at Punaluʻu, where Palikapu spent part of his youth. The land is now surrounded by the golf course and buildings of a resort put up in the 1970s by C. Brewer and Company, heirs to the sugar industry that has ruled Kaʻū life for the last hundred years.

The resort is rather modest, in this age of megaresorts, but the developers plan to enlarge in the near future. When this first increment of the resort was built, in the 1970s, many local residents protested. C. Brewer maintained that as a company with long roots in Kaʻū, it felt a strong commitment to the area. It would provide jobs for local residents. It would include a cultural center in the resort. Before I met with Palikapu, I had walked through the cultural center. It held some yellowing photographs of turn-of-the-century Punaluʻu village, a diorama of the bay as it might have looked in ancient times, and a case full of calabashes and a few other artifacts. Everything looked dusty and neglected. Last year, after another bitter fight, C. Brewer was granted a rezoning so that they could expand the resort. Again they assured local residents that they had the good of Kaʻū very much in mind. A few months later, the company sold the resort to a Japanese consortium.

So far the buildings do not entirely obscure what is one of the most majestic views on the island. Long stretches of black cinder beach and rugged lava coastline sweep to the right and left, forming a broad, shallow bay that offers some protection from the ocean swells that break against the south end of the island. Huge groves of coconut trees surround ancient fishponds at the east end of Punaluʻu beach. The brackish ponds are fed by springs that also seep out along the coast

A view showing one of the strange flat-topped hills above Punalu'u, in Ka'ū. The intensive taro cultivation depicted here suggests a large population in the area at this time. Engraving by M. Dubourg after drawing by Thomas Heddington, artist with the Vancouver expedition. 1794. Courtesy of Bishop Museum.

below the water line. From these springs, Palikapu tells me, Punalu'u ("diving spring") takes its name. The original inhabitants filled their water gourds by diving down to the spots where fresh water leaked out under salt. Here, as in all of Ka'ū district, water was precious.

The ruins of a very large *heiau* cover the promontory at the east end of the bay. Another *heiau* crowns the lava cliffs at the west end. Punalu'u must have been an important place, since it offered one of the rare places that a canoe could be landed along this rough coast. Perhaps the first human footprints in the Hawaiian Islands were made here on these black sands by those ancient voyagers from a distant southland.

Inland from Punalu'u, the land slopes up into belts of intense green—sugar cane—and to a series of strange hills shaped like flat-topped pyramids. Above their heads, which are bathed in mist, rain and clouds obscure the great bulk of Mauna Loa behind them. These hills are sentinels to the transformative power of this land: they are the last remnants of an old shield volcano now almost completely covered by the lava flows of Mauna Loa.

For the Hawaiians of Ka'ū, one hill, Makanau, has a deeper meaning. As Palikapu Dedman tells the story, there was a Ka'ū chief who treated his people poorly, who was more interested in war and conquest than in their welfare. He ordered the building of a large *heiau* on the flat top of Makanau ("surly eyes"). The chief took the people from their fields and fishing and had them carry up thousands of baskets of small water-worn stones to pave the new temple. But when he ordered the people to drag to the top an enormous *'ōhi'a* log to be carved into an image of a war god, the workers were driven to rebel. The hated chief stood below as they hauled the log with ropes up the steep sides of Makanau. With one accord the workers let go the ropes, so that the log slid down and crushed the chief beneath it.

The hill is both a memorial to the fierce independence of Ka'ū's people, and to the end of that independence. In the 1790s, Ka'ū's beloved chief Keoua, last of the district's hereditary chiefs, met a delegation from Kamehameha at this *heiau*, and agreed to the fatal meeting that ended with his body sacrificed to the war god at Kawaihae. The fierce spirit of the people was broken, as they adjusted to rule by a hated conqueror.

Still, Kamehameha's appointed chiefs might have ended up ruling well had it not been for the arrival of the *haole* foreigners. The chiefs here and throughout the Islands quickly developed an insatiable desire for foreign goods. They pressed the commoners into supplying a continuous flow of items to trade, though their own crops went neglected. The patterns of traditional life were disrupted, even in regions as remote as Ka'ū and Puna. The breakdown of the *kapu* system in 1819 contributed to neglect of the food sources the people relied on. Fishing, for example, was no longer regulated by traditional religious observances, and some of the richest fishing grounds were soon fished out.

Then in 1848 the tribal land use system was destroyed, at the instigation of foreigners who wanted to own land.

Hawaiians believed the lands belonged to the gods. The chiefs controlled the use of lands, paying tributes to the gods for the privilege. Commoners worked the land—generally by extended families—and tithed to the chiefs in a rather benign version of feudalism. People were free to move to another chief's land if not treated well by their own. Each land division controlled by a chief ran from the mountaintop to the sea, and commoners had hunting and gathering rights throughout the land division.

In 1848 Kamehameha III, whose government by then was dominated by Westerners, instituted a new land system called "the Great Mahele" ("division"—"The Great Land Grab" as many Native Hawaiians now call it). The Great Mahele divided the lands into (1) those allotted to the chiefs, (2) those reserved for the government, (3) those considered the king's personal or "crown" lands, and (4) those for the commoners. The last were a tiny portion of the whole—less than 1 percent, in fact, of the total land area. Foreigners were for the first time permitted to own land, and they bought at a prodigious rate from both chiefs and commoners, who had a hard time grasping the implications of private ownership. (Gavan Daws notes, in his history of the Islands, *Shoal of Time,* that some natives thought survey instruments bore some relationship to the long, carved poles that represented gods during the Makahiki harvest festival.)[1]

The commoners were busy enough simply trying to survive. Besides being demoralized by the disruption of their customary lives, they were prey to foreign diseases—venereal disease, then whooping cough, influenza, and measles—often fatal to a people with no immunity. It is now considered a conservative estimate that forty years after Cook's arrival the general population of the Islands had declined by as much as 80 percent.[2] And it continued to shrink, even in remote areas like the Ka'ū district. A missionary census of the Ka'ū population in the 1830s estimated the number to be around 6,000, a fraction of what the huge quantity of archeological sites suggests it once was. In 1872 a census recorded 1,829 Hawaiians and 35 "foreigners."

About that time, sugar, the industry that dominated Ka'ū until very recently, brought a new form of feudalism—the plantation economy—and an influx of outsiders. An 1884 census lists 1,543 Hawaiians and part-Hawaiians out of a total population of 3,483.[3] As Palikapu Dedman sees it, only the strong identity the Ka'ū Hawaiians feel with the land has kept them from being submerged completely. The customary tribal life on the land is now mostly a memory; and in the last century many of the visible remnants of traditional culture have been destroyed. The *heiau* of Makanau is gone now, the stones used for road building, and sugar cane is planted on the hilltop.

In the foreground, between myself and the view of Makanau, was parked Palikapu Dedman's truck. A bumper sticker on the back fender read, "*Kapu Ka'ū.*" Being used to bumper stickers requesting one to "Save" or "Help," I was intrigued by this slogan. One sees the word *kapu,* or "tabu," on signs posted on private property all over Hawai'i. It means, in the modern vernacular, "No trespassing; keep out."

Kapu Ka'ū is the name of a group of Ka'ū residents, mostly Hawaiian, who have been involved in various local battles to keep resort development out, to preserve coastal access, to protect important archeological sites, and generally to preserve the rural lifestyle of Ka'ū. Like its sister organization the Pele Defense Fund (Palikapu is active in both), the group's underlying purpose is to confront land use issues from a Hawaiian cultural perspective. In terms of local environmental politics, both groups are somewhat "separatist," reflecting the unfortunate division here in the Islands between environmentalists and "locals," particularly Native Hawaiians. Environmentalist groups, particularly local chapters of national groups—Sierra Club, Audubon, The Nature Conservancy, and so on—whose membership is predominantly urban, white-collar, *haole,* have often been ignorant of or insensitive to local traditions. They have tended to fight small pitched battles to save specific resources or to conserve certain lands, a style of defense that has allowed little time to consider larger issues of nature and culture.

Many Native Hawaiians and locals have viewed such efforts with suspicion as "token" gestures rather than a true concern for the land. Locals tend to focus on cultural concerns—traditional rights of access, of hunting or gathering. Hawaiians, particularly, are concerned about loss of ancestral lands and of aboriginal rights, and ultimately, about loss of their culture. They feel that they themselves should be listed at the top of the state's "endangered species" list.

Even when the concerns of environmental groups and locals have been similar, deep-seated antagonisms and misunderstandings have sabotaged cooperative efforts. A unified vision was badly needed— one that carried those who cared deeply about the region beyond the context of economic or humanistic concerns, and into a recognition of the spirit, even the *will* of the land itself. A vision that bows to place, not person, as the source of wisdom.

I wondered if the wording on the bumper sticker—"*Kapu Ka'ū*"— did not express that need for a vision that came from the land itself: *kapu* in its traditional meaning, "Forbidden; set apart; sacred."

For the past few years Palikapu Dedman has been chief spokesperson for the Pele Defense Fund. This group of Native Hawaiians and their supporters formed in response to the threat of geothermal development—wells and electricity-generating power plants—on the east rift zone of Kīlauea. Citizen and environmental groups had rallied to oppose the first commercial project, which was to have been developed on land adjacent to Volcanoes National Park. Most of these groups did not oppose all geothermal development, but they wanted it moved to a less environmentally sensitive area and they wanted strict guidelines drawn up for quality control. Palikapu Dedman and others felt that there were more fundamental issues to address.

There was a gap, the Native Hawaiians decided, between their vision of proper destiny for the lands of Ka'ū and Puna, and the vision of environmental groups. "Call it a psychological gap," said Palikapu Dedman, "or call it a religious one. Because for us Hawaiians that is what this land is—our religion, and our history. You cannot separate the land from Hawaiian culture. The land shaped us to speak for it; we are what the land made us, we are its soul."

The group that later formed the Pele Defense Fund felt that the environmental groups did not argue for the spiritual value of the land, because they still thought of land as property. As long as people understood land only in that way, there was always the chance that they might bargain or "sell out."

The land considered for geothermal development was owned by Campbell Estate, a huge landholding trust managed for the heirs of an early *baole* businessman. The area in question had been zoned "conservation" in the 1960s during what was then considered a pioneer program in state land use planning. In 1981 Campbell Estate petitioned for rezoning of 5,000 of its 26,000 acres on the east rift zone to allow for exploratory drilling.

These 5,000 acres were, in fact, superb native *'ōhi'a* forest, harboring several endangered species of plants and birds, including the *'ō'ū,* a very rare Hawaiian honeycreeper. The park had long hoped to acquire this land, knowing that its own small holdings of rainforest were not large enough to offer adequate protection to a rainforest ecosystem.

Campbell's plans projected 200 wells and five power plants. Half the wells would sit within a thousand feet of park boundaries. Park officials and environmentalists were alarmed for several reasons. The drilling towers with their steam plumes would tower above the forest. Drilling operations would be very noisy. Toxic emissions from the wells during venting could adversely affect both humans and biota. Miles of roads would intersect the forest, inevitably introducing exotic weeds into a fragile ecology.

216

Park officials and several citizen and environmental groups contested the rezoning of the land as a "geothermal resource subzone" on the basis of these concerns. They also raised the issue of volcanic hazard. Representatives of Campbell Estate had argued that the level of risk for Kīlauea's east rift zone was one eruption approximately every twenty years. Geologist Dick Moore pointed out that for the upper part of the rift zone the rates were much higher—closer to one eruption every three years.

The most disturbing issues raised by the geothermal project were the hardest to address directly. To environmentalists and Hawaiian activists alike, the state's willingness to rezone several thousand acres of conservation land for commercial use seemed to call into question how meaningful such designations are, if they can be so easily changed to suit private interests. As local Sierra Club activist Nelson Ho pointed out to me, "The geothermal scheme has derailed the state's land use plan. Business and industrial forces have succeeded in dismantling a key component in land-use policy—which ranked land according to value *and* environmental impact. This returns us to value alone. It sets a dangerous precedent."

The other troubling issue was raised by the scale of Campbell Estate's petition. The developer was asking for zoning to permit enough wells to generate up to 250 megawatts of electricity. Current electrical needs for the Big Island are less than half of that amount. Campbell Estate, it seemed, was banking on one (or both) of two possible futures: large-scale industrialization or development of the Big Island, or the Deep-Water Cable.

Since the early 1980s, the state had been supporting the idea of a deep-water cable to carry geothermally generated electricity from the Big Island to Maui and O'ahu. In 1981 the state successfully lobbied for $1.4 million of federal funding to develop the formidable technology to lay cable on ocean floor over 7,000 feet deep. The cable (which would cost in the billions to build) would carry 500 megawatts of "Pele power," as the proponents were calling it, through the longest and deepest-laid underwater power conduit in the world in order to meet O'ahu's soaring energy needs. Even though costs would be extremely high—and probably would be passed on to the public through taxes and rates—O'ahu's power monopoly, Hawaiian Electric, was arguing that the cable was a healthy move toward energy self-sufficiency for the state.

Cable opponents pointed out that not only would Hawai'i County (which comprises the entire Big Island) be bearing the environmental impact of a project that would benefit another island, but also all the state's taxpayers would have to pay for what could be "an economic boondoggle." They argued that both the rift zone where the wells would be located and the ocean floor the cable crossed presented high geologic risk from both eruptions and earth movement.

State officials on Oʻahu supporting the cable project seemed singularly blind to the geologic risks—and to the effects of such a major development on the Big Island's environment. In 1988 Senator Daniel Inouye suggested in an interview that the "destiny" of the Big Island should be to become the "energy source" for Oʻahu and Maui. One recognizes in this statement—and in other plans the state has come up with for use of Big Island lands—the common urban Western attitude toward land as expendable resource. For years now the state and the U.S. Department of the Interior have been jointly developing plans to mine the mineral-rich seabed that surrounds the Hawaiian Islands. The state has targeted Puna as the best location for the smelting plants. To overcrowded Oʻahu, the native forest and lava lands of the Big Island are simply empty lands that should be put to use. Apparently the formidable presence of the volcanoes is no longer enough to deter development of the last large region of rural and wilderness lands in the archipelago.

For the most part, the various environmental groups involved in the geothermal conflict were concerned about pollution of their own neighborhoods and damage to the rainforest or to the National Park, and were anxious to maintain control over development at the county level. Some groups took the position of advocating modest, carefully regulated geothermal development for local use. And members of a few groups suggested that the state facilitate a land swap with Campbell for nonforested state lands farther down the rift zone, in an area of less volcanic risk that already contained roads and subdivisions.

In late 1982, after lengthy hearings, the state Board of Land and Natural Resources (BLNR) authorized Campbell Estate to begin "exploratory drilling" on Estate land adjacent to the National Park. A few weeks later, on January 3, 1983, the Puʻu ʻŌʻō eruption began. Lava flowed over a section of the land authorized for geothermal development. Had the project been in place, lava would have buried nearly half the wells, destroyed one of the power plants, and assured that at least two of the remaining four plants were shut down almost continuously during the next few years. It is possible that many of the wells would have free-vented toxic fumes into the atmosphere for an indefinite period of time.

In the face of Pele's activity, the state proposed a land exchange—not for nonforested land but for 28,000 acres of state forest reserve land farther down the rift zone for the 26,000 acres of Campbell Estate land, now partially buried by lava. Why some of the environmental groups that had spearheaded the opposition agreed to endorse this exchange is a bit hard to understand, since such a concession was remarkably short-sighted. Park officials and others primarily concerned with impact on the park felt it answered that immediate concern. Other environmental groups were exhausted and demoralized by a battle that had stretched over years. They allowed the state once again to rezone conservation lands in a near-pristine forest watershed. For some Native Hawaiians and a few of the other opponents of geothermal development, this was proof that at least some environmental groups could not be trusted to see beyond their own immediate backyards.

Palikapu Dedman and Emmett Aluli, a medical doctor and long-time advocate of Native Hawaiian rights, filed an appeal of the BLNR's land swap and rezoning decision. This action was the birth of the Pele Defense Fund. Even though they knew they would have to break new legal ground to succeed, they decided to address the issue of land use solely from the viewpoint of native rights. As a strategy, their decision had its risks, but for Dedman and Aluli—and the Pele Defense Fund—the two issues, land use and native rights, were inseparable. Hawaiian cultural values, which are based on what Hawaiians term *aloha 'āina*, "love and respect for the land," could not be addressed within Western legal concepts, which assign only commodity value to land.

For some Hawaiians, the issue of development in the volcanoes region was even more personal. "Some of us are members of the Pele clan," said Palikapu Dedman. "In the Hawaiian scheme of things, we call the gods into existence, and it is our responsibility to keep them alive. If Pele is your *'aumakua* ['family god'], then you have a special trust to everything that is part of her."

Palikapu Dedman and Emmett Aluli filed their appeal to the state Supreme Court on behalf of "Pele worshippers." They argued that "like [mainland] Native Americans, our religion is in Nature. . . . On the Big Island, the goddess Pele appears to us daily in all her forms. She is the volcano, the lava, the steam, the heat. Her family is present in the fern, certain shrubs, certain native trees. She is the land itself." All the lands of active volcanism, they maintained, were sacred areas as part of the body of Pele and the source of spiritual power for her worshipers. Any development would "desecrate sacred land" and interfere with the religious practices of Native Hawaiians. "Pele influences and informs the daily physical and spiritual life of Pele practitioners," they stated in their deposition. "It is essential to them that Pele not be violated and degraded, and that she be allowed to exist in her unaltered form and in a pristine natural environment."[4]

The Pele Defense Fund was using the word *desecrate* in its original meaning, to deconsecrate, to take away the sacredness. As poet Gary Snyder writes in several recent essays on "the good, the wild, the sacred" in nature, the concept of sacred ground is common to nonurban cultures. But for the urbanized West this idea is a ghostly memory, retained only in myths about sacred groves of the early Greeks and the grottoes of Druids. In a world ruled by corporate agriculture and urbanization, the land is secularized, released from the gods to become a human commodity. In Western culture, "good" land is land that is productive. "Wild" land is uncultivated, uninhabited, a waste, a wilderness. Yet we have an ambiguous relationship with the "wild," perhaps because it still awakens an ancient sense of awe, a faint memory that such lands were once the dwelling places of gods. But the memory is too dim to affect our sense of the value of land: we admire wilderness, but only when it is "controlled" within the boundaries of our parks.

"We knew," Lehua Lopez, another member of the Pele Defense Fund told me, "that we were going into the courts of the Western legal system, where land is only one thing—property. And that we were introducing a "foreign" concept—that land can be sacred—it can belong to the gods. And that Hawaiians have a spiritual claim to the land that still exists, even if our lands have been taken away from us. But we felt that somehow we had to get that into the dialogue. All this talk about the environment means nothing without it."

The very slim precedent for what the Pele Defense Fund was trying to do rested on the efforts of Native American Indians to retain their rights to traditional spiritual practices. First Amendment rights to "freedom of exercise" of religion form what one would assume to be a solid constitutional basis for such claims. Nevertheless, Native Americans have fought a long battle for recognition that their religion is "legitimate." A major victory in that battle was won in 1978, when Congress passed the American Indian Religious Freedom Act, which reaffirms that "Native American religions are an integral part of Native American life, and are indispensable and irreplaceable to the continuation of native traditional cultures."

The right to traditional practice was defined in the act as including *but not limited to* [my emphasis] "access to sites, use and possession of sacred objects, and the freedom of worship through ceremonials and traditional rites." "What we found out in testing this law," states Palikapu Dedman, "is that things were still defined in terms of Western religion. By sites they meant church ground, or maybe a cave where someone had a vision of a saint. But our church, our saints, are nature. Our sites are the land itself, not just the temples we built."

The Pele Defense Fund appealed to a legal organization called the Native American Rights Fund (NARF) for help with their appeal. NARF was also active in another case that the Native Hawaiians hoped would broaden the interpretation of "religious sites" to include "sacred ground." The case involved sacred sites of the Eureka Native American tribe in the high country of the Six Rivers National Forest, in northern California. The Forest Service wanted to put a logging road through the area. The Indians claimed that the sites were, essentially, a "sacred geography" stretching from one mountaintop to another. The California State Supreme Court supported the tribe's claims.

The Forest Service, however, appealed the case at the federal level, and won their appeal. Three justices dissented, and one wrote the following conclusion:

> Today, the Court holds that a federal-land use decision that promises to destroy an entire religion does not burden the practice of that faith in the manner recognized by the Free Exercise Clause. . . . Given today's ruling, that freedom [to maintain religious beliefs] amounts to nothing more than the right to believe that their religion will be destroyed. The safeguarding of such a hollow freedom not only makes a mockery of the "policy of the United States to protect and preserve for American Indians their inherent right to believe, express, and exercise traditional religions," it fails utterly to accord with the dictates of the First Amendment.[5]

To their appeal in front of the state Supreme Court, the Pele Defense Fund brought Hawaiian religious experts and teachers of chant and hula to testify to the belief that Pele, in all her forms, is sacred. "What hurt the most about that courtroom scene," said Palikapu Dedman, "is that our beliefs weren't even taken seriously. We might as well have been arguing about parking tickets." Their appeal was denied on the basis that there were no known religious sites that would be affected by the geothermal development—therefore the Hawaiians could not show "burden of proof" that development would interfere with their religious practices. "Our practice," said Palikapu, "is in our values, our standards. The evidence is there in our chants and traditions. They [the judges] are saying that there is something called practice that is separate from belief."

The Pele Defense Fund filed with the Ninth Circuit Court of Appeals. On April 25, 1988, the appeal was denied—one week after the federal court overturned the California State Supreme Court's decision to recognize the sacred geography of the Six Rivers high country in northern California.

In early 1989 the Pele Defense Fund filed a second appeal at the federal level "against loss of ceded lands from the Trust obligations of the state and federal governments, which should be used to benefit Native Hawaiians and allow traditional gathering and subsistence use of the forests."[6] "Ceded lands," comprising about 1.7 million acres, are those lands that were established, in the Great Mahele of 1848, as belonging to the Hawaiian monarchy and "ceded" to the U.S. government after the fall of the monarchy. "By focusing on this issue, we are returning to the underlying problem," Palikapu Dedman told me. "We would not have to fight to have our spiritual claim to the land recognized as legitimate if our sovereign rights were recognized."

Many Hawaiians regard these lands as taken illegally from them, an argument that is hard to deny. These "crown and government lands" were in possession of the Hawaiian monarchy until 1893, when a coalition of U.S. businessmen led a bloodless coup, backed by the big guns of a U.S. warship that was in Honolulu harbor at the time. Queen Lili'uokalani, ruler of Hawai'i, was placed under house arrest. The aging queen, fearing for the safety of her people, abdicated the throne several weeks later.

The businessmen set up a "provisional government" and lobbied for U.S. protection. In 1898, Hawai'i was annexed to the United States. The crown and government lands were turned over, or "ceded," to the new territorial government. In 1959, when Hawai'i became a state, these lands were reclassified as state lands "to be held in public trust for the people of Hawai'i" (except for nearly 400,000 acres, to which

222

the federal government retained title). A clause of the State Admissions Act recognizes a particular responsibility toward "the betterment of the conditions of Native Hawaiians" with a portion of the proceeds from use of these lands.

Other than from a small portion of the most marginal lands—set aside by Congress for homesteading by Hawaiians in the Hawaiian Homes Commission Act of 1921—Hawaiians cannot be said to have benefited at all from these lands. The aboriginals of Hawai'i have ended up essentially a landless people.

In the last two decades, Native Hawaiians have been encouraged to seek redress by the qualified success Native American Indians have had in restoring lands alienated from them by breached treaties. Thus far, the case put forward for land reparations has been met with the argument that the United States signed no treaties with the Hawaiians, which is true: Queen Lili'uokalani, under duress, simply abdicated. No treaties were offered at the time.

What form restoration of some portion of sovereignty to the Hawaiians might take is a matter of hot debate these days, but the general consensus among Native Hawaiians actively protesting their current status is that the state should return title to a major portion of the "ceded lands." Reestablishing a land base is essential, many Hawaiians feel, if they are to survive as a culture. Although the majority of Hawaiians are now urbanized, they draw their spiritual resources from those landscapes, fast dwindling, that still reveal the lineaments of pre-Western times.

For these reasons, Hawaiians have a special stake in protecting the volcanoes region, where the land still echoes so vibrantly with the presence of the people and their gods. They feel that recognizing and honoring the link between the land and traditional culture may be the only way to preserve at least one region of Hawai'i from becoming one more Western outpost.

The heart of the volcanoes region is Hawai'i Volcanoes National Park. Most of the 200,000 acres that make up the National Park were "ceded lands"—lands transferred to the federal government when Hawai'i was annexed to the United States. Lands that were formerly in the possession of the Hawaiian monarchy.

Hawai'i Volcanoes National Park was primarily the brainchild of two men—volcanologist Thomas Jaggar and Lorrin Andrews Thurston.

Thurston, grandson of one of the earliest missionary families, played a leading role in the overthrow of Queen Liliʻuokalani. While subsequently in Washington lobbying for the United States to annex the Hawaiian Islands, he also urged the designation of a national park in the volcanoes region.

Thurston, an amateur volcanologist, was primarily interested in the geological scenery of the area. His concern with nature as "spectacle" and recreational resource was common to most of the founders of our national parks system. As the word *park* suggests, these lands were set aside primarily for their recreational or scenic value. Awareness of the crucial role parks play as ecological preserves has only come in the last few decades, and the responsibility it entails, at least in the case of Hawaiʻi Volcanoes National Park, has been accepted rather reluctantly. As late as the 1970s, an HVNP superintendent—transferred here recently from the mainland—reiterated that the park's *raison d'être* was primarily as *geological* preserve. Neither the park's physical boundaries nor its administrative framework lend themselves readily to its new role.

The park has had even more difficulty defining its role as a cultural preserve. On the continent, national parks were generally created out of lands from which the aboriginal inhabitants had long since been removed. Here park lands were carved out of a region in which rural Hawaiians still maintained strongly traditional ways.

In the 1930s park officials, recognizing the rich archeological resources of the southern coastlands below Kīlauea, lobbied for an addition to the park. In 1938, the park lands were extended toward the small Hawaiian fishing village of Kalapana. Acknowledging that the land appropriated was in the midst of an area where Hawaiians still practiced traditional lifestyles, supplementing subsistence agriculture with hunting and gathering, the act retained for Native Hawaiians fishing rights along the newly acquired coastlands. It also gave the secretary of the interior "discretionary authority to allow homesite leases within the Kalapana extension of the Park."

The visions of the role the park might play in fostering Hawaiian culture were idealistic and decidedly paternal. As one park ranger wrote around that time, "The Puna district is the one remaining section which has least felt the coming of the white man, and should be protected to keep it as unchanged as possible." Such sentiments were tainted by romanticized notions of what role Hawaiians should play, as one sees from what this ranger had in mind:

A Hawaiian village could be built by the Hawaiians themselves in the Park area around Kalapana, if given proper stimulus and protection, and fresh and saltwater ponds could be made and stocked for use as food. They could have substantial grass huts and could build up a good industry making *lauhala* [pandanus] hats, mats, pocketbooks, or useful articles and souvenirs. Proper protection and assistance of the kind possible only under Park administration would give these people opportunity to prosper and would do a great deal to prevent the race from dying out as it is now doing.

The park ranger reveals the colonialist underpinnings of his vision of "prospering" Hawaiians in his last paragraph:

They could have their gardens and taro patches. When there were visitors, they could have an exhibition of their arts and wares, and give little playlets with native music, singing and dancing. Extension courses could be given them to teach them weaving, cooking, sewing, carpentry, etc. Proper religious guidance could be given or encouraged.[7]

Not surprisingly, the Hawaiians were suspicious of such vestiges of the paternal system they had endured since the arrival of the missionaries. No one in her right mind, for one thing, would choose to live in the traditional grass house in an area now well populated by the insects and vermin that had hitchhiked to the Islands on various foreign ships. There were no applications for home site leases within park lands until the 1970s, when the Hawaiian activist movement renewed some interest in subsistence farming. At this time the park clung to the same narrow vision of "traditional use," refusing to take into account that not only the culture but the very land itself had been altered by the advent of Westerners.

The park has made some effort to employ local people as park rangers and interpreters, but those gestures are mostly token. Like most federal entities, the park has been administered by a rotating staff of outsiders, fostering an attitude that is both colonial and continental—ignorant of the unique qualities of the region.

An incident Palikapu Dedman relates illustrates, on the level of the ludicrous, the depth of park bureaucracy and insensitivity to local conditions. Two years ago, the park installed fee booths. Local people resented losing free access to a region they considered "theirs," and Hawaiians were incensed at being required to pay to walk on their own "sacred lands" or to gather traditional plants for ceremonies or hula performances. The park was autocratic, in the way that only a federal agency can be, and no attempt was made to respond to the local outcry.

There were several confrontations at the new fee booths between Hawaiians and park rangers. Palikapu Dedman recalls driving up to the gate, and noting that the fee schedule proclaimed "senior citizens free." How strange, he remembers thinking, that old people should be given special status and the genuine "special status" of aboriginals ignored. At the fee booth, Dedman said that he was going to Kīlauea caldera for religious worship, and did not feel obligated to pay the fee. The ranger argued, then finally had him fill out a long form and let him through, if he would agree not to use the "facilities," which were "federal property." "As far as I could see," said Palikapu Dedman, smiling, "that must have meant the toilets. Kind of shows how self-defeating their rigid rules can be."

Thus the park continues to operate within an insular, "continental" rather than "island" viewpoint, although it has become painfully obvious that it cannot adequately fill its many roles in splendid federal isolation, that its own health is inescapably linked to the health of the region. What is puzzling is that the park already has in hand a blueprint for change. In 1981, HVNP was designated a Biosphere Reserve under the auspices of the United Nations (UNESCO) Program for Man [sic] and the Biosphere. With this hefty honorific, the park joined over 260 "natural area preserves" worldwide that have been nominated since 1971 to UNESCO's pioneer program. Each Biosphere Reserve, it is hoped, will help to preserve indigenous nature *and* culture in a unique "biogeographic region."

One might ask what good, in a world that already has more than 140 categories of "protected areas," can more names or categories do? But the Biosphere Reserve program is unique—even revolutionary—in its focus on the interaction between nature and culture. While "protected" areas generally curtail human use in order to preserve biota, Biosphere Reserves are set up as experiments in finding ways to manage bioregions that benefit both nature and humans. Implicit in the concept is an acceptance of the wisdom of regional people and their traditional uses of the land.

At the core of a Biosphere Reserve is a "protected area" of a "representative territorial environment." The core area must be large enough to contain and preserve genetic diversity. HVNP was chosen because it is the only major portion of land in Hawai'i already under protection that encompassed most of the terrains and climate conditions in the Islands. In addition, the interaction between native biota and volcanism made park lands and adjacent rainforests an unparalleled laboratory for studying evolution.

Thus far, in its objectives, the Biosphere Reserve does not differ significantly from the park. But the reserve is much more than the protected wilderness that forms its core. Ideally the core area should be surrounded with a "buffer zone" of multiple uses, including (1) areas suitable for experiments in "appropriate development" (that is, development beneficial to the health of the bioregion; (2) "examples of harmonious landscapes resulting from traditional patterns of land-use"; and (3) "examples of modified or degraded ecosystems that are suitable for restoration to natural or near-natural conditions." As well as all or part of the above, the buffer zone may include "zones of co-operation"—areas of "unspecified multiple use" that are compatible with the basic goal: preservation of cultural as well as genetic diversity.[8]

Biosphere Reserves worldwide now harbor hunting and gathering populations (Siberut in Indonesia, Manu in Peru, Rio Platano in Honduras, and some Australian Reserves), herding populations (Lake Turkan in Kenya, Boule Loop in Mali, Asbaran in Iran), and traditional farming cultures (in many reserves). But the interpretation of "traditional use" is dynamic rather than static, calling for "judicious modification or supplementation of these practices using methods which respect and build upon their cultural traditions." What is "judicious" and what isn't is something only the people within a bioregion can decide.

What is truly revolutionary about the Biosphere Reserve concept, then, is its open-ended approach, this recognition that human culture and nature are inseparably linked, but woven together in a variety of unique ways. From this great web of nature and culture we draw our knowledge of the land and the way to nurture it, or be taught by it. Each place has its special knowledge to offer, if it is allowed to. A UNESCO poster proclaims the Man and the Biosphere credo as "conserving the unknown":

Because we don't know what we are losing.
Because we don't know what we'll need.
Because we don't know what we'll want and love.

Lofty dreams, these, but can we implement them, particularly in a region where traditional land use patterns have very nearly disappeared?

Although Hawai'i Volcanoes National Park has been a Biosphere Reserve for eight years now, I found only one park employee—Chuck Stone—who had given serious thought to its ideas. Stone is a research biologist, and from his position the park's difficulties in simply preserving its native biota seem staggering—an escalating guerrilla war against foreign invaders. Fountain grass here, kikuyu grass there. Invasions of blackberry, Christmas berry, Koster's curse. Seeds carried everywhere by the feral pigs, who root up the native seedlings as well. The research time (what's left over) going to identifying what we've got here—the native biota we don't even know about. Before we lose it.

The Biosphere Reserve is a designation only, a plaque on the wall, Chuck Stone pointed out. Great ideas, yes, but no funds and no warm bodies. And so far neither the superintendent of Volcanoes Park nor the Western Regional Parks office had shown interest in the Biosphere Reserve ideas. "You have to understand that the parks system in this country is a slow-grinding federal bureaucracy," Stone said. "It's very insular—it was never set up to respond to local conditions."

In the United States, there are now forty-three places nominated as Biosphere Reserves (most of them are National Parks), but few have progressed very far in implementing the ideas. In a sense, thus far, they haven't really had to: in a rich country, with low population pressure and land to spare, it has been easier to ignore the fact that conservation ultimately depends on the cooperation of the local populace and the health of the region. Even though, like HVNP, these designated reserves may be beset by problems that originate outside their borders, long-established patterns of isolation prevail.

The Biosphere Reserve concept was developed in response to the problem of conservation in Third World countries, where it has been obvious that natural reserves cannot function in isolation. Mapimi Biosphere Reserve in northern Mexico, for example, was created in an area where peasants had been forced to supplement a meager subsistence by hunting nearly to extinction the largest species of land turtle in North America. From the beginning, Mapimi has made "fostering and improving traditional agriculture" a major part of its plan. Members of local peasant groups and cattle ranchers serve on its board, working out goals to protect the turtle in the core area and to improve varieties of native plants useful to those making a living on the land.[9]

Hawai'i bears more resemblance to a Third World country than it does to the continental United States. The archipelago is a small, fragile world. It is not yet—not entirely—Westernized. And it has a surviving indigenous population whose wisdom and traditions are essential to any understanding of the land. Unlike most continental North Americans (excluding Native Americans), who are migrants or the grandchildren of migrants, Hawaiians are a people who define themselves by the land. Yet they have been deprived of any real voice in the land's destiny.

Native Hawaiians may need to establish some form of sovereign claim to the land before they will be given a major voice in bioregional discussions. There are some interesting precedents. When Kakadu National Park was proposed in Northern Australia, the Aboriginals' land claims were settled by an agreement that the native peoples would retain title to proposed parklands, but lease the land to the national park system. The Aboriginals continue to use the parklands and to participate in decisions involving the land.

In American Samoa, the National Parks committee has been negotiating with Samoan tribal chiefs to establish a National Park that would partly encompass tribal lands. The new park would be administered jointly by head chiefs and the National Parks Service and would encourage traditional arts of farming, hunting, and gathering within its boundaries.

The Biosphere Reserve approach cannot resolve the sovereignty issue for Native Hawaiians, but it can initiate a bioregional dialogue among all elements of the population. What such a dialogue might uncover is that what we perceive as "special interest groups"—such as Native Hawaiians, the parks administration, Sierra Club, and the Audubon Society—have common fundamental goals: an environment that nurtures both nature and human culture; and a voice in the decision-making process. Clearly a common ground is needed. Without a unified view, the small defenses, "brush fires" fought to save the native birds or the rainforest, beaches or customary fishing places, traditional ways, may all fail. The Biosphere Reserve concepts may provide the best blueprint thus far for regional self-determination.

After Palikapu Dedman drove off in his pickup, obscuring for a moment the *Kapu Ka'ū* bumper sticker in a cloud of exhaust, I sat on the beach of Punalu'u for a while, thinking of how easy it is to get lost in the meshes of history and myth, in the many conflicting visions of this land. One can argue that Hawaiians are not really "Hawaiian" any more. One can say, with truth, that many Hawaiians could care less about the old lineaments of land and culture. One can say that indigenous culture is dead, only an exhibit in museums now. One can argue that the real history never got told. One can contemplate Palikapu, spokesman for Hawaiian culture as living tradition—wearing the ubiquitous Japanese rubber sandals that are now so much a part of Island culture. Korean-made sunglasses. Smoking Kents. Looking, as he is, only a small part Hawaiian.

Or one can argue, as Palikapu does, that being "Hawaiian" has to do with a somewhat intangible spiritual inheritance. Or with a real kinship with place, an acceptance of the land that is identical to an acceptance of one's ancestors. This is a wisdom that the twentieth-century nomad has—almost—forgotten: that the land itself can be law and revelation, that it can be, if you acknowledge its claim on you, the deepest part of yourself.

Sacred Darkness

Pele is my goddess,
a chiefess of sacred darkness
and of light.

Fragment of chant recited
at dawn and dusk by
Mary Kawena Pukui's grandmother

Enter not prayerless the house of Pele.

From chant translated
by Emerson in *Pele and Hiiaka*

*A*t its highest point, the scarp of the Hilina Pali plummets 1,200 feet to a broad lava plain. To the east, the plain declines gently and then sweeps up again, like a nearly cresting wave, to the back of Pu'u Kapukapu. Pu'u Kapukapu is what geologists call a *horst*—a piece of land left high and dry as fault systems all around it allowed its surrounding terrain to sink downward. To either side of Kapukapu, the land slopes more gently to the coast. Out of sight, in the shadow of the horst's seaward cliffs, is Halapē, the once-idyllic cove and stand of coconut trees, much of the land now submerged, the broken remnants of trees immersed in water at high tide. But the beach there is slowly filling in again, and small new palms have sprouted, hiding the scars of the land shattered by the 1975 earthquake under their green fronds.

From here at the top of the Pali, one can see more than forty miles of coast. To the southeast, basalt seacliffs emerge again beyond the shadow of Pu'u Kapukapu, and curve into points and shallow bays until they vanish in a volcanic haze. To the southwest, the land bends outward and disappears into the horizon at the distant point of Ka Lae. The rain clouds that have shrouded Kīlauea for the last two weeks are breaking up just to the northwest, and a rainbow arches from them, falling over the edge of the Pali. Thunder and rain season, the inseminating rain of Lono.

There are four of us here at the top of Hilina Pali, eyeing the first steep switchback of the trail down. Archeologist Laura Carter. Fay-Lyn Jardine, a tall, graceful backcountry park ranger of Hawaiian-Portuguese blood. And Tamar Elias, an athlete and jill-of-all-trades, currently employed changing the recording papers on the seismographs at the observatory.

We are headed into the midst of the lava plain below us to find two lava tube caves containing petroglyphs and cultural remains. The caves were discovered in the 1970s. No archeologist has visited them since, and Laura wants to see how they are faring, and to leave a sign in one of them reminding hikers that might stumble on the site to leave the remains undisturbed.

The trail down the Pali makes a dozen turns down the rocky face, over stretches of rubbly *a'ā*. Halfway down, Fay-Lyn points out the place where a Park Service packhorse named Battle Star got off the trail and tumbled "ass-over-teakettle" fifty feet down to the next switch-back, emerging, miraculously, with just a few scrapes, but a strong aversion to packing.

At the bottom of the Pali, we take an altimeter reading, then fan out across the rough country to look for the caves. Waist-high grass masks jagged flows of *a'ā*, in between billowy mounds of *pāhoehoe;* the land dips and sways like a choppy sea. The "cave" opening is actually the fallen roof of a lava tube, so its entry will be from a depression in the ground; in this country, one could walk within ten yards of it and not see it.

But I come across it just as I think we may have walked too far. The collapsed roof of the lava tube has created a pit thirty feet or so wide, and a low opening yawns at the north end. It is like a thousand such "caves" in the layered lava of this country, but the pile of stones at the entrance is arranged into a low wall. I climb down to the wall, and find that its top is laid with water-worn stones, here, three to four miles inland. In front of the wall, an area of the rocky pit has been leveled and thin, flat stones upended in a square to form a hearth.

The petroglyphs cluster so thickly at the entrance that at first I don't perceive them. Then my eyes register the darker, incised rock on the mottled, vitreous surface of the cave's inner walls, and human figures startle me, crowding forward from the darkness.

The shapes are cut or pecked into the thin, glazed coating left by the molten river that once flowed through the lava tube. Perhaps because this surface is easier to work, these petroglyphs are richer in detail than others I have seen: many of the human figures have fingers and toes; some have spiky hair or headdresses. There is a hawk-headed man with bird feet and an arrow-shaped penis. Turtles, dogs, and chickens. And three life-sized incised feet, the broad shovel-shape of Hawaiian feet, good for walking on lava.

The archeologists who explored the cave a decade ago uncovered more petroglyphs under rubble and midden. Charcoal in the midden furnished a date of plus or minus 300 years. No historic artifacts (such as nails) were found in this cave, and none of the petroglyphs are of European motifs (horses, for instance), suggesting that use of this site ceased before Western settlement. These caves may have provided seasonal water and shelter, as a large number of water gourds found in a nearby cave would seem to indicate; crops may have been grown nearby at times in the year, and water carried down to fishing villages on the coast. But these figures spilling from the darkness hint at other uses than water and shelter, at other powers felt or honored here.

Perhaps the hawk-headed figures are a key to the *mana* of this particular place, for, though not unknown elsewhere, such petroglyphs are rare, and there are several here. But what secrets the cave holds it does not readily reveal. The figures thin out and then stop some twenty feet into the cave. Forty feet farther, the cave narrows down to a space one could crawl through, painfully, with some padded clothes. My flashlight is not strong enough to penetrate the night beyond.

We return to the caved-in pit and open sky to eat our lunches, next to the heart with its surrounding midden of *'opihi* (limpet) shells, evidence of meals eaten here long ago. Then we explore the south entrance to the lava tube, crawling over the fallen rocks that narrow the opening. A few petroglyphs cluster at the entrance, but the glazed walls farther in are empty of figures. The lava tube appears to continue on into a pitch blackness. Laura and Fay-Lyn and Tamar turn back to the entrance, determining to go search for the other cave mentioned in the archeological report, the one that contained fragments of many water gourds.

I linger behind, deciding on impulse to do something I've never done alone before, to follow that dark passage.

Left to myself, I reconsider. Beyond the reach of my light, the tube opening is a dense, black maw. I have one flashlight, no spare batteries. But if I watch carefully to make sure the tube does not branch anywhere, I could feel my way back out if I had to. I have long since lost all but a reflex anxiety, in this country, about predatory animals or snakes. The only large animals that frequent the lava tubes are feral goats, who shelter in them, and in sickness or old age may crawl into their recesses to die.

Indeed, fifty feet in, at the furthest reach of the light from the entrance, a goat skull and bones are scattered across the floor, white remnants of a natural death, but I can't stifle an inner shiver that makes me read them as sentinel or warning to the dark passage beyond. Some deep-seated reflex in me links darkness with death, but it has come to seem less like a primal response and more like a cultural legacy. I am reminded once more of H. Rider Haggard's nightmare journey, in his novel *She,* into the caverns of earth somewhere in darkest Africa. There his hero found a savage tribe inhabiting vast catacombs, ruled by a strangely immortal female given over to a cult of death. A fantastical story, but compelling, as it must have been to Haggard himself, who wrote it, it is said, in six weeks, as though it poured in some great stream from the unconscious.

Haggard's images are crude, as dreamscapes often are, but disturbingly familiar, as though they tap a deep vein in the Western mind where the shadow side of the natural world has been replaced by an inner darkness. The darkness, loosed from its moorings in the natural cycles of birth and death, no longer something we can reach or touch, or make our peace with, terrifies us from within, elicits rage and fear toward all that is alien or wild or "other," all that reminds us of the tenuousness of human control.

Armed only, as in Haggard's dreamscape, with a sense of the darkness as unholy, one would find in this landscape only a mirror of inner terrors. But other visions rise from the land, and are given voice in Hawaiian myth: images, prolific in this volcanic world, of the deep-rooted, creative powers of darkness:

An incandescent river pours through a black labyrinth, streams briefly into the light at the edge of a seacliff, cools to steaming black at the edge of an ocean wave, shatters from the pressure of its still-molten heart, and is flung back on shore as tiny grains of glistening jet. "Born was the island, it grew, it sprouted, it flourished, lengthened, rooted deeply, budded." From the black maws of the lava of last year, tiny ferns sprout like lambent green flames. As the legends of the land tell, the mouths of darkness, like the wombs of women, are the channels through which flows *"Pō nui hoʻolakolako,"* "The great night that supplies."

I walk into the black tunnel of the lava tube. The walls curve gently to the right, ridged horizontally like striations of muscles, marking the levels of the molten lava as it diminished and narrowed. The tube must once have been filled to the brim with a fiery river; as it drained, it cascaded and pooled, creating intricate, molded patterns on the floor. When the molten rock subsided, the residue on the ceiling hardened into smooth, conical drips, teat-shaped, like some vast statuary of a many-breasted mother goddess.

For a few hundred paces, the smooth musculature of the cave makes walking easy, but then the ceiling narrows to a crawlspace. I shut off the light and lean against the laminated wall.

Absolute night surrounds me, warm, moist, palpable—the pressure of amniotic fluid, or of the eyelid on the eye. It is a nonhuman presence so overwhelming that it threatens to dissolve the fragile boundaries of self. Nothing in it seems benign or disposed toward humans. Nor indisposed. Simply there, a vast mystery behind every element of this landscape. I switch the flashlight back on quickly. *"Enter not prayerless the house of Pele."* Some great current seems to flow from the inner recesses, propelling me back toward the entrance.

And into an astoundingly noisy outer world, where the darkness fractures into a million forms. The wind is hissing through grass, and for the first time I hear in its lower register the base note of waves pounding the coast. I glance at the crowd of human figures at the north mouth of the lava tube. Midway between the light and the darkness, arms akimbo, some pointing up, some pointing down, guarding the passage, or pointing the way.

Notes

For a general introduction to volcanology, see Robert and Barbara Decker, *Volcanoes* (San Francisco: Freeman, 1981) and Peter Francis, *Volcanoes* (New York: Penguin, 1976). See H. W. Menard, *Islands* (New York: Scientific American, 1986) for a comprehensive explanation of island chain volcanism. The indispensable text on Hawaiian volcanism is G. A. MacDonald, A. T. Abbott, and F. L. Peterson, *Volcanoes in the Sea: The Geology of Hawaii* (Honolulu: University of Hawai'i Press, 1983). See also the papers collected in R. W. Decker, T. L. Wright, and P. H. Stauffer, eds., *Volcanism in Hawaii,* vols. 1 and 2, U.S. Government Professional Paper 1350 (Washington, DC: U.S. Government Printing Office, 1987).

1: TEN VIEWS OF MAUNA LOA

1. Archibald Menzies, *Hawaii Nei 128 Years Ago* (Honolulu: Wilson, 1920), pp. 196–199.
2. For quotations from the letters of David Douglas, see Athelstan George Harvey, *Douglas of the Fir* (Cambridge, MA: Harvard University Press, 1947); and James Jarves, *Scenes and Scenery of the Sandwich Islands* (Boston: Tappan and Bennett, 1843). For biographical information on Douglas, see also William Norwood, *Traveller in a Vanished Landscape* (New York: Potter, 1973).
3. Sarah Joiner Lyman, *The Lymans of Hilo,* edited from her journals (Hilo, HI: Lyman House Museum, 1979), p. 64.
4. The phrase is from Jarves, p. 258.
5. This and following quotations from the unpublished letters of Isabella Bird are from a transcript of the originals in the Edinburgh Library, passed on to me by the late Victorian scholar Alfons Korn. Permission to quote from the letters was graciously granted by Bird's publishers, John Murray, London.
6. Titus Coan, as quoted by William T. Brigham, *The Volcanoes of Kilauea and Mauna Loa* (Honolulu: Bishop Museum, 1909), p. 391.
7. C. F. Gordon-Cumming, *Fire Fountains,* vol. 1 (Edinburgh: Blackwood, 1883), p. 145.
8. Quoted in Brigham, *The Volcanoes of Kilauea and Mauna Loa,* p. 391.
9. See Charles Wilkes, *Narrative of the U.S. Exploring Expedition during the Years 1838, 1839, 1841, 1842,* vol. 4 (Philadelphia: Lea & Blanchard, 1845) and Charles Wilkes, *Autobiography of Rear Admiral Charles Wilkes, U.S. Navy 1798–1877* (Washington, DC: Department of the Navy, 1978). For background on the Wilkes expedition, see Herman J. Viola and Carolyn Margolis, eds., *The Magnificent Voyagers: The U.S. Exploring Expedition, 1838–1842* (Washington, DC: Smithsonian Institution Press, 1985). See also Russell A. Apple, *Mountain Trails: The 'Āinapō and Mauna Loa,* typescript, Hawai'i Volcanoes National Park Library, 1973.
10. Isabella Bird, *Six Months Among the Palm Groves, Coral Reefs and Volcanoes of the Sandwich Islands* (London: Murray, 1881).

Notes

2: "UNSTABLE WAS THE LAND"

1. Stephen Jay Gould, *Time's Arrow, Time's Cycle* (Cambridge, MA: Harvard University Press, 1987), p. 43. For other discussions of the origins of geology as a science, see John McPhee, *Basin and Range* (New York: Farrar, Strauss & Giroux, 1980); and John C. Greene, *The Death of Adam* (Iowa: Iowa State University Press, 1959).
2. Daniel E. Appleman, "James D. Dana and the Origins of Hawaiian Volcanology," in Decker, Wright, and Stauffer, eds., *Volcanism in Hawaii*, vol. 2, p. 1608.
3. Appleman, "James D. Dana," p. 1616.
4. For background on Jaggar, see Russell A. Apple, "Thomas A. Jaggar, Jr. and the Hawaiian Volcano Observatory," in Decker, Wright, and Stauffer, eds., *Volcanism in Hawaii*, vol. 2, pp. 1619-1644; G. A. MacDonald, "Thomas Augustus Jaggar," *Volcano Letter*, no. 519 (1953), pp. 1-4; and Joan Abramson, *Photographers of Old Hawai'i* (Honolulu: Island Heritage Press, 1977), pp. 165-168.
5. Thomas A. Jaggar, *Volcanoes Declare War* (Honolulu: Paradise of the Pacific, 1945), p. 16. The poem "Kilauea" was published in *Paradise of the Pacific, 38*, no. 12 (December 1925), 87.
6. Jaggar, *Volcanoes Declare War*, pp. 2-3.
7. As quoted in Abraham Fornander, *Fornander's Collection of Hawaiian Antiquities* (Honolulu: Bishop Museum, 1916-1920), p. 363.
8. Traditional Pele chant, translated by Marjorie Sinclair in *The Path of the Ocean* (Honolulu: University of Hawai'i Press, 1982), p. 34.
9. For an analysis of the sources of the myths and collation of various versions, see H. Arlo Nimmo, "Pele's Journey to Hawai'i, An Analysis of the Myths," *Pacific Studies 11*, no. 1 (November 1987), 1-40. For a discussion of the Pele myths in relation to other Hawaiian myths, see the classic work by Martha Beckwith, *Hawaiian Mythology* (Honolulu: University of Hawai'i Press, 1970). Originally published 1940.

3: THE LAVA LAKE

For a scientific account of the Pu'u 'Ō'ō eruption see Edward W. Wolfe, Michael D. Garcia, Dallas B. Jackson, et al., "The Pu'u 'Ō'ō eruption of Kilauea Volcano, Episodes 1–20," in Decker, Wright, and Stauffer, eds., *Volcanism in Hawaii*, vol. 1, pp. 471–508. As well as the books on volcanology listed previously, John McPhee's *Basin and Range* was an important source for the history of plate tectonics. I found two articles particularly helpful on the Hawaiian "hot spot": G. Brent Dalrymple, Eli A. Silver, and Everett D. Jackson, "Origin of the Hawaiian Islands," *American Scientist 6*, no. 3 (May–June 1973), pp. 299–308; and David A. Clague and G. Brent Dalrymple, "The Hawaiian-Emperor Volcanic Chain, Part I: Geologic Evolution," in Decker, Wright, and Stauffer, eds., *Volcanism in Hawaii*, vol. 1, pp. 1–54.

1. Thomas Jaggar, *My Experiments with Volcanoes* (Honolulu: Hawai'i Volcano Research Association, 1956), pp. 178–179.
2. Harry Hess, "History of Ocean Basins," in A. E. J. Engel, Harold L. James, and B. F.

Notes

Leonard, eds., *Petrologic Studies: A Volume in Honor of A. F. Buddington* (New York: Geological Society of America, 1962), pp. 599–620.

3. Actually, according to Tina Neal, Iceland is located both over the Mid-Atlantic Ridge *and* a "hot spot."

4. Louis-Sebastien Mercier, an eighteenth-century scientist influenced by alchemy. As quoted in Barbara Stafford, *Voyage into Substance* (Cambridge, MA: MIT Press, 1984), p. 63. On alchemy and the world as *magna mater,* see Mircea Eliade, *The Forge and the Crucible* (Chicago: University of Chicago Press, 1962), and Morris Berman, *The Reenchantment of the World* (Ithaca: Cornell University Press, 1981). On alchemy and sexual symbolism, see also Gaston Bachelard, *The Psychoanalysis of Fire* (Boston: Beacon Press, 1964).

4: VOLCANIC GENESIS

For an overview of island ecology, see Sherwin Carlquist, *Hawaii: A Natural History,* 2nd ed. (Honolulu: Pacific Tropical Botanical Garden, 1980); and John Culliney, *Islands in a Far Sea* (San Francisco: Sierra Club Books, 1988).

Useful guides: Otto Degener, *Plants of Hawaii National Parks (Ann Arbor, MI: Braun-Brumfield, 1930);* and Andrew J. Berger, *Hawaiian Birdlife* (Honolulu: University of Hawai'i Press, 1972).

For an excellent discussion of conservation problems in Hawai'i, see Charles P. Stone and Danielle B. Stone, eds., *Conservation Biology in Hawai'i* (Honolulu: University of Hawai'i Cooperative National Park Resources Study Unit, 1989). Also, see *Bioscience 38,* no. 4 (April 1988), an issue discussing Hawaiian conservation.

1. Charles Darwin, letter written to John Dalton Hooker, director of Kew Gardens, in 1850. From F. Darwin, ed., *More Letters of Charles Darwin* (London: Murray, 1930), p. 459.

2. Stephen Jay Gould discusses Darwin's evolution as an evolutionist in *The Flamingo's Smile* (New York: Norton, 1985); and in *The Panda's Thumb* (New York: Norton, 1980).

3. Estimates of population at time of Western contact have run from 250,000 to 800,000, the latter number argued recently by David Stannard in *Before the Horror: The Population of Hawai'i on the Eve of Western Contact* (Honolulu: University of Hawai'i Press, 1989).

4. William P. Mull, "Hawaii's Magnificent Minutiae," *Defenders 50,* no. 6 (December 1975), 490.

5. Thomas Berry, *A Dream of the Earth* (San Francisco: Sierra Club Books, 1988).

6. Martha Beckwith, *The Kumulipo* (Honolulu: University of Hawai'i Press, 1971), p. 58. Originally published 1950.

7. John Charlot, *The Kamapua'a Literature* (La'ie, Hawai'i: Institute for Polynesian Studies, Brigham Young University, 1987).

8. This and the following quotations from *The Kumulipo* are from the translation and study by Rubellite Kawena Johnson, *Kumulipo: Hawaiian Hymn of Creation,* vol. 1 (Honolulu: Topgallant, 1981), pp. 3–4.

9. Beckwith, *The Kumulipo,* p. 97.

Notes

5: THE VOLCANO AS WESTERN METAPHOR

Two books by Paul Shepard greatly influenced my thoughts on the Western vision of nature: *Man in the Landscape* (New York: Knopf, 1967); and *Nature and Madness* (San Francisco: Sierra Club Books, 1982).

1. M. G. Bosseront d'Anglade, *A Tree in Bud: The Hawaiian Kingdom 1889–1893* (Honolulu: University of Hawai'i Press, 1987), p. 123.
2. Bachelard, *The Psychoanalysis of Fire*, p. 7.
3. Norman O. Brown, *Life Against Death* (Middletown, CT: Wesleyan University Press, 1959), p. 316.
4. Emerson as quoted by Frank Lentriccia in *After the New Criticism* (Chicago: University of Chicago Press, 1980), p. 215. Lentriccia comments on the volcano image as "a metaphor for the great expressive hope of the romantics."
5. See Mario Praz's classic study of British nineteenth-century art and literature, *The Romantic Agony* (New York: Meridian, 1956). Praz notes, among other things, the age's preoccupation with female power in the image of the *femme fatale*.
6. Eric Neumann, *The Great Mother* (Princeton, NJ: Princeton University Press, 1955).
7. Sandra Gilbert, "Haggard's Heart of Darkness," *Partisan Review 50,* no. 3 (1983), 444–453.
8. Adrienne Rich, *The Dream of a Common Language* (New York: Norton, 1978), p. 30.
9. William Ellis, *Polynesian Researches* (Honolulu: Tuttle, 1969), p. 287. Originally published 1829.
10. Robert Dampier, *To the Sandwich Islands on H.M.S. Blonde* (Honolulu: University of Hawai'i Press, 1971), pp. 61–64.
11. For references on Peale, see Viola and Margolis, eds., *Magnificent Voyagers;* and Jessie Poesch, *Titian Ramsay Peale* (Philadelphia: American Philosophical Society, 1961).
12. Bird, *Six Months in the Sandwich Islands,* p. 257. Also see Chapter 1, Note 5.
13. The Volcano House Register, from the transcription at Hawai'i Volcanoes National Park library.
14. Twain: Volcano Register passage and dream can be found in Walter Francis Frear, *Mark Twain and Hawaii* (Chicago: Lakeside Press, 1947), pp. 126–127 and 251–255. See also A. Grove Day, *Mark Twain's Letters from Hawaii* (New York: Appleton, 1966), p. 15.
15. See Gordon-Cumming, *Fire Fountains,* vol. 1, pp. 141–175.
16. On the "volcano school" painters, see the introductory essay by David Forbes in *Hilo 1825–1925* (Hilo, HI: Lyman House Museum, 1984); and Helen Maxon, *David Howard Hitchcock* (Honolulu: Topgallant, 1986).

6: "THE ASTONISHING FOOD OF THE LAND"

There is one brief but interesting book on Hawaiian petroglyphs: J. Halley Cox and Edward Stasack, *Hawaiian Petroglyphs* (Honolulu: Bishop Museum Press, 1970).
1. E. S. C. Handy and Mary Kawena Pukui, *The Polynesian Family System in Ka'ū, Hawai'i* (Rutland, VT: Tuttle, 1972), p. 226.
2. Handy and Pukui, *The Polynesian Family System,* p. 28.

Notes

7: MYTH AND MYSTERY AT THE SCENE OF THE ERUPTION

1. The journal of Joseph Goodrich, *Missionary Letters,* vol. 3, pp. 900–901, transcript held at Hawaiian Mission Children's Society library, Honolulu, Hawai'i.
2. As Jocelyn Linnekin points out in her chapter "Women and *Kapu,*" *Sacred Queens and Women of Consequence: Rank, Gender, and Colonialism in the Hawaiian Islands* (Ann Arbor: University of Michigan Press, in press.) From the typescript provided by the author, pp. 113–114.
3. K. R. Howe, *Where the Waves Fall: A New South Sea Islands History from First Settlement to Colonial Rule* (Honolulu: University of Hawai'i Press, 1984), p. 66, as quoted by Caroline Ralston in her introduction, "Sanctity and Power: Gender in Polynesian History," *Journal of Pacific History 12,* no. 3 (July 1987), 115.
4. Barbara Bennett Peterson, ed., *Notable Hawaiian Women* (Honolulu: University of Hawai'i Press, 1984), p. 200.
5. Charles S. Stewart, *A Visit to the South Seas in the United States Ship "Vincennes"* (New York: Haven, 1833), p. 92.
6. Ellis, *Polynesian Researches,* p. 311.
7. Ellis, *Polynesian Researches,* p. 277.
8. Hiram Bingham, *A Residence of Twenty-one Years in the Sandwich Islands* (Hartford, CT: Huntington, 1847), pp. 254–255.
9. William Westervelt, *Hawaiian Legends of Volcanoes* (Rutland, VT: Tuttle, 1963), p. 158. Originally published 1919.
10. Alfred, Lord Tennyson, *The Poems of Tennyson,* ed. Christopher Ricks (New York: Norton, 1969), p. 1450.
11. Charlotte Yonge, *A Book of Golden Deeds* (London: Macmillan, 1908), p. 423. Originally published 1864.
12. Joseph B. Emerson, "The Lesser Hawaiian Gods," *Hawaiian Historical Society Papers,* no. 2 (Honolulu, HI: Hawaiian Historical Society, 1978), p. 7.
13. John Cameron, *John Cameron's Odyssey* (New York: Macmillan, 1928), p. 222. For a brief biographical note on Princess Ruth, see Peterson, ed., *Notable Hawaiian Women.* See also Kristin Zambucka, *The High Chiefess Ruth Ke'elikōlani* (Honolulu: Mana, 1977).
14. Oliver Stillman is quoted by Eugene Burns in "He recalls Princess Ruth," *Honolulu Star Bulletin,* May 20, 1939.
15. Gordon-Cumming, *Fire Fountains,* vol. 2, pp. 267–269.

8: UNREDEEMED NATURE; UNREDEEMED GODDESS

1. John Stokes, "Notes on Hawaiian temples." Page 590 of manuscript in the Bishop Museum library, Honolulu, Hawai'i.
2. Thegn Ladefoged, Gary F. Somers, and M. Melia Lane-Hamasaki, *A Settlement Pattern Analysis of a Portion of Hawaii Volcanoes National Park,* Western Archeological Center Publications in Anthropology, no. 44 (Tucson: National Park Service, 1987), pp. 56–58.
3. Valerio Valeri, *Kingship and Sacrifice* (Chicago: University of Chicago Press, 1985), pp. 326–332.

Notes

4. Valeri, *Kingship and Sacrifice,* p. 19.
5. As anthropologist Jocelyn Linnekin sums up Valeri's view in *Sacred Queens and Women of Consequence.* From the typescript provided by the author, p. 35.
6. E. S. C. Handy, *Polynesian Religion* (New York: Kraus Reprint, 1971), p. 47. Originally published 1927.
7. Jocelyn Linnekin covers this ground expertly in a chapter called "Pollution Revisited," in *Sacred Queens and Women of Consequence.*
8. Handy, *Polynesian Religion,* p. 43.
9. Valeri, *Kingship and Sacrifice,* p. 114.
10. F. Allan Hanson, "Female Pollution in Polynesia?" *Journal of the Pacific Society 91,* no. 3 (September 1982), 335–381.
11. Caroline Ralston, introduction, "Sanctity and Power," p. 118.
12. Valeri, *Kingship and Sacrifice,* p. 114.
13. Beckwith, *Hawaiian Mythology,* p. 125.
14. Marshall Sahlins, *Historical Metaphors and Mythical Realities: Structure in the Early History of the Sandwich Island Kingdom* (Ann Arbor: University of Michigan Press, 1981), pp. 11–12.
15. Valeri, *Kingship and Sacrifice,* p. 217.
16. See Valeri, *Kingship and Sacrifice,* p. 222.
17. Sahlins, *Historical Metaphors and Mythical Realities,* p. 18–19. See also Marshall Sahlins, "Hierarchy and Humanity in Polynesia," in Antony Hooper and Judith Huntsman, eds., *Transformations of Polynesian Culture* (Auckland, New Zealand: Polynesian Society, 1985).
18. Samuel H. Elbert, "The Chief in Hawaiian Mythology," Indiana University, 1950, pp. 167–176.
19. E. S. C. Handy and Elizabeth Green Handy, *Native Planters of Old Hawai'i* (Honolulu: Bishop Museum Press, 1972), p. 311.
20. Handy and Handy, *Native Planters,* p. 556.

9: THE MANY BODIES OF THE GODDESS

For general references on the hula, see Dorothy B. Barrère, Mary Kawena Pukui, and Marion Kelly, *Hula: Historical Perspectives,* Pacific Anthropological Records, no. 30 (Honolulu: Bishop Museum, 1980); and Nathaniel B. Emerson, *The Unwritten Literature: The Sacred Songs of the Hula,* Bureau of American Ethnology Bulletin, no. 38 (Washington, DC: Smithsonian Institution, 1909). John Charlot has also written on the meaning of chant and hula in *Chanting the Universe:* Hawaiian Religious Culture (Honolulu: Emphasis International, 1983) and in "The Hula in Hawaiian Life and Thought," *Honolulu Magazine 14,* no. 5 (November 1979), 49–56.

1. Marshall Sahlins, *Islands of History* (Chicago: University of Chicago Press, 1985), p. 14.
2. Samuel H. Elbert and Noelani Mahoe, *Nā Mele o Hawai'i Nei* (Honolulu: University of Hawai'i Press, 1970), p. 62.
3. Linnekin, *Sacred Queens and Women of Consequence,* p. 84.

Notes

4. Sahlins, "Hierarchy and Humanity," p. 211.
5. "Granddaughter of Keahi remembers," interview with 'Iolani Luahine, *Honolulu Advertiser,* November 15, 1978.
6. As quoted by John Charlot, in a brochure for the "Arts of the Land" exhibit, East-West Center, Honolulu, Hawai'i.
7. Beckwith, *Hawaiian Mythology,* p. 186.
8. Emerson, "The Lesser Hawaiian Gods," p. 8.
9. Handy and Pukui, *The Polynesian Family System,* p. 124.
10. Beckwith, *Hawaiian Mythology,* p. 180.
11. The Rev. Henry Kahalakili, as quoted in the *Honolulu Advertiser,* April 25, 1987.
12. Nathaniel Emerson, *Pele and Hiiaka: A Myth from Hawaii* (Honolulu: Star Bulletin Press, 1915).
13. Emerson, *Pele and Hiiaka,* p. 130.
14. This and the following quotation are from Beckwith, *Hawaiian Mythology,* p. 176.
15. Marjorie Sinclair, *The Path of the Ocean,* p. 32.
16. Elbert, *The Chief in Hawaiian Mythology,* p. 167.

10: PELE AND THE PIG GOD

1. Currently, the definitive source on Hawaiian archeology is Patrick Kirch, *Feathered Gods and Fishhooks* (Honolulu: University of Hawai'i Press, 1985).
2. Henry M. Lyman, *Hawaiian Yesterdays* (Chicago: McClung, 1906), p. 160.
3. Beckwith (*Hawaiian Mythology,* p. 201) is quoting from a translation by Queen Lili'uokalani.
4. Charlot, *The Kamapua'a Literature,* p. 87.
5. Handy and Handy, *Native Planters,* p. 138.
6. Handy and Handy, *Native Planters,* p. 620.
7. See Beckwith, *Hawaiian Mythology,* p. 212.
8. Lilikalā Dorton, "A Legendary Tradition of Kamapua'a, the Hawaiian Pig God," unpublished master's thesis, University of Hawai'i, 1982, pp. 197–198.

11: RIFT ZONES

1. As quoted in Brigham, *The Volcanoes of Kilauea and Mauna Loa,* p. 479.
2. F. S. Lyman as quoted by Brigham, *The Volcanoes of Kilauea and Mauna Loa,* p. 102.
3. *Pacific Commercial Advertiser,* 1868, as quoted by Harry O. Wood, "On the Earthquakes of 1868 in Hawaii," *Bulletin of the Seismological Society of America 4,* no. 4 (December 1914), 106.
4. Dr. William Hillebrand, as quoted by Wood, "On the Earthquakes of 1868," p. 201.
5. As quoted in Handy and Handy, *Native Planters,* p. 567.
6. Harold T. Stearns, "The 1823 lava flow from Kilauea volcano, Hawaii," *Journal of Geology 34,* no. 4 (May–June 1926), 340.

Notes

7. This and the following quotation are from Arthur D. Little, Inc., *Evaluation of the Potential for Space-related Activities in the State of Hawaii* (Honolulu: Little, 1987), pp. IV–26 and IV–9.

8. From a Royal Gardens brochure on file at the Hawai'i County Planning Department, Hilo, Hawai'i.

9. Gavan Daws and George Cooper, *Land and Power in Hawaii* (Honolulu: Benchmark Books, 1985).

10. "Rural Plan Is Promising," *Honolulu Star Bulletin,* April 24, 1964.

11. Daws and Cooper, *Land and Power,* p. 271.

12. Daws and Cooper, *Land and Power,* p. 274.

13. Donal R. Mullineaux, Donald W. Peterson, and Dwight R. Crandell, "Volcanic Hazards in the Hawaiian Islands, in Decker, Wright, and Stauffer, eds., *Volcanism in Hawaii,* vol. 1, pp. 599–624.

14. Richard B. Moore, "Hualalai Volcano: A preliminary summary of geologic, petrologic, and geophysical data," in Decker, Wright, and Stauffer, eds., *Volcanism in Hawaii,* vol. 1, pp. 571–586.

15. *Hawaiian Riviera Resort Final Environmental Impact Statement* [EIS] (Honolulu: Belt Collins and Associates, December 1987), p. II–11.

16. V. R. Bender, "Mauna Loa erupts again," *National Parks Magazine 24,* no. 103 (1950), 140.

17. *Hawaiian Riviera EIS,* p. IV–9.

18. P. W. Lipman, "Rates of Volcanic Activity along the Southwest Rift Zone of Mauna Loa, Hawaii," *Bulletin of Volcanology 43* (1980), 708.

19. *Hawaiian Riviera EIS,* Appendix, p. 12.

20. *Hawaiian Riviera EIS,* p. IV–5.

21. John McPhee, *The Control of Nature* (New York: Farrar, Strauss & Giroux, 1989), p. 145.

12: *"KAPU KA'Ū"*

1. Gavan Daws, *Shoal of Time* (Honolulu: University of Hawai'i Press, 1968), p. 127.

2. Some estimates have been higher. See David Stannard, *Before the Horror.*

3. See Handy and Pukui, *The Polynesian Family System,* pp. 244–248.

4. *Dedman and Aluli* v. *Ono,* December 20, 1985.

5. *Lyng* v. *Northwest Indian Cemetery Association,* April 19, 1988.

6. *Ulaleo and Pele Defense Fund* v. *Paty,* August 22, 1989.

7. Park ranger Everett Brumaghin, "Letter to Park Supt. E. P. Leavitt, March 23, 1933. Hawai'i Volcanoes National Park Library Ethnology Pamphlet No. 22.

8. The information here is taken from UNESCO's *Nature and Resources 10,* no. 4 (October 1984), 1–12. See also Francesco di Castro and Jane Robertson, "The Biosphere Reserve Concept: 10 Years After," *Parks 6,* no. 4 (January–March 1982), 1–10.

9. See Gonzalo Halffer, "The Mapimi Biosphere Reserve: Local Participation in Conservation and Development," *Ambio 10,* nos. 2–3 (1981), 93–96.

A Brief Chronology

400–500 C.E. Earliest evidence of Polynesian settlers in Hawai'i.

1300–1400. According to tradition, new emigrants from Tahiti, led by the priest Pā'ao, arrive in Hawai'i, bringing with them a highly structured ritual system involving rigid tabus, worship of the war god Kū-ka'ili'moku, and the practice of human sacrifice. Archeologists characterize this time as the beginning of the "expansion period": for the next two hundred years or so, the population appears to have grown very rapidly.

1778. The English captain James Cook discovers Hawai'i.

1790. An explosive eruption in Kīlauea caldera. Part of the army of Keoua, hereditary chief of Ka'ū, is killed, presumably by a ground surge of poisonous fumes, while traveling a few miles south of the caldera.

1790–1791 (?). Keoua is invited to Kona by Kamehameha, where he is slain as he steps from his canoe to the shore and sacrificed on the altar of Kamehameha's newly finished war temple. Kamehameha becomes ruler of all Hawai'i Island.

1810. Kamehameha recognized as ruler of all the Islands.

1819. Kamehameha's heir, Liholiho, dismantles the traditional *kapu* (tabu) system and religious worship at state temples.

1820. The first missionaries—New England Protestants—arrive in Hawai'i.

1823. The Reverend William Ellis (English) tours the island of Hawai'i and provides the first Western account of the volcanoes region.

1824. The female chief Kapi'olani, a Christian convert, visits Kīlauea caldera and sings hymns to honor the Christian god.

1834. Scottish botanist David Douglas climbs Mauna Loa.

1840. U.S. South Seas Exploring Expedition (the Wilkes expedition) reaches Hawai'i.

1848. The "Great Mahele": Kamehameha III, at the urging of Westerners, institutes a system of private property, with the result that most Hawaiians are alienated from traditional and use rights.

1866. Mark Twain visits Kīlauea volcano.

1868. Major fault block movement on Mauna Loa's southwest rift zone is accompanied by severe earthquakes and eruptions of Kīlauea and Mauna Loa. The strongest earthquake causes a tidal wave that destroys villages along the south coast of Hawai'i.

1880. Princess "Ruth" Ke'elikōlani prays to Pele to stop the lava flow threatening Hilo. The Mauna Loa eruption, which had been continuous for months, stops the next day.

1893. Queen Lili'uokalani is forced from the throne in a "bloodless revolution" organized by U.S. businessmen.

1898. The Hawaiian Islands are annexed to the United States.

1912. Founding of the Hawaiian Volcano Observatory, with Thomas Jaggar as director.

1959. Hawai'i becomes a state.

1975. Major fault block movement, or "slumping," on the south flank of Kīlauea produces a magnitude 7.2 earthquake. Two campers are killed on the south coast of the Big Island by the resulting tidal wave.

1983. Kīlauea volcano's Pu'u 'Ō'ō eruption begins.

Glossary

Here is a rudimentary key to Hawaiian pronunciation.
The basic sounds for the five vowels are

    a "ah" as in *car*
    e "eh" somewhere between *led* and *laid*
    i "ee" as in *fleece*
    o "oh" as in *sole*
    u "oo" as in *moon*

Vowel combinations glide into one smooth sound, but the stress is on the first vowel: as in *pau* = "pAHoo" ("all done, or finished").

Glottal stops, however, indicate a total break in sound: *a'ā* = "ah-ah."

The main accent of a word in Hawaiian usually falls on the next-to-the-last syllable. This means that in words of only two syllables, the first half is generally stressed: *moa* = "MOH-ah" (chicken).

Any vowel marked with a macron, however, is given stress, no matter where it is located in the word: *'ōhelo* = OH-HEH-low.

a'ā: See list of geologic terms.

ahu: A cairn of piled rocks, used mainly as a trail marker.

akua: God, spirit, supernatural being. Can apply also to ghosts or to images believed inhabited by gods.

'ama'u: *Sadleria,* a genus of ferns endemic to the Hawaiian Islands. It is usually the first plant to grow on new lava flows.

'aumakua: Family or personal god or spirit.

hale o Papa: House or temple where women chiefs worshiped, located adjacent to the temples of human sacrifice dedicated to the god Kū.

haole: Traditionally, foreigner, but contemporary meaning is "white person."

hāpu'u: *Cibotium,* three species of native tree fern. A very common plant in the rainforest, the tree fern can reach a height of forty feet.

heiau: Traditional Hawaiian place of worship or shrine.

kahuna: Priest.

kaona: In Hawaiian poetry, hidden meaning.

kapa: Cloth made from bark that is soaked and beaten thin. Hawaiians most commonly used *wauke* or paper mulberry, or *māmaki,* a member of the nettle family.

kapu: Tabu or prohibition; sacred, forbidden.

kī: A woody plant (*Cordyline terminalis*) known throughout Polynesia as *ti,* and introduced to the Hawaiian Islands by the early Polynesian settlers.

kinolau: "Many bodies"; the many forms that can be assumed by the Hawaiian gods. For Pele, these included human and animal forms as well as all the forms of volcanism.

kīpuka: A pocket of older land surrounded by younger lava flow(s).

koa: *Acacia koa,* a beautiful native tree that can grow to a height of 100 feet. It is usually found in drier forest, ranging from 1,000- to 6,000-foot elevation.

kukui: *Aleurites moluccana,* a large tree also called "candlenut," probably introduced to Hawai'i by early Polynesian settlers. The seeds are rich in oil, and were strung on midribs from palm leaves to make a "candle."

kumu hula: Hula teacher.

Kumulipo: Origin, genesis, source of life. Name of a Hawaiian creation chant.

loa: Great, long, tall.

luakini heiau: A temple of human sacrifice dedicated to the god Kū.

māmaki: *Pipturus hawaiiensis,* the "nettleless nettle," a large native shrub or small tree common to the lower rainforest. The bark was used by the Hawaiians to make *kapa.*

mana: Supernatural or spiritual power.

mauna: Mountain.

mo'o: Supernatural beings, often linked to places, and associated especially with bodies of water.

'ōhelo: *Vaccinium reticulatum,* a small native shrub with red or yellow berries, a member of the cranberry family. The berries are considered sacred to Pele.

'ōhi'a: *Metrosideros collina,* a common, extremely adaptable native tree, a member of the myrtle family, found from coast to alpine level. The flowers are called *lehua,* and the tree is often referred to as *'ōhi'a lehua.*

pāhoehoe: See list of geologic terms.

palai: *Microlepia setosa,* a native fern with lacy, somewhat hairy fronds. Associated with Laka, the goddess of hula.

pali: Cliff.

piko: Umbilical cord or stump.

pō: Night, darkness; cosmic birthing place, realm of the gods.

poi: A sticky, pastelike food, made from the root of the taro plant, which provided the main staple of the Hawaiian diet.

puʻu: Hill.

wahine: Woman.

wauke: The paper mulberry (*Broussonetia papyrifera*), introduced to the Hawaiian Islands by the Polynesian settlers, and used to make bark cloth (*kapa*) clothing and bedclothes. When available, this plant was preferred to the *māmaki,* since it produced a finer and more durable "cloth."

GEOLOGIC TERMS

aʻā: Lava characterized by a rough, jagged, clinkery surface.

caldera: A large circular depression, usually at the summit of a volcano. A caldera can form either from volcanic explosion or from collapse as underground magma drains away, leaving the ground unsupported.

cinder cone: A conical hill that forms when cinders propelled into the air by a volcanic eruption fall back around the vent, piling up into a mound.

crater: A basin-like depression in the ground. Craters formed by explosive eruptions are often found at the top of cones. Pit craters may result from collapse when underground magma drains away and leaves the ground unsupported.

diapir: In hot spot theory, a rising plume of molten or partially molten rock that feeds volcanic activity at the earth's surface.

fault: A fracture or zone of fractures in the earth's crust.

fault block: A discrete unit of crustal rocks bounded partially or completely by faults, often structurally isolated from the surrounding terrain.

fault scarp: A cliff or steep slope resulting from earth movement along a fault.

fissure: A fracture or crack in the rocks of the earth's crust, common in volcanic terrain where a fissure may serve as an eruptive or fumarolic vent.

flank eruption: An eruption that occurs on the side of a volcano, rather than at the summit.

fumarole: A vent in the earth from which volcanic gases escape to the surface.

guyot: A flat-topped seamount.

harmonic tremor: A continuous ground vibration caused by the movement of molten rock underground.

hot spot: A fixed zone of anomalously high heat flow tens of miles below the earth's surface, where molten rock is continuously rising from the earth's depths. The Hawaiian hot spot is the source of the volcanic activity that has built the Islands.

lava tube: A tunnel that forms within a lava flow. As the flow cools on all sides, the molten interior is insulated and continues to flow freely. When the eruption ceases, the remaining molten lava in the tube flows out, leaving an empty tube of solid lava.

magma: Molten rock beneath the earth's surface. When magma erupts above ground, it is called *lava.*

magma chamber: A reservoir beneath or within a volcano in which magma is stored.

magnetic field reversal: An abrupt switch in the earth's polarity in which the north and south magnetic poles are reversed. Several such reversals have taken place in the past, one 700,000 years ago, another 25 million years ago.

mid-ocean ridge: A linear belt of mountains and valleys superimposed on a broad swell on the ocean floor. It is the site of extensive submarine volcanic activity, where new oceanic crust is created.

olivine: A translucent green or brownish-green mineral, composed mostly of silicon, oxygen, iron, and magnesium, that commonly occurs in Hawaiian lava. Olivine of gem quality is called *peridot.*

pāhoehoe: Lava characterized by a smooth surface, which may be ropy, wrinkled, or billowy.

phreatomagmatic explosion: An explosion that results when ground water is heated rapidly to steam by contact with magma. Portions of the eruptions of Kīlauea in 1790 and Mount St. Helens in 1980 were phreatomagmatic; typically, ash is produced, and fragments of old and new rock are ejected.

plate tectonics: Earth dynamics described by the theory that the earth's outer rigid shell is divided into about a dozen plates that move slowly about, causing faulting, volcanism, earthquakes, and mountain building along their margins.

rift zone: A linear belt of highly fractured rock on the flank of a volcano, a belt from which eruptions can occur.

sea floor spreading: The concept that some ocean basins, such as the Atlantic, are expanding as new crustal material is added by volcanic activity at the mid-ocean ridges. The rates of sea floor spreading range between 1 and 10 centimeters (0.4–4 inches) per year.

seamount: A submarine mountain rising at least 3,000 feet above the adjacent ocean floor.

seismometer: An instrument placed on the ground to sense earth vibrations, such as those caused by earthquakes and harmonic tremor. The vibrations can be transmitted to a recording seismograph, where a pen makes a continuous trace on a rotating, paper-covered drum.

slump: A landslide or downslope movement of a discrete block of earth.

shield volcano: A volcano with gently sloping sides, having the shape of a broad dome, similar to a Roman shield. Very fluid lava flows produce such a shape. The Hawaiian volcanoes are classic shield volcanoes.

subsidence: The gradual or sudden lowering of the ground due to a variety of processes, including withdrawal of subsurface magma or ground water, or earthquake-related fault slippage.

tumulus: A dome or mound formed on the crust of a *pāhoehoe* lava flow resulting when pressure builds up in the molten lava underneath. This happens when the molten core of the flow is impeded and cannot flow freely.

tiltmeter: An instrument that detects changes in the slope of the ground, used to measure inflation or deflation of a volcano resulting from the filling or draining of the magma chamber.

vent: An opening in the ground through which volcanic materials reach the surface.

Index

Index

Index

Index

Index